FREEDOM
UNDER THE
WORD

FREEDOM
UNDER THE
WORD

KARL BARTH'S
Theological Exegesis

Edited by

Ben Rhodes
and Martin Westerholm

Baker Academic
a division of Baker Publishing Group
Grand Rapids, Michigan

Published by Baker Academic
a division of Baker Publishing Group
PO Box 6287, Grand Rapids, MI 49516-6287
www.bakeracademic.com

Printed in the United States of America

Library of Congress Cataloging-in-Publication Data
Names: Rhodes, Ben, 1983– editor.
Title: Freedom under the Word : Karl Barth's theological exegesis / edited by Ben Rhodes and
    Martin Westerholm.
Description: Grand Rapids : Baker Publishing Group, 2019. | Includes bibliographical references
    and index.
Identifiers: LCCN 2018034274 | ISBN 9780801098819 (pbk.)
Subjects: LCSH: Barth, Karl, 1886–1968. | Bible—Criticism, interpretation, etc. | Theology,
    Doctrinal.
Classification: LCC BX4827.B3 F734 2019 | DDC 230/.044092—dc23
LC record available at https://lccn.loc.gov/2018034274

ISBN 978-1-5409-6162-4 (casebound)

19   20   21   22   23   24   25   7   6   5   4   3   2   1

*Dedicated to the memory
of John Webster (1955–2016)*

Contents

Abbreviations

CD   Karl Barth, *Church Dogmatics*, 4 volumes in 13 parts, ed. and trans. G. W. Bromiley, T. F. Torrance et al. (Edinburgh: T&T Clark, 1956–69).

GA   Karl Barth Gesamtausgabe (Zurich: Theologischer Verlag Zürich, 1971–).

I   *Predigten*

II   *Akademische Werke*

III   *Vorträge und kleinere Arbeiten*

IV   *Gespräche*

V   *Briefe*

KD   Karl Barth, *Kirchliche Dogmatik*, 4 volumes in 13 parts (Frankfurt am Main: Fischer-Bücherei, 1932–67).

Romans II   Karl Barth, *The Epistle to the Romans*, trans. Edwyn Hoskyns (Oxford: Oxford University Press, 1933).

Römer I   Karl Barth, *Der Römerbrief, Erste Fassung (1919)*, ed. Hermann Schmidt, GA II 16 (Zurich: Theologischer Verlag Zürich, 1985).

Römer II   Karl Barth, *Der Römerbrief, Zweite Fassung (1922)*, ed. C. van der Kooi and Katja Tolstaja, GA II 47 (Zurich: Theologischer Verlag Zürich, 2010).

Introduction

BEN RHODES AND MARTIN WESTERHOLM

Do we really need another book on the theology of Karl Barth? After so much commentary, is there anything left that is worth saying? It is of course not surprising that the decisive figure of twentieth-century theology continues to generate debate and discussion, but one question that we might ask ourselves in considering the future of these discussions is how far they are faithful to the criterion by which Barth himself wished to be judged. Barth claimed that his theology consisted in listening to Scripture and telling his readers what he heard; he made clear that fidelity to Scripture is the appropriate criterion for evaluating its success. Yet reception of his thought has been marked by a peculiar hesitance to engage directly with his exegesis. The first wave of responses to Barth's work, concentrated on his commentaries on Romans, included extensive engagement from biblical scholars, but these figures tended to devote the bulk of their attention to Barth's method. Subsequent theological scholarship has struggled to make a turn to sustained consideration of exegesis. Study of Barth's work in recent decades was dominated for a time by heavily conceptualized debates that turned not on attention to the particularities and surprises of Barth's exegesis but on the capacity of particular master concepts to facilitate a systematizing of the whole of Barth's thought. Among the casualties of these debates was patient attention to the way that the twists and turns of Barth's theology are themselves reflections of his attempt to listen to the complex voice of Scripture. A series of recent conferences on Barth's exegesis, including two from which the majority of

the essays in this volume originate, suggest that the focal point of attention
to Barth's work may be shifting, but as we near the hundred-year anniversary
of Barth's landmark work on Romans, scholars working in this sphere are
having to play a measure of catch-up.

   This book aims to engage with Barth on the terms of his preferred criterion
by presenting studies of his exegetical work. There are at least a couple of
reasons why this task is important. In a more narrow sense, the task is crucial
to consideration of the legacy and future potential of Barth's theology. The
fruitfulness of Barth's work today is best measured by the contributions that
it makes to contemporary interpretation and presentation of Scripture. But
beyond narrower questions regarding Barth's legacy, attention to his exegesis
is important as an element in the ongoing task of learning what it means
to read Scripture well. The question of the kind of interpretation that aids
the church's proclamation is the question of theological interpretation of
Scripture. Just how this interpretation is to function is among the crucial
questions facing theologians and biblical scholars today. Interest in theological interpretation has grown exponentially in recent years, but it has not
produced agreement either among theologians or between theologians and
biblical scholars on the nature and function of this practice. Debates that
expose the continued fragmentation of contemporary theology by driving
confessional and disciplinary divisions to the surface continue. One resource
available to contemporary thinkers as they attempt to make progress in these
debates is the example of past masters. Study of the exegetical habits of leading figures in the Christian tradition is thus something of a growth industry at
present. Alongside renewed interest in, say, the exegesis of Thomas Aquinas,
consideration of Barth's exegesis is a tool that may be deployed for the sake
of advancing our understanding of theological interpretation more generally.

   In the interest of contributing not only to evaluation of Barth's work,
but also to the wider task of bringing theologians and biblical scholars together in consideration of what it means to read Scripture well, this volume
presents essays from a range of specialists in both Barth's work and biblical
studies. The bulk of the essays in this book are drawn from two sources: a
study group focusing on Barth's exegesis that ran from 2013 to 2015 within
the Evangelical Theological Society and a conference that took place in 2015
under the auspices of the Institute for Bible, Theology, and Hermeneutics at
the University of St. Andrews. Though the contributors to this volume did
not encounter one another's essays beyond the exposure that these conferences facilitated, and their conclusions vary widely in detail, a measure of
consensus emerged around a series of interrelated notions. First, Barth's exegesis, often carried out at great length in the fine-print sections of the *Church*

Dogmatics, as well as the many lectures on Scripture given throughout his academic tenure (to say nothing of his early years as a pastor in Safenwil), is crucial for understanding his theological work, and consideration of the latter cannot responsibly proceed without attention to the former. Second, though responsible consideration of Barth's theological claims depends on attention to his exegetical work, fair evaluation of Barth's work as a united whole requires acknowledgment of a cyclical movement through which exegetical work grounds theological conclusions and theological conclusions in turn inform exegetical work, with the result that disciplined grappling with Barth's work requires dynamic attention to a spiraling give-and-take between exegetical and theological reflection. Third, though the theological reading of Scripture that results from the spiraling relation of exegesis and dogmatics in Barth's work is robust and remains a salutary challenge for critically inclined modes of exegesis, some difficulties do appear to arise on particular exegetical questions like the role of Israel and the Old Testament background to New Testament material, and on broader procedural questions about the influence of doctrinal decisions on exegetical work. These areas of consensus are of course quite broad, but they may perhaps serve as points of departure for further dialogue between biblical scholars and theologians as they continue to reflect on Barth's legacy and theological interpretation today.

Five sections structure the contribution that this volume seeks to make. In a first section, two essays provide a background against which Barth's exegesis can be understood by treating key elements in his theology of Scripture. Exegetical practice is always shaped by convictions regarding what Scripture is and how it functions. Some sense of Barth's theology of Scripture is thus crucial to understanding and evaluating his exegesis. In the first essay, Martin Westerholm aims to facilitate engagement with Barth's exegesis by sketching the development of Barth's theology of Scripture. Because the essays in this volume treat elements of Barth's exegesis from across the breadth of his career, a sketch of the way that Barth's understanding of Scripture developed is useful as background to the different exegetical moments that the other authors take up. In a second introductory essay, Ben Rhodes provides a more concerted look at Barth's theology of Scripture in its most systematic exposition in *CD* I/2. This essay aims to provide a dogmatic treatment of Barth's theology of Scripture that stands alongside the developmental perspective that Westerholm develops. In so doing, it suggests constructively that the classical distinction between the Spirit's work of original inspiration and subsequent illumination of Scripture, a distinction which Barth rejected, gives better dogmatic grounding to Barth's actual exegetical practice than some of Barth's own alternatives.

After an introductory section that treats Barth's theology of Scripture, four sections appear that divide treatments of Barth's exegetical work into chronological groups. The first section contains three essays that consider the earlier exegetical work through which Barth first made a name for himself and began to develop his theological convictions. These essays concentrate on Barth's work on Romans, in particular on the first two editions of his commentary, published in 1919 and 1922, and on the exegetical lectures that he delivered through the 1920s. Francis Watson considers how far Barth's work on Romans can fairly be considered commentarial. In examining the way that the first two editions of Barth's *Epistle to the Romans* handle the first seven verses of Paul's letter, Watson argues that in fact the little-known first edition of Barth's book is a better example of commentary and is therefore deserving of wider attention. In the second essay, John Webster examines Barth's recently published lectures on Ephesians, originally delivered during the winter semester of 1921–22, and gives a careful account of a complex two-sided relation: the way that Barth's efforts to develop cogent theological positions shape his reading of the text, on one side, and the way that his reading of the text furthers his theological development, on the other. Finally, Carsten Card-Hyatt considers the lectures on the Epistle of James that Barth gave at a couple of points during the 1920s. Though little known, these lectures stand as an important counterpart to Barth's work on Romans. The Pauline convictions that Barth develops through his work on Romans might appear to render James, with his moral exhortation, a difficult conversation partner for Barth, and the interplay that Card-Hyatt traces between Paul and James yields important results. We learn a great deal about Barth's sensitivity to the danger of "mastering" biblical texts, willingness to challenge Protestant interpretive consensus, and interest in reckoning seriously with the moral and spiritual dynamics of the life of faith. These lessons illustrate how far understandings of Barth's thought may continue to grow through consideration of exegetical work that is only now becoming available.

After this look at Barth's earlier exegesis, the third section in this volume presents a group of four essays that are linked chronologically and thematically. These essays range widely within Barth's corpus, concentrating especially on exegetical work that developed in Barth's work during the 1920s and came to fruition in the landmark theology of election that appears in CD II/2. They pose a set of interrelated questions about Barth's handling of the Hebrew Bible and interpretation of the place of Israel in the economy of salvation. In the first essay, Wesley Hill charts Barth's exegesis of the Johannine Prologue from work beginning in 1925 to the extended treatment that appears in Barth's theology of election, and asks if Barth's construal of John's

Logos language is sufficiently sensitive to the Old Testament background to New Testament concepts. In a similar vein, Stephen Fowl examines Barth's exegesis of Ephesians 1:4 in lectures delivered during the early 1920s and then in exegetical work in *CD* II/2 and asks if Barth is sufficiently alert to the role that God's election of Israel plays in conditioning Paul's understanding of election. The critical questions raised in these essays are then balanced by a more positive account of Barth's relation to Israel and to the Hebrew Bible that is developed by Mark Gignilliat, who ranges across the full scope of the *Church Dogmatics* in arguing that, in considering Isaiah's depictions of the messianic, Barth works hard to be faithful both to Isaiah's letter and to a measure of christological spirit. But in the final essay in this section, the questions raised by Hill and Fowl are pushed to their sharp point by Susannah Ticciati, who raises explicit concerns regarding supersessionism in the exegesis of Romans 9–11 that shapes Barth's mature theology of election. Ticciati's essay adds remarkable depth to the scene that Hill and Fowl sketch by arguing that, while Barth works hard to avoid problematic forms of Christian triumphalism, his theology continues to be marked by subtle forms of supersessionism. Ticciati's essay lays a foundation for further inquiry by showing that important work remains to be done regarding theological understandings of Israel both within and beyond Barth's framework of thought.

The fourth section of the book presents three essays that engage with exegetical work from the theology of creation in *CD* III. The first two of these essays helpfully further conversation regarding Barth's handling of the Hebrew Bible by considering his interpretation of the creation narratives in Genesis. Both Andrew Torrance and Christina Larsen attend to the way Barth's interpretation of Genesis is shaped by conceptions of Christ, grace, and church; both essays help us to think further about Barth's way of engaging the Hebrew Bible. Following these essays on Genesis, Christopher Green swings to the other end of the canon and takes up a new set of themes by working through the exegesis of Revelation 4–5 that appears as part of the theology of providence in *CD* III/3. Within the wider sphere of Barth scholarship, the whole of *CD* III, and in particular the exegetical work that it contains, remains relatively neglected. Green helps us to see that the volume contains untapped exegetical riches by describing the treatment of angels and their exemplification of holy theology-as-praise that Barth develops through Revelation 4–5.

The final section in this volume contains three essays that consider the exegetical work that informs Barth's mature theology of reconciliation. Much of the work in this section concentrates on material in *CD* IV, but Grant Macaskill opens the section with a treatment of Barth's understanding of the

Christ-Adam dialectic that draws heavily from Barth's 1956 *Christ and Adam according to Romans 5*. Macaskill offers a masterful blending of exegetical and theological reasoning in critically scrutinizing Barth's account of Christ and Adam and charting points of continuity with and constructive challenge to contemporary Pauline scholarship. Turning next to more concerted engagement with *CD* IV, David Nelson offers an essay that complements the account of moral agency presented by Carsten Card-Hyatt by examining the eschatological mode of human agency, centering around a dialectic of faith and hope, that the mature Barth develops through exegesis of Hebrews 11. Finally, Paul Nimmo draws the volume to a close by locating Barth's interpretation of Jesus's compassion for the crowds within Barth's doctrine of reconciliation and analyzing its dogmatic entailments. Nimmo helpfully depicts Barth's combination of critical scriptural exposition and creative theological construction as a living conversation between exegesis and dogmatics. Though his essay brings the conversation marked out by this volume to a close, the volume as a whole is intended to contribute to the wider continuation of discussion regarding theological readings of Scripture.

This account of the structure of the book and the topics of the essays is but a brief sketch; each essay repays attention to its particular claims. Readers' attention should perhaps not be diverted any longer, but it is important in closing for us to say a word about John Webster's contribution both to this volume and to our wider work. Webster was among the original presenters at the 2015 conference on Barth's exegesis that took place in St. Andrews, and he was of course an important voice calling out in the wilderness for greater attention to Barth's exegesis. Webster's presentation at the conference focused on Barth's theology of Scripture and its connection with his exegetical practice; unfortunately, his sudden passing in 2016 left a final version of his paper unavailable for inclusion in this volume. In its place is a recent introduction that Webster penned to Barth's lectures on Ephesians.[1] This latter piece examines exegetical material that would otherwise not have been treated in this volume. It is hoped that its appearance here will expand the circle of readers who have access to it and that its characteristic patience and erudition will encourage readers to turn to wider work by both Webster and Barth.

Webster supervised both of our doctoral dissertations at the University of Aberdeen and was a true mentor, both personally and theologically. He is deeply missed. This collection is dedicated to his memory.

---

1. The essay first appeared as "'A Relation beyond All Relations': God and Creatures in Barth's Lectures on Ephesians, 1921–22," in Karl Barth, *The Epistle to the Ephesians*, ed. R. David Nelson (Grand Rapids: Baker Academic, 2017), 31–49.

PART 1

Barth's Theology of Scripture

ONE

Barth's Theology of Scripture in Developmental Perspective

MARTIN WESTERHOLM

Introduction

Given the education and inclinations of the young Karl Barth, it was not a given, humanly speaking, that biblical exegesis would be central to his theological contributions. Barth's father worked for a time at a small college in Switzerland that sought to train "scriptural" preachers;[1] he later arranged for Barth to attend the conservative-leaning university in Bern, where he himself held a chair funded by the traditionally inclined branch of the Swiss church. But the young Barth found neither classical Protestant theologies of Scripture nor typically Protestant emphases on exegesis compelling. Barth's interest in theology had come to life through confirmation classes that impressed upon him the dubious nature of the "later orthodox theory of the literal inspiration of the Bible";[2] he was unhappy in Bern and pressed his father to

---

This essay is a condensed and revised version of material that was first published in Stephen Westerholm and Martin Westerholm, *Reading Sacred Scripture* (Grand Rapids: Eerdmans, 2016).

1. Eberhard Busch, *Karl Barth: His Life from Letters and Autobiographical Texts* (London: SCM; Philadelphia: Fortress, 1976), 1.

2. Karl Barth, "Karl Barth and Oscar Cullmann on Their Theological Vocation: On Systematic Theology," *Scottish Journal of Theology* 14 (1961): 225.

permit him to attend more liberal institutions. Having finished his education, he began work as a minister without a sense of the "worth" of the Bible.[3] His early preaching and teaching reflect the emphases of the liberal theology of his day. Faith and religion appeared as matters of experiential encounter with God; the significance of Old Testament figures was taken to lie in their religious personalities; and the Old Testament as a whole was treated as significant only because it formed Jesus's own religious consciousness. The New Testament, in turn, was viewed as so many accounts of the apostles' experience of faith, and reading Scripture was understood as a means of sharing in this experience. Stronger claims about the inspiration of Scripture were treated as aberrations that are absent from the best elements of the early church and Luther and unable to account for the "variations, losses, mistakes" in Scripture.[4]

Careful engagement with Scripture itself was formative of Barth's turn away from these notions. This engagement came about in part because it was demanded by Barth's pastoral work. Barth wrote later that, whatever his own inclinations, his task was "above all to preach the Bible,"[5] and that, viewed retrospectively, "it was extremely fruitful for me, as I entered upon twelve years in the pastorate, to be compelled to engage myself much more earnestly than ever before with the Bible as the root of all Christian thinking and teaching."[6] Barth's job demanded a measure of attention to Scripture, but this attention may not have shifted his thinking had he not faced pressure from other quarters. Engagement with Scripture became crucial for Barth not only because of the weekly sermon but also because his basic convictions came to seem inadequate in the face of class struggles and the tumult of the First World War. "Real problems of real life" drove Barth to think through the foundations of his various positions and eventually to make what he later called a "turn back to the Bible."[7] A commentary on Romans, published first in December 1918 (and cited as published in 1919) and then again in a revised edition in 1922, was the most substantial fruit of this turn. The 1922 edition in particular marked a turning point in Barth's life, for it catapulted him to the center of theological debate. This work was widely seen as announcing the end

3. Karl Barth, "Gespräch mit Mennoniten (13.12.1967)," in *Gespräche 1964–1968*, ed. Eberhard Busch, GA IV 28 (Zurich: Theologischer Verlag Zürich, 1996), 432.

4. Karl Barth, "Konfirmandenunterricht 1909/10," "Konfirmandenunterricht 1910/11," in *Konfirmandenunterricht, 1909–1921*, ed. Jürgen Fangmeier, GA I 18 (Zurich: Theologischer Verlag Zürich, 1987), 10–16, 60–69 (my translation).

5. Karl Barth, "Entretiens de Bièvres," in *Gespräche 1963*, ed. Eberhard Busch, GA IV 41 (Zurich: Theologischer Verlag Zürich, 2005), 409 (my translation).

6. Barth, "Barth and Cullman on Their Theological Vocation," 226.

7. Karl Barth, *Final Testimonies* (Grand Rapids: Eerdmans, 1977), 23.

of the theological project that marked nineteenth-century neo-Protestantism. It stands as a seminal work in twentieth-century theology.

The task of this chapter is to trace the theology of Scripture that emerged as Barth executed a "turn back to the Bible" and to trace the development of this theology as Barth's thinking matured. The essays that appear in this volume treat aspects of Barth's exegesis that are ranged across the whole of Barth's career. It will be useful for us to be able to situate this exegesis in relation to the theology of Scripture that shaped Barth's work at various points. On one level, Barth's theology of Scripture is striking in the degree to which its basic building blocks remained stable from the early 1920s onward. Yet, on another level, some of the idiosyncrasies of the exegesis that we will encounter in this volume make better sense against the backdrop of shifts in the way that these foundational building blocks are configured. Barth's work is noteworthy in part because he possessed a remarkable capacity to allow himself to be surprised by Scripture. Openness to surprise brought with it an openness to rethinking just how Scripture is best understood and interpreted. Attention to the movement of this process as preparation for considering his exegesis is the task of this chapter.

Barth's Early Understanding of Scripture

The first question for us concerns the understanding of Scripture that informed Barth's work between 1915 and 1921. For reasons we will come to in due course, explicit attention to a theology of Scripture was secondary during this period to consideration of the content of Scripture itself, but this work on theology of Scripture marks a turning point in theological history and reflects a set of instincts about the nature of Scripture that are foundational for Barth's later thought.

The focal point of Barth's thinking at this point was his account of just what the Bible presents. In 1917, Barth gave a lecture that took up the questions: "What is in the Bible? What sort of house is it that the Bible is a door to? What sort of land spreads out before our eyes when we open up the Bible?"[8] Barth's answer was that the Bible presents the activity of God as a sovereign reality that constitutes a new world. "'What is in the Bible?' . . . In the Bible there is a new world, the world of God."[9] The new world that is grounded in the activity of God stands in absolute opposition

---

8. Karl Barth, "The New World in the Bible, 1917," in *The Word of God and Theology*, trans. Amy Marga (London: T&T Clark, 2011), 16.
9. Barth, "New World," 18.

to an "old" world made up of morality, religion, culture, and all else that issues from human activity. Far from complementing and completing these human realities, divine activity represents "a blast of trumpets from another world" that "interrupts your reflections about yourself, and your life, . . . the nurturing of your religious thoughts and feelings."[10] It asserts the sovereignty of God over against all human speaking and doing. "A new world stands in the Bible. God! God's sovereignty! God's honor! God's inconceivable love! Not the history of humanity but the history of God."[11] "It is certain that the Bible, if we read it with careful attention, leads us exactly to the point at which we must decide to accept or disavow the royal sovereignty of God. This is precisely the new world of the Bible."[12] The Bible is the place that human beings go to learn again to speak of the sovereignty of God, to recognize that "God is God."[13]

The suggestion that the decisive content of the Bible is a new world that stands opposed to the "old world of war and money and death" presents a kind of scaffolding around which Barth's understanding of Scripture is constructed.[14] The first point that issues from it is an account of the divine activity that is required if creatures are to grasp the true content of the Bible. Barth declares that, because human activity belongs to the "old, sick world" of human striving, the new world of divine activity may be apprehended only through the work of the divine Spirit.[15] "The Bible is 'understood' neither through this nor that 'mental or intellectual faculty,' but by the power of the Spirit, who is the same as its content, and that in faith."[16] The "hidden things" of the new world are "inaccessible to sensible perception"; they are "displayed" by the "Spirit of God."[17] They belong to a sphere of spirit that is inaccessible to the eyes of flesh and must be understood "spirit through spirit."[18]

A particular understanding of biblical inspiration follows from this emphasis on the Spirit's work. In the preface to the first edition of his commentary on Romans, Barth writes that he would side with the "venerable doctrine of inspiration" if forced to choose between it and historical-critical

---

10. Barth, "The Righteousness of God, 1916," in *Word of God and Theology*, 4.

11. Barth, "New World," 26.

12. Barth, "New World," 23.

13. Barth, "New World," 27; cf. Barth, "The Christian in Society, 1919," in *Word of God and Theology*, 66; Barth, "Righteousness of God," 11.

14. Barth, "Righteousness of God," 13.

15. Barth, "New World," 29.

16. Karl Barth, "Fifteen Answers to Professor von Harnack," in *Beginnings of Dialectical Theology*, vol. 1, ed. James M. Robinson (Richmond: John Knox, 1968), 167.

17. Karl Barth, "The Preface to the Third Edition," in *Romans II*, 20.

18. Barth, "Biblical Questions, Insights, and Vistas, 1920," in *Word of God and Theology*, 86, alluding to 1 Cor. 2:13.

study. This contrast might appear to reflect a kind of category mistake, for teaching about inspiration generally treats the way that the text came into being while the historical-critical method finds tools to understand the text today, but Barth supposes that in fact these realities may be placed side by side. On his terms, the doctrine of inspiration is concerned with the "labour of apprehending" rather than the formation of the text.[19] It is a functional doctrine that establishes principles for understanding Scripture. At the heart of these principles is the stipulation that grasping the content of Scripture requires a "spiritual apprehension" grounded in the work of the divine Spirit. The doctrine of inspiration codifies the notion that "penetrating the heart of a document" is a matter of presuming "that its spirit will speak to our spirit through the actual written words."[20] It secures a "correlation of 'Scripture' and 'Spirit'" that ensures that the latter is not displaced as the principle of the comprehension of the former.[21]

What does exegesis that is carried out in light of this principle look like? Barth's answer to this question revolves around a contrast between Calvin's work as a biblical commentator and the work of modern biblical scholars who follow in Schleiermacher's wake. In pioneering the modern study of hermeneutics, Schleiermacher proposes that interpreting a text is a matter of deploying exhaustive grammatical and psychological study for the sake of reconstructing the thought that underlies the written words of a text. Study of this kind aims to overcome the historical gap between the writer and the reader. As Barth presents it, this understanding dominates modern exegesis, with the result that contemporary exegetes fixate on the historical, grammatical, and psychological aspects of the text: "Recent commentaries contain no more than a reconstruction of the text, a rendering of the Greek words and phrases by their precise equivalents, a number of additional notes in which archaeological and philological material is gathered together, and a more or less plausible arrangement of the subject-matter in such a manner that it may be made historically and psychologically intelligible."[22]

Lost in this attention to the grammatical, psychological, and historical is the actual subject of the biblical text itself. "Real struggling with the raw material of the Epistle," "reconsideration of what is set out in the Epistle, until the actual meaning is disclosed," is given short shrift.[23] Fixation on grammatical

19. Karl Barth, "The Preface to the First Edition," in *Romans II*, 1.
20. Barth, "Preface to the Third Edition," 18.
21. Barth, "An Answer to Professor von Harnack's Open Letter," in *Beginnings of Dialectical Theology*, 177.
22. Karl Barth, "The Preface to the Second Edition," in *Romans II*, 6.
23. Barth, "Preface to the Second Edition," 8.

or historical elements means that the text as a whole "still remains largely unintelligible."[24]

By contrast, Barth proposes that Calvin is a model of the "tenacious" exegete who grapples with the true subject matter of the gospel. Calvin begins with an attempt to establish "what stands in the text" in grammatical and historical terms, but he recognizes that this is nothing more than "preparatory" work and moves "energetically" beyond it in an attempt to "rethink the whole material and wrestle with it." He engages in a "conversation" with Paul that "moves round the subject-matter" until the barriers of the grammatical, historical, and psychological disappear, "the walls that separate the sixteenth century from the first become transparent," and the "actual meaning" of the text is disclosed. The subject matter of the text, rather than the thought of the one who wrote it, is the object of Calvin's interest. Concentration on the subject matter means that "the man of the sixteenth century" is able to hear when Paul speaks.[25]

In attempting to engage in conversation with Paul about his subject matter, Calvin models biblical interpretation that derives its principles from the doctrine of inspiration. Modern critics dismiss Calvin's exegesis as a reflection of the "compulsion of inspiration," but Barth suggests that those who dismiss the hermeneutical force of the doctrine of inspiration in this way "betray" the fact that they have "never worked upon the interpretation of Scripture." They condemn themselves to a preoccupation with textual elements that does not permit a grasp of the text's subject matter as the reality that gives sense to the whole. Lacking a perception of the whole, they are quick "to dismiss this or that difficult passage as simply a peculiar doctrine or opinion of Paul," attributable to the idiosyncrasies of Paul's personality and historical location. By contrast, Calvin shows "tenacious determination to understand and to interpret" the subject matter in light of which Paul's letter as a whole has its sense.[26]

Barth himself employs the exegetical principles that he associates with Calvin.[27] He writes that, in accordance with the hermeneutical direction contained in the doctrine of inspiration, "my whole energy of interpreting has been expended in an endeavour to see . . . into the spirit of the Bible, which is

24. Barth, "Preface to the Second Edition," 7.
25. Barth, "Preface to the Second Edition," 7.
26. Barth, "Preface to the Second Edition," 8.
27. Barth discusses Calvin in the preface to his commentary on Romans largely in order to elucidate his own approach. In lectures on Calvin delivered during 1922, Barth told his students that Calvin's exegesis "provided an external model for my own special study of Romans." Karl Barth, *The Theology of John Calvin*, trans. Geoffrey Bromiley (Grand Rapids: Eerdmans, 1995), 393.

the Eternal Spirit."[28] This endeavor requires the kind of attempt to "rethink the whole material" through "conversation" between the first century and the present that Calvin exemplifies. It mandates that commentary on Scripture be understood not as a matter of commentary "on" a text, as if the author and the text were ends in themselves, but rather commentary "with" Paul, "standing by Paul's side" in an effort to apprehend the object of which Paul speaks.[29]

> Proper concentration of exegesis presses behind the many questions to the one cardinal question by which all are embraced. . . . When an investigation is rightly conducted, boulders composed of fortuitous or incidental or merely historical conceptions ought to disappear almost entirely. The Word ought to be exposed in the words. Intelligent comment means that I am driven on till I stand with nothing before me but the enigma of the subject-matter; till the document seems hardly to exist as a document; till I have almost forgotten that I am not its author; till I know the author so well that I allow him to speak in my name and am even able to speak in his name myself.[30]

"Paul knows of God what most of us do not know; and his Epistles enable us to know what he knew."[31] Through "creative straining of the sinews," "the matter contained in the text" can be "released."[32]

The challenge to the standards of modern biblical exegesis that accompanied Barth's commendations of Calvin occasioned no small amount of criticism. Barth was accused of imposing his own theological framework on Paul's text. His response points back to the contrast between old and new worlds as the structuring principle of his thinking about Scripture. He writes that his exegesis presumes no framework other than what Kierkegaard calls the "infinite qualitative distinction" between the divine and the creaturely.[33] Echoing the comments in his early lecture on "The New World in the Bible," he asserts again that an absolute distinction of this kind is the decisive "theme" of the Bible and suggests that this distinction is the only assumption that he brings to the text.[34] It is his understanding of the Bible's essential content, and not general principles regarding textual interpretation or reflection on the task of reconstructing another's thinking, that supplies his interpretive framework. Barth concedes that this understanding may come into question

28. Barth, "Preface to the First Edition," 1.
29. Barth, "Preface to the Third Edition," 17–19.
30. Barth, "Preface to the Second Edition," 8.
31. Barth, "Preface to the Second Edition," 11.
32. Barth, "Preface to the Second Edition," 8.
33. Barth, "Preface to the Second Edition," 10.
34. Barth, "Preface to the Second Edition," 10–11.

in the course of actual exegesis, but he insists that, as a question of interpretive principle, his critics do more violence to the text by approaching it with hermeneutical precepts derived from various branches of modern study than he does in attempting to interpret it in light of its own subject matter.[35]

Barth's conception of a contrast between old and new worlds permits him to respond to two other criticisms of his work. In the first place, it positions him to resist the charge that he is an "enemy of historical criticism" who wishes to return to a naive precritical biblicism.[36] Barth claims that—"fortunately"—he need not choose between a doctrine of inspiration and the principles of historical-critical study.[37] The latter concern the text as a quantity shaped by the old world of human activity. The critical scholar uses the results of historical, archaeological, and grammatical analysis to present a picture of the text as it reflects the elements of human language and activity. This endeavor is "both necessary and justified" as "preliminary work" that facilitates the reconstruction and comprehension of the text, but it is of strictly penultimate significance because it has no purchase on the new world of God.[38] The tools used by the critical scholar can yield the conclusion that a human agent acted in a particular way, but they rest on assumptions about the causal continuity of all events in time in a way that precludes access to the activity of God. The standards used by historical scholarship permit it to speak to the old world of human being and doing but not the new world of God.

By contrast, the doctrine of inspiration calls the reader to understand the text in terms of the new world of the activity of God. Whereas historical-critical work seeks to understand Scripture "apart from the 'Spirit,'" which is Scripture's proper object, the doctrine of inspiration secures the "correlation of 'Scripture' and 'Spirit'" and ensures that understanding Scripture is a matter of discerning "in spiritual fashion what is spiritually intended."[39] Crucially, restoring this "correlation" does not involve "repristination" of precritical modes of exegesis, but rather a call to scholars to take their critical work to its proper end.[40] True criticism means "the measuring of words and phrases by the standard of that about which the documents are speaking"; thus, "the critical historian needs to be more critical" by moving beyond criticism of the text in light of historical inquiry to criticism in light of the text's subject

35. Barth, "Preface to the Second Edition," 10–11.
36. Barth, "Preface to the Second Edition," 6.
37. Barth, "Preface to the First Edition," 1.
38. Barth, "Preface to the Second Edition," 6–7.
39. Barth, "Answer to von Harnack's Letter," 177; Barth, "Preface to the Third Edition," 19.
40. Barth, "Answer to von Harnack's Letter," 176–77.

matter.[41] Barth thus supposes that, rather than opposing critical inquiry, his work shows a "meaningful way of incorporating it into theology" by permitting it to do its work, and then inviting it to complete itself in engaging in criticism in light of the subject matter of the text itself.[42]

A similar radicalization of the position of his critics appears in Barth's response to a second concern that was raised regarding his exegesis. A century before Barth, Schleiermacher had suggested that exegesis involves a critical procedure through which the reader identifies the authentic core of a text and then applies this core as a standard in relation to which authentic and inauthentic elements may be distinguished within the text as a whole. Readers of Barth's commentaries faulted him for failing to make use of a similar procedure so that aspects of Paul's letters—Paul's apparent reliance on Old Testament teaching about Adam and Paul's attitude toward secular authority, for example—could be shown to be incidental to his true theme. Yet Barth claims that a grasp of the contrast between old and new worlds makes this critical procedure inappropriate. On one level, all the words of the Bible are human words that belong to the old world of human speaking and doing. On another, all the words may point to the new world of the activity of God and help readers to recognize its reality. Barth's critic supposed that, through careful study, the words of the true "Spirit of Christ" must be separated out from the words of "other spirits" within Paul's letters. Barth responds:

> I must go farther than [my critic] does and say that there are in the Epistle no words at all which are not words of those "other spirits." . . . Is it really legitimate to extract a certain number of passages and claim that there the veritable spirit of Christ has spoken? . . . It seems to me impossible to set the Spirit of Christ—the veritable subject-matter of the Epistle—over against other spirits, in such a manner as to deal out praise to some passages and to depreciate others where Paul is not controlled by his true subject-matter. Rather, it is for us to perceive and to make clear that the whole is placed under the KRISIS of the Spirit of Christ. The whole is litera, that is, voices of those other spirits. The problem is whether the whole must not be understood in relation to the true subject-matter, which is—The Spirit of Christ.[43]

In effect, Barth's contrast between old and new worlds means that there are two ways in which the Bible can be read. On one level, the realities associated with the old world of human activity—history, morality, and religion—are to

41. Barth, "Preface to the Second Edition," 8.
42. Barth, "Answer to von Harnack's Letter," 176–77.
43. Barth, "Preface to the Third Edition," 16–17.

be found in the Bible.[44] On this level, it can be said that "the Bible contains the literary monuments of an Ancient Near Eastern religion and of a religious cult of the Hellenistic epoch. As a human document like any other, it can lay no a priori dogmatic claim for special attention or consideration."[45] Historical-critical work as well as moral, psychological, and religious inquiry have their justification in the fact that the Bible may be read for its creaturely history, morality, and religion. But on another level, the fact that the true subject matter of Scripture is the new world of the activity of God means that those who approach the Bible on these terms miss its decisive element. Barth writes that the Bible ultimately confounds the historian, the moralist, and the religious thinker because history, morality, and religion are interrupted in the seminal events in which God acts. History "temporarily stops" because events cannot be explained in terms of causes within the creaturely world, moral reflection is confounded because the Bible speaks of divine rather than human activity, and religion meets its end because the Bible presents God's thoughts about human beings rather than human thoughts about God.[46]

The final point to be made about Barth's early exegesis is that, while he is willing to grant legitimacy to historical, moral, and religious inquiry into Scripture, he is also insistent that the divine Spirit may unmask this inquiry as a strategy used by human readers to evade encounter with the new world of God. One of the consistent themes of Barth's work is that, through the divine Spirit, Scripture itself has an agency through which it turns human questions back onto the questioners and prods them beyond evasion to acknowledgment of the reality of God. Barth writes that we might in fact do better not to ask "what is in the Bible?" for the question "has a mortifying way of turning into the opposing question: 'Well, what do you want?'"[47] "We will find in it only as much as we are looking for: great things and divine things if we look for great and divine things, or inane and 'historical' things if we look for inane and 'historical' things."[48] The Bible "gives to each one what fits him," but there is an agency at work in Scripture that does not leave readers free to rest with the penultimate versions of the content of Scripture that they construct: "The Bible says quickly, very clearly, and in a very friendly manner about the certain 'versions' we make of it: 'So this is you, but not me! Now this is what

44. Barth constructs his lecture on the new world in the Bible in part around the affirmations that history, morality, and religion are all to be found in the Bible, and then in calling the importance of these affirmations into question. See "New World," 20, 21, 24.

45. Barth, "Biblical Questions," 79.

46. Barth, "New World," 22–25.

47. Barth, "New World," 18; cf. Barth, "Biblical Questions," 74.

48. Barth, "New World," 18.

perhaps in fact fits you very well, your emotional needs, your views. . . . See, you wanted to mirror yourself in me, and sure enough you have rediscovered your image in me! But now go and search for me! Look for what is there!'"[49]

The Development of a Theology of Scripture

The instincts regarding the theology of Scripture that are present in Barth's early work figure centrally in his mature work, but it is significant that these early notions resist summation into doctrinal formulation. Two reasons may be given for this. The first is that, in Barth's view, formulation of a theology of Scripture risks appearing as an evasion of encounter with the reality that Scripture wishes to present. Inquiry into the nature of Scripture as such may betray that one's commitment to the text is in fact limited, for a truly "loyal" reader does not make the text an object of interest for itself but seeks rather to understand all of its elements in terms of its "veritable subject-matter."[50] The second is that Barth's own understanding of Christology, the work of the Holy Spirit, and the way that creaturely realities like the sacraments, Scripture, and preaching mediate the presence of God is underdeveloped. A strong opposition between divine and creaturely reality is central to his thinking. He has not yet worked through the ways that differing elements within the creaturely sphere mediate the presence of the divine.

Barth became painfully aware of the limitations of his theological background when, in 1921, he was invited on the basis of his work on Romans to take up an honorary professorship at the University of Göttingen. He found himself required to teach subjects with which he had little familiarity, and worked with extraordinary energy to fill gaps in his own understanding. During his first several years in Göttingen, his courses were confined to scriptural exegesis and historical theology. Through his work in historical theology in particular, Barth began to develop the conceptual tools that shape his mature theology of Scripture.

Two elements in this process are important for us. The first is the theology of Scripture that Barth found in the Reformed tradition and in Calvin's work in particular. Through lecture courses on Calvin's theology and the theology of the Reformed confessional statements, Calvin became for Barth a special guide to the theology of Scripture in the same way that Paul had been a guide to Scripture's meaning. This occurred in part because, as we have seen, Barth had already found in Calvin's exegesis an approach to Scripture that was

49. Barth, "New World," 19.
50. Barth, "Preface to the Third Edition," 17.

companionable with his own concerns, but more systematic study of Calvin and the Reformed tradition also served to push Barth beyond his existing notions to sharper understanding of the theology of Scripture.

This dynamic emerges first in the way that engagement with Calvin filled out Barth's understanding of inspiration. In his early work, Barth tended to functionalize the notion of inspiration, treating it as a clue to the way that Scripture is to be understood by the contemporary reader. This tendency continues to be reflected at points in his lectures on Calvin,[51] but Calvin also presents Barth with an understanding of inspiration as a "twofold" divine act that is typical of Barth's own later work.[52] According to this understanding, there is a speaking of the Spirit among the writers of Scripture and a corresponding speaking of the Spirit among contemporary readers of Scripture. On the basis of the Spirit's movement "there and then" it may be said that "the Holy Spirit is in the letter" of the text. But the corresponding work of the Spirit "here and now" means that Scripture becomes "certain and authoritative" not merely by "an enforcing of the dictate of the letter" but also by the "voice of truth that makes itself heard . . . in the believing reader."[53] This paired set of acts of divine speech means that inspiration appears in a "living sense" as "a conversation of the truth with itself."[54] Elements in the later Reformed tradition go astray, on Barth's telling, by so emphasizing the speaking of the Spirit among the prophets and apostles that the biblical text is treated as identical with the speaking of God, but Calvin remains reliable in insisting that the Spirit must speak again through the text if the Word of God is to be found in Scripture.

On a related front, study of Calvin's work moves Barth toward a principled affirmation of the authority of Scripture as a decisive element within the church's life. In his earlier work, Barth insisted on the authority of the subject matter of the text in order to resist those who emphasized the authority of a method of study,[55] but he tended not to move from asserting the normative force of the subject to acknowledging the authority of the text itself. This changed as Barth began to absorb an insight that he took to be characteristic of Reformed theology generally. As he presented it, the Reformed tradition is distinguished by the development of a consistent "Scripture principle" that

---

51. Barth asks what, for Calvin, the doctrine of inspiration "amounts to in practice but the hypothesis that in some sense the text is trustworthy, the premise that there has to be a meaning in it, a meaning, indeed, in its wording?" (Barth, *Theology of John Calvin*, 391).

52. Barth, *Theology of John Calvin*, 167.

53. Barth, *Theology of John Calvin*, 167.

54. Barth, *Theology of John Calvin*, 167.

55. Barth, "Answer to von Harnack's Letter," 176.

affirms "the Word of God in the Bible as the norm of faith and life" within the church.[56] This affirmation rests on a threefold movement of thought. It asserts that God alone is the subject of the knowledge of God, progresses to the claim that God is therefore known only as he gives himself to be known, and concludes that Scripture is authoritative because it is in Scripture that God gives himself to be known.[57] On these terms, acknowledgment of the authority of Scripture is derived from confession of the sovereign uniqueness of God as the only subject of the knowledge of God. "The Bible's isolated normativity" is understood as an "image" of the "isolated authority of God."[58] This sequence of thought allowed Barth to move away from the worry that identification of an authoritative element in the creaturely sphere—the sphere in which Scripture is found—detracts from the sovereignty of God. By grounding the authority of Scripture in the sovereign uniqueness of God, the Reformed tradition equipped Barth to acknowledge the former without threatening the latter.

The final front on which study of Calvin and the Reformers advanced Barth's theology of Scripture concerns the conceptual tools that allowed Barth to work through the relation between the divine and the creaturely in Scripture. Barth's early work is marked by an opposition between the divine and the creaturely in which the former is present in the latter only in episodic moments of revelation, but Barth finds in Calvin a notion that helps him to think through the perdurance of Scripture's authority without collapsing the distinction between the divine and the creaturely. This notion emerges from Reformation debates about the sacraments, in which the mode of divine presence in creaturely reality was precisely the issue. As Barth presents it, Calvin is able to see further than his contemporaries on this question because his work is shaped by a proper understanding of the difference between the Creator and the creature. "No Reformer is shaped by the opposition between time and eternity as strongly as he is."[59] Calvin rejects Lutheran notions of the real presence of the divine in the sacraments as a denial of this antithesis; he suggests instead that God is present in the sacraments in his promise to be present. God promises his presence; it is this promise that is present to the church; it is itself not a mere set of words but a positive form of the very presence that is promised. God is present in his promise in a form that is proper to life in

56. Barth, *Theology of John Calvin*, 386; Karl Barth, *The Theology of the Reformed Confessions*, trans. Darrell L. Guder and Judith J. Guder (Louisville: Westminster John Knox, 2002), 38–40.
57. Barth, *Theology of John Calvin*, 386–88; Barth, *Theology of the Reformed Confessions*, 38–64.
58. Barth, *Theology of the Reformed Confessions*, 49.
59. Barth, *Theology of John Calvin*, 125.

time. Promise is, for Calvin, the "supreme and proper form in which God now draws near to us."[60] "What we as Christians can be and have is wholly and exclusively promise, promissio, and nothing more."[61]

This understanding of promise as the proper mode of divine presence in time means that the uniqueness of Scripture is to be understood in terms of its connection with divine promise. The words of Scripture issue from the speaking of the divine Spirit "there and then." Though the words themselves are a creaturely reality that is not to be identified with divine speech, they come with the promise that the Spirit's speaking "there and then" will be accompanied by a speaking "here and now."[62] This promise is itself the proper mode of God's relation to the words of Scripture. Equipped with this notion, Barth believes that he can affirm the authority of Scripture without weakening the distinction between the divine and the creaturely. Understanding promise as a positive mode of divine presence provides a conceptual anchor for the Reformed Scripture principle and grounds the hope that the "twofold" reality of the act of inspiration will be fulfilled. In its connection with Barth's understanding of the inspiration and authority of Scripture, it is a hinge point in the maturation in Barth's doctrine of Scripture that follows from his encounter with the Reformed tradition in the early 1920s.

Barth's burgeoning theology of Scripture is further fleshed out through lectures on the Gospel of John that he delivered during the mid-1920s. These lectures position Barth to give a well-grounded account of a notion that is central to his theology of Scripture. We have begun to see that Barth's understanding of Scripture revolves around the notion that Scripture points beyond itself to the sovereign reality of God. The words of the Bible are not to be identified with divine speech; instead, the relation between the two is to be understood in terms of promise. From the early 1920s onward, Barth adopted the language of "witness" to characterize this relationship.[63] Though not the speech of God itself, Scripture is a witness to the reality and activity of God that is accompanied by the presence of God in promise. The notion of witness plays a central role in Barth's theology of Scripture from the early 1920s, but it is sharpened through Barth's study of the opening chapter of John's Gospel in particular. Two elements in this chapter are important. The

---

60. Barth, *Theology of John Calvin*, 175.

61. Barth, *Theology of John Calvin*, 125.

62. Barth holds that word and sacrament go together as the essential elements of the church's life because sacrament is the sign of the promise that accompanies the preaching of the word.

63. See, e.g., Karl Barth, *The Göttingen Dogmatics: Instruction in the Christian Religion*, vol. 1, ed. Hannelotte Reiffen, trans. Geoffrey W. Bromiley (Grand Rapids: Eerdmans, 1991), 201–11.

first has to do with the presentation of John the Baptist. The second has to do with the theology of creation more generally.

In the first place, the description of John the Baptist that appears in John 1 captures Barth's attention as a "paradigm" of the work of witness that Scripture performs.[64] Barth supposes that the Evangelist discusses John the Baptist, who came "to bear witness to the light," in order to clarify the work of witness that he himself performs in writing a Gospel. "[The Evangelist] instructs his readers regarding his own relation to his object insofar as he instructs them in the same relation with regards to John the Baptist. He wants to create clarity about what he, the evangelist, does and does not do as such, can and cannot do, is and is not."[65] John 1 is thus, for Barth, the definitive statement of the terms on which Scripture itself wishes to be understood. "More clearly than anywhere else in the Bible . . . it is said to us here just what the Bible is: witness to revelation that is related to but also distinct from revelation itself."[66] The two-sided "related to" but "distinct from" that appears here is foundational to Barth's understanding of Scripture. In Scripture's own account of its relation to its object, there is on the one hand "the great Yes" with which Scripture affirms its relation to the speaking of God, but there is alongside it a "But" with which Scripture insists that it must be distinguished from the event of God's own speech.[67] "Witness is truly and in the best sense speaking about a subject, describing it exactly and fully, pointing to it, confirming and repeating it, and all in such a way that the subject remains itself and can speak for itself. . . . Only where we have both supreme concern to speak with maximal proximity to the object and supreme concern to permit the object its distance so that it may speak for itself do we have witness."[68]

Barth fleshes out this account of the work of witness by clarifying the dangers of confusing the witness with the reality to which it points. He suggests that the writer of the Fourth Gospel has a special reason for using John the Baptist to clarify the relation of the witness to its object, for a "Baptist sect" had arisen in the first century that effaced the distinction and honored John the Baptist as the revealer.[69] In the face of this situation, Barth suggests that the Evangelist seeks, first, to ward off this misunderstanding by insisting that the Baptist "was not the light, but came to bear witness to the light" and, second,

64. Karl Barth, *Erklärung des Johannes-Evangelium (Kapitel 1–8)* (Zurich: Theologischer Verlag Zürich, 1976), 19.
65. Barth, *Erklärung des Johannes-Evangelium*, 19.
66. Barth, *Erklärung des Johannes-Evangelium*, 21.
67. Barth, *Erklärung des Johannes-Evangelium*, 21.
68. Barth, *Erklärung des Johannes-Evangelium*, 64.
69. Barth, *Erklärung des Johannes-Evangelium*, 19–21.

to use Jesus's discussion of John's work as a "witness to the truth" to show the "danger" of the misunderstanding.[70] This latter discussion shows "what should not happen in the situation between the revealer, the witness, and the hearer."[71] Jesus's hearers rejoiced "for a little while" in the light of John the Baptist, but they do not acknowledge Christ. That they rejoiced in John and ignore Christ shows that they have confused the witness with the reality. The hopelessness of their situation shows the danger of mistaking the witness to the light for the light itself. Driving the same point home in an exposition of 1 Corinthians, Barth writes that followers of Peter and Paul find themselves at odds in the church in Corinth because they have confused the witness of Peter and Paul with the Word that may be spoken by God alone.[72] For Barth, religious turmoil and fractiousness in the church are what believers ought to expect when the witness to revelation is confused with revelation itself.

Engagement with John 1 permits Barth to go on to ground his account of the work of witness in the theology of creation. Barth interprets the emphasis in John 1 on the coming into being of all things through the Word as an attempt to provide the ontological framework within which the notion of witness may be understood. That "all that is" came into being through the Word indicates, first, that "all that is" is creaturely and not divine. It belongs within the "circle of becoming" and so is not "immediate" to God.[73] "There is in the entire world no immediacy to God"; thus the witness cannot be treated as identical with the Word of God itself.[74] The origin of creaturely reality through the Word then means, second, that all creaturely being and activity is dependent on the Word. "Its existence cannot be understood in any other way than through the Word. Its own function is absolutely bestowed by the Word, by the Word that is God."[75] Barth argues that John introduces this notion in order to establish a "criterion" in relation to which the Baptist's work of witness may be understood. The witness may not be taken to be identical with the Word; it also cannot be thought to possess a freestanding significance separable from the activity of the Word itself. Only by continual reference to the reality of the Word itself may the witness be understood. The witness thus functions within the parameters that are proper to it in its creatureliness only when it does not claim significance for itself but seeks instead to point

70. Barth, *Erklärung des Johannes-Evangelium*, 19–20, 65–66; cf. John 5:30–47.
71. Barth, *Erklärung des Johannes-Evangelium*, 20.
72. Karl Barth, *The Resurrection of the Dead*, trans. H. J. Stenning (Eugene, OR: Wipf and Stock, 2003), 13–16.
73. Barth, *Erklärung des Johannes-Evangelium*, 41.
74. Barth, *Erklärung des Johannes-Evangelium*, 41.
75. Barth, *Erklärung des Johannes-Evangelium*, 41–42.

beyond itself to the one through whom it came into being. Equipped with an understanding of the difference between the creature and the Creator and the dependence of the former on the latter, Barth thinks that the Evangelist is positioned to show that, in serving as a witness to the light, John fulfills the function that is proper to him as a creature.

Barth's Mature Theology of Scripture

To this point we have encountered the fundamental building blocks of Barth's mature theology of Scripture. One further aspect of Barth's lectures on John is useful for us in making a turn to this theology. In opening these lectures, Barth reflects on the force of the notion that God is known through God alone for the reading of Scripture.[76] It is this notion that he identified earlier as the basis of the Reformed Scripture principle. He suggests now that it has significant hermeneutical implications. It implies that Scripture is always encountered in "a concrete determined situation" that is shaped by divine rather than human activity, and that the factors that constitute this situation—the nature of the gospel message as good news that human beings cannot create for themselves, the presentation of this good news in the words of other human beings who are able to speak the truth only as illumined by God, the demand for faith that the Bible places on its readers—represent "the fundamental elements of a biblical hermeneutics."[77] The affirmation that God is known through God alone means that the elements of biblical hermeneutics are found not in grammatical and psychological principles that facilitate apprehension of the human thinking that underlies the text but rather in the divine activity that creates the "situation" in which the faithful reader encounters Scripture. The Reformed Scripture principle means that understanding Scripture requires consideration of the economy of divine activity.[78]

Barth's mature theology of Scripture is constructed in and around an account of the economy within which Scripture is what it is. Scripture first appears in the *Church Dogmatics* as the basis for the possibility of theology at all. Barth opens his magnum opus with an inquiry into the "way of knowing" that is to be taken in theology. He writes that the theme of his treatment of the question will be the topic that "the older Protestant theology . . . treated

---

76. This comes to the fore through Barth's invocation of 1 Cor. 2:14 ("The natural man does not receive the gifts of the Spirit of God" [RSV mg.]), a verse that Barth sees as an expression of the principle that God alone knows God and God alone gives himself to be known. See Barth, *Erklärung des Johannes-Evangelium*, 1.

77. Barth, *Erklärung des Johannes-Evangelium*, 4–12.

78. Barth, *Erklärung des Johannes-Evangelium*, 4.

under the title On Holy Scripture," and is "materially the same as the assertion of the authority and normativeness of Holy Scripture."[79] Scripture is thus presented as the basis of the theological enterprise. All that is to be said about the possibility of theology is to be said in reference to the reality of Scripture, but Barth goes on to say that "what falls to be said about Holy Scripture . . . needs a comprehensive elucidation of context." It must be situated within an understanding of the theology of revelation generally, which in turn requires treatment of "the whole doctrine of the Trinity and the essentials of Christology."[80] Understanding Scripture requires a comprehensive account of God's revealing activity that is rooted in an understanding of God. The 1,400 pages of volume I of the *Church Dogmatics* are thus in one sense nothing more than a development of the claim that human speech about God finds its basis in the authority of Scripture. But, in a further sense, the development of this claim involves a comprehensive account of the being and activity of the triune Revealer as the "context" in which the authority of Scripture may be understood.

The claims regarding Scripture that are developed in *CD* I—that Scripture is, for instance, one "form" of revelation alongside the church's proclamation and the event of revelation itself—are among the best known, if not always best understood, features of Barth's theology. I will bypass further comment on them here; the content and contours of the theology of Scripture that Barth presents in *CD* I are treated in a further essay in this volume by Ben Rhodes. I propose to turn instead to some of the decisions regarding the theology of Scripture that mark the later volumes of the *Church Dogmatics*. The importance of these decisions ought not to be overlooked. Though the material in *CD* I represents Barth's most systematic treatment of the theology of Scripture, some readers hold that in fact later volumes of the *Church Dogmatics* present this theology in its most fruitful forms as Barth engages in concerted use of Scripture and considers Scripture as a theme only in an ad hoc way as engagement with the text itself demands.[81] The full sweep of the *Church Dogmatics* offers a treasure trove of concepts regarding the theology of Scripture; unfortunately, we must content ourselves with summary indications of a series of notions developed in the work as a whole.

Perhaps the most significant aspect of the *Church Dogmatics* in its entirety is its grounding in and saturation by Scripture. The work contains more than two thousand exegetical discussions in an extraordinary range of forms: con-

79. *CD* I/1, 43.
80. *CD* I/1, 43–44.
81. See, e.g., Hans Frei, *The Eclipse of Biblical Narrative* (New Haven: Yale University Press, 1974), vii–viii.

sideration of key biblical terms, typological discussions of the way that Old Testament figures point to the christological shape of God's act of election, discussions of the way that apparent differences in manuscript sources in Genesis are in fact pointers to matters of theological significance. In one sense, the *Church Dogmatics* appears as "nothing other than a sustained meditation on the texts of Holy Scripture."[82] At a number of points, its content is decisively shaped by submission to Scripture's authority. In his theology of election, Barth writes that he would have liked to follow Calvin's doctrine quite closely, but that "as I let the Bible itself reach to me on these matters, as I meditated upon what I seemed to hear, I was driven irresistibly to reconstruction."[83] In his theology of creation, he suggests that it is not self-evident that a theology of the Word of God, which has the relation between God and human creatures as its essential concern, should include a discussion of angels, but that "the teacher and master to which we must keep in this matter can only be the Holy Scriptures of the Old and New Testament," and Scripture itself points to treatment of angelology as an element in a proper understanding of the relation between God and creatures.[84]

The prevalence of Scripture in the *Church Dogmatics* reflects Barth's sense that the theologian is tasked with inciting in readers "an interest and love" for Scripture as the "inexhaustible real ground and epistemological basis of the science of systematic theology."[85] Barth expressed growing concern about the neglect of Scripture in the life of the church and the individual believer. "Today theologians are always travelling. Instead of their staying at home, I fear that a great majority of them are out there sitting in cars, in waiting rooms, in trains or in airports. When do they ever find time to read the Bible?"[86] "We need to take time again for Scripture. . . . Gather around the table to study Scripture together!"[87] "Every believer needs to get used to reading continuous passages. . . . For me as a theology professor, it is a daily duty. . . . One needs to accustom oneself to reading the Bible."[88]

Barth's later work emphasizes that the significance of Scripture is rooted in the irreducible significance of Christ himself. Barth is perhaps best known for a theological Christocentrism that mandates that all aspects of Christian teaching are to be rooted in Christology. In the sphere of the theology of

---

82. Francis Watson, "The Bible," in *The Cambridge Companion to Karl Barth*, ed. John Webster (Cambridge: Cambridge University Press, 2000), 57.
83. *CD* II/2, x.
84. *CD* III/3, 369–72.
85. Barth, "Barth and Cullman on Their Theological Vocation," 226–27.
86. Barth, "Gespräch mit polnischen Christen," in *Gespräche 1964–1968*, 390.
87. Barth, "Interview von S. Findeisen (26.5.1964)," in *Gespräche 1964–1968*, 171.
88. Barth, "Interview von. Fr. Klopfenstein (30.4.1966)," in *Gespräche 1964–1968*, 243.

Scripture, Barth's Christocentrism issued in an increased emphasis on Christ as the decisive center in relation to which all other aspects of Scripture are to be understood. Barth writes that, if we ask "concerning the one point upon which, according to Scripture, our attention and thoughts should and must be concentrated, then from first to last the Bible directs us to the name of Jesus Christ."[89] "When Holy Scripture speaks of God it concentrates our attention and thoughts upon one single point and what is to be known at that point."[90] Even then, in approaching scriptural teaching about creation, the material is to be interpreted christologically. The "impregnable basis" of a doctrine of creation "is indeed the fact that it is in the Bible"; yet a further step needs to be taken to the recognition that the Bible "gives us a reliable basis for our knowledge and confession" because "it gives us witness to Jesus Christ."[91] "Its word in all words is this Word. . . . If, therefore, we are rightly to understand and estimate what it says about creation, we must first see that—like everything else it says—this refers and testifies first and last to Him. At this point, too, He is the primary and ultimate object of its witness."[92]

Barth supposes that it is a Christocentrism of this kind that secures the uniqueness of Scripture in the face of the demand of critical scholars that it be read "like any other book." He develops this notion by suggesting that, beside "the right and necessary and central biblicism," there is a "scattered and peripheral" biblicism that "does not know that the Bible is a totality and that it is meant to be read in all its parts in the light of its unity, i.e., of the One of whom it everywhere speaks."[93] This latter biblicism takes the "verbal doctrine of inspiration" to mean that all elements of Scripture possess a freestanding significance that may be grasped apart from reference to Christ. "The question of Jesus Christ ceases to be the controlling and comprehensive question and simply becomes one amongst others."[94] Where this occurs, "secretly the book of revelation is being treated and read like other books," for it is "divorced from the living Word" and made "readily apprehensible as though it were an object of secular experience."[95] Scripture has its uniqueness in its witness to Christ; where it is read apart from this decisive center, it is reduced to a "repository of all sorts and degrees of pious knowledge" that might just as well be found elsewhere.[96]

89. CD II/2, 53.
90. CD II/1, 52.
91. CD III/1, 23.
92. CD III/1, 23.
93. CD III/1, 24.
94. CD IV/1, 368.
95. CD IV/1, 368.
96. CD III/1, 24; IV/1, 368.

Barth anchors his account of the christological shape of "the right and necessary and central biblicism" in a new christological emphasis in his theology of inspiration. From the early days of his lectures on Calvin, Barth understood inspiration as a "twofold" reality that consists in correspondence between an act of divine speaking among the prophets and apostles and a further act of divine speaking among contemporary readers of the prophetic and apostolic witness. Through the opening volumes of the *Church Dogmatics*, this divine speaking is understood in terms of the work of the Holy Spirit, but the later volumes of the *Church Dogmatics* guard against a doctrine of inspiration that permits aspects of Scripture to float free of Christology by folding an account of inspiration into an understanding of the communicative quality of Christ's work. In the last part-volume of the *Church Dogmatics* that Barth completed, he develops the claim that Christ's work is marked by a prophetic character through which it is inherently communicative.[97] "As he lives, Jesus Christ speaks for Himself. . . . He is His own authentic witness. . . . Of Himself He grounds and summons and creates knowledge of Himself."[98] Christ's life is "eloquent and radiant";[99] the "twofold" reality of inspiration is a function of this radiance. On the one side, "the word of the prophets and apostles" has its truth from the fact that they themselves "participated in the history of Jesus Christ" and had their word "formed and guided" by the one Word of God.[100] On the other side, the contemporary reader of Scripture is enlightened by Christ's prophetic work, for the Christ whose life is light is the risen Christ who is not bound by history.[101] This christological account of inspiration ensures that no part of Scripture might be taken to possess a significance that can be abstracted from Christ.

In contrast to a sequence of thought that marks the work of other modern figures like Schleiermacher, a christocentric account of inspiration does not lead Barth to crowd the Old Testament out of the Christian canon. Barth makes clear that, while Christ "fulfils" and "transcends" the history of Israel,[102] this history is not in any way "outmoded, replaced or dissolved."[103] This history

---

97. This affirmation belongs to Barth's deployment of the classical notion that Christ's work can be understood in terms of a "threefold office." As the anointed one of God, Christ performs the functions associated with the three offices in the Old Testament that required anointing: prophet, priest, and king. Volume IV of *CD* has the division of Christ's work into prophetic, priestly, and kingly aspects as one of its structuring principles.

98. *CD* IV/3.1, 46.

99. *CD* IV/3.1, 79.

100. *CD* IV/3.1, 113–14.

101. *CD* IV/3.1, 46.

102. *CD* IV/3.1, 49–52.

103. *CD* IV/3.1, 70.

can be seen as "a type and prefiguration" of the revelation of Christ, but, crucially, it may be seen in this way only when it is grasped as an interconnected whole.[104] Barth furthers his polemic against a "peripheral biblicism" by suggesting that dissimilarity outweighs similarity when particular Old Testament figures or events are compared to Christ, but that considerable structural similarity between the history of Israel and Christ's own history may be seen when the Old Testament is grasped "in its totality and interconnection as planned, initiated, controlled and determined by Yahweh."[105] In its totality, the history of Israel mirrors and anticipates Christ's history in that it "has its basis in an address, promise, command, order, and summons of Yahweh"; it has a universal significance for the lives of all nations; it is "overarched and stabilised and ordered by the grace of the covenant" in such a way that it is a history of reconciliation; and it presents a mediating reality between God and creation.[106] In mirroring the structure of Christ's history in this way, the history of Israel is "co-ordinated" with Christ's history as a "definite pre-history" marked by expectation of the promised Messiah.[107]

One final aspect of Barth's theology of Scripture is connected to the emphasis on history that marks his handling of Israel and Christology. The notion of history brings with it a host of questions that were formative of Barth's intellectual context. In what sense do the biblical texts present historical events? Is revelation identical with particular events in history? If so, is historical study best suited to discovering the truth about God? Influential voices in the generation that preceded Barth insisted that historical study is the proper means for understanding Christianity; this insistence was then taken by some to mean that Christianity cannot claim absolute significance, for realities that are known through historical study are made relative by the fact that they are understood in relation to and analogy with other events. We have encountered elements of Barth's early response to these assertions in his claim that, while there is history in the Bible, history "stops" at the point where the new world of God breaks into the old world of flesh, for events rooted in divine activity are not conditioned by other causal forces and cannot be understood through analogy with other events. Further elements are found in Barth's later work as he engages with aspects of Scripture that raise the question of history in an acute form.

Four kinds of biblical texts are central in raising for Barth the question of revelation and history: discussions of creation, angels, miracles, and the

104. *CD* IV/3.1, 53.
105. *CD* IV/3.1, 52–69.
106. *CD* IV/3.1, 53–63.
107. *CD* I/2, 70.

resurrection. Barth is consistent is suggesting that these discussions present a form of "'non-historical' history." They present history in one sense because they do not refer to abstract, timeless realities to which narrative form is an incidental pointer. They refer to events in space and time that have no meaning apart from their spatiotemporal occurrence, but they are to be understood as "'non-historical' history" because divine activity is their essential "content," and they are thus inaccessible to historical study.[108] They are not the work of one agent alongside others in continuous causal connection. They are not analogous to other events in time, and they cannot be understood through consideration of the set of possibilities that is known to human agents.[109] Because they have their basis in divine activity, they are "beyond the reach" of straightforward historical depiction and historical research.[110] Barth writes that "the whole history of the Bible . . . intends to be and is real spatio-temporal history," but it has a "constant bias" toward a "non-historical" form of history because of its proximity to the activity of God.[111] "Every history is in fact 'non-historical'" where it stands "in immediacy to God."[112]

Barth proposes that the term "saga" best corresponds to this kind of "'non-historical' history." Saga presents "imaginative," "poetic" descriptions of events that evade "historical depiction."[113] "Saga in general is the form which, using intuition and imagination, has to take up historical narration at the point where events are no longer susceptible as such of historical proof."[114] It is "an intuitive and poetic picture of a non-historical reality of history."[115] How could anything other than a poetic picture be deployed, Barth asks, when Scripture deals with "the history of the work and revelation of God, which . . . is not confined to the sphere of ordinary earthly analogies?"[116] It is entirely in order that, in seeking to deal with the singular activity of God,

---

108. *CD* III/1, 78–81; III/2, 446–47.

109. *CD* III/3, 374–76.

110. *CD* III/2, 452. It is important to note that Barth's work is shaped quite heavily by a particular account of the principles used in proper historical research. In the generation prior to Barth, it was proposed that historical study is possible only where events exist in an interconnected network of causal forces and can be comprehended through analogy with known events in time (see Ernst Troeltsch, "Historical and Dogmatic Method in Theology," in *Religion and History* [Edinburgh: T&T Clark, 1991]). In his own day, Barth responded critically to those who continued to suppose that only events that could be understood on these terms count as history (see *CD* III/2, 446–47).

111. *CD* III/3, 375–76.

112. *CD* III/1, 80.

113. *CD* III/1, 81; II/2, 452; IV/1, 508.

114. *CD* IV/1, 508.

115. *CD* III/1, 81.

116. *CD* III/3, 376.

the biblical writers should reach for language, concepts, and images that are imaginative and poetic, but this does not mean that "we are in the sphere of Red Riding Hood and her grandmother and the wolf, or the stork that leaves babies, or the March Hare and Father Christmas."[117] In the first place, the events themselves are not less real because they evade the categories of ordinary historical description. "Why should not imagination grasp real history, or the poetry which is its medium be a representation of real history, of the kind of history which escapes ordinary analogies?"[118] Second, the narratives themselves are not arbitrary and haphazard because they are imaginative. There is "meaningful as well as meaningless imagination . . . disciplined as well as undisciplined poetry . . . good saga and bad. . . . Both imagination and poetry can be ordered by orientation to the subject and its inner order."[119] The reality to which the biblical writers attempt to give witness has a rationality of its own. Where this rationality forms the witness of the biblical writers, it gives coherence, meaning, and truth to their "divination . . . imagination and poetry."[120]

How is the reader to approach events that are presented in the form of saga? Barth insists that these events "are not to be taken as 'history' in our sense of the word," which is to say that they are not to be thought capable of historical study or proof.[121] Attempts to harmonize differing accounts of the resurrection, or to read 1 Corinthians 15:3–8 as an attempt to "prove" the resurrection, are "amusingly incongruous."[122] Attempts to relate the Genesis narrative "either favorably or unfavorably to scientific palaeontology, or to what we now know with some historical certainty concerning the oldest and most primitive forms of human life," miss "the unprecedented and incomparable thing" that Genesis seeks to relate.[123] These attempts "do violence to the whole character of the event in question" by suggesting that it can be approached as a historical puzzle analogous to the questions raised regarding Hannibal's journey across the Alps.[124] Barth suggests that, because the Bible speaks of events that stand outside of all continuity and analogy with

117. CD III/3, 376.
118. CD III/3, 374. It is a "false conclusion" to assume that, because an event must be presented in the form of saga, the event itself "could not have occurred." "It is sheer superstition to suppose that only things which are open to 'historical' verification can have happened in time" (CD III/2, 446–47).
119. CD III/3, 376.
120. CD III/3, 376.
121. CD III/2, 452.
122. CD III/2, 452.
123. CD IV/1, 508.
124. CD III/2, 452.

other historical realities, "if we really want to know and understand the accounts, . . . we too shall have to make that divinatory crossing of the frontier of historicism and enter the sphere of imagination and poetry."[125] For readers, grasping the significance of the activity of God requires an imagination ordered by the inner logic and rationality of the activity of God. This, for Barth, involves taking the narratives literally, "not in a shallow but in a deep sense."[126] The hasty reader supposes that taking the material literally means treating it as straightforward historical narrative, but Barth supposes that this view reduces the God presented in Scripture to an agent whose acts can be recounted and understood through the same categories used in relation to all other acts. From the early days of his wrestling with Romans, Barth's reading of Scripture was shaped by the notion that, in his sovereignty, God stands in an infinite difference from all that is creaturely. The claim that grasping God's sovereign activity requires an imagination that is attuned to the rationality of this activity represents a working out of the consequences of this notion. It echoes Barth's earlier claim that understanding Scripture requires discerning "in spiritual fashion what is spiritually intended."[127] In both Barth's early and late work, a mode of spiritual comprehension is required to grasp the work of an agent who stands in infinite difference from all that is creaturely. It requires the activity of the Holy Spirit, which speaks "now" in correspondence to its speaking "then" in a completion of the living circle of biblical inspiration.

125. CD III/3, 374–75.
126. CD III/1, 84.
127. Barth, "Preface to the Third Edition," 19.

TWO

Barth's Theology of Scripture in Dogmatic Perspective

BEN RHODES

Introduction

Karl Barth's doctrine of Scripture is more often criticized than seriously considered.[1] Some of this is probably Barth's fault, since he wrote so very much. But some of the difficulty lies in Barth's manner of writing—his seemingly interminable dialectical spirals, exhaustively working through a theological

---

1. There are exceptions. Most recently, see *Reading the Gospels with Karl Barth*, ed. Daniel Migliore (Grand Rapids: Eerdmans, 2017). For a broad sampling, see *Thy Word Is Truth: Barth on Scripture*, ed. George Hunsinger (Grand Rapids: Eerdmans, 2012). John Webster has highlighted the importance of Barth's exegetical lectures for a better account of Barth's development; his essay on Barth's lectures on the Gospel of John, reprinted in *Thy Word Is Truth*, is a good example, though see also his *Barth's Earlier Theology* (Edinburgh: T&T Clark, 2005). Considering his original audience, Bruce McCormack's bravura performance "The Being of Scripture Is in Becoming: Karl Barth in Conversation with American Evangelical Criticism" in *Evangelicals and Scripture*, ed. Vincent Bacote, Laura Miguelez, and Dennis Okholm (Downers Grove, IL: InterVarsity, 2004), 55–75, is impressive. What McCormack calls Barth's "dynamic infallibilism" may appear in the same dogmatic location as inerrancy (a notoriously contested term, especially nowadays) does within North American evangelicalism, both of which certainly do "give rise to a very high view of Biblical authority," and this may make Barth a useful ally of American evangelicals (73–74). However, the doctrinal differences between Barth and American evangelicals seem rather deeper than simply the results of varying philosophical commitments (as McCormack argues).

point only to pivot to consider a different facet of the doctrine from yet another perspective. This prolix style is meant to indicate the infinite depths of God's perfect triune being as Father, Son, and Holy Spirit and the endless quest for finite and fallen humans to witness to the riches of God's self-revelation, ultimately disclosed in the person of Jesus Christ, who is the object of Scripture's witness, spoken of in the proclamation of the church, as critically tested in the activity of dogmatics. This means that summarizing Barth can be a tediously boring affair, stilling the movement that makes actually reading Barth so fascinating, or simply misleading, presenting his main points in bullet form, abstracted from their fluidly actual execution.

This general rule is nowhere as true as when it comes to consideration of Barth's doctrine of Scripture, particularly when considered in comparison with his actual exegetical practice. The main purpose of this essay is therefore to situate the content of this book, multiple essays that grapple with Barth's exegesis in careful detail. Here I will simply describe the general features of Barth's doctrine of Scripture as straightforwardly as possible, make a few critical comments about its adequacy—particularly regarding the relation of inspiration to illumination—and then get out of the way, because Barth's actual exegetical practice turns out to be more interesting than his theoretical remarks.

The typical evangelical understanding of (or at least doctrinally conservative Christian understanding, since the term "evangelical" is increasingly contested and politically controversial) Barth's doctrine of Scripture centers on two basic points. First, Barth says that Scripture has to *become* the Word of God by the action of God, which is often understood to mean that Scripture is not the Word of God before or apart from this action. Second, this actualistic conception of Scripture renders the possibility—or even reality—of errors in the (human) words of the Bible irrelevant. Reactions to this understanding tend to be strong. Those who are committed to inerrancy often accuse Barth of having abandoned any sense of the authority of Scripture, while others welcome Barth's claim with relief, finding that such a doctrine of Scripture permits dismissal of apparently archaic notions of inerrancy or infallibility. While there is a grain of truth in this understanding of Barth's doctrine of Scripture—he does make both claims—it misses the connection between what Barth says and how he says it, ignores the vast majority of Barth's full doctrine of Scripture (much of which I think ought to be highly congenial to doctrinally conservative Christians), and never investigates how Barth actually exegetes Scripture.

A better approach to Barth's doctrine of Scripture might begin by noting Barth's first ten years as a pastor in Safenwil, tasked with preaching Scripture to an audience largely unimpressed with his education or politics.[2] Or we might observe that Barth came to fame by publishing a commentary on Romans, the preface of which famously proposed that, if forced to choose, Barth would opt for the venerable doctrine of inspiration over the historical-critical method—though Barth believed he did not have to choose.[3] Or we might quote Barth's parting advice to his students in Bonn, as the Nazis forced him to return to Switzerland: "Exegesis, exegesis, and yet more exegesis!"[4] While all these observations are important, the best approach requires us to engage directly with Barth's most sustained "theoretical" presentation of the doctrine of Scripture, the place where he makes those inflammatory dialectical comments for which he is most well-known: §19 of *Church Dogmatics*, "The Word of God for the Church."[5]

An Outline of Barth's Doctrine of Scripture in *Church Dogmatics* I/2

The four chapters that constitute the first prolegomenal volume (I/1 and I/2) of the *Church Dogmatics* are structured with some care and are all located under the title "The Doctrine of the Word of God." Barth's famous three-fold conception of the Word of God—Jesus Christ, Scripture, and church proclamation—appears here in §4, its unity in distinction said to be analogous only to the Trinity (a curiously formal comparison that Barth later wisely drops).[6] The question of authority is at stake throughout, which is one of the reasons that Barth includes material theological exposition within his prolegomena, perhaps most famously a long sketch of the doctrine of the Trinity in chapter II ("The Revelation of God") as well as a highly compressed Christology, pneumatology, and anthropology (§§13–18). Chapter III ("Holy Scripture") contains three paragraphs: §19, "The Word of God for the Church"; §20, "Authority in the Church"; and §21, "Freedom in the Church." The secondary and derivative authority of the church in its proclamation

2. See Eberhard Busch, "Comrade Pastor," chap. 3 in *Karl Barth: His Life from Letters and Autobiographical Texts*, trans. John Bowden (London: SCM; Philadelphia: Fortress, 1976), 60–125.

3. *Romans II*, 1. Barth concludes his 1932 preface to the English edition by stating that "the purpose [of the book] was and is to direct [readers] to Holy Scripture, to the Epistle of Paul to the Romans, in order that, whether they be delighted or annoyed, whether they are 'accepted' or 'rejected,' they may at least be brought face to face with the subject matter of the Scriptures. . . . Primarily, and above all else, it must serve that *other* Book where Jesus Christ is present in His Church. Theology is *ministerium verbi divini*. It is nothing more nor less" (x).

4. Busch, *Karl Barth*, 259.

5. *CD* I/2, 457–537.

6. Most clearly in §4.4, "The Unity of the Word of God" (*CD* I/1, 120–24).

(chap. IV, "The Proclamation of the Church") rests on the relation between the Word of God and Scripture; since dogmatics is the critical testing of the church's proclamation in comparison with the Word of God, this relationship is the linchpin of the prolegomena. At its heart is Barth's description of inspiration as a miraculous circle extending from the production of the text of Scripture to the response of the reader or hearer. The entirety of that circle is an act of God, especially appropriated to the Holy Spirit. Barth is everywhere concerned to begin with actuality and only then proceed to analyze the conditions of possibility: we might say that a classic mark of Barth's theological reasoning is to theorize ex post facto, dogmatics as thinking after (*nachdenken*), primarily after the fact and in light of the reality of Jesus Christ.

Section 19 itself is divided into two subsections; Barth first speaks of "Scripture as a Witness to Divine Revelation" and then of "Scripture as the Word of God." "Witness" is one of Barth's favorite concepts; here he deploys it to demarcate the ontological status of Scripture. As a witness, the Bible is part of divine revelation, necessarily possessing a special status in the church; this is something we cannot establish, but can only confess.[7] But the Bible is not revelation itself; that Scripture is written in human words is what justifies serious historical study and confirms its status as witness: pointing beyond itself as a sign of divine revelation.[8]

The bulk of Barth's doctrine of Scripture in §19 is devoted to six points clarifying the meaning of the statement that Scripture is the Word of God. First, that Scripture is the Word of God is a canonical judgment by the church, a recognition that Scripture is already given.[9] Second, Scripture is a unified witness to the divine revelation of Jesus Christ in the Old and New Testaments.[10] We cannot philosophically systematize Scripture, because this unified witness is not at our disposal: "revelation is no more and no less than the life of God Himself turned to us, the Word of God coming to us by the Holy Spirit, Jesus Christ."[11] Third, the Bible's claim to be inspired is grounded by the true humanity of Jesus Christ, which includes within itself the humanity of the authors of Scripture, who are set apart by the divine summons to repeat in human words what God

---

7. *CD* I/2, 460.

8. *CD* I/2, 463. Incidentally, Barth takes this notion of human words as sign and witness to be in keeping with the hermeneutical self-understanding of Scripture (and not a general hermeneutic previously achieved and then subsequently applied to Scripture), but he suggests that it might profitably contribute to our reading of any text, patiently listening for the subject matter of the text instead of striving to dominate the text (465–72).

9. *CD* I/2, 473.

10. *CD* I/2, 482.

11. *CD* I/2, 483.

has said.[12] Fourth, the form and content of Scripture is indissoluble: divine revelation cannot be separated from the human words of the Bible.[13] Barth thinks that historical criticism is mistaken if it ignores this indirect identity, but insists that historical investigation is valuable when it is (re)oriented to the goal of understanding texts for their own sake, since the revelation to which they attest is not behind but in these texts.[14] Fifth, Scripture is authoritative over the church because it attests to God—the only absolute authority—in proclaiming the assault of the divine law on our existence, law that contains the mercy of the gospel within itself, the revelation of God in Jesus Christ.[15]

Barth's sixth point is his longest, containing the most sustained historical and exegetical excursus of §19. Curiously, the argumentative crux is perhaps the simplest to express: this priority or authority of Scripture is the result of a divine disposing that we cannot control.[16] Our response ought to be a circling around the center of the Word of God attested in Holy Scripture in past recollection and future expectation that God will act again in our present.[17] Barth argues that the two classical New Testament passages about the inspiration of Scripture support this claim. Second Timothy 4:14–17 shows that the relationship between God and Scripture is an inaccessible mystery of free grace in which the Holy Spirit is present and active before and above and in the Bible.[18] Second Peter 1:19–21 tells us that Scripture is not given by the will of man, but as men were moved by the Holy Spirit, who is therefore the real author of Scripture—though our knowledge of the way in which the Spirit acts makes it clear that the human authors made full use of their human capacities.[19] The biblical concept of *theopneustia* indicates the special obedience of those who are specially elected—pointing us to the present, the event that occurs for us, without itself being that presence.[20] Our belief in the inspiration of the Bible is a result of being overmastered by God, which is obviously a miracle and cannot be guaranteed or assured apart from faith. Barth summarizes: "*Theopneustia* is the act of revelation in which the prophets and apostles in their humanity became what they were, and in which alone in their humanity they can become to us what they are."[21]

12. *CD* I/2, 490.
13. *CD* I/2, 492.
14. *CD* I/2, 494.
15. *CD* I/2, 500.
16. *CD* I/2, 502.
17. *CD* I/2, 503.
18. *CD* I/2, 504.
19. *CD* I/2, 505.
20. *CD* I/2, 506.
21. *CD* I/2, 507.

Barth then turns from this enormous excursus to conclude with eight positive propositions about Scripture as (*als*) the Word of God. First, the Bible is the Word of *God* and thus not under our control.[22] Second, the Word of God is the *work* of God, which refers to an event; our knowledge of this event depends on our willing approach to that which is promised us as an event. Third, the Word of God is the *miracle* of God, which begins a new series of events, none of which are under our control.[23] Fourth, this miracle does not compromise the *humanity* of the Word of God; "every time we turn the Word of God into an infallible biblical word of man or the biblical word of man into an infallible Word of God we resist that which we ought never to resist; i.e., the truth of the miracle that here fallible men speak the Word of God in fallible human words."[24]

Barth explicitly opposes this statement about the humanity of the Word of God to claims for the inerrancy of Scripture. Fifth, since this miracle is an *event*, "we cannot regard the presence of God's Word in the Bible as an attribute inhering once for all in this book as such," but rather inconceivably present, "not as a third time between past and future, between recollection and expectation, but as that point between the two which we cannot think of as time."[25] Sixth, and here Barth returns to the primary referent of the phrase "Word of God" (Jesus Christ), the Word of God *himself* decides when and how the Bible shows itself to us in this event, so that we are "absolved from trying to force this event to happen,"[26] and the "presence of the Word of God is not an experience, precisely because and as it is the divine decision concerning us."[27]

The last two of Barth's eight propositions concern the concept of the inspiration of Scripture more broadly. Barth insists that, seventh, we must think of a *twofold* reality here. First, God really speaks in these concrete human words, in the ordinary language of men and women, and second, this is a "matter of the event or the events of the presence of the Word of God in our own present: not the experience of its presence, but its actual presence. . . . Faith in the inspiration of the Bible stands or falls by whether the concrete life of the Church and of the members of the Church is a life really dominated by the exegesis of the Bible."[28]

22. CD I/2, 527.
23. CD I/2, 528.
24. CD I/2, 529.
25. CD I/2, 530.
26. CD I/2, 531.
27. CD I/2, 532.
28. CD I/2, 533.

Therefore, eighth, the inspiration of the Bible cannot be *reduced* to our faith in it. "We do justice to [the inspiration of the Bible] by believing and resting on the fact that the action of God in the founding and maintaining of His Church, with which we have to do in the inspiration of the Bible, is objective enough to emerge victorious from all the inbreaks and outbreaks of man's subjectivity."[29]

The formal conclusion points to the importance of confession. In a neat turn of phrase, Barth says: "The Bible must be known as the Word of *God* if it is to be *known* as the Word of God. The doctrine of Holy Scripture in the Evangelical Church is that this logical circle is the circle of self-asserting, self-attesting truth in which it is equally impossible to enter as it is to emerge from it: the circle of our freedom which as such is also the circle of our captivity."[30]

Barth ends the entire paragraph with a pointed quotation of D. F. Strauss's criticism of the Protestant scholastic Alstedt, who claimed that the authority of Scripture rests solely on the testimony of the Holy Spirit. Strauss noted that nobody in his day was able to attest to the divinity of this witness, concluding that this revealed the Achilles' heel of Protestantism. Barth's rejoinder is that Protestantism is without a system and must embrace (and confess!) this weak point as the location of its greatest strength.[31]

Analysis of Barth's Doctrine of Scripture in *Church Dogmatics* I/2

The typically actualistic character of Barth's theological convictions is clearly on display throughout §19—he strenuously argues against any conception of the holiness of Scripture as a predicate or quality that inheres in these texts themselves and repeatedly urges at crucial junctures that the Holy Spirit must act for these human words to become the Word of God, as they have in the past and will in the future, by virtue of the divine promise alone. Barth thinks that the correct human response here is simply to confess that Scripture is the Word of God rather than strenuously exerting ourselves to secure such status. Furthermore, the proper human attitude is one of prayer, a stance that enables a truly serious consideration of the historical nature of these texts. Because Scripture is witness, it is *indirectly* identical to revelation, which means that any attempt to collapse the space between and make Scripture directly identical with revelation is an evasion of the God who speaks, a flight from the miracle that God speaks here. This absolves us from any mistaken

29. *CD* I/2, 534.
30. *CD* I/2, 535.
31. *CD* I/2, 537.

effort to force God's presence and is real wholly apart from our experientially
varied faith that God speaks in Scripture, neatly walking the very narrow path
between false objectivity and overworked subjectivity. As always for Barth,
salvation is *extra nos*.

Barth claims that this conception of Scripture flows from the truly biblical
basis of inspiration as promised grace, stating that "the doctrine of inspiration will always have to describe the relation between the Holy Spirit and
the Bible in such a way that the whole **reality** of the unity between the two is
safeguarded no less than the fact that this unity is a free act of the **grace** of
God, and therefore for us its content is always a **promise**."[32] Thus, as Barth
puts it when commenting on Paul's account of the Spirit's role:

> The circle which led from the divine benefits to the apostle instructed by the
> Spirit and authorized to speak by the Spirit now closes at the hearer of the
> apostle, who again by the Spirit is enabled to receive as is necessary. The hearer,
> too, in his existence as such is part of the miracle which takes place at this
> point . . . the mystery of God, now entrusted to the human witness, will still
> remain a mystery . . . if its self-disclosure does not go a step further . . . if the
> same Spirit who has created the witness does not bear witness of its truth to
> . . . those who **hear** and **read**. This self-disclosure in its totality is *theopneustia*,
> **the inspiration of the word of these prophets and apostles**.[33]

The dogmatic key to the doctrine of Scripture presented in §19 is this miracle
of the circle of inspiration, where the same Spirit who inspired the prophets
and apostles inspires later readers and hearers in a singular act.[34] The move

32. CD I/2, 514. I have restored the emphasis (in bold) present in the original German (see
KD I/2, 571).
33. CD I/2, 516 (I have restored Barth's original emphasis in bold). Cf. KD I/2, 573: "wenn
seine Selbsterschließung nicht weiter geht, nun auch in seiner Gestalt als menschliches Zeugnis,
wenn nicht derselbe Geist, der dieses Zeugnis als solches geschaffen, den Menschen, den **Hör-
ern** und **Lesern** Zeugnis gibt von dessen Wahrheit. **Diese Selbsterschließung in ihrer Totalität
ist die Theopneustie, die Inspiration des Propheten- und Apostelwortes**." The translator has
introduced the phrase "if the same Spirit who has created the witness does not bear witness of
its truth to those who hear and read," but it represents the kind of idiomatic wordplay (here
with Zeugnis) that so often disappears in English translation of Barth.
34. The words "circle" and "miracle" appear frequently, and in key places in the paragraph,
where Barth is speaking of the content of this event. Apart from the above passage, *Kreis* (circle)
is used four times: generally, to describe the closing of the circle of our knowledge of God's
graciousness as revealed in Scripture (KD I/2, 553) and three times in deliberate punning summary of the logically circular (*logische Zirkel*) nature of the doctrine of Scripture, the circle of
freedom that is as such the circle of our captivity (KD I/2, 595; CD I/2, 535, quoted above). Barth
uses the verbal form (*kreist* or *kreisen*) four times on p. 558 to describe the restless dogmatic
response to the event of God's action as the Word of God in Scripture. Barth also describes the
failure of the early church to maintain this circle (*Kreislauf*) four times. "Miracle" (*Wunder*

is negatively supported by an enormous amount of critical diagnostic work in historical theology; although Barth spends some time exegeting four classic New Testament passages (2 Tim. 3:16; 2 Pet. 1:19; 2 Cor. 3:4–18; 1 Cor. 2:6–16), the balance is markedly tilted toward historical critique. The strong weighting of historical theology over exegesis here is significant. Carefully reading this section can produce the impression that Barth is less engaged in deriving a doctrine of Scripture from the Bible than he is in illustrating his doctrine of Scripture by appealing to certain texts.

Such a strong charge needs to be defended. After all, we might suspect that this relentless assault on any stable quality of Scripture owes something to the politically fraught context in which *CD* I/2 was written.[35] Barth's historical analysis of the perennial temptation to adduce "external" reasons for believing that Scripture is the Word of God extends from the early church to a sidelong glance at his Christian contemporaries, who were in the midst of succumbing to National Socialism while he delivered the lectures. And indeed, Barth's application of what I call Feuerbach's razor (in parallel with Ockham's prescription against the unnecessary proliferation of causal entities) is here in 1937 more sharply laid against the neck of any perceived attempt to reduce theology to anthropology. As the German Christians fell increasingly into the inevitably idolatrous results of this anthropological substitution, Barth explicitly observes that taking the Scriptures seriously in their historicity means recognizing their "Jewishness," pointedly quoting Jesus's words in John 4:22 that "salvation is of the Jews."[36] Shortly after the release of *CD* I/2 in 1938 by Barth's new Swiss publishing firm, all of Barth's writings were banned in Germany.[37] Such potent theological claims about the Jewishness of

---

and its various forms) is scattered throughout the last section of the paragraph, substantially beginning (as a description of God's action and in contrast to the impossibility of any human capacity to effect this event) after Barth's exegesis of the scriptural passages (mentioned above) and continuing until the last of his eight positive propositions about the doctrine of Scripture.

35. Barth gave the lectures that would be published as *CD* I/2 from 1933 to 1937, during which time he was dismissed from his teaching post at Bonn and moved back to Switzerland (May 1935).

36. *CD* I/2, 511. There, the hostility of the world to Jewish blood reveals its stupidity and blindness (if the church cooperates, it does as well), because to reject the Jew is to reject God (p. 511). See also: "For the Bible as the witness of divine revelation in Jesus Christ is a Jewish book. It cannot be read and understood and expounded unless . . . we are prepared to become Jews with the Jews" (p. 511). Cf. *KD* I/2, 567: "Indem die Bibel als das Zeugnis von Gottes Offenbarung in Jesus Christus ein jüdisches Buch ist . . . wenn wir nicht bereit sind, mit den Juden Juden zu warden."

37. Busch, *Karl Barth*, 289. Barth said much the same in a public lecture in Zurich by way of response to Kristallnacht: "Anyone who is in principle hostile to the Jews must also be seen as in principle an enemy of Jesus Christ. Antisemitism is a sin against the Holy Spirit," quoted on the next page (290).

the Bible and the powerful claim that we must simply confess that we trust
the Holy Spirit to "make" Scripture the Word of God are impressive. We
ought to respond with respect to Barth's protest against anti-Semitism and
(especially today) take to heart his evergreen concern about the temptation to
find other, perhaps more politically acceptable, grounds for our belief in the
truth of Scripture. But Barth's claims for Scripture are not in fact qualitatively
new, not generated from the dangerous times in which he lived. Instead, Barth
had made the dogmatic claims that underlie this understanding of Scripture's
historicity as early as 1924.

Barth's "Earlier" Doctrine of Scripture

While much has been written about the course and contours of Barth's theological development in his first three academic appointments (1921–25 in
Göttingen, 1925–30 in Münster, 1930–35 in Bonn), it is sufficient for my purposes here to simply affirm the scholarly consensus that many of the major
dogmatic decisions that shape (especially the early volumes of) the *Church
Dogmatics* are already in place and on display in Barth's 1924–25 lectures
in dogmatics at Göttingen.[38] This is certainly true for Barth's doctrine of
Scripture: the dogmatic and historical argument of §19 in *CD* I/2 is present
in Göttingen[39] and remains the same in the slightly longer 1927 version of
Die christliche Dogmatik im Entwurf.[40] The increase in length[41] is largely due
to Barth's multiplication of historical investigations, but what is fascinating
is that he derives both the basic dogmatic structure and essential historical
presentation from Heinrich Heppe's *Reformed Dogmatics*.[42] The argument
can be accurately summarized with surprising brevity.

38. Here I entirely elide the debates about the extent of Barth's revision of the doctrine of
election.
39. Published posthumously in three volumes under the original lecture titles as *Unterricht in
der christlichen Religion*, I–III (Zurich: Theologischer Verlag Zürich, 1985–2003), in the ongoing
Gesamtausgabe. The first half, §§1–18, was translated as *The Göttingen Dogmatics: Instruction
in the Christian Religion*, vol. 1, trans. Geoffrey Bromiley (Grand Rapids: Eerdmans, 1991).
40. *Die christliche Dogmatik im Entwurf, erster Band, Prolegomena zur christlichen Dogmatik: Die Lehre vom Worte Gottes* (Munich: Kaiser, 1927). I quote from the 1982 critical edition
from Theologischer Verlag Zürich, ed. Gerhard Sauter (GA I 14).
41. In the German critical edition, §8, "The Scripture Principle," of the 1924 lectures runs
for 31 pages (with 35 mostly short footnotes); in 1927, the equivalent §20, "God in the Witness
of the Prophets and Apostles," is 38 pages (with 87 rather longer footnotes and some critical
apparatus). Since Barth introduced the small-print convention in the *Kirchliche Dogmatik*, the
98 pages of *KD* I/2, §19 are almost triple the earlier length.
42. Heinrich Heppe, *Schriften zur reformierten Theologie, Band II: Die Dogmatik der
evangelisch-reformierten Kirche* (Elberfeld: R. L. Fridrichs, 1861), rev. and ed. by Ernst Bizer

Heppe claims that the older Reformed theologians distinguished between the Word of God and Holy Scripture, but that later Protestant scholastics collapsed the distinction, further making inspiration refer not to God's act of revelation but to the authorial recording of that revelation.[43] In describing the authority of Scripture, Heppe observes that "we must of course never forget that Scripture has neither authority nor validity apart from the direct opening of our minds by the Holy Spirit. The same Spirit which inspired the authors must inspire us, if Scripture is to be Scripture for us as for them."[44]

Heppe believes this is the positive content of Calvin's *testimonium Spiritus sancti*, the ultimate (and, rightly understood, only) proof of Scripture's authority or *autopistia*.[45] I will return to this claim about Calvin, but here we can simply note that in his lectures at Göttingen, Barth agrees with Heppe on each of these points. Barth further finds the dogmatic solution to the decline from the Reformers in a return to identifying inspiration as "a single, timeless—or, rather, contemporary—act of God (its *communication*, too, is really an act) in *both* the biblical authors *and* ourselves. It is an act in which Spirit speaks to spirit, and spirit receives the Spirit."[46]

By the time of *CD* I/2, this "timeless act" of God has become the miracle of the circle of inspiration, the Holy Spirit's mysterious presence in the present, which the church cannot command but to which it looks back in recollection and forward in expectation. Apart from the phrasing and length, the structure in Göttingen is the same as in the *Church Dogmatics*.

Conclusion

What are we to make of all this? Barth's insistence on grounding his doctrine of Scripture in an explicit affirmation of the work of the Holy Spirit

---

in 1935, trans. by G. T. Thomson as *Reformed Dogmatics* (London: George Allen & Unwin, 1950), and published in the US by Baker in 1978.

43. Heppe, *Reformed Dogmatics*, chap. 2, "Holy Scripture," §5 (canon), 15.

44. Heppe, *Reformed Dogmatics*, chap. 2, "Holy Scripture," §6 (inspiration), 18.

45. Heppe, *Reformed Dogmatics*, chap. 2, "Holy Scripture," §10 (authority), 22.

46. Barth, *Göttingen Dogmatics*, 1:225. Cf. *Unterricht in der christlichen Religion I*, 274: "Im Blick auf den heiligen Geist also ist zu sagen, daß man die Inspiration auffassen muß als einen einzigen zeitlosen oder vielmehr gleichzeitigen Akt Gottes (!! auch die **Vermittlung** der Offenbarung ist nur wirklich im Akt!!) an den biblischen Autoren **und** an uns, ein Akt, in dem der Geist zum Geiste redet, der Geist den Geist vernimmt." While "simultaneous" is a better rendering of *gleichzeitigen* than "contemporary" and the translation elides Barth's emphasis on the mediation of revelation, as well as missing the pairing of speaking and hearing (*vernimmt*), the main idea does come across.

is commendable. But this unitary understanding of inspiration collapses the work of the Spirit in an unhelpful way, because even in Barth's strongest affirmations of the church's proclamation as the third form of the Word of God, he is careful to distinguish preaching from both Jesus Christ and Scripture. The Spirit works on us as readers of Scripture differently from the prophets and apostles; that is why we are not ourselves new prophets or apostles. The canon is closed. This distinction is at the heart of Barth's equal-opportunity criticism of the Roman Catholic Church and "enthusiasts" of all ages. On Barth's account, to appeal to the magisterium's tradition of reading this text (or an individual's charismatic sermon) as the Word of God is to make Scripture directly identical with revelation, to assert our control over God. This mistaken identification is not something that can be avoided by simply being more actualistic: that would force Barth into occasionalism, as critics have often claimed. Barth himself is aware of this problem, as his famous comment evidences: "God may speak to us through Russian Communism, a flute concerto, a blossoming shrub, or a dead dog. We do well to listen to Him if He really does." The question is how to retain the emphasis of the next sentence (in the original German, the next half of the same sentence): "But, unless we regard ourselves as the prophets and founders of a new Church, we cannot say that we are commissioned to pass on what we have heard as independent proclamation."[47] The church's proclamation is bound to the biblical witness in a unique way, but Barth's conception of inspiration as singular cannot adequately anchor the Christian need to attend to these words (and not others) as authoritative. Barth knows and affirms that the voice of the Spirit in Scripture is qualitatively different from the Zeitgeist; it is not accidental that Tillich is the target in the small-print section immediately before the preceding quotation. Yet Barth's famous dialectic seems to fail here by collapsing inspiration into a simple circle of miracle. Why?

Precisely determining Barth's motivations for his dialectical juxtapositions is difficult, much less discerning why or where the dialectic ends. Proof in these matters is unlikely to be without any shadow of a doubt, but we can name at least two influential accomplices. First, Barth's original lectures in Göttingen were composed under great pressure, and he never revised his (unfortunately) insufficiently critical acceptance of Heppe's historiography. That flawed account of the Reformed tradition remained intact in the *Church Dogmatics*, even if it is less clear there that Heppe is the source. Second, although Barth softened later in life, he retained a strong skepticism toward his Pietist in-

47. *CD* I/1, 55.

heritance, which likely prevented him from seeing the value of the traditional distinction between inspiration and illumination.[48]

Ironically, the classical distinction between the original inspiration of the Holy Spirit in producing Scripture and the subsequent, ongoing illumination that the Spirit gives to readers and hearers preserves the unity in differentiation for which Barth is searching. In sum: the same Spirit who spoke in and through the prophets and apostles is at work in our hearing of Scripture today—but not in the same way. That these are different works is in fact what Barth's touchstone in his Reformed doctrine of Scripture turns out to actually be arguing: Calvin's famous appeal to the internal testimony of the Holy Spirit concludes with his emphatic claim that until the Spirit "illumines their mind, [readers] ever waver among many doubts."[49] Calvin had very little patience with charismatic interpretations of Scripture, but he was insistent that illumination is necessary for interpretation, and that illumination is not the same work as inspiration, through both works are done by the Holy Spirit. Though Barth is extremely leery of any positive description of this "enlightenment by the Spirit" (in the phrasing of the *Leitsatz* to §16) because he thinks the temptation to narcissistic self-contemplation is almost irresistible, he is clear that the Spirit does point toward Christ, whom we know primarily through Scripture.[50] Although I would want to say more about how the Spirit so directs us, that admission is enough to open up room for the distinction between inspiration and illumination (or enlightenment). As Barth puts it earlier in the same volume: "The Holy Spirit certainly comes to us, not by an independent road . . . but by the Word and its testimonies . . . [we] are bound to the sign-giving."[51]

48. The best source for this background is Eberhard Busch, *Karl Barth and the Pietists*, trans. Daniel W. Bloesch (Downers Grove, IL: IVP Academic, 2004). Donald Dayton's foreword is invaluable in setting the context for North American readers, many of whom have a rather different sense of Pietism than Europeans like Barth.

49. John Calvin, *The Institutes of the Christian Religion* 1.7.4, ed. John McNeill, trans. Ford Lewis Battles (Philadelphia: Westminster Press, 1960). The Latin reads: "quia donec mentes illuminet, semper inter multas haesitationes fluctuant." For exhaustive demonstration of the kind of continuity between Calvin and later Protestant scholastics on this and other doctrinal matters, see the work of Richard Muller, who seems to have been driven to his historiographical labors at least partially out of sheer frustration with the inadequacies of Heppe.

50. I describe this pattern in Barth, which might be called a Johannine interpretation of the ostensive work of the Holy Spirit, at much greater length in my doctoral thesis, "The Spirit of Fellowship: Karl Barth's Pneumatology and Doctrine of Sanctification" (University of Aberdeen, 2012).

51. *CD* I/2, §16, "The Freedom of Man for God," 236. Even here Barth claims that the Word is not so bound, since God could create new prophets and apostles if God wished, which seems an unhappy instance of insisting on the sort of speculation that Barth elsewhere denounces as backward. Christian theology must proceed from God's actuality to any in-principle possibilities; what God has done is more important than what God could have done.

This being bound to the sign-giving is another reason to prefer the classical distinction between inspiration and illumination, because it more firmly secures our attention to this text.[52] Barth himself makes an almost offhand comment to similar effect after insisting that only God can make Scripture the Word of God because this door can be opened only from within. And yet:

> It is another thing whether we wait at this door or leave it for other doors, whether we want to enter and knock or sit idly facing it . . . faith in the inspiration or the Bible stands or falls by whether the concrete life of the Church and of the members of the Church is a life really dominated by the exegesis of the Bible. If the biblical text in its literalness as a text does not force itself upon us, or if we have the freedom word by word to shake ourselves loose from it, what meaning is there in our protestation that the Bible is inspired and the Word of God?[53]

That is precisely right, and it is a virtue of Barth's actual exegetical practice that he does not so shake himself loose from the biblical text. I have nowhere found Barth to identify any detail of Scripture as erroneous in order to dismiss or ignore a difficult passage. On the contrary, he often seems to delight in discovering difficult passages and interpreting them in ways that bring the power of the Word to bear on theological matters or practical concerns. Yet there is nothing in his unitary notion of inspiration that warrants such close attention to these texts, even with an elevated dose of actualism.

We can appreciate the force and contextual reasons for Barth's powerful dialectic without mistaking the nearly paradoxical claim that God can use erroneous human words to testify to himself for a satisfactory dogmatic conclusion, much less the theoretical foundation for Barth's exegetical practice. Distinguishing between inspiration and illumination provides a more substantial dogmatic foundation for the kind of attention to the actual text of Scripture that Barth himself displays. It also more firmly situates us as contemporary readers or hearers of Scripture in the church, not as new apostles, but as those who are under authority, those who need the ongoing work of the Holy Spirit, in company with other fallible humans looking for the light of the life of the world in dark times. We cannot force that illumination, but it is something for which we can and must pray.

---

52. Though Barth considerably mollifies his forceful opposition to natural theology in CD IV/3 (see especially section 2, "The Light of Life," in §69, "The Glory of the Mediator," where Barth speaks of little lights outside Scripture that display or mirror the one true light of Jesus Christ), he insists that Scripture remains canonical and authoritative: in fact, he deliberately refuses to specify any concrete instances of these little lights (see 135).

53. CD I/2, 533.

Speaking of illumination as the act proper to the Spirit's work on us as readers of Scripture further specifies precisely the kind of prayer that Barth says must have the last word:

> We can remember that the Bible has really already been for ourselves and others the place of this act. We can and should expect this act afresh. We can and should cling to the written word, as Jesus commanded the Jews, and as the people of Berea did. We can and should search the Scriptures asking about this witness. We can and should therefore pray that this witness may be made to us. But it does not lie—and this is why prayer must have the last word—in our power but only in God's, that this event should take place and therefore this witness of Scripture be made to us. We are therefore absolved from trying to force this event to happen. This does not allow us to be unfaithful or indolent.[54]

What we are praying for is that God would illumine our hearts and minds in the reading of His Word, not that he would inspire us to become (new) prophets or apostles. Our prayer is therefore action-guiding, productive of vigorous work, and definitively ordered. Illumination is no less miraculous than inspiration, but it is more appropriate to our existence in the church as ordinary Christians. Barth worries too much about the assimilation of illumination to purely subjective, non-scripturally determined experience.[55] His tireless repetition of the dictum that "abuse does not prevent right use" deserves to be applied here: the classical (especially Reformed) distinction between illumination and inspiration better grounds Barth's actual exegetical practice. As I believe that the essays in the remainder of this collection make clear, Barth's exegesis is remarkably valuable, beyond the somewhat less happy specifics of his much more well-known doctrine of Scripture. *Tolle lege*.

54. *CD* I/2, 531.
55. See, e.g., *CD* I/2, 519 and passim. For a larger account of Barth's theological commitments here, as well as a defense of his position against his many critics, see Rhodes, "The Spirit of Fellowship."

PART 2

Barth's Early Exegesis

THREE

Rewriting Romans

Theology and Exegesis in Barth's Early Commentaries

FRANCIS WATSON

Introduction

Published in 1933, the English translation of Karl Barth's commentary on the Letter to the Romans opens with a preface in which Barth addresses himself to his new English-speaking readers. The tone is uncharacteristically defensive. Although the book is only eleven years old, "it seems to have been written by another man to meet a situation belonging to a past epoch."[1] Readers are kindly requested "not to bind the Professor at Bonn too tightly to the Pastor of Safenwil."[2] Barth's growing ambivalence toward the work that made him famous is already evident in the preface to the fifth German edition in 1926, where he admits at one point that "I have often wished I had not written it."[3] But he did write it and he did authorize the English translation, and in the new preface he seeks to guide his readers' response to it. One thing he wishes to make quite clear is that this commentary on Romans really *is* a commentary on Romans, genuinely concerned with the interpretation of Paul's text:

1. *Romans II*, vi.
2. *Romans II*, vi.
3. *Römer II*, xxvi.

In writing this book, I felt myself bound to the actual words of the text, and did not in any way propose to engage myself in free theologizing. . . . Proper criticism of my book can be concerned only with the interpretation of the text of the Epistle. . . . Of my friendly readers I ask that they should take nothing and believe nothing from me which they are not of themselves persuaded stands within the meaning of what Paul wrote. . . . The purpose was and is to direct them to Holy Scripture, to the Epistle of Paul to the Romans.[4]

In reality, readers of Barth, whether in English or German, have found it virtually impossible to follow this authorial directive. The work seems to stretch the commentary genre to breaking point, treating the text as the pretext for precisely the "free theologizing" that Barth denies that he intends.

At Romans 1:18 Paul announces the revelation from heaven of "the wrath of God" directed against all human unrighteousness. The treatment of this point in other widely used commentaries of the period highlights the difficulty Barth's work would pose to those who read it in its new English guise. Such readers are likely to be aware of the Romans commentaries of William Sanday and A. C. Headlam, published in 1895 in the International Critical Commentary series, and of C. H. Dodd, published in 1932 in the commentary series based on the New Testament translation of James Moffatt (1913).[5] Sanday and Headlam devote a single paragraph to the *orgē theou*, tracing its roots in the Old Testament covenant relationship, its association with the "day of the Lord" in the prophets, and its predominantly eschatological usage in the New Testament. References are provided to illustrate each point, and the reader is directed to Albrecht Ritschl's *Rechtfertigung und Versöhnung* for discussion of the theological issue.[6] C. H. Dodd points to the "impersonal" nature of many of the Pauline references to "wrath" (e.g., Rom. 5:3; 7:8, 13), arguing that it refers to a process of retribution for sin operating immanently within the created order and that Paul attributes to God an "all-embracing" love and mercy that leaves no place within the divine character for "the irrational passion of anger."[7] These English-speaking commentators are aware of theological issues posed by Paul's terminology, but they seek to address them by historical and exegetical argumentation.

4. *Romans II*, ix–x.
5. W. Sanday and A. C. Headlam, *A Critical and Exegetical Commentary on the Epistle to the Romans* (Edinburgh: T&T Clark; New York: Scribner, 1895); C. H. Dodd, *The Epistle of Paul to the Romans* (London: Hodder & Stoughton, 1932).
6. Sanday and Headlam, *Romans*, 41.
7. Dodd, *Romans*, 50.

Not so Karl Barth, whose lengthy comment on Paul's reference to "the wrath of God" opens as follows in Sir Edwyn Hoskyns's translation:

> **The wrath of God** is the judgement under which we stand in so far as we do not love the Judge; it is the "No" which meets us when we do not affirm it; it is the protest pronounced always and everywhere against the course of the world in so far as we do not accept the protest as our own; it is the questionableness of life in so far as we do not apprehend it; it is our boundedness and corruptibility in so far as we do not acknowledge their necessity.[8]

Rhetorically powerful though this may be, it poses a challenge to the reader who has been requested by Barth not to regard his commentary as "free theologizing" and to assess it as "interpretation of the text of the Epistle." The wrath of God is the divine judgment of, or protest against, our failure to recognize that divine judgment or protest. Paradoxically, it becomes a reality insofar as its reality is denied. Equally paradoxically, we may escape it by affirming its reality and our own subjection to it. The intention is ostensibly to paraphrase Paul, but it is not clear how the Pauline statement can be said to generate such conclusions; indeed, the relation between text and comment appears to require a further level of exegesis, focused primarily on Barth's own text. Throughout the commentary, the reader is confronted with the double difficulty of getting inside the omnipresent paradox and relating the comment to the text of Romans. Barth may insist that his commentary on Paul's Letter to the Romans really *is* what it purports to be, but he is, perhaps, simply wrong. This *Römerbrief* is a historically important monument to Barth's early theology, but contrary to his intentions we learn little or nothing from it about Paul himself. The voice of the author has been drowned out by the voice of the commentator.

That assessment of Barth's *Römerbrief* has long been taken for granted. It is all too easy to claim that this celebrated or notorious work is not really a commentary at all. It is less easy to explain *why* its form and its content appear to diverge so widely. One possible line of inquiry is to look behind the 1922 second edition to its predecessor, the neglected first edition of 1919. We might anticipate that Barth's first attempt at a commentary on Romans would maintain a more direct and explicit connection to the text than the radically rewritten version of 1922. Barth's relation to the biblical text may become clearer if we can retrace the route that took him from the first to the second edition. His prefaces are a good place to start.

8. *Romans II*, 42 (boldface original).

I

Barth wrote and discarded three draft prefaces for the 1919 version of his commentary.[9] The first of these consists in a single paragraph that Barth appears to have written directly after completing his exposition of Paul's text.[10] It opens as follows:

> Das vorliegende Buch ist ein Versuch, anders in der Bibel zu lesen, als wir es auf Universitäten unter der Herrschaft der Theologie der neunziger Jahre im Ganzen gelehrt worden sind. Gefragt: inwiefern anders? möchte ich antworten: Sachlicher, inhaltlicher, wesentlicher, mit mehr Aufmerksamkeit und Liebe auf den Sinn der Bibel selbst eingehend. Ich rede nicht nur in meinem Namen. Denn wenn ich mich auch nur mit Wenigen darüber verständigt habe, so weiß ich doch aus vielen Anzeichen, daß eine ganze Generation von jüngeren Pfarrern und Studenten im Nachrücken ist, hinter denen auch genug Nicht-Theologen stehen, die in Bezug auf den positiven Sinn der Bibel Fragen auf dem Herzen haben, die im gegenwärtigen wissenschaftlichen Betrieb der Theologie sozusagen nicht zur Sprache kommen.[11]

The present book is an attempt to read the Bible otherwise than it is generally taught in universities under the dominance of the theology of the 1890s. If asked in what sense "otherwise," I would answer: with more concern for what is objective, substantial, essential, inquiring into the meaning of the Bible itself with greater attentiveness and love. I do not speak purely on my own behalf. Although I have shared these concerns only with a few, I see many indications that a whole generation of younger pastors and students—and also a number of nontheologians—are raising profound questions about the positive meaning of the Bible about which current academic theology remains silent.

As Barth writes these words in the summer of 1918, the outcome of the war remains undecided, but revolution is in the air.[12] More clearly than in the many prefaces to follow, the thirty-two-year-old village pastor presents himself as the spokesman for a generational conflict in which the young rise up against the authority of their theological teachers and accuse them of

9. *Römer I*, 581–98. As enumerated in the Barth Gesamtausgabe (II 16), the three drafts are represented by I (581–82); II (588–94), which is a fair copy of Ia (582–88); and III (594–98). The published preface is V (600–602), of which IV is a first draft (599–600).

10. *Römer I*, 581n.

11. *Römer I*, 581. Except where specified, translations in this paper are my own.

12. In Russia but also closer to home. In a letter to Barth dated June 24, 1918, Eduard Thurneysen reports: "In Basel hat es eine kleine Revolution gegeben, an der unsere sozialistischen Freunde beteiligt sind." *Karl Barth-Eduard Thurneysen Briefwechsel, Band I: 1913–1921*, GA V 3 (Zurich: Theologischer Verlag Zürich, 1973), 283.

providing a stone when asked for bread. In this case, as Barth proceeds to explain, the unsatisfactory fare consists in a view of the Bible as the "classic document of piety,"[13] a record of the human religious quest in which we too may participate more fully as we study the biblical texts in the light of modern knowledge and insights. With all due acknowledgment of its achievements, Barth says, we must utterly reject this theological outlook as a travesty of the biblical message.[14]

Alongside this first draft preface, two later prefaces were also to be discarded. In them Barth attempts to explain his method of working and to counter in advance the objections he expects to receive. What is striking about these drafts is their exclusive focus on the Bible. The coming revolution is to be a revolution in the understanding of the Bible, which will be perceived no longer as a human religious classic but in terms of its essential content. Surprisingly perhaps, the Bible is mentioned far more frequently than God in the sequence of four prefaces.[15]

In the preface that Barth finally published, attention is focused not so much on the Bible as such but on the specific biblical author with which this commentary is concerned. The first word is given to Paul himself:

> Paulus hat als Sohn seiner Zeit zu seinen Zeitgenossen geredet. Aber viel wichtiger als diese Wahrheit ist die andere, daß er als Prophet und Apostel des Gottesreiches zu allen Menschen aller Zeiten redet. Die Unterschiede von einst und jetzt, dort und hier, wollen beachtet sein. Aber der Zweck der Beachtung kann nur die Erkenntnis sein, dass diese Unterschiede im Wesen der Dinge keine Bedeutung haben.[16]

> Paul, as a child of his time, spoke to his contemporaries. Far more important than this, however, is the fact that as prophet and apostle of the kingdom of God he speaks to all people of all times. The differences between then and now, there and here, should be noted. But the aim of doing so can only be the recognition that these differences have no essential significance.

There is no doubt here that Barth wants to speak of Paul and the Pauline text. No reference is made to contemporary events or issues: the Great War, for example, entering its final stages as Barth writes in neutral Switzerland not far from some of the action, or the resulting crisis for faith and theology. Barth

---

13. *Römer I*, 582.
14. *Römer I*, 582 ("als unsachlich, formal, unwesentlich, im letzten Grund als unaufmerksam und lieblos gegenüber der Bibel").
15. The term *Bibel* is used 18 times; the term *Gott* is used 5.
16. *Römer I*, 3.

speaks instead of his "joyful discovery" (*Entdeckerfreude*) of "the mighty voice of Paul" (*die kräftige Stimme des Paulus*).[17] Apart from a passing reference to Barth's father, Fritz Barth, Paul is the only individual to be mentioned here by name—although the preface does include an unattributed quotation from Goethe. Barth thus positions himself as the mouthpiece or representative of the powerful figure whose address to the people of our own time he will strive to articulate.

In the 1922 preface the situation has changed utterly. Barth's second edition is in effect a new work. As he puts it, with an allusion to the earlier preface, the original work

> hat ihren "bestimmt umschränkten Dienst," wie ich damals zu hoffen wagte und doch fast nicht hoffen konnte, getan. Einige auf Paulus und auf die Bibel überhaupt aufmerksam zu machen, die es vorher so nicht waren. Sie kann heute mit ihren Vorzügen und Fehlern vom Schauplatz verschwinden.[18]

> has performed its "definite, limited service," as I then dared to hope and was barely able to hope: to persuade a few people to attend to Paul and the Bible as a whole who had not previously done so. With its strengths and weaknesses, it can now disappear from the scene.

The first commentary did indeed disappear. In the 1922 preface Barth explains that he has continued to reflect on Paul and that the new edition represents his latest findings. But he also acknowledges the influence of his further reading: to Paul's name are added the names of Overbeck, Plato, Kant, Kierkegaard, and Dostoevsky.[19] There is also a new family member to acknowledge: in place of Barth's theologian father, Fritz, reference is now made to a philosopher brother, Heinrich.[20] There is a certain distancing from the initial *Entdeckerfreude*, an expression that Barth now acknowledges was somewhat naive.[21] The change of perspective does not stem only from Paul:

> Wenn ich einen "System" habe, so besteht es darin, dass ich das, was Kierkegaard den "unendlichen qualitativen Unterschied" von Zeit und Ewigkeit genannt hat, in seiner negativen und positiven Bedeutung möglich beharrlich im Auge behalte. "Gott ist im Himmel und du auf Erden." Die Beziehung *dieses*

17. *Römer I*, 4. *Kräftig* replaces *merkwürdig*, which appears in the first draft of this preface (*Römer I*, 599).
18. *Römer II*, vi.
19. *Römer II*, vii.
20. *Römer II*, vii.
21. *Römer II*, xvii: "etwas romantisch."

Gottes zu *diesem* Menschen, die Beziehung *dieses* Menschen zu *diesem* Gott ist für mich das Thema der Bibel und die Summe der Philosophie in Einem.[22]

If I have a "system," it consists in this: that I keep in view as consistently as possible what Kierkegaard has called the "infinite qualitative difference" between time and eternity, in both its negative and its positive significance. "God is in heaven and you upon earth." The relation of *this* God to *this* humanity, and of *this* humanity to *this* God, is for me both the theme of the Bible and the essence of philosophy.

The difference between the two published prefaces is striking. The first announces a rediscovery of the Bible in general and of Paul in particular. It belongs to a time when Barth believes himself to be reentering what he calls "the strange new world of the Bible." In a lecture under that title delivered in the autumn of 1916, Barth begins by posing the questions: "What sort of house is it to which the Bible is the door? What sort of country is spread before our eyes when we throw the Bible open?"[23] It is such questions as these from which the first Romans commentary derives. The equation of the message of the Bible with the essence of philosophy is absent. Here, then, is a potential and partial answer to the question why the commentary of 1922 is so unlike a biblical commentary: in the second edition a systematic principle has been imposed on the "biblicism" of the first. The difference is virtually acknowledged by Barth himself, if each of the two prefaces is read in the light of the other. At the same time, however, the difference is covered over: for the 1919 preface was reprinted in the 1922 commentary, in the hope that the "mighty voice of Paul," prophet and apostle of the kingdom of God, would resound still more effectively in the new work than in its predecessor. The old preface is salvaged from the earlier work, which Barth otherwise discards, and is reattached to a significantly different work determined—according to Barth himself—by a systematic principle that is supposed to reduce the whole of the Bible and the whole of philosophy into the pithy formulations of Kierkegaard and Ecclesiastes. Kierkegaard's "infinite qualitative difference" represents philosophy, the Bible is represented by Qoheleth's "God is in heaven and you upon earth," and the two citations together are supposed to represent the convergence of the two fields.

If the 1919 commentary represents the phase of the "strange new world of the Bible" and the 1922 commentary that of the "infinite qualitative difference,"

22. *Römer II*, xiii (emphasis original). Accused by a reviewer of the first edition of imposing a "system" on Paul's text, Barth takes the opportunity of asserting the systematic principle underlying the new edition of his commentary.

23. Karl Barth, *The Word of God and the Word of Man* (New York: Harper & Row, 1957), 28.

we have a possible answer to the question why the later work seems so un-commentary-like. Initially, Barth writes a theological commentary on Romans in which his main concern is indeed to recover "the mighty voice of Paul," which "speaks to all people of all times." As it is rewritten in the light of the new commitment to the infinite qualitative difference, it retains only the outward appearance of a commentary on a biblical text and becomes instead a series of free meditations arising out of the text rather than expounding the text. That, at least, is the working hypothesis that now needs to be tested to see how far it is adequate to the data.

II

The standard Greek letter opening takes the form: "*A* to *B*, Greeting." This format also underlies the Pauline letter openings, although here it is typically extended and elaborated. Only in the Thessalonian letters does Paul introduce himself simply as "Paul" (1 Thess. 1:1; 2 Thess. 1:1). Elsewhere he presents himself as a "servant of Christ Jesus" (Phil. 1:1), a "prisoner of Christ Jesus" (Philem. 1), an "apostle of Jesus Christ by the will of God" (2 Cor. 1:1). It is in Romans that the self-introduction is most extensive: Paul has so much to say about his gospel and his commission that it is only at Romans 1:7 that the addressees are at last identified and greeted: "To all who are in Rome beloved of God, called to be saints, Grace and peace from God our Father and the Lord Jesus Christ." The format is still "*A* to *B*, Greeting," but the *A* element overwhelms the other two. It is as though Paul wishes to ensure that key words and concepts should be laid out on the table at the earliest possible opportunity: not only apostleship but also gospel, God, Scripture, Spirit, resurrection, sonship, grace, faith, Gentiles:

> Paul a servant of Christ Jesus, called to be an apostle, set apart for the gospel of God which he promised beforehand through his prophets in the Holy Scriptures, concerning his Son, born of the seed of David according to the flesh, installed as Son of God in power according to the Spirit of holiness by resurrection from the dead, Jesus Christ our Lord, through whom we have received grace and apostleship to bring about the obedience of faith among the Gentiles, to all who are in Rome beloved of God, called to be saints: Grace to you and peace from God our Father and the Lord Jesus Christ. (Rom. 1:1–7)

Given this concentration of theologically significant vocabulary, it is to be expected that major themes in Barth's commentaries will also come to expression in his treatment of the letter opening. That is already likely to be the case in the first edition, and in the second we should expect to see early indications of the new themes that have occasioned the thoroughgoing rewriting of its predecessor. In both works Barth's exegetical technique is to focus on successive words and phrases, considered in relative isolation from one another. Only rarely does he step back and introduce or summarize the contents of a longer passage, and still more rarely does he offer a justification for the interpretive positions he takes. As he rewrites both Paul's text and his own earlier work, Barth everywhere strives to confront his reader with what he takes to be the *Sache* of the text, its fundamental theme and object and demand, that which makes it directly relevant to modern readers no less than to the Roman readers of the first century. These are not commentaries "on" Paul's text, maintaining a certain distance between the apostle and his interpreter. Rather, these commentaries *commandeer* Paul's text, speaking from within it so that—as Barth acknowledges—the interpreter almost forgets that he himself is someone other than Paul.[24] The intention is to disclose "the Word in the words," the divine speaking to which the text bears witness,[25] and the method is to attend closely to what—according to Barth—the text's key words say and do not say.

We will therefore follow Barth as he encounters key words or concepts for the first time in the text's exordium and as he revisits the same key words in the process of rewriting. Paul is commissioned to proclaim "the gospel of God" (Rom. 1:1). The content of the gospel is Jesus Christ, "born of the seed of David according to the flesh and installed as Son of God in power according to the Spirit of holiness, by resurrection from the dead" (Rom. 1:3–4). We will subject Barth's successive comments on God and Christ to close scrutiny, in the hope of understanding how the second commentary has risen from the ashes of the rejected first.

Paul introduces himself as "set apart for the gospel of God" (Rom. 1:1). In the 1919 commentary, Barth finds occasion here to present his fundamental contrast between the self-communicating God of the Bible and the current focus on religion as a human phenomenon:

> Eine Botschaft von *Gott* hat er auszurichten, keine menschliche Religionslehre. Also ein lebendiges, aus seinem Ursprung fortwährend sich neu erzeugendes Wort, kein ausgeklügeltes, fertiges System. Eine objektive Erkenntnis, nicht Erlebnisse, Erfahrungen und Empfindungen.[26]

> [Paul] has a proclamation from God to deliver, not a human theory of religion. Thus, a living Word continually renewed from its origin, not an artfully

24. *Römer II*, xii.
25. *Römer II*, xii.
26. *Römer I*, 12.

constructed, self-contained system. An objective knowledge, not ecstasies, experiences, or emotions.

The relative simplicity of these statements makes them valuable for analytical purposes. In each of the three sentences cited, an affirmation is paired with a negation. The affirmations paraphrase the Pauline text. Barth interprets Paul's apostolic commission in prophetic terms: Paul is the human mouthpiece of the divine Word that declares the original and ultimate truth about the world and makes it accessible to human knowing. The negations sharpen the affirmations by showing them to be at odds with current academic and popular assumptions about the phenomena of religion: that religion can be theorized or systematized, that its primary manifestations lie in the sphere of subjective experiences of the ineffable, and above all that talk of "God" must be bracketed within the wider context of discourse about religion as a human practice. It does not matter that Paul himself was entirely unfamiliar with the post- or sub-Schleiermacherian themes toward which Barth here gestures. Interpretation of a canonical text as canonical is bound to concern itself both with what the words mean and with their contemporary significance, which may lie well beyond the horizons of the original author. As theologically motivated exegesis, Barth's remarks here cannot be faulted.

In the later version of this passage, the negations multiply. To clarify the nature and extent of the alterations, the passage may be divided into three parts, with I. representing its original 1919 form and II. the 1922 expansion, with the substantive new elements italicized.

I. Eine Botschaft von G o t t hat er auszurichten

II. Die "Heilsbotschaft Gottes" hat Paulus auszurichten: *zu Handen der Menschen die ganz und gar neu, die unerhört gute und frohe Wahrheit Gottes.* Aber eben: "Gottes"![27]

I. He has a proclamation from God to deliver

II. Paul has the "saving proclamation of God" to deliver: *to pass on to human hands the absolutely new and unheard of good and joyful truth of God.* But precisely: "of God"!

The new emphasis on absolute and unanticipated novelty is in some tension with the Pauline claim that the gospel was "promised beforehand by his

---

27. *Römer II*, 4 (emphasis original).

prophets in the holy Scriptures" (Rom. 1:2). Can a truth be absolutely new and unheard of if it has been promised beforehand? While Barth evidently believes that it can, the question is whether the tension created by the emphasis on novelty is present in the Pauline text. Since the first thing Paul says about the gospel of God is that it was "promised beforehand," the motif of absolute novelty seems to have been imported from elsewhere. In what follows, however, this motif is subordinated to that of divine unknowability:

I. keine menschliche Religionslehre. Also ein lebendiges, aus seinem Ursprung fortwährend sich neu erzeugendes Wort, kein ausgeklügeltes, fertiges System.

II. Also keine religiöse Botschaft, *keine Nachrichten und Anweisungen über die Göttlichkeit oder Vergöttlichung des Menschen, sondern Botschaft von einem Gott, der ganz anders ist, von dem der Mensch als Mensch nie etwas wissen noch haben wird und von dem ihm eben darum das Heil kommt. Also kein direkt zu verstehendes, einmalig zu erfassendes Ding unter Dingen, sondern das unter Furcht und Zittern* immer neu zu vernehmende, weil immer neu gesprochene Wort des Ursprungs aller Dinge.[28]

I. not a human theory of religion. Thus, a living Word continually renewed from its origin, not an artfully constructed, self-contained system.

II. Thus, no religious proclamation, *no information or instruction concerning human divinity or divinization, but the proclamation of a God who is wholly other, of whom humans as such can never know or possess anything, and from whom for that very reason salvation comes.* Thus, *no directly perceptible, graspable once-for-all object among objects*, but the always newly perceived because always newly spoken Word of the origin of all things, *to be received with fear and trembling.*

In this passage Barth's original negations seemed directed against certain forms of current theological discourse. In the new version the emphasis lies on God as the "wholly other," a phrase borrowed from Rudolf Otto, whose book *Das Heilige* (1917) Barth read and appreciated in the early summer of 1919.[29] The divine otherness is understood in terms of unknowability: remarkably, this unknowability and unavailability is now seen as the content of the gospel. To see through illusions about human godlikeness and to peer into the

---

28. *Römer II*, 4 (emphasis original).
29. Letter to Eduard Thurneysen, 3.6.19, *Barth-Thurneysen Briefwechsel I*, 330. Barth wrote: "Ich las diese Woche mit ziemlicher Freude *Das Heilige* von Otto. Die Sache ist zwar psychologisch orientiert, weist aber deutlich über die Grenze hinaus auf das Moment des 'Numinosum,' dem rational nicht beizukommen ist, weil es das 'Ganz Andre,' das Göttliche an Gott ist."

originary divine abyss is actually to experience the salvation the gospel seeks to communicate. The "good and joyful truth of God" is to be "received with fear and trembling," a paradox that may be related to Otto's awe-inspiring *mysterium tremendum*, which also "shows itself as something uniquely attractive and *fascinating*."[30] The new emphasis on wholly otherness has been shaped by Barth's reading of Otto and others, and it evidently has little or nothing to do with any ongoing engagement with the Pauline text. In Barth's version of this motif, the divine wholly otherness is self-communicating, and what it communicates is simply itself as wholly other.

I. Eine objektive Erkenntnis, nicht Erlebnisse, Erfahrungen und Empfindungen.

II. Also nicht Erlebnisse, Erfahrungen und Empfindungen, *und wären es solche höchsten Ranges*, sondern schlichte objektive Erkenntnis *dessen, was kein Auge gesehen, kein Ohr gehört.*[31]

I. An objective knowledge, not ecstasies, experiences, or emotions.

II. Thus, not ecstasies, experiences, or emotions, *even of the highest order*, but simple objective knowledge *of what no eye has seen nor ear heard*.

In the first version of this passage, objective knowledge was played off against subjective experience. The opposition is maintained in the second version, but the content of the objective knowledge is now said to be a not-knowing in the face of the divine ineffability. The reference to "what no eye has seen nor ear heard" is, however, an allusion to Paul (cf. 1 Cor. 2:9). Here and elsewhere, a basis for divine otherness in the Pauline texts may not be entirely lacking. Yet it does seem here that the specificities of what Paul strives to communicate to his Roman readership are obscured by the imposition of the systematic principle that Barth traces back not to Paul but to Qoheleth and Kierkegaard: God is in heaven whereas we are upon earth, and there is an infinite qualitative difference between the two. In principle, of course, there is no reason why a theological interpretation of a biblical text should not be enhanced by engagement with, say, Kierkegaard. Barth is right: the theological interpretation of Scripture must be far more than just the laborious reproduction of an authorial meaning within the limits of its original context. The problem lies not so much with the hermeneutical theory as with the execution.

30. R. Otto, *The Idea of the Holy: An Inquiry into the Non-Rational Factor in the Idea of the Divine and Its Relation to the Rational* (Oxford: Oxford University Press, 1931), 31 (emphasis original).
31. *Römer II*, 4 (emphasis original).

In all this there is a certain irony. The published prefaces to the first, second, and third editions of Barth's Romans commentary have become a kind of locus classicus for those seeking to practice a theological interpretation of Scripture characterized in terms of its difference from the so-called historical-critical method.[32] As we have seen, the first preface (together with its unpublished predecessors) articulates precisely this distinction, arising from the rediscovery of the "strange new world of the Bible" and the revolt against an academic theology that had allegedly transformed the Bible into a human religious classic. Barth had this preface reprinted in his later editions, elaborating the hermeneutical stance he had adopted in 1919 in the subsequent prefaces. Yet it is the 1919 commentary that is concerned with recovering the message of the Bible. In the 1922 version, this earlier "biblicism" has been compromised by the imposition of a theological dialectic only tenuously related to Paul. There is, then, a mismatch between the initial rediscovery of "the mighty voice of Paul" and the Romans commentary in its definitive 1922 form.

III

According to Paul, the gospel of God was promised in the prophets and has as its content God's Son, "born of the seed of David according to the flesh and installed as Son of God in power according to the Spirit of holiness, by resurrection from the dead, Jesus Christ our Lord" (Rom. 1:3–4). Here the concentration of names and titles (Son of God, Jesus, Christ, Lord) and the reference to a double origin from flesh and Spirit invite the interpreter to reflect on Paul's Christology. In both versions of the commentary Barth bases his exposition on the expression "Jesus Christ our Lord," with which the Pauline statement concludes. Although there are three terms here, Barth is primarily interested in the distinction between the human life *kata sarka* and the resurrected life *kata pneuma hagiosynēs*, and he superimposes this duality onto the terms "Christ" and "Lord" in *Römer I* and onto "Jesus" and "Christ" in *Römer II*. In the 1919 commentary he writes as follows:

> Es handelt sich um "Jesus Christus, unsern Herrn." Wir nennen ihn "Christus," Messias, den Gesalbten Israels, weil in ihm das Wort jener Worte der alten Zeit gesprochen, weil in ihm die Erfüllung der Weissagung erschienen ist. Wir nennen

32. See my article "Does Historical Criticism Exist?," in *Theological Theology: Essays in Honour of John Webster*, ed. R. David Nelson, Darren Sarisky, and Justin Stratis (London: Bloomsbury T&T Clark, 2015), 307–18.

ihn "unsern Herrn," weil in ihm die Wende der neuen Zeit, in der wir stehen, vollzogen ist. Zwei Welten, zwei Geschichten gehört er an, und die eine ist in der andern abgeschlossen und überwunden durch ihn.[33]

The concern is with "Jesus Christ our Lord." We call him "Christ," Messiah, the Anointed of Israel, because in him the content of those words of the old era has been spoken, because in him the fulfillment of prophecy has been manifested. We call him "our Lord," because in him has taken place the turn to the new era, in which we stand. He belongs to two worlds, two histories, and through him the one is concluded and superseded by the other.

Here a contrast is drawn between what is true of Jesus as the Christ and as Lord. The Christ is the Messiah, "a member of the Israelite people of God and its royal household, as such an heir of divine promises, but as such also born into the need and weakness of his time, his race, and a whole world that has not yet attained its fulfillment."[34] Barth here takes seriously the fact that Paul sets the human life of Jesus in the context of traditional Jewish messianic expectations. He also takes seriously the Pauline sequence: Jesus Christ is *first* born of the seed of David, and *subsequently* raised from the dead and appointed as Son of God in power. In the resurrection of Jesus there is a "turn" from one history to another, from an old era to a new. The "two worlds" to which Barth also refers are related to each other temporally rather than spatially. Here Paul's initial christological statements are interpreted eschatologically; the interpretation is broadly convincing as exegesis of the scriptural text.

In the 1922 version of this passage, the key terms are no longer "Christ" and "Lord" but rather "Jesus" and "Christ," with "Jesus" correlated with the fleshly human life and "Christ" with the resurrection. The Jewish messianic context disappears from view, and so too does the recognition of temporal sequence. The "two worlds" are no longer "two histories," an old and a new, but "two planes," a known and an unknown:

In diesem Namen begegnen und trennen sich zwei Welten, schneiden sich zwei Ebenen, eine bekannte und eine unbekannte. Die bekannte ist die von Gott geschaffene, aber aus ihrer ursprünglichen Einheit mit Gott herausgefallene und darum erlösungsbedürftige Welt des "Fleisches," die Welt des Menschen, der Zeit und der Dinge, unsre Welt. Diese bekannte Ebene wird geschnitten von

33. *Römer I*, 13.
34. *Römer I*, 13: "Angehöriger des israelitischen Gottesvolkes und seines Königshauses, als solcher Erbe göttlicher Verheißungen, aber als solcher auch hineingeboren in die Not und Schwachheit seiner Zeit, seines Geschlechts und einer ganzen, der Erfüllung noch nicht teilhaftigen Welt."

einer andern unbekannten, von der Welt des Vaters, der Welt der ursprünglichen Schöpfung und endlichen Erlösung.[35]

In this name two worlds meet and divide, two planes intersect: a known and an unknown. The known is the one created by God but fallen from its original unity with God and so in need of redemption: the world of the "flesh," the world of humans, time, and things, our world. This known plane is intersected by another, which is unknown: the world of the Father, the world of the original creation and final redemption.

The sequential relationship between the old era and the new is here replaced by a spatial relationship between a horizontal plane intersected at right angles by a second plane and thus producing a line of intersection (*Schnittlinie*) that runs through human history but becomes visible at a single point: the life of Jesus, culminating in his resurrection. And even this visibility remains indirect. It is not the visibility of the so-called historical Jesus, available and accessible to some degree through refined methods of scholarly analysis. Insofar as it is embedded within its own time and place, the life of Jesus remains an ordinary piece of historical occurrence, in no way elevated above whatever else took place before, after, and around it. It is in the resurrection that, through the Holy Spirit, the transformative significance of this life is revealed:

> Jesus als der Christus ist die uns unbekannte Ebene, die die uns bekannte senkrecht von oben durchschneidet. Jesus als der Christus bringt die Welt des Vaters, von der wir innerhalb der historischen Anschaulichkeit nichts wissen und nie etwas wissen werden. Die Auferstehung von den Toten aber ist die Wende, das "Einsetzen" jenes Punktes von oben und die entsprechende Einsicht von unten. Die Auferstehung ist die Offenbarung, die Entdeckung Jesu als des Christus, die Erscheinung Gottes, und die Erkenntnis Gottes in ihm.[36]

> Jesus as the Christ is the plane that is unknown to us, intersecting the known plane vertically from above. Jesus as the Christ brings the world of the Father, which we do not and can never know from within the sphere of what is historically visible. It is the resurrection from the dead that is the moment of transition, the "installation" of that point from above and its corresponding perception from below. The resurrection is the revelation, the discovery of Jesus as the Christ, the appearance of God and the knowledge of God in him.

We recall how, in the preface to the 1933 English translation, Barth asks his English-speaking readers to accept that his concern was not to engage in

35. *Römer II*, 7.
36. *Römer II*, 6.

"free theologizing" but to interpret the Pauline text.[37] In this christological passage, however, "free theologizing" is exactly the right expression. "Free" does not mean that the commentary bears *no* relation to the text. The terms on which it reflects—Jesus, Christ, resurrection—are all present within Paul's text. Yet Barth acts with an extraordinary degree of freedom in the way he handles them. As a symptom of this, we note the virtual absence from the discussion of the term "Son of God." For Paul, the resurrection is the moment when Jesus Christ, the Messiah descended from David, is appointed or installed as Son of God. For Barth, the resurrection is the moment when the historical Jesus becomes and is disclosed as the Christ.[38] The christological concept on which Paul lays the greatest emphasis, that of Jesus as Son of God, is precisely the one that Barth avoids.

Here too, the 1919 commentary is more obviously commentary-like than its better-known successor. In the earlier work, the Pauline transition from Jesus's life in the flesh to his risen life as Son of God is accurately registered, and the link between explicit Christology and implicit eschatology is rightly emphasized:

> Als er seinen Lauf vollendet als Glied jener alten Welt, brach sein eigentliches, inneres Wesen in Kraft hervor in seiner Auferstehung von den Toten, wurde ihm der Platz zugewiesen, der ihm nach der Absicht Gottes, der ein Neues ins Sein rufen wollte, zukam: als Gottes Sohn, in dem die Geschichte einer andern Menschheit eröffnet ist. Denn indem dieser Eine wurde, was er von Gottes wegen war, indem der Bann des Todes, der ihn mit aller Kreatur gefangen hielt, zerbrach durch die Kraft, die sich in seiner Auferstehung als wirksam erwies, ist der neue Äon, das Zeitalter des Geistes angebrochen für die ganze Welt.[39]

> As he completed his course as a participant in the old era, his true innermost reality burst forth in power in his resurrection from the dead. Thus he received the status assigned to him in the purpose of God, who wills to call a new world into being: as God's Son, in whom is disclosed the history of another humanity. Because this one became what he was before God, because the sway of death—which had held him and every creature captive—was shattered by the power manifested in his resurrection, the new aeon which is the age of the Spirit has broken in for the whole world.

This is an effective theological paraphrase of Paul's statements.

37. *Romans II*, ix.
38. The expression "Jesus as the Christ" is later systematically developed by Paul Tillich in *Systematic Theology*, vol. 2 (London: SCM, 1978), "Part III: Existence and the Christ," 97–138.
39. *Römer I*, 13.

In contrast, the later treatment drifts away from exegesis in the direction of the "free theologizing" that Barth is so anxious to deny: the two planes, the line of intersection, and the point at which this line becomes visible constitute an arresting if puzzling image, but its relation to Paul's text is tangential. It is not so much that Barth is using Paul's Letter to the Romans as the pretext or occasion for this free theologizing. Rather, the pretext or occasion is provided by his own earlier commentary. A new and intense conviction of divine wholly otherness is superimposed onto that commentary, converting it into a work *sui generis* in which the author strives to articulate *his own* understanding of the topics covered in the scriptural text even without direct authorization from the text.

In the 1922 Romans commentary, the commentator and the theologian are at odds with one another. A decade later Barth will achieve a more stable account of their relationship, as he embarks—after yet another false start—on the *Kirchliche Dogmatik*, which was to occupy the rest of his theological career:

> Darum fragt die Dogmatik als solche nicht nach dem, was die Apostel und Propheten gesagt haben, sondern nach dem, was "auf dem Grunde der Apostel und Propheten" wir selbst sagen sollen. Diese Aufgabe kann uns auch durch die notwendig vorangehende Erkenntnis des "Schriftgrundes" nicht abgenommen sein.

> Thus dogmatics as such does not ask what the apostles and prophets said, but what we ourselves should say "on the foundation of the apostles and prophets." The necessary prior knowledge of the "scriptural foundation" does not exempt us from this task.[40]

Barth refers to the example of Calvin in support of this hard-won distinction between theology and exegesis. It is a distinction embedded even in the formatting of the *Church Dogmatics*, in which "what we ourselves should say" is carefully differentiated from the exegetical basis provided in the small-print sections that follow. In a certain sense, the *Church Dogmatics* actually practices the "free theologizing" that causes Barth such anxiety as he contemplates the appearance of the 1922 commentary in its English guise: "free" not in the sense that dogmatics can dispense with a scriptural basis but in the sense that it remains underdetermined by that basis. In retrospect, the commentary can be understood as a kind of workshop in which Barth develops a conceptuality that finds its proper home in the orderly world of the *Church Dogmatics*, not in the disorderly series of theological meditations that Barth imposes ostensibly on Paul's Letter to the Romans, but above all on his own earlier commentary.

40. *KD* I/1, 15; *CD* I/1, 16. The allusion is to Eph. 2:20.

FOUR

"A Relation beyond All Relations"

God and Creatures in Barth's Lectures on Ephesians, 1921–22

JOHN WEBSTER

I

Over the course of his relatively brief but extraordinarily active tenure of the newly founded chair of Reformed theology in Göttingen from 1921 to 1925, Barth lectured in three areas of the theological curriculum: historical theology, dogmatics, and New Testament exegesis. The publication of a good number of the historical and dogmatic lectures in the Barth Gesamtausgabe over the last quarter century has made abundantly clear how formative the time in Göttingen proved to be, not only for the decade or so before the appearance of the first volume of the *Church Dogmatics*—during which Barth deepened, clarified, and refined the theological positions that he had begun to adopt in the middle of the Great War as he distanced himself from Herrmann and later liberal Protestantism—but also for his mature work in the three decades in Basel. His teaching in Reformed historical theology led him to acquaint himself more thoroughly with the confessional and theological writings of

This essay originally appeared in Karl Barth, *The Epistle to the Ephesians*, ed. R. David Nelson (Grand Rapids: Baker Academic, 2017), 31–49.

that tradition—the Heidelberg Catechism, the Reformed confessions, and the works of Calvin, Zwingli, and Schleiermacher[1]—and on that basis to take up a stance toward and formulate his own interpretation of the material in which he was obligated to provide instruction. He quickly identified what he took to be the marks of Reformed theology and Christian practice: astonishment before and responsibility to divine revelation as a present, entirely uncontainable occurrence; commitment to the Scripture principle and corresponding dedication to the task of biblical exegesis and exposition; an eschatological moralism in which divine majesty at one and the same time evokes and relativizes action in the world. In dogmatics, Barth's Göttingen lectures were the beginning of what was to be a lifelong task of setting out a comprehensive account of Christian teaching in a quite different register from that of his teachers, one that required him to reconceive the objects, cognitive principles, and ends of dogmatics and to recast and reorder its various *loci*.[2]

Recognition of the importance of the Göttingen lectures in biblical exegesis has been quite slow, largely because of the unavailability of much of the material: although the lectures on 1 Corinthians 15 were published in 1924,[3] and a revised version of those on Philippians, originally given in 1924 and then delivered in Münster, appeared in 1927,[4] those on James and Ephesians have been published only recently,[5] and those on 1 John, Colossians, and the Sermon on the Mount

1. See Karl Barth, *The Theology of John Calvin*, trans. Geoffrey W. Bromiley (Grand Rapids: Eerdmans, 1995); Barth, *Die Theologie Zwinglis, Vorlesung Göttingen 1922/23*, ed. Matthias Freudenberg, GA 40 (Zurich: Theologischer Verlag Zürich, 2004); Barth, *The Theology of the Reformed Confessions, 1923*, trans. and ed. Darrell L. Guder and Judith J. Guder (Louisville: Westminster John Knox, 2002); Barth, *The Theology of Schleiermacher: Lectures at Göttingen, Winter Semester of 1923/24*, ed. Dietrich Ritschl, trans. Geoffrey W. Bromiley, with "Concluding Unscientific Postscript," trans. George Hunsinger (Grand Rapids: Eerdmans, 1982).

2. Karl Barth, *"Unterricht in der christlichen Religion,"* I: *Prolegomena, 1924*, ed. Hannelotte Reiffen, GA II 17 (Zurich: Theologischer Verlag Zürich, 1985); Karl Barth, *"Unterricht in der christlichen Religion,"* II: *Die Lehre von Gott / Die Lehre vom Menschen, 1924/25*, ed. Hinrich Stoevesandt, GA II 20 (Zurich: Theologischer Verlag Zürich, 1990); Karl Barth, *"Unterricht in der christlichen Religion,"* III: *Die Lehre von der Versöhnung / Die Lehre von der Erlösung, 1925/26*, ed. Hinrich Stoevesandt, GA II 38 (Zurich: Theologischer Verlag Zürich, 2003). The final lectures in the series, on eschatology, were delivered in Münster. The first volume of the *"Unterricht"* is available in English as Karl Barth, *The Göttingen Dogmatics: Instruction in the Christian Religion*, vol. 1, ed. Hannelotte Reiffen, trans. Geoffrey W. Bromiley (Grand Rapids: Eerdmans, 1991).

3. Karl Barth, *Die Auferstehung der Toten: Eine akademische Vorlesung über 1.Kor. 15* (Munich: Kaiser, 1924); trans. H. J. Stenning as *The Resurrection of the Dead* (New York: Revell, 1933). The English translation is inaccurate and incomplete.

4. Karl Barth, *Erklärung des Philipperbriefes* (Munich: Kaiser, 1928); trans. James W. Leitch (from the German 6th ed., 1947) as *Epistle to the Philippians: 40th Anniversary Edition* (Louisville: Westminster John Knox, 2002).

5. Karl Barth, *Erklärungen des Epheser- und des Jakobusbriefes, 1919–1929*, ed. Jörg-Michael Bohnet, GA II 46 (Zurich: Theologischer Verlag Zürich, 2009).

remain unpublished. Many of the standard accounts of Barth's early work say little of his exegetical labors beyond *The Epistle to the Romans*, and a good deal of the literature on his hermeneutics and exegetical practice confines itself to *Romans* or to the *Church Dogmatics*, though there is increasing recognition of the importance of Barth's study of and teaching about Paul in the decisive phase of his theological development.[6] If the lectures on historical theology were, inter alia, exercises in *ressourcement* and critical retrieval of elements of the Reformed tradition, those on New Testament texts were exercises in commentarial exposition of Christian teaching, setting forth the content of Christian belief neither by free theologizing nor by topical, systematic anatomy but by the attempt to articulate what Barth took to be the matter indicated by the biblical text. This was undertaken on the basis of a conviction that theology is derivative from and governed by exegesis and directed toward exposition. Exegesis and exposition are necessary because they are the activities through which access to biblical instruction is constantly to be sought. As Barth states in a lecture on Calvin,

> The relation to the Bible is a living one. The spring does not flow of itself. It has to be tapped. Its waters have to be drawn. The answer is not already there; we have to ask what it is. The Bible calls for objective study. What is in it is, of course, known already insofar as it is a matter of the relation about which we cannot ask without first knowing it, but because it is a matter of the form and order of this relation in time, we do not yet know what is in the Bible, and, as is unavoidable in time, we have to seek and find this by work. The Bible is thus opened and listened to with a readiness to receive what is not yet known, not for the purpose of finding again what is known already.[7]

Moreover, objectivity in theology—attentiveness to theology's *Sache* in its otherness from the expectations of religious and theological subjectivity—requires constant and concentrated exercise of expectant, untrammeled exegetical intelligence. Barth continues: "This is what gives Calvin's expository skill its first distinctive feature: its extraordinary objectivity. We can learn from Calvin what it means to stay close to the text, to focus with tense attention on what is actually there. Everything else *derives* from this. But it has to derive from *this*. If it does not, then the expounding is not real questioning and readiness to listen."[8]

6. See Nina-Dorothee Mützlitz, *Gottes Wort als Wirklichkeit: Die Paulus-Rezeption des jungen Karl Barth (1906–1927)*, Neukirchener Theologie (Neukirchen-Vluyn: Neukirchener Verlag, 2013); Martin Westerholm, *The Ordering of the Christian Mind: Karl Barth and Theological Rationality* (Oxford: Oxford University Press, 2015).
7. Barth, *Theology of John Calvin*, 388–89.
8. Barth, *Theology of John Calvin*, 389 (emphasis original).

The lectures on Ephesians were delivered in Barth's first semester in Göttingen, and he was much occupied with this New Testament text in the final period of his pastorate in Safenwil. In a letter to Eduard Thurneysen in March 1918, he reported that he had been studying the text with his confirmation candidates,[9] and from May to September of the following year he delivered a series of sermons on the epistle.[10] Later that same year he produced a translation and brief interpretation of Ephesians, which became the basis for an adult Bible study in the parish in the following spring. From this emerged a written text, consisting of a translation and notes on the letter, into which are interpolated summaries of the sermons that Barth had earlier delivered.[11] The Göttingen lectures on Ephesians are the culmination of this extended engagement.

The lectures are especially valuable for the light they shed on one of Barth's principal preoccupations in Göttingen (and, arguably, well beyond Göttingen in his mature theology of covenant)—namely, the relation between God and creatures. Many of Barth's concerns in that concentrated, vivid period of development turn on that relation: his understanding of history, his eschatology, his theology of the resurrection, his theology of revelation and its associated hermeneutics, his ethics, and his interpretation of the differing emphases of the Lutheran and Reformed wings of the Reformation. In accounts of Barth's early theology, his way of articulating the relation of God and creatures is commonly designated "dialectical." Though Barth himself makes quite frequent appeal to the term, it is probably best to use it sparingly in characterizing his work. Partly this is because the term has been used in rather different ways in some of the controversies in the reception of Barth's writings; partly, again, because its deployment as an overarching interpretive category may inhibit close observation of the variety and scope of what Barth has to say about the relation of God and creatures in the various genres in which he was working.

In the lectures on Ephesians, we can observe Barth's thinking about the matter firsthand. More particularly, we can see him trying to learn from this New Testament text how to think about God's presence to and relation with creatures in rather less starkly oppositional terms than those to which he makes much appeal in the second edition of *The Epistle to the Romans*, completed just as he left Safenwil for Göttingen.

9. *Karl Barth—Eduard Thurneysen Briefwechsel I: 1913–1921*, ed. Eduard Thurneysen, GA V 3 (Zurich: Theologischer Verlag Zürich, 1973), 268–69.
10. Karl Barth, *Predigten 1919*, ed. Hermann Schmidt, GA I 39 (Zurich: Theologischer Verlag Zürich, 2003), 173–334.
11. This material is available in Barth, *Erklärungen des Jakobusbriefes*, 3–44.

II

Barth's exegesis of Ephesians presupposes, and occasionally makes explicit, an understanding of the relation between divine communication and the causality of its creaturely media. Though he does not bring to the exercise anything like a comprehensive theology of revelation and Scripture, he does have some working principles to which he turns on those occasions when, in the course of interpreting the text, he thinks himself required to give attention to its origin and its primary speaker.

In his final lecture on the prologue to Ephesians, Barth remarks on this "compendium of the fundamental Pauline framework":

> It offers a glimpse into the unprecedented revolution that must have occurred in the hearts and minds of this group of people in the first century and the impression it must have made upon them—upon both Paul and his readers, whom he considered capable of understanding such ideas! It is impossible on the basis of historical analysis to perceive the essentially imperceptible event that occurred here, or anywhere. . . . However, I hope that I have convinced you that it is possible to enter sympathetically with Paul and not only to see along with Paul but to think along with him at that point where *the subject matter* [*Gegenstand*], *the incommensurable, Jesus Christ*, speaks and becomes his own interpreter.[12]

Barth reads Ephesians as an apostolic text, whose origin lies in the attempt on the part of its author to indicate the wholly incommensurable reality and presence of God, and which is now the means whereby its readers are drawn before that reality and presence. The lectures on Ephesians antedate his engagement with the Reformed Scripture principle in lectures on the Reformed confessional writings,[13] and he does not characterize the nature and function of the text by appeal to the theological categories deployed by that principle. Rather, he thinks of the text, in both its origin and its effect, as arising from and indicative of realities that may not be drawn within the regularities of history.

This does not mean that Barth is wholly indifferent to the literary properties of the text. As in the other Göttingen exegetical lectures, the text enjoys a good deal more prominence than it does in either of the first two editions

---

12. Karl Barth, "Exposition of Ephesians, Winter Semester 1921–22," trans. Ross M. Wright, in *The Epistle to the Ephesians*, 126 (emphasis original).

13. Barth, *Theology of the Reformed Confessions*, 38–64; see also Karl Barth, "Das Schriftprinzip der reformierten Kirche," in *Vorträge und kleinere Arbeiten 1922–1925*, ed. Holger Finze, GA III 19 (Zurich: Theologischer Verlag Zürich, 1990), 500–544.

of the *Romans* commentary (despite the fact that both editions are indeed intended to be *commentaries*). If in *Romans* the relation between what the text says and what Barth says that the text says is not always transparent, in Ephesians the governance of the text is much more direct and explicit. The text is not simply the occasion for the articulation of Barth's theological convictions (prompted and informed by the text, perhaps, but not always demonstrably bound by and directed toward it). Rather, the text of Ephesians is that to which Barth attempts to direct his hearers' attention and whose course he seeks to follow. He does not devote a great deal of time to linguistic, grammatical, and stylistic matters or to a review of exegetical options; his attention is much more gripped by the matter of the text. Nevertheless, what he offers his hearers is not a set of theological variations on topics in Ephesians; it is, rather, theology in exegetical and expository mode.

Barth remains ambivalent, however, toward the value of historical investigation of the text and its provenance for coming to understand its matter. It is important not to attribute to Barth some principled indifference to history or an "anti-historical" attitude, either in reading biblical texts or more generally in historical theology.[14] Barth does consider it necessary to devote some time at the beginning of the lecture series to questions of authorship and recipients, though he does not find such matters engaging, and he concludes his review of the phrase ἐν Ἐφέσῳ early on in the third lecture on a weary note: "I believe that I have discharged my duty by making you aware of all these possibilities, and I leave it to you to decide which of them is the least improbable."[15]

Barth's sense of the restricted applicability and fruitfulness of historical inquiry in biblical interpretation arises from what he takes to be the matter of the text and the communicative act of which the text forms an element. He considers that Ephesians sets before its readers a reality that exceeds historical intelligence, even as it presents itself in a textual form inextricable from (though not wholly exhausted by) historical processes of authorship and reception. Both the matter of the text and the way in which the textual indication of that matter comes into being point to the limits of historical description and explanation.

The matter to which exegetical intelligence is to be directed, on Barth's account, is not simply the historical quantities of the religious lives, situation,

14. In this connection, Barth's remarks on "history as life's teacher" in his opening lecture on Calvin in the 1922 series are illuminating (see Barth, *Theology of John Calvin*, 1–9). See further Hinrich Stoevesandt, "Barths Calvinvorlesung als Station seiner theologischen Biographie," in *Karl Barth und Johannes Calvin: Karl Barths Göttinger Calvin-Vorlesung von 1922*, ed. Hans Scholl (Neukirchen-Vluyn: Neukirchener Verlag, 1995), 107–24.

15. Barth, "Exposition of Ephesians," 72.

or beliefs of its author and original recipients but an "eschatological" reality. If exegesis terminates on some interim reality, it has not run its full course. Lecturing on Ephesians 1:20 ("[God] raised him from the dead") on February 16, 1922, for example, Barth notes that when the author speaks of resurrection, "he means an event . . . that is more nearly impossible and unhistorical than historical. He means the impossible event κατ' ἐξοχήν . . . an event that takes place precisely at the *boundary* between what is possible and what is impossible, what is historical and what is unhistorical, time and eternity."[16] "Boundary" is an important term here: it is not that the matter of Ephesians is transcendent *tout court* but more that—in its difference from the temporal— that matter points beyond itself "in" time, though not as a contingent temporal happening but as the displacement of time, as time's outer edge. What is given in Jesus Christ, Barth says,

> is given in *history*, therefore not as something other than history, removed from history, in addition to history, removed from history—not as a Platonic idea, as popularly conceived. It is given as an idea in the fullest sense, that is, as the idea or conception of *God*, therefore as the origin of all *origins*, the inaccessible in the immediate, the wholly other in the human, the beyond in *this life*. But note: it is given as an *event* in history, as *the other side* of this world, as an event that is in history but not *of* it—not a mere object of history but history's fundamental origin and absolute boundary. This boundary and origin are of a different order than anything that can be explained on *the basis of history* or examined within *the established order of knowledge*, even the most extraordinary and unprecedented event.[17]

Such is the incommensurability of the resurrection that it cannot be grasped through categories such as "miracle" or "vision," which draw the resurrection within the domain of historical experience: "The reality that Paul describes here is not experienced the way we experience anything else. It would be far more faithful to Paul to say that we do not experience it at all."[18] Historical-critical research offers a negative testimony to this: precisely by advertising the contradictions in the biblical accounts of the resurrection, it reveals "just how improbable, implausible, and historically impossible the event is."[19] Similar attempts by Barth to discriminate the matter of the text from anything experientially or historically available and familiar recur throughout the lectures. What he finds himself struggling to articulate to his audience

16. Barth, "Exposition of Ephesians," 132–33 (emphasis original).
17. Barth, "Exposition of Ephesians," 133 (emphasis original).
18. Barth, "Exposition of Ephesians," 134.
19. Barth, "Exposition of Ephesians," 134.

is, quite simply, nonpareil, that to which we cannot stand in any accustomed historical relation.

Something similar is found in the account of the authorship of Ephesians with which Barth opens the lecture series. Starting from the letter's first word, Παῦλος, he gives a brief survey of the *status quaestionis* concerning Pauline authorship, concluding that though he himself "would defend the authenticity" of the letter, he does not "have any great interest in the question," preferring to follow Bengel: *Noli quaerere quis scripserit sed quid scriptum est*.[20] If Bengel is attractive to Barth, it is because to accord priority to *quid scriptum est* is to detach study of the Bible from inquiry into religious personality[21] and instead to devote attention to the revelatory matter of which the Bible is sign and embassy.

There is, doubtless, a certain externality in this account of the relation of the matter of the Bible and its human authorship. The decisiveness with which Barth separates *quis scripserit* from *quid scriptum est* may suggest that the natural properties of the author (e.g., cultural setting; moral, spiritual, and intellectual gifts; virtues and experiences) are not sanctified or caused to serve the presentation of the *res* of the text but are little more than occasion for the acts of another agent, having no instrumental role. On the other hand, it may be that as he tries to dispose himself before the text, Barth is not eliminating or suspending the human author so much as characterizing the kind of human authorial activity that occurs in the sphere of (eschatological) reality in which Ephesians is caught up.

This, at least, is what Barth attempts in his account of the second word of Ephesians, ἀπόστολος:

> The apostolic vocation splits the person, so to speak. He is an apostle not on the basis of anything he is in and of himself but on the basis of what he is *not*. A demand of a very *different* order is made on him, and a demand of a very different order directs him to his fellow human creatures. There is something exceptional and impossible about him, but it is not his genius, his experience, his unmediated knowledge, or anything that can be accounted for psychologically as greatness or character. What makes him an apostle is his mission, his instructions, and the service he is to offer, which are not, from a psychological point of view, even *his own matter* but the matter that *has him* and sends him.[22]

20. Barth, "Exposition of Ephesians," 58–59.
21. See here the 1917 lecture "The New World in the Bible," in Karl Barth, *The Word of God and Theology*, trans. Amy Marga (London: T&T Clark, 2011), 15–29.
22. Barth, "Exposition of Ephesians," 59–60 (emphasis original).

The apostle is defined by the demands laid upon him, by vocation rather than by inherent or even bestowed capacity.[23] The being and act of the ἀπόστολος are wholly a function of Χριστοῦ Ἰησοῦ, both because the apostle is defined by reference to Jesus Christ as the substance of his vocation and because the apostle shares in the paradox of "Immanuel! God with us!"[24] The incarnation is revelation *sub contrario*, in the *coincidentia oppositorum* of God and flesh; and "the existence of an ἀπόστολος is a repetition and variation of the same theme in a subordinate position, where it is possible to serve, to point, and to witness."[25]

Again, reflecting on the phrase "by the will of God" (Eph. 1:1), Barth stresses that apostleship entails abandonment of human privilege and capacity. The divine will "necessarily includes negation in the form of renunciation. Paul renounces all natural protection." The apostle is outside the "composite of well-ordered functions," which we indicate by the term "society." The apostle calls into question the human needs and concerns that cluster around "religion." The apostle gives up "the shelter and protection that he was due by virtue of his human authority," along with "self-honor." In short, the apostle "negates himself."[26]

The denials are forceful and resonant. Their positive intent is to draw attention to the objectivity of apostolic existence and work:

When [Paul] calls himself ἀπόστολος διὰ θελήματος θεοῦ and addresses his readers on this basis, it is not in order to draw attention to his personal attributes, not even his so-called religious personality, or to flaunt his experience or experiences, or to impress them with his knowledge. He has no reason to linger on these human factors, be they good or evil. His relationship to his readers is determined by his office. He has an objective message to convey, and on the basis of the phrase διὰ θελήματος θεοῦ he appeals to his hearers to receive it objectively.[27]

If there is a weakness here, it is that Barth's eagerness to lift apostleship out of the realm of natural religious personality may inhibit him from speaking not only of the judgment of human nature and powers but also of their sanctification for divine service. In his eagerness to acknowledge the originality of God in relation to the biblical testimony, Barth may at times veer toward

23. A little later, however, Barth notes briefly that apostles are "envoys who are instructed and equipped with power" (Barth, "Exposition of Ephesians," 61).
24. Barth, "Exposition of Ephesians," 61.
25. Barth, "Exposition of Ephesians," 61.
26. Barth, "Exposition of Ephesians," 62–63.
27. Barth, "Exposition of Ephesians," 64.

a kind of extrinsicism. Yet he also finds that Ephesians presses beyond the antithesis of the divine and the creaturely to speak of their association and of a strange but real human correlate to revelatory divine activity. To this we now turn.

III

In his exegesis and exposition in these lectures, Barth, we have seen, considers attention to the historical properties of the text to be necessary (in a relatively minimal way) but by no means sufficient for understanding of and intelligent participation in the communicative act of which the apostolic text forms an element. This view of the text and its setting and function in divine revelation is bound up with a set of wider convictions about God and God's relation to creatures, convictions that Barth both takes to the text and finds confirmed by it. They are not given any systematic formulation in the lectures, but they are articulated at various points as he proceeds, sometimes in passing, sometimes more expansively.

As he reads Ephesians, Barth's attention is frequently drawn to the way in which the letter resists any treatment of God as a correlate of human religious or moral culture. Even to speak of God as the object or cause of human knowing, experiencing, and acting is to reduce God to being one term in a pair, folding God into the created reality to which God is related and failing to acknowledge God's entire incommensurability. Commenting, for example, on Ephesians 1:2 ("Grace be with you and peace from God our Father and the Lord Jesus Christ"), Barth stresses that grace and peace are wholly to be understood in terms of God rather than in terms of the subjectivities of believing recipients: "It is *God* we are dealing with here. . . . The realities about which [grace and peace] speak are hidden in *God*, and *God* himself guarantees that they are genuine realities."[28] God himself is

> the incomprehensible *Nevertheless!* at the heart of both terms. . . . When Paul refers to God as the giver of grace and the source of our peace, he is not thinking about a conspicuous metaphysical object. When he calls God our "Father," he is using the ultimate parable to express the inexpressible and unimaginable, namely, our origin. *Our* origin: *we* human creatures, although thoroughly human, are related to him, who is most wonderful, who is not and never will be simply a contingent object, who is unknown, who is holy, the *Deus absconditus*.[29]

28. Barth, "Exposition of Ephesians," 76–77 (emphasis original).
29. Barth, "Exposition of Ephesians," 77 (emphasis original).

As often in Barth's early writings, the term "origin" here has a double resonance. In part—as we will see shortly—it indicates the singular character of God's relation to creatures. But it is also a term that Barth uses to reach toward the idea that God is in himself ungrounded, *a se*. In the lectures, Barth has little to say about God's inner life, perfection, and beatitude. Partly this is because he does not find textual prompts to talk about such matters. Partly, again, it may be because what Barth says about God in his writings from this period is still to some degree shaped by the liberal Protestant tradition of which it is sometimes the reverse image; having issued a denial that God is a correlate of human religious life, he does not go on to talk of God's immanent being and acts. When he lectured on Ephesians, Barth had not yet immersed himself in the post-Reformation dogmatics of the inner divine nature and processions, which he was to discover at the prompting of Heinrich Heppe. Moreover, Barth's acute awareness that a theological metaphysics of the divine essence may be a close cousin of idolatry increases his reluctance to make use of such categories in his exposition. For such reasons, rather than talking of God *in se*, Barth usually limits himself to statements about God's relation to creatures, which draw attention to the sheer difference of the *relata* and so to the way in which that relation is unlike any contingent relation, most of all because it is devoid of the mutual presence and exchange that characterize the reciprocal life of creatures. God's relation to creatures is "beyond all relations."[30]

How is this singular relation to be described? A characteristic comment from Barth (he is considering the relation of divine purpose and human approbation in Eph. 1:5–6) runs:

An infinite qualitative distinction separates the action of the creator from that of the creature. However, this infinite distinction is precisely what unites the creature and the creator. God can bless man only as his creature; man can bless God only as his creator. The recognition of this infinite distinction is precisely what makes the blessing and the praise both meet and right. Recognition of God's divinity establishes the divine Otherness, the "*aliter*"; and precisely by being established, it is sublated.[31]

It is important to note that Barth does not think that Ephesians presents either an unrelieved antithesis between or an easy coordination of God and creatures. Rather, as he reads the text, he finds that it compels attention to the acts in which God sets himself before creatures and creatures before himself,

30. Barth, "Exposition of Ephesians," 97.
31. Barth, "Exposition of Ephesians," 80–81.

on the basis of which their respective natures and the character of their relation in some measure may be perceived.

Barth most commonly describes these acts in the idiom of revelation, understood as the divine act of indirect and interruptive communication, unforeseen and unassimilable, and as an event of manifestation rather than a condition of revealedness. Commenting on "the mystery of [God's] will" in Ephesians 1:9, Barth remarks that the divine will cannot be the object of direct perception "on the basis of what is observable and concrete."[32] He continues: "Because our vision is occluded, an act of revelation is necessary. Every veil must be rent; all human reality must be upended. *God* must speak, and God must *speak*, if we are to understand his will."[33] Immediate knowledge of the will of God is "impossible, even unimaginable for us"; what is vouchsafed to creatures is an event in time, an "incomparable today" in which "time is split" and "the will of God *meets* us."[34] "The *disiecta membra* of this world-reality *do have* a unity. This is so because of *God's* reality, *God's* act, *God's* revelation."[35] The term "revelation" condenses a range of Barth's convictions about the inexhaustibility of God and his unavailability for apprehension on terms other than those in which he presents himself as well as about the instability of creaturely knowledge of God and the impossibility of detached observation or cognitive accumulation and possession.

It is, once again, important to recognize that Barth's demarcations, vigorous and determined though they are, are intended not to deny God's communicative presence but to specify its conditions and the manner of its occurrence. The spiritual blessings of which the apostle speaks in Ephesians 1:3 are not "the presence of God in the form of visible, direct immediacy, which is the domain of gods and idols";[36] they do not simply add to our store of experiential goods. Rather, as the *Spirit's* blessings, they are "God's unmediated presence for us, . . . God in his inapproachability, inaccessibility, and hiddenness. God, who cannot be known, surrounds, besieges, storms, and reorders the domain of my knowing."[37] Spiritual blessings are an event of divine giving, not a given commodity. Again, Barth resists conceptions of a causal relation between God and creatures, which he fears would reduce God to being the first of a series; God is, rather, "beyond the world, beyond all causality."[38] Or

32. Barth, "Exposition of Ephesians," 111.
33. Barth, "Exposition of Ephesians," 111 (emphasis original).
34. Barth, "Exposition of Ephesians," 112 (emphasis original).
35. Barth, "Exposition of Ephesians," 112 (emphasis original).
36. Barth, "Exposition of Ephesians," 89.
37. Barth, "Exposition of Ephesians," 89.
38. Barth, "Exposition of Ephesians," 97.

again, the relation established by God between himself and creatures must be differentiated from "domesticated piety, which regards *living* with God to be more important than living with *God*."[39] But none of this is intended to negate the relation of God and creatures: the fact that divine presence cannot be made a function of human self-presence "does not obliterate, neutralize, or obviate anything that is mine, positive or negative; but the relativity of all that is mine is clearly revealed, or to be precise, *related* to its origin, measured according to the standard by which all things are decided. . . . What I am, I am in relation to God."[40]

The lectures on Ephesians are an early instance of the way in which, in his theological work in Göttingen, Barth often reaches toward an account of the relation of God and creatures that neither reduces God to a correlate of the human subject nor, by way of correction, simply segregates or opposes God and creatures. In effect, if not in intent, Barth offers a kerygmatically charged appropriation of the scholastic conception of a "mixed" relation between God and creatures—what might be termed an eschatological theological metaphysics of that relation. Properly understood, Barth notes in a comment on Ephesians 1:12, "ἔσχατον . . . refers not only to the last things but also to the first and most important thing in each moment."[41] At this very fertile stage in his development, observes Christopher Asprey,

> Barth's theology . . . proceeds from the conviction that human beings exist before God *eschatologically*. Human ontology is not a settled condition, a "nature" of any kind, but a response to the imposing presence of God, who summons me to live beyond myself. What defines this God most fundamentally is not his superiority over all other beings, nor his providential governance of history, but his *encounter* with human beings as their *God*. Both aspects are indispensable: God is not conceived in abstraction from his creation, yet he meets it in such commanding superiority that, just as importantly, *it* may not extract itself from *him*. This encounter is what is meant by revelation.[42]

A closely similar pattern of thought is evident in Barth's christological remarks in the lectures. At the opening of the letter, the author speaks of himself as ἀπόστολος Χριστοῦ Ἰησοῦ; and "Jesus Christ"—a proper name set together with an office of universal scope—"means the unification of all that is inherently incompatible, the *coincidentia oppositorum*, and the

39. Barth, "Exposition of Ephesians," 102 (emphasis original).
40. Barth, "Exposition of Ephesians," 89 (emphasis original).
41. Barth, "Exposition of Ephesians," 123.
42. Christopher Asprey, *Eschatological Presence in Karl Barth's Göttingen Theology* (Oxford: Oxford University Press, 2010), 24 (emphasis original).

complete riddle of Christology."[43] Incarnation does not mean peaceful co-ordination of divine and human natures: in Christ, opposites coincide but remain opposites (an early expression from Barth of the instinct behind the *extra Calvinisticum*, perhaps). Further, the reality that the name indicates does not present itself as a matter for calm contemplation. It is an assault: "the message of the incarnation is not proclaimed as an idea . . . ; rather, the word from the peaceful kingdom enters the world as a battle cry, as a declaration of war. Here, the δύναμις τοῦ θεοῦ speaks. Here, the One God demands an acknowledgment. . . . Here, the One God determines to rule as monarch, and *all* other demands with which life confronts us are called into question by him. Here, it is a matter of God's decisive battle against idols."[44] The very humanity in which revelation takes form subverts any attempt to integrate it into an existing experience or scheme: "in order to . . . prevent us from turning it into a religious or philosophical truth, to impress upon us that the truth comes to us only in the eternal moment of knowledge, the concrete subject matter of this gospel and its most characteristic trait is a human face, the completely mysterious face of one who suffers, is rejected, and dies—the face of Jesus of Nazareth, who was crucified."[45] Yet this is not a disavowal of God's presence in Christ but an attempt to spell out its origin and its distinctive properties. "Ἐν Χριστῷ means Immanuel! God with us! Ἐν Χριστῷ God draws near in his self-revelation, while remaining distant, strange, and incomprehensible: the *Deus absconditus*. In Christ is thus *the* proximity of God, which always means eternity and never merely the temporal extension of what is palpable, comprehensible, or perceptible. Precisely because the proximity of God is ultimate reality, it can only be believed—and the belief itself is the wonder of its revelation."[46] Because in Christ divine revelation is asymptotic, it breaks the assumption, which Barth found to be deep-seated in the exegesis, dogmatics, and ethics of the liberal Protestant tradition, that the real is the historical-experiential.

God is beyond—not constituted by—all relations; nevertheless, he sets himself before creatures and brings them into relation to himself. In what ways does this relation take creaturely form?

Barth is markedly reluctant to say much about how objective relation to God coincides with creaturely subjectivity, because he is recoiling from theologies in which religious subjectivity enjoys priority. Commenting on "sealed with the Holy Spirit of promise" (Eph. 1:13), for example, he does

43. Barth, "Exposition of Ephesians," 60.
44. Barth, "Exposition of Ephesians," 61.
45. Barth, "Exposition of Ephesians," 61.
46. Barth, "Exposition of Ephesians," 82–83.

not take the occasion to speak of the Spirit as the agent of the realization of divine benefits in the believer, and he emphasizes contingency rather than appropriation:

> Humanity and everything human is questionable. What is not in question is the relation of humanity and everything human to *God*. The more we recognize humanity's uncertainty, the more we recognize the certainty of man's relation to God. Indeed, the reason human existence in and of itself is dubious is precisely because humanity is originally related to God. Everything that is contingent and temporal is relative. What is not relative is the actual relation to the *Absolute*. The more clearly we recognize this relation for what it is, the more clearly we understand the relativity of all things.[47]

Because contingency is by far the most important attribute of creaturely relation to God, the creatures of divine grace are defined not by divinely given powers to act or dispositions or forms of life and experience but by reference to their origin in God, the counterpart to which is a lack of creaturely extension.

What, Barth asks in his lecture on Ephesians 1:7, does it mean that we "have" (ἔχομεν) redemption and other divine blessings? In considering this "having," we are not to think that "our feet touch the familiar ground of human being, having, and doing, where we can catch our breath for a moment," for here "our familiar human being, having, and doing are called into question from beyond."[48] Our having is not possession but rather the (unfinishable) process of coming to have, incessant reception. "We have what only God has, what we [can] have only in God, who unites time and eternity. In other words, we have what we must receive continuously from God in each present moment."[49] This triggers some critical remarks on the "Biblical Realism" of J. T. Beck; though Barth had learned from Beck's unease with critical theology in the school of F. C. Baur and had made use of Beck's work on Ephesians,[50] he is troubled by the way in which Beck's "realism" drifts into a noneschatological subjectivism. Beck's concern to go beyond the extrinsicism of some Protestant theologies of justification and speak of the intrinsic reality of divine grace threatens to become "simply a form of naturalism."[51] "The Word of God does not become more real by being refashioned into human

---

47. Barth, "Exposition of Ephesians," 123–24 (emphasis original).
48. Barth, "Exposition of Ephesians," 103–4.
49. Barth, "Exposition of Ephesians," 107.
50. J. T. Beck, *Erklärung des Briefes Pauli an die Epheser: Nebst Anmerkungen zum Brief Pauli an die Kolosser* (Gütersloh: Bertelsman, 1891).
51. Barth, "Exposition of Ephesians," 107.

reality. We should be content with its own reality rather than trying to make it conform to ours."[52]

An important corollary here is that the creature's relation to God does not follow an ordered temporal course; it is not discursive but always at the beginning. The knowledge with which the apostle (in Eph. 1:15–23) asks that his recipients be blessed is—precisely as "the blessing of *God*"—"completely new each new moment,"[53] a constantly renewed divine act of giving, such that "we must return continually to the source and origin. This origin does not exist in the world or within time," and so "the human creature must repeatedly *call upon* God as God."[54] As often in his earlier (and sometimes in his later) writing, Barth makes much of the idea of newness in order to emphasize that life in relation to God is not an amplification of natural being in time, for God's action is punctiliar, not durative. "Any truth that is *not new* does not qualify as God's truth. Likewise, when redemption ceases to be an object of hope and becomes something we possess or consume, it is no longer redemption."[55] "If we regard [God's] name, kingdom, and will as no more than the evolution, extension, or continuation of what already exists—then obviously we do not know what we are saying when we say 'God.'"[56] Relation to God is marked above all not by the accumulation and enjoyment of spiritual goods but by prayer for fresh acts of grace: "A new day has dawned. Yesterday's discovery must be sought anew today."[57]

Similar patterns of thought recur throughout Barth's comments on Christian existence in the course of the lectures. Early on, he considers the apostle's designation of his recipients as τοῖς ἁγίοις τοῖς οὖσιν . . . καὶ πιστοῖς ἐν Χριστῷ Ἰησοῦ (Eph. 1:1). Neither holiness nor faithfulness may on Barth's reckoning be understood as modifications of human subjectivity in time: "Ἅγιος signifies a place, object, or person, which, although situated in the known world, belongs not to this world but to the rule of God's power and splendor";[58] it thus indicates "a *negation*, a cordoning off, the imposition of a blockade, an attack that creates a void, like the crater formed from an exploding shell."[59] Moreover, both its cause and its effects are unavailable for direct perception. "The one who makes them holy . . . does not appear as such, occupying time and space. . . . There is no way to directly identify the state of holiness as

52. Barth, "Exposition of Ephesians," 108.
53. Barth, "Exposition of Ephesians," 128.
54. Barth, "Exposition of Ephesians," 129 (emphasis original).
55. Barth, "Exposition of Ephesians," 129 (emphasis original).
56. Barth, "Exposition of Ephesians," 129.
57. Barth, "Exposition of Ephesians," 129.
58. Barth, "Exposition of Ephesians," 65.
59. Barth, "Exposition of Ephesians," 65 (emphasis original).

such! Holiness that is conspicuous, tangible, or perceptible (humanly speaking) is not holiness."[60] And so Barth once again counters what he regards as a deleterious historical stability by insisting on the interruptive, occasional character of God's relation to the creature and the irregularity of its creaturely complement. "Holiness," he writes,

> is a relationship with *God*. This relationship is established by *God*. It is never simply a given. It is never a finished event. For the human creature, it will always remain a quest and goal; but as free grace, it becomes more than a quest and goal. It exists wonderfully, moment by moment, on the basis of God's eternal election; and absolutely *no* law could possibly be at work, above or apart from God's *beneplacitum*, diverting the course of this election. To *call a person holy* is to say that God eternally disturbs him and fills him with joy, that God has laid his hand upon the creature. The creature is attacked and wounded where he is most vital, in his subjectivity, his existence. Existentially, he is no longer his own. He himself no longer lives. He resembles an off-centered wheel, which no longer revolves around its own center.[61]

Moreover, the action and presence of God are entirely invisible and generate no creaturely form: "all we can see is the creature, living in sin and death."[62] Yet, crucially for Barth, the absence of historical form or visibility betokens not divine absence but simply the mode of God's relation to the creature: "unlike all gods and idols, he draws near while maintaining his infinite distance."[63] Because of this, *malgré tout*, we may say that there is a human reality of holiness, that "in Christ, the human creature is sanctified."[64] Such holiness is real not as an "experience" or "condition"[65] but because of its divine basis, which Barth describes as "the human creature's *eternal* relation to God, *the* relation in which the person *is* eternal and will become what he certainly never was and *becomes* what he eternally is: God's possession, instrument, servant, and child. This relation is real only because it begins where *everything* comes to an end, in *the* life that comes from death."[66]

Similarly, reflecting on the description of the recipients of the letter as πιστοῖς, Barth steers away from any correlation of God and creatures. "The idea of polarity, equipoise, or balance between divine and human action is

60. Barth, "Exposition of Ephesians," 65–66.
61. Barth, "Exposition of Ephesians," 66 (emphasis original).
62. Barth, "Exposition of Ephesians," 66.
63. Barth, "Exposition of Ephesians," 67.
64. Barth, "Exposition of Ephesians," 67.
65. Barth, "Exposition of Ephesians," 67.
66. Barth, "Exposition of Ephesians," 67 (emphasis original).

absent from Paul's thought; wherever 'faith' is spoken of in such a fashion, it leads to simplistic and false dogmatics."[67] Barth admits that πιστοῖς does in some way refer "to a truly subjective human state,"[68] but the concession is immediately qualified:

> Faith is the action of the new person in me, the person *I am not*, the new person whose identity within me is the source of the greatest possible honor. Faith is a fundamental and eternal event that is beyond all temporal processes. Faith is God's work in us. It takes place in us, to be sure; it is not some invisible metaphysical reality, independent of our recognition of God's mercy, enclosed in his holiness. But it takes place only as God's work, as the eternal moment hidden within the temporal moment; it is one with what occurs in us.[69]

IV

It would be relatively easy to judge Barth's lectures, both in what they say about divine revelation and its apostolic media and in their presentation of Christian existence in relation to God, as often trapped by the malign contrast: *aut gloria Dei aut gloria hominis.* Such an opposition is not Barth's intention: the lectures (along with those on Calvin from the following semester) are in part a struggle to articulate a relation between the "vertical" and the "horizontal" that is neither antithesis nor synthesis. So intense is Barth's concern to draw attention to the nongiven, nonrepresentable character of God's presence that he allows himself to say rather little about the human forms and acts by which divine revelation and saving action are communicated and received and about the ways in which they shape and order human life and activity—beyond some highly charged descriptions of the dislocation that they engender. Together with Barth's instinctive occasionalism and his insistent rhetoric, this intensity runs the risk of denying what, after many qualifications, he is trying to affirm. In the *Church Dogmatics*, Barth will leave this difficulty behind in his long descriptions of God's economic acts and the human moral history that they evoke and sustain. Here, however, his principal concern is to refuse to think of God and creatures as reciprocal, commensurable terms; yet in so doing, he sometimes appears to subvert not only commensurability but all relation.

What Barth is reaching toward in his exegesis and exposition is an understanding of God and creatures in which, because God is perfect, simple, and

67. Barth, "Exposition of Ephesians," 68.
68. Barth, "Exposition of Ephesians," 68.
69. Barth, "Exposition of Ephesians," 68–69 (emphasis original).

uncompounded, God's relation to creatures is not constitutive of his being. The protest against any settled forms of creaturely relation to God is directed against the idea that God is merely one *res* alongside another. To issue the protest, Barth often appeals to one or another element of the theology of divine grace, but grace is identified primarily with divine freedom rather than with the communication of goods or with an ever-fresh act of divine giving rather than with its creaturely effects. An account of the matter less concerned to voice dissent might make its appeal to divine goodness—to the beneficence that flows from God's fullness of life and that enacts his purpose to cause, sustain, and bless creaturely life in its integrity and continuity. Yet there is a reminder in what Barth struggled to articulate to his audience almost a century ago: only when we have come to know that God is beyond all relations may we understand and enact the relation to him in which we have been caused to stand.

FIVE

The Call to Repentance
Is the Call of the Gospel

Barth, the Epistle of James, and Moral Theology

CARSTEN CARD-HYATT

Introduction

Karl Barth's legacy as an exegete will always be foremost as an interpreter of Paul, and rightly so. The unhappy consequence of this fact, along with the exigencies of publishing and translating Barth's *Nachlass*, is that his consistent engagement with non-Pauline and Gospel texts throughout the 1920s (with 1 Peter making a late appearance in 1938) has garnered little attention. Among these, it is the lectures on the Epistle of James that are likely to hold the greatest interest for those interested in the scope of Barth's exegetical activities beyond his work on Romans, as well as for students of Barth's development.

An earlier version of this paper was presented as part of the "Theology of Karl Barth" panel at the 2015 Evangelical Theological Society Annual Meeting. I am grateful to Ben Rhodes for inviting me to present on the panel and encouraging me to work on Barth's lectures on James. Along with him, I am grateful to David Robinson and Rebecca Card-Hyatt for providing valuable comments that have improved the paper immensely.

In part, these lectures are significant because this particular scriptural text seems to offer so little in form or content to which Barth would gravitate, yet he returned to the text twice in his first decade of teaching. When he first lectured on James during the winter semester of 1922–23 in Göttingen he gave it a sympathetic reading, but, as he confessed to Eduard Thurneysen, he found James "one-sided" and looked forward to going back to something "Pauline."[1] When he lectured on James again in Münster six years later, he did a fair amount of revision of his original lectures, all the while maintaining the substance of his key judgments.[2] By 1942 Barth evidently saw the text in a more positive light, asserting that "there is no New Testament text that presents the Gospel to men so emphatically and unwaveringly, so consistently from the standpoint of the divine claim, as the Epistle of James."[3] All this to say, of the non-Pauline texts on which Barth lectured during the 1920s, James presents his clearest interpretive challenge, and yet his labors also seem to have borne fruit in changing his appreciation of this difficult text.

Beyond the interests of *Barthiana*, Barth's reading of James offers a full presentation of what makes him such an engaging reader of Scripture, yet one who is nonetheless often an unwelcome presence at the exegete's table. Barth's frank admission that reading the Bible is primarily a spiritual and moral enterprise, one for which humanity and the church are not obviously suited, seems to threaten the removal of interpretation from the demands of reason altogether. As Adolf von Harnack declaimed in the early days of dialectical theology, if Barth was successful, then the teaching of the gospel would be "exclusively handed over to revival preachers, who freely create their understanding of the Bible and who set up their own dominance."[4] In retrospect this can only strike us as somewhat hysterical, but even though Barth moved away from the prophetic mode that characterized *Romans II* to

1. Karl Barth, letter to Eduard Thurneysen, January 23, 1923, in *Karl Barth-Eduard Thurneysen Briefwechsel II: 1921–1930*, GA V 4 (Zurich: Theologischer Verlag Zürich, 1974), 134.
2. Barth presented them a third time, with no substantial revision, in Bonn during the summer semester of 1930. Barth scholarship owes a great debt of thanks to Pastor Bohnet, who scrupulously prepared the two versions of the lecture texts and presented them in parallel so that it is readily apparent where Barth made changes. See Karl Barth, *Erklärung des Epheser- und Jakobusbriefes*, GA II 46, ed. Jörg-Michael Bohnet (Zurich: Theologischer Verlag Zürich, 2009). He also published a brief summary of the "character" of the epistle in 1927, "Der Charakter des Jakobusbriefes," in *Almanach 1927* (Munich: Kaiser, 1927), 7–14. Barth's only other significant work on James came when, as a young pastor in Genf, he preached on the epistle in 18 sermons from Jan. 9 to Aug. 7, 1910. These sermons remain unpublished.
3. *CD* II/2, 588.
4. Adolf von Harnack, "An Open Letter to Professor Karl Barth," in *The Beginnings of Dialectical Theology*, vol. 1, ed. James M. Robinson (Richmond: John Knox, 1968), 174.

the less paraphrastic interpretive method we find in the university lectures, Harnack's fear may not be groundless. What I will argue in this essay is that the power of Barth's reading of James is in its conviction that the epistle lays a claim on the reader that preempts the claims of dogmatic systems or assumptions about coherence to which interpretation putatively aspires. It is obvious that this leaves Barth open to the charge of only being able to assert, rather than justify, his interpretation.[5]

Any response to such charges must take the form of thinking with Barth's own exegesis, and to that end I aim to do three things in this essay. First, I show how Barth substantiates his claim that the unifying standpoint of the epistle is a summons to see faith in its explicitly moral register, which Barth calls repentance. Second, I will argue that Barth's attention to James's rhetoric allows him to rehabilitate a form of Christian moral communication, while separating himself from an influential stream of theological ethics and its account of the moral subject. Finally, I will show how Barth's understanding of the epistle's "call to repentance" informs his critique of certain habits of theological interpretation in his exegesis of the passage on faith and works.[6]

Neither a comprehensive account of Barth's revisions between the two lecture cycles nor an evaluation of his exegesis in light of other scholarship can be attempted here. Further, Barth's treatment of the material is truncated, and the limitations of these lecture texts are evident if one is seeking a comprehensive overview of James. Nearly all of Barth's exegetical lectures from this period have an accordion-like structure—alternately expansive and compressed—and in neither cycle does he comment in detail on anything beyond chapter 2. With these limitations in mind, my primary hope is that this essay will encourage further, more extensive study of this material.

The Call to Repentance

Following Barth's lead, a close reading of his exposition of James 1:2–4 will tell us how he arrives at the notion that repentance is the dominant motif of the letter and how he understands the letter to be theological speech. Because

5. For a discussion of the charge that Barth's exegetical practice is authoritarian, see Donald Wood, *Barth's Theology of Interpretation* (Aldershot, UK: Ashgate, 2007), 74–86.
6. Given the complex relationship between the earlier and later versions of these lectures, this essay will exclusively reference the later, 1928–29 material. This decision is largely a pragmatic one, as Barth's revision produced a clearer, cleaner text, but, as will become apparent, it also allows us to draw connections to other work by Barth from around the same time.

Barth's exegesis of these opening verses is central to his reading of the entire epistle, it will be helpful to have the text to hand:[7]

Πᾶσαν χαρὰν ἡγήσασθε, ἀδελφοί μου, ὅταν πειρασμοῖς περιπέσητε ποικίλοις, γινώσκοντες ὅτι τὸ δοκίμιον ὑμῶν τῆς πίστεως κατεργάζεται ὑπομονήν. ἡ δὲ ὑπομονὴ ἔργον τέλειον ἐχέτω, ἵνα ἦτε τέλειοι καὶ ὁλόκληροι ἐν μηδενὶ λειπόμενοι.

Haltet es für völlige Freude, meine Brüder, wenn ihr in vielerlei Versuchungen fallt, in der Erkenntnis, dass die Erprobung eures Glaubens Beharrlichkeit bewirkt. Die Beharrlichkeit aber soll es zum vollendeten Werk bringen, damit ihr vollkommen und ganz seid, in keinem Stück im Rückstand.

Consider it complete joy, my brothers, when you fall into all sorts of temptations, in the knowledge that the testing of your faith produces perseverance. But perseverance should be brought to completion, so that you will be perfect and whole, in no part lacking.

Before coming to Barth's comments on these verses directly, a word is in order about his exegetical approach generally. Induced by his theological conviction that the meaning of the biblical text must make reference to the singular divine subject that is its occasion, as well as his own habit of mind, Barth tended to seek a unifying idea for the texts he interpreted. As a rule, this did not result in his exegesis becoming a deductive exercise but rather allowed him greater freedom to notice the odd detail and digression while unfolding a coherent whole. The Epistle of James appears unsuited to this approach on two fronts. First, its theological commitments are notoriously minimal. Outside of a reference to Jesus Christ in the first verse (a reference whose authenticity is contested), God seems only an occasional, perhaps somewhat abstract, presence in the epistle. Second, it is difficult to find a unifying theme among the disparate prescriptions and warnings that fill its chapters. It earns its appellation as "the Proverbs of the New Testament" not only for its recommendation of moral rectitude but also for the allegedly unsystematic deployment of its advice. To underscore the text's apparently haphazard assemblage, there is no scholarly consensus as to the identity of

7. Greek text from *Novum Testamentum Graece*, 28th rev. ed., ed. Barbara Aland et al. (Stuttgart: Deutsche Bibel Gesellschaft, 2012). German text from Barth, *Erklärung des Jakobusbrief*, 211. The English, here and in block quotations below, is my own translation of Barth's German, which departs in some important ways from the standard English renderings. See, e.g., the same passage in the NRSV: "My brothers and sisters, whenever you face trials of any kind, consider it nothing but joy, because you know that the testing of your faith produces endurance; and let endurance have its full effect, so that you may be mature and complete, lacking in nothing."

the author, leaving open the possibility it is a redacted assemblage of oral tradition.[8]

On the second point, Barth rejected the notion that in order to recognize a unity of purpose in a text, the identity of the author had to be historically substantiated. The lack of historical consensus as to the identity of the author of James is a point that Barth exploits in his typically subversive fashion toward the claims of historical scholarship. Questions of a historical nature were never incidental for Barth, but always relative and at best preparatory, serving by their very limited character to move the reader toward the demands of the text itself. In this case, the impossibility of definitively resolving the question allows Barth to argue that if interpretation is not to revolve around problems whose solutions are out of reach, it must begin by asking what claim the author, whoever he or she might be, is laying on the reader. This claim is not simply a product of the moral obligation that exists between persons, but as a biblical text it bears witness to God's Word, which is always and definitively obligating. This means that, though Barth takes the reference to Christ in 1:1 to be significant, he can find in James's mode of address a standpoint and orientation that are fundamentally theological and that unify the disparate elements of the epistle.

Barth thinks that this mode of address is the "call to repentance," and that this call gives the epistle both its theological character and its unity. Barth offers an initial definition as follows:

> Characteristic of James's personality, as he encounters us in his letter, is the *call to repentance* (*Bußruf*). I do not say: active Christianity (*Tatchristentum*) or practical Christianity, which is what one often hears. This does not touch on the matter. It also is not in the act for James, not in praxis, not in a second [thing], but in God. But he speaks of God in the form of the call to repentance and not, or nearly not, anything else. I say "call to repentance" in a biblical sense, which does not call upon the impious, not the outsiders, not the ungodly, rather the pious, the insiders, the Jews, the Jewish-Christians or Christians, in any event, calling those already standing in fellowship with God, to return (*Umkehr*) to God.[9]

Echoing a point that he will make formally elsewhere about the relation between dogmatics and ethics, the basic claim here is that moral exhortation is not an appendix to theology proper. When he denies that James is

8. For an overview of the various theories of authorship, see Rainer Metzner, "Der Lehre Jakobus: Überlegungen zur Verfasserfrage des Jakobusbriefes," *Zeitschrift für Neutestamentliche Wissenschaft* 104 (2013): 238–67, esp. 238–42.

9. Barth, *Erklärung des Jakobusbrief*, 185 (emphasis original).

commending "active" or "practical" Christianity, he is not saying that moral theology has neither active nor practical consequences, but rather that in so being it does not pass over into a different domain that can be established on general terms. The primary interpretive challenge is then to show how the rhetoric of paraenesis is, contrary to expectation, within the domain of theological description.

Barth's lapidary summary of James as a whole captures this challenge well: "If you really hear the call to repentance, how could you not hear the Gospel?"[10] It also suggests the means by which he will prosecute his case. If moral exhortation is to be theological, then it must at root communicate the gospel, with the terms of its summons falling within the sphere of that message. Though James does not use "repentance," nor discuss it explicitly, we can see why Barth found it suitable to his interpretation. As he uses it here, we can define it as the movement of faith in its explicitly moral register. Much of Barth's energy in the first part of these lectures is given to articulating this movement.

Following a comment on the authorship question, then, it is Barth's task to show how he finds the theological dynamics that govern the entire epistle in 1:2–4. He begins by noting that the initial command, to take joy, is in response to a specific moral situation. The nature of this situation determines the sphere in which an appropriate response operates. Barth's first significant interpretive choice, then, is to render πειρασμός as "temptation" (*Versuchung*) rather than "trial," which is the standard choice of contemporary English translations. In doing so he also departs from Luther, who prefers a more general scope to πειρασμός in his choice of "Anfechtung." Barth's translation is not only defensible but also precludes a "stoic" reading of this verse by signaling the spiritual sphere in which the ensuing command operates.[11] The moral conflict in which the audience is expected to be involved is best rendered "temptations" instead of the more neutral "trials," thinks Barth, because for the Christian moral conflicts are fundamentally spiritual: "The full actuality of temptation belongs also to the concrete situation and precisely to the Christian. Where belief is, there is also the possibility of unbelief. . . . The enemy schemes. Even in this their situation, indeed with the presence of the

10. Barth, *Erklärung des Jakobusbrief*, 245.

11. Cf. Oliver O'Donovan on the "voluntarist" character of translations that render πειρασμός in 1:2 as "trial" and in 1:12 as "temptation," leaving "no encouragement for the 'tempted' and nothing but congratulation for the 'tried.'" Barth avoids the voluntarism by keeping to the moral and spiritual tenor of both uses of πειρασμός, though his account may not give sufficient attention to the "context of world-time" that O'Donovan would like to see preserved in understanding temptation. See O'Donovan, *Finding and Seeking*, vol. 2 of *Ethics as Theology* (Grand Rapids: Eerdmans, 2014), 168.

enemy they should rejoice, not just partly rejoice, but completely and wholly rejoice, and consider it properly the apex of Christian joy."[12]

It is not immediately obvious why temptation should specifically target belief, unless we see how Barth situates the moral conflict and the command in terms of the ends of a specifically Christian perfection. In the first place, if the πειρασμοῖς into which the believer falls will serve for the betterment of faith, then the conflict must be a spiritual one. In turn, the moral response to this spiritual conflict is directed toward the end of a specifically spiritual perfection, whose meaning is determined by the gospel rather than a generic account of moral rectitude. As such, the command to take joy in response to temptations is not one command alongside others but is basic to the dynamics of Christian moral action. This is what makes the call to repentance the unifying motif of James, thinks Barth. To repent is to see one's moral acts as a Christian not as separate from but as within the movement of faith, the end of which is a spiritual perfection.

By situating moral action within faith, Barth can go on to show why he thinks repentance is properly speech about God. Put differently, the subjective end of moral action is only explicable in light of its objective correlate, which is God's work of salvation:

> That [James] exhorts repentance does not prevent, but rather assures that he exhorts joy no less than Paul in Philippians. . . . In this he *reminds* them, falling into temptation is to be *held* as joy, and, in what must immediately mean to them their separation from the power and blessing of God, to *see* their nearness in the actuality of the difficult and serious battle in which they stand and in which he wants them to see themselves standing, to assess it as [an] already accomplished victory . . .[13]

Citing the Swabian Pietist C. H. Rieger, Barth goes on to say that the command to take joy could not be spoken without "belief in the cross of Christ."[14] Barth's claim that moral action is part of the movement of faith now has greater specificity. It is not a faith in a benevolent God who "gives to all generously" (1:5), does not tempt (1:13), and is the source of "every perfect gift" (1:17). Rather, for Barth, it is quite determinately the God of the gospel and justification by faith that are the basis for James's moral exhortation.

This way of thinking of repentance is not unique to the James lectures, but is also present in other key writings from around the time that Barth

12. Barth, *Erklärung des Jakobusbrief*, 219.
13. Barth, *Erklärung des Jakobusbrief*, 215–17 (emphasis original).
14. Barth, *Erklärung des Jakobusbrief*, 217.

was making revisions for the second cycle. Repentance appears perhaps most prominently in this period in an extended discussion in his lectures on ethics in Münster, under the broader heading of humility, as the response to the command of God the Reconciler. There, repentance is the "return to right thinking," the possibility to think "the miracle (*Wunder*) of mercy, which obviously is higher than all reason [Phil. 4:7]."[15] Though not in explicit reference to James, Barth sounds the most Jacobean note in *Die christliche Dogmatik*: "That we are in [the Spirit] holy and joyful, therein we conduct ourselves confidently, that we at all times may give God the right against ourselves. Nothing here is understood from oneself, since the same Spirit that compels us also makes us free, free in repentance to *believe*, which we can only do in *repentance*, only in *obedience*."[16]

What is characteristic of Barth's use of repentance in both his ethics lectures and *Die christliche Dogmatik* is that it is the movement of faith that corresponds to moral action. In each of these cases, repentance involves a double movement, both against oneself as in need of mercy and reconciliation, and, in the freedom reconciliation brings, taking moral action that leads toward the spiritual end furnished by God's redemptive work.

Thus far, we have observed two important points in Barth's reading of James. First, there is an underlying theological unity to the Epistle of James in virtue of the underlying presupposition of a basic movement that all Christian moral action shares, which Barth calls repentance. Second, Barth's understanding of repentance is doctrinally informed, but in a way that is not necessarily specific to the epistle itself, as witnessed by his discussion of it elsewhere without reference to James.

These points prompt at least two critical questions, one about the interpretive suitability of Barth's moves, the second about their theological probity. As an interpretive move, even if we allow that "temptations," "faith," and "joy" furnish the context, means, and ends of an irreducibly theological account of moral action, we might wonder if granting such significance to an at best implicit framework threatens to flatten Barth's reading of the remainder of the text. More pointedly, might not an appeal to justification by faith skew one's reading in an overtly doctrinal and Pauline direction, smoothing over James's unusual mode of address and its consistent deployment of command and chastisement? The question of the theological probity of Barth's moves is closely

15. Karl Barth, *Ethik II*, GA II 10, ed. Dietrich Braun (Zurich: Theologischer Verlag Zürich, 1978), 281–82; trans. G. W. Bromiley as *Ethics* (Edinburgh: T&T Clark, 1981), 415–16.
16. Karl Barth, *Die christliche Dogmatik im Entwurf I: Die Lehre vom Worte Gottes; Prolegomena zur christlichen Dogmatik*, GA II 14 (Zurich: Theologischer Verlag Zürich, 1982), 432–34, esp. 434 (emphasis original).

aligned with these worries. By making faith the root of moral action, does Barth blunt the immediacy of the command and the spiritual challenge of obedience, to say nothing of prejudicing any reading of the passage on faith and works?

These questions are acute for Barth, not least because what he finds valuable in the epistle is its theological and stylistic independence. That these two elements are of a piece is, as we shall see, one of Barth's central theological convictions about the nature and limits of theological interpretation. In the next section, I will show how Barth's analysis of the rhetorical posture of James informs his theological evaluation of the ethical content of the epistle. Then, in the third section, we will see him apply this evaluation to theological interpretation, by way of the conflict over faith and works.

Rehabilitating Exhortation

Once Barth has established that James presumes a soteriological framework that is recognizable in other New Testament writers (even if not exclusively Pauline), he turns to the uniqueness of the epistle's rhetoric. Why, if justification by faith is implicit in James's approach, does the author bypass all but the barest suggestion of this reality in favor of repeated ethical demands? Barth answers this question by way of a comparative analysis of the epistle's mood, which in turn provides an insight into its theological significance.

The epistle's preferred mood, Barth notes, is the imperative rather than the indicative. This choice is of rhetorical rather than semantic significance, a point that Barth demonstrates by a comparison of James 1:2–4 and Romans 5:3–4.[17] Both passages exhibit an overlapping line of thought, from the trial of faith that leads to perseverance and ultimately the realization of a spiritual good, and Barth considers the substance of these verses to be the same. Yet Paul is essentially descriptive, and the dynamics of suffering, endurance, and hope are cast by him in the indicative. There is no command involved, simply a presentation of the reality that follows from the work of the Spirit pouring out the love of God in the believer's life.[18] The difference here between Paul and James is "not in the matter, but in the words."[19]

This rhetorical difference is not decorative, however, but conceals a difference in intent that is crucial for understanding the epistle's aim. The shift in mood exhibited in 1:2–4 bears this out. Barth notes that the command to

---

17. "And not only that, but we also boast in our sufferings, knowing that suffering produces endurance, and endurance produces character, and character produces hope" (NRSV).
18. Barth, *Erklärung des Jakobusbrief*, 225–27.
19. Barth, *Erklärung des Jakobusbrief*, 227.

take joy in 1:2 is given in the imperative, while the ends of that action are the perfection described in the indicative in 1:3–4. The ordering of imperative and indicative are suggestive, he thinks, of how James orients the command to the ends of action:

> In any event James writes from a psychological orientation, as one would put it today, a *way*, a concrete path in the human situation, whose possibility he writes of to his readers in verse 3 as indicative, yet insistently placed before their eyes on the highest level as imperatival . . . verse 3 then means that the author who in verse 2 touched on the problematic of the Christian life would now dig in deeper, to its true meaning, if not to uncover it, yet still, as is appropriate in the psychological sphere in which he moves, to make it plain and in this way bring it close to his readers so that they can see the concrete problematic of their lives in the light of that joy.[20]

Barth's writing here is somewhat clotted, but the basic point is clear enough: the imperative mood is not incidental but possesses an immediacy fitting to the moral tension that characterizes spiritual existence. Even when shifting to the indicative to describe the objective ends of that existence, the author contrives to remain direct and specific to the ethical situation. As a linguistic device, James's rhetoric is in keeping with the author's own position in relation to moral thinking, a position Barth enigmatically calls a "psychological orientation." Given remarks made about psychological approaches to theology elsewhere (such as his evident suspicion of the psychological in theology in *Romans II*[21] and his withering remarks about his Göttingen colleague Georg Wobbermin's psychology of religion method[22]), such a description invites further investigation.

Initially, we should note that despite Barth's general suspicion that psychology tends to overstep its bounds, his view is in fact not universally negative.[23] In the lectures on ethics that he delivered the same year, Barth

20. Barth, *Erklärung des Jakobusbrief*, 227 (emphasis original).
21. See *Romans II*, 182.
22. "Dann mit Abscheu gelesen: *Wobbermin*, 'Das Wesen der Religion,' gänzlich einsichtsloses, breitspuriges Geschwätz, das keinen Schritt weiterführt, sondern auf einen Eiertanz zwischen dem hl. Schleiermacher, der Veda-Religion und einigen andern hottentottischen Unerheblichkeiten hinausläuft, mit einer 'Widerlegung' von Feuerbach, daß Gott erbarm." Barth, circular letter of January 23, 1923, in *Karl Barth-Eduard Thurneysen Briefwechsel II: 1921–1930* (Zurich: Theologischer Verlag Zürich, 1974), 129. Barth is referring to the second volume of Wobbermin's *Systematische Theologie nach religionspsychologischer Methode* (Leipzig: J. C. Hinrichs, 1921).
23. Barth's sense that psychology tends to improperly combine and overtake distinct theoretical domains may have its roots in the Marburg neo-Kantians. See Johann Friedrich Lohmann, *Karl Barth und der Neukantianismus* (Berlin: De Gruyter, 1995), 122–27.

notes that "psychology is not in itself an objectionable matter" provided it does not attempt to be an answer to the ethical question.[24] In a 1925 lecture on the work of his former teacher Wilhelm Herrmann, Barth says that it is a matter of achieving the proper order between theology and psychology, and once it was recognized that between God and humanity there is a "*single* act" of Christ, "*afterward*, this *principium theologiae* having been acknowledged, the 'religious-psychological circle' can always be put to use."[25]

As Barth's lecture on Herrmann suggests, when Barth gives a positive evaluation to psychology, it does not designate an anthropological domain independent from Christ's vicarious action. As a clue to what Barth means by it in the James lectures, we might begin with what he means by "orientation." As recent scholarship encourages us, we will be aided in understanding Barth's meaning by turning to Kant.[26] In his essay "What Does It Mean to Orient Oneself in Thinking?" Kant notes that when humans orient themselves in space, the fixed points on the horizon would be useless for providing spatial awareness unless one can orient oneself by the "feeling" one has of right and left. Similarly, in thought, we orient ourselves by a "subjective principle" when "objective principles of reason are insufficient for holding something true."[27] I take Barth to be thinking along these lines, even if he does not strictly adhere to Kant's technical meaning. To speak from a "psychological orientation" is just to reckon the objective reality of God's acts for one's immediate context and its ethical demands.

If the indicative is suitable for communicating the objective acts of God and the imperative is suited to the agonistic immediacy of subjective ethical existence, we might wonder if, in his reading of James, Barth is exhibiting a broader inability to sufficiently correlate God's objective acts and the subjective reality of Christian existence. As some critics of Barth's theology of this period hold, while the moral subject may be secure in Christ, when Barth comes to speak of the moral life of faith as a present, concrete reality—from

24. Barth, *Ethik I*, 115–16; *Ethics*, 70–71.

25. Barth, "Die dogmatische Prinzipienlehre bei Wilhelm Herrmann," in *Vorträge und kleinere Arbeiten 1922–1925*, GA III 19, ed. Holger Finze (Zurich: Theologischer Verlag Zürich, 1990), 597–603; trans. Louise Pettibone Smith as "The Principles of Dogmatics according to Wilhelm Herrmann," in *Theology and Church: Shorter Writings 1920–1928* (London: SCM, 1962), 266–71, here 266, translation altered.

26. See Martin Westerholm's lucid account of Barth's use and adaptation of Kant's conception of rationality in *The Ordering of the Christian Mind: Karl Barth and Theological Rationality* (Oxford: Oxford University Press, 2015).

27. Immanuel Kant, "What Does It Mean to Orient Oneself in Thinking?," in *Religion within the Boundaries of Mere Reason and Other Writings*, trans. A. Wood and G. di Giovanni (Cambridge: Cambridge University Press, 1998), 4–6, esp. 6.

a "psychological orientation"—his account of the moral subject is punctiliar and its relation to God tending toward occasionalist.[28] We can go further and suggest that such limitations have their formal expression in the proverbial mode of James with its unsystematic approach to moral exhortation. It may be that Barth is coming up against the limits of the epistle's theological categories as well as his own. As we shall see, there is an aspect of this critique to which Barth can only too happily agree. Against a powerful line of modern Protestant moral theology, Barth will hold that the imperative is a valid form of Christian ethical discourse, its tendency toward lurching immediacy notwithstanding.

Before we pursue this line of thought, however, we can see that Barth does not find in James such a wholly deracinated subject. Barth draws attention to the connection made between the "concrete" ethical situation and the "perfection" promised in 1:3–4. Because the joy that is to be completed is given as the end of moral action, we ought to take such talk of perfection, thinks Barth, not as an ideal but as a "possible and realizable goal."[29] As when Christ calls the disciples to be "perfect, therefore, as your heavenly Father is perfect" (Matt. 5:48 NRSV), claims Barth, so in James it is not a call to attain the perfection of God, as "this would make the imperative pointless, but rather as God is perfectly divine, so also we humans should exist no less satisfied with the exhaustion (*Erschöpfung*) of our human possibilities."[30] We should not suppose Barth to be saying here that grace perfects nature, but simply that the ends of the moral actions that humans undertake are defined as creaturely ends. Those ends are disposed not by their nature as creatures, however, but by God's purposes for fellowship with humanity. Undertaking faithful moral action is not realizing immanent capacities, but directing attention to the purpose conferred on those capacities by God's redemptive decree. Barth writes that "James is concerned here with Christian completeness as a *signum electionis*. But this is established after the foregoing: that the faith that is within you is always proved in the testing of the act, in obedience, in the corresponding work."[31] Barth appropriates a bit of classic Reformed teaching in suggesting that the certainty of election can only be had *a posteriori* in order to underline that the subjective end of Christian moral life is not the unfolding of an internal

28. See, e.g., Christopher Asprey, *Eschatological Existence in Karl Barth's Göttingen Theology* (Oxford: Oxford University Press, 2010), 190–93.

29. Barth, *Erklärung des Jakobusbrief*, 241. We might note in passing that this passage is largely the same in both lecture cycles, though in 1928–29 Barth adds the modifier "human" to "possibilities."

30. Barth, *Erklärung des Jakobusbrief*, 241.

31. Barth, *Erklärung des Jakobusbrief*, 243.

principle.[32] Put differently, the moral existence that is possible in faith is not alien to the nature of the creature, but is still given *extra nos*.

With this understanding of the imperative in view, we are prepared to see how it cuts against the grain of a prominent strand of modern Protestant theology. Where Barth holds that the imperative is compatible with an ethics rooted in the movement of faith, this sets him apart from a stream of nineteenth-century Protestant ethics that held the reverse to be true. Friedrich Schleiermacher is the most significant example. In very brief compass, for Schleiermacher Christian ethics is an essentially descriptive task, and the historical development of ethical thought means that the New Testament imperatives should be understood as holdovers of the "spirit of the law" that characterized the ethical immaturity of the Old Testament, whose time has now passed.[33] The problem, thought Schleiermacher, was not that the Bible could not play a normative role in Christian ethics, but that the imperative mood was not suited to Christian ethics. Ethical guidance that takes the form of the imperative reintroduces the "attitude of obedience" typical, on Schleiermacher's account, of Roman Catholic ethics, and does not reflect the Protestant understanding of justification by faith.[34]

Wilhelm Herrmann's 1891 essay "The Repentance (*Buße*) of the Lutheran Christian" takes up Schleiermacher's line of thought in relation to the imperative and the unity of the moral subject.[35] He reads post-Reformation theology (principally Lutheran) as a failure to recognize Luther's radical insight on the relation between faith and genuine moral change in the life of the Christian. Luther's breakthrough, claims Herrmann, was to locate true repentance entirely within the life of faith. As a result, Protestant Christians could have a genuinely moral life because they are no longer caught up in the unending cycle of transgression, confession, and absolution that characterized Roman Catholic moral teaching. This cycle was morally destructive to individuals because it cut them off from the ethical demands that were to shape them by making the demands external, leaving them no personal

---

32. Cf. Cocceius: "The sign of election is true faith in God through Christ, which being explored and proved by trials affords the faithful sure hope, consolation and glorying in the hope of glory." Heinrich Heppe, *Reformed Dogmatics*, ed. Ernst Bizer, trans. G. T. Thompson (London: George Allen & Unwin, 1950), 177.

33. Friedrich Schleiermacher, *Die christliche Sitte*, ed. Wolfgang Erich Müller, 2nd ed. (1844; repr. Waltrop: Spenner, 1999), 12–15. Cf. Poul Henning Jørgensen, *Die Ethik Schleiermachers* (Munich: Kaiser, 1959), 144; Oliver O'Donovan, *Self, World, and Time*, vol. 1 of *Ethics as Theology* (Grand Rapids: Eerdmans, 2013), 84–86.

34. See Kevin M. Vander Schel, "Grace and Human Action: Distinctively Christian Action in Schleiermacher's *Christian Ethics*," *Journal of Religion* 96 (2016): 10.

35. Wilhelm Herrmann, "Die Buße des evangelischen Christen," *Zeitschrift für Theologie und Kirche* 1 (1891): 28–81.

character as the basis of action. In short, on Herrmann's account, Roman
Catholicism produced a fractured moral subject. But if knowledge of and
relationship to the good are only proper to the life of faith, this no longer
need be the case. The good could then in a qualified sense become internal
to the life of the believer.[36]

To a degree, thought Herrmann, the architects of Lutheran Orthodoxy
sustained this insight, clearly specifying that repentance from wrongdoing by
those who had no faith would not be effective and would lead to no genuine
moral change.[37] But, crucially, they failed to specify how the Christian is to
determine whether or not one's own moral awareness is an instance of true
repentance. After all, the experience of a range of penitential emotions is the
exclusive property of neither the believer nor the unbeliever. It is here that
the Lutheran Orthodox provide no clarity, which for Lutherans has meant
a reliance on religious technique and eventually a backward slide into the
"*contritio violenta*" of Roman Catholicism.[38] The source of this corrosive
lack of clarity is the failure to see that it is the relationship that is established
in faith that forms the basis of moral change, instead dealing with faith as
though it were itself an external law. Quite to the contrary, faith is a wholly
personal relationship, as Herrmann argues:

> Certainly, a person can easily be brought by any fear to be prepared to accept
> the doctrine that Christ has carried his punishment and fulfilled the law. But
> what has he thereby achieved? Certainly not a reconciling with God. . . A true
> repentance steps spontaneously (*unwillkürlich*) in the development of faith, in
> which we seek and find God. Once we step into this moment of faith's develop-
> ment, we find the capability to not only take up the doctrine of reconciliation,
> but rather Christ himself as reconciler.[39]

Appropriating the personal relationship with Christ was essential in order to
prevent the fragmentary moral existence that Herrmann took to be the result
of external moral commands. If the act of repentance is not to contribute
to this fragmentary, cyclical moral existence, then it must arise not from an
external source but from the personal relationship established in faith. So for
Herrmann, too, the imperative is inapposite in Christian ethical discourse.
The personal relationship with Christ is the root of ethics, and appropriating
that relationship is sufficient to shape action.

36. Herrmann, "Buße," 65.
37. Herrmann, "Buße," 78.
38. Herrmann, "Buße," 79.
39. Herrmann, "Buße," 80–81.

Two powerful arguments against the use of the imperative in Christian ethical discourse are evident here. First, for Protestant thought, the centrality of justification by faith would suggest that the imperative reintroduces obedience to the law in a way that compromises the sufficiency of justification. The second argument is derivative of the first, but more pertinent to Barth's reading of James. It holds that the imperative produces a faulty account of moral reasoning, because the moral subject can never achieve coherence as its normative standards always remain external and detached.

In sharp contrast, Barth would rehabilitate the rhetoric of exhortation. Most prominently, he sees in justification by faith precisely the basis for the command and his well-known priority of gospel over law.[40] While this serves as the theological foundation of much of what he has to say about the imperative in James,[41] the exhortative rhetoric is a fitting form of moral communication, precisely because it is fitting to the creaturely sphere of action. To be a Christian is to be *in medias res* in a double sense. In one sense it is to find oneself in spiritual-moral conflict, and so always facing an ethical demand. But it is also to find one's moral existence ordered to a reality beyond one's self, the ends of which are not replaced by that reality but established by it. As such, the exhortative stance is apposite to the particularity of the Christian moral existence, but the imperative can also be issued in the confidence that the moral subject is not burdened to be self-constituting. Indeed, the exhortative rhetoric militates against such pretensions to self-establishment.

To be able to commend the imperative in such terms is also an interpretive advantage. Both Schleiermacher and Herrmann were clear that their conceptions of theological ethics had interpretive consequences and that those passages in the New Testament that contain direct commands are something of an embarrassment. For Schleiermacher, they are products of the early disciples' immaturity, signaled by their reliance on Jewish forms of moral discourse.[42] For Herrmann, they are purely rhetorical, designed by Jesus not to be an external command but to be internalized as a personal duty. Commands cannot be taken directly because they would compromise the basic goal of moral development, and so "what sounds like a command on [Jesus's] lips is always only a stimulus urging on the disciples to make clear to themselves

---

40. These are explored at length by Gerald McKenny in *Analogy of Grace: Barth's Moral Theology* (Oxford: Oxford University Press, 2010), 167–200.

41. Barth writes that "Gospel and Law are not separated for this preacher of repentance." See Barth, *Erklärung des Jakobusbrief*, 217.

42. Jørgensen, *Die Ethik Schleiermachers*, 145–46.

what they ought to do."[43] Over against interpretive positions such as these, Barth's recommends itself for its simplicity in taking the form to be straight-forwardly expressive of the author's intent.

Despite some concerns raised earlier in this essay, Barth's strongly theo-logical reading seems better able to retain something closer to the plain sense of James than the work of some of his forebears. Moreover, it does not minimize the force of the command, but rather serves to reinforce its urgency without tending into legalism. In the final section of this essay, we will take up this double theme of interpretation and moral discourse in what must be the test case for judging these issues, the conflict over faith and works in James 2:14–26.

Against the Paulinists

When Barth turns to James 2:14–26, he is more interested in the moral dy-namics of reading this passage within its canonical context than he is in whether or not there are two different accounts of justification in James and Paul. Indeed, as we have already seen, at one level the question is moot, as justification by faith alone is the presupposition for James's whole approach to the moral imperative. We might consider this simply another instance of Protestant exegesis that refuses to entertain the suggestion that James might be indicating an alternative to forensic justification. Yet Barth would reject the terms of this critique. He would reject the idea that when reading this passage one should principally be concerned with the *doctrine* of justification, but more significantly, he would reject the interpretive standpoint that presumes to establish a resolution between James and Paul on a doctrinal level in the first place. Barth begins his consideration of the passage by quoting the Swiss Reformed pastor Paul Geyser, who blustered that "those who carry the train of Jezebel and the antichrist see a conflict here between James and Paul."[44] Barth begs to differ: "Without returning the scolding, I would say in contrast: whomever does not see or would not see a conflict here between Paul and James has not read the text calmly and desires without [the text] to master it with his dogmatics."[45] What it means to "master" the text with dogmatics is Barth's concern in this section. We will first look at Barth's account of the passage, then at his critique of the theological interpretation that seeks to establish doctrinal unity between James and Paul.

43. Wilhelm Herrmann, "The Moral Law," in *Faith and Morals*, trans. Donald Matheson and Robert W. Stewart (London: Williams & Northgate, 1904), 184.
44. Barth, *Erklärung des Jakobusbrief*, 475.
45. Barth, *Erklärung des Jakobusbrief*, 475.

Unlike most Protestant theological commentators, Barth holds that 2:14–26 is intended by the author of James to be in conflict with Paul's thought.[46] It is important to recognize that this is not a pseudo-conflict in which James and Paul appear to have different teachings on the doctrine of justification, but can in fact be shown as unified. Nor, however, is it the bare opposition of two different accounts of Christian existence that cannot be sustained within one confession, as Luther held. As we shall see, Barth holds both of these approaches to be guilty of the same error. By considering 2:14–26 in intentional opposition with Pauline thought, Barth moves the conflict into a different register. If James is largely ignorant of Paul, or seeks only to emphasize a different feature of a unified doctrine of justification, then the conflict merely requires some exegetical legwork to make the pieces fit. Yet Barth's argument that James is being intentionally critical of Paul, or a Pauline element in the early church, leads the conflict away from the conceptual register to the moral-spiritual dynamics of reading the Bible. On Barth's reading, James is an intervention against a spiritually dangerous pattern of thought that is incubated in the dominant voice of the New Testament.

Barth thinks the primary target of James's criticism is a kind of "Paulinism," whose roots lie not in any overt claims of Paul, but in a kind of thinking that may result from privileging Paul above the rest of the New Testament. This allows Barth to be cagey and ultimately noncommittal as to whether or not James is going after Paul specifically. The real danger is equating Paul's thought with the substance of the gospel. We might think that this takes the teeth out of the conflict that Barth is at pains to emphasize, if in reality it is no more than a misunderstanding of Paul's thought that James is after. But this would miss Barth's point. James's articulation of the relationship between faith and works is the consequence of the preaching of repentance from a psychological orientation. It is therefore a pattern of thought that gets expressed as a criticism of Paul because Paul's pattern of thought may lead to adopting a false theological standpoint. The mastery of the text that Barth wants to criticize is a species of just such a tendency.

How does such a desire to master the text come about? As theological interpreters confront the biblical text and its internal criticism, they seek some

---

46. Though it has long been the case, certainly post-Reformation, that most commentators assumed an *apparent* conflict with Paul on justification, it was not typical to think that James intended to put himself in conflict with Paul or Paul's thought unless one holds a fairly late date of composition, which Barth does not. Martin Hengel, who argues a position similar to Barth's, including an early dating and apparently without knowledge of Barth's lectures, is unusual among modern commentators in this regard. See Martin Hengel, "Der Jakobusbrief als antipaulinische Polemik," in *Paulus und Jakobus: Kleine Schriften III* (Tübingen: Mohr Siebeck, 2002), 511–48, esp. 525n42.

ground for unity. Following Paul's privileging of the indicative, they secure this unity through doctrinal constructions that then become the actual focus of attention in the interpretation rather than the text itself.[47] The trouble here is not doctrine per se, but that doctrine becomes a tool for evading the specific claim of Scripture that preempts other considerations. Barth's accusation against theological interpreters is not that they make doctrinal claims but that they adopt a theological standpoint that determines in advance the reading of the text.

Such a position would seem to narrow the exegetical task to an individual encounter and seriously undermine the church's capacity to have its teaching unified by the biblical canon. Yet it is here that Barth claims that to affirm the canon is to relativize the claims of doctrine in just this way: "Precisely when we read the Bible as a canonical text we must say: *we*, insofar as we have constructed a Christian or theological standpoint following the instruction of Paul, meet the counter-word, the contradiction by James. He must contradict Paul, must stand as such a contradictor of Paul in the canon, and must be thoroughly understood by us as such so that we, insofar as we are perhaps Paulinists, and perhaps are more Paulinists than Christians, are contradicted."[48]

On this evidence, the distinction between "doctrine" and "canon" is between that which is posited by human reason and that which is acknowledged in faith. By canon, then, Barth simply means the Bible itself in its occasioning and commissioning by God. Therefore, acknowledging canon, unlike the "mastery" of the text, is understood not to be derived from human reason but given in the Spirit.[49] The sort of "mastery" of two opposing texts that Barth opposes conceals a spiritual error, which consists in reading the text as though it could be completely assimilated into human knowledge:

> It was and is an error of orthodoxy not to be retained and not to be renewed that the sentence "the Bible is the Word of God" is interpreted to mean that it is unified in itself as a closed system of explicit truths, in which the individual components must chime in the human hearer as they do in God as the *auctor scripturae*, when in fact they doubtless only cohere in God beyond Paul and James. A true hearer of the biblical word as the Word of God hears at every step precisely that which at *this* step is said to *him*.[50]

47. Barth, *Erklärung des Jakobusbrief*, 475–77.
48. Barth, *Erklärung des Jakobusbrief*, 477.
49. Indeed, Barth suggests that finding Paul and James in the same canon allows a reading that presupposes a "proper conception of the inspiration, yes of the verbal inspiration of Holy Scripture" (Barth, *Erklärung des Jakobusbrief*, 479).
50. Barth, *Erklärung des Jakobusbrief*, 477 (emphasis original).

Barth is doing more here than affirming that the classic distinction between archetypal and ectypal theology holds for the content of Scripture as much as it does for any doctrinal system. He is claiming that the interpretation of Scripture is no less an act taking place in the immediacy of the "temptations" that are ever-present to faith, and thus no less initiates the interpreter into a spiritual conflict. The movement of faith that responds to this conflict preempts the systematic movements of the interpreter, even if it does not wholly preclude them.

Barth's reading of the passage on faith and works has the air of a provocation. A number of questions are left unanswered, such as whether the kind of tension between the immediate demands of the text and a broader, systematic reading are possible to maintain consistently, or if the "error of orthodoxy" barb actually finds its mark. Yet by stressing the moral-spiritual register of the interpretive task, Barth is able to encourage recognition of the individuality of biblical texts, indicating how they might maintain the specificity of their witness even within a unified canon.

Conclusion

In this essay, we have seen Barth's reading of James as a "preacher of repentance." We saw how Barth takes this as accounting for the thoroughgoing rhetoric of exhortation in the epistle, which Barth seeks to rehabilitate as a legitimate form of Christian moral communication. Against some prominent voices in modern theology, Barth affirms that such rhetoric accords with both the freedom and the limits of moral action that God makes possible in the creature. Finally, we saw how this account of moral action informed a critique of certain habits of theological interpretation and sought to preserve the specificity of the claim that each biblical text makes on the reader.

As I argued, this allows Barth to preserve the individual character of James, and more broadly the topographical variety of Scripture as a whole, so often thought to be flattened by appeals to canon. These interpretive moves sit within a broader account of the nature of the moral subject and the character of Christian moral action that affirms that the moral subject is in a real sense outside herself. Much of the moral drama of scriptural interpretation then comes from submission to the text's authority, which is at once the interpreter's denial that the foundation of her moral self lies within and the renewal of her freedom to be responsive to the divine command.

Harnack's worry about "dominance" comes in at just this point, where submission to the text's authority may or may not be easily distinguished from interpretive authority. Barth's commitment to the individual claim made by the text on the reader is not without the danger of being elided with the claim of this or that interpreter on another's reading. Already in this period Barth recognizes that the public character of the Bible's authority is a check on individual enthusiasm, and the sheer patience he has with the text itself militates against charismatic manipulation.[51] Nonetheless, it may be that such worries as Harnack's can never be put to rest by Barth, for the simple reason that the task as he conceives it is never without risk.

51. See especially Barth's discussion of canon and church authority in *Die christliche Dogmatik I*, 481–84.

PART 3

Barth's Doctrine of God in Exegetical Perspective

SIX

The Logos Is Jesus Christ

Karl Barth on the Johannine Prologue

WESLEY HILL

Introduction

Karl Barth is a theologian whose theology is inextricable from biblical exegesis.[1] One can scarcely read a page of the mature Barth, even apart from the small-print excurses of the *Church Dogmatics*, without encountering a theology rooted in scriptural reading. As a theologian, Barth's "aim was to interpret Scripture."[2] But such scriptural engagement raises the question of which came first, the chicken of Barth's powerful theological imagination or

1. See Paul McGlasson, *Jesus and Judas: Biblical Exegesis in Barth* (Atlanta: Scholars Press, 1991); Mary Kathleen Cunningham, *What Is Theological Exegesis? Interpretation and Use of Scripture in Barth's Doctrine of Election* (Valley Forge, PA: Trinity Press International, 1995); Richard E. Burnett, *Karl Barth's Theological Exegesis: The Hermeneutical Principles of the Römerbrief Period*, Wissenschaftliche Untersuchungen zum Neuen Testament 2/145 (Tübingen: Mohr, 2001); Francis B. Watson, "Barth's Philippians as Theological Exegesis," in Karl Barth, *The Epistle to the Philippians*, trans. James W. Leitch (repr., Louisville: Westminster John Knox, 2002), xxvi–li; John Webster, "Karl Barth," in *Reading Romans through the Centuries*, ed. Jeffrey P. Greenman and Timothy Larsen (Grand Rapids: Brazos, 2005), 205–23; Mark S. Gignilliat, *Karl Barth and the Fifth Gospel: Barth's Theological Exegesis of Isaiah*, Barth Studies (Aldershot, UK: Ashgate, 2009).
2. As he wrote in the preface to the English translation of his famous *Römerbrief: Romans II*, ix.

the egg of Barth's biblical exegesis? Is exegesis mainly ornamental, a kind of "ruminative overlay,"[3] to Barth's theology, or is there some indication that exegesis was generative for it?

In what follows, I wish to engage that question by way of examining what Barth said about certain selected portions of the Prologue to the Fourth Gospel. Matthias Gockel's judgment that Barth's exegesis of the Johannine Prologue "is not simply the result of the retrospective attempt to find exegetical backing for [his] christological revision" is one that needs demonstration.[4] With that need in view, then, I want to describe two key instances of Barth's grappling with the Johannine Prologue and also say something about the importance of that exegesis to Barth's larger understanding of Christology and election. Finally, I will conclude by offering some suggestions for what a critical engagement with Barth on these scores might look like.

Barth's Reading of the Johannine Prologue

The first time Barth engaged extensively with John 1 was in the winter semester of 1925–26 when he lectured for four hours a week on the Fourth Gospel. By that time, he had already been lecturing for four years on various biblical texts, including Ephesians, James, 1 Corinthians 15, Philippians, Colossians, and Matthew 5–7, treating them to a form of theological exegesis that attempted to engage classic questions of Reformed theology by means of scriptural interpretation (and vice versa). The same would prove to be true of his reading of John 1. As John Webster remarks, "[Barth's] reading of the Johannine Prologue . . . shows the extent to which Barth had schooled himself in the Calvinist divines over whose writings he pored in Göttingen."[5] According to Webster, by the time of the lectures on John 1, Barth had become especially interested in considering the relation between God and creatures and had found himself committed to "restor[ing] a theology of divine prevenience as the ground of the encounter of God and creatures."[6] And yet, at the same time, Barth's reading of John 1 helped shape his engagement with

3. The phrase is Ephraim Radner's, as quoted in Stanley Hauerwas, *Matthew*, Brazos Theological Commentary on the Bible (Grand Rapids: Brazos, 2006), 18.
4. Matthias Gockel, *Barth and Schleiermacher on the Doctrine of Election* (Oxford: Oxford University Press, 2007), 170.
5. John Webster, "Witness to the Word: Karl Barth's Lectures on the Gospel of John," in *The Domain of the Word: Scripture and Theological Reason* (London: T&T Clark, 2012), 65–85, here 68.
6. Webster, "Witness to the Word," 79.

those historical and systematic questions, leading him into some creative moves within and beyond that historical tradition.

In that early engagement with the Johannine Prologue, Barth's most pronounced emphasis is, arguably, on the transcendent distinction of the Logos from creation: "His being as such is not one that comes into being. It is not temporal; it is the eternal being that in principle precedes and encloses and originates all time."[7] This means that the Logos shares in the essential deity (θεότης) of the Father and is ranged with the Father over all contingent creaturely reality.[8] "[He] stands over against the human world with all the superiority of the creator."[9] From there, Barth goes on to locate the world's origin, and not only its redemption, in the Logos, in an interpretation of John 1:3: "[There is no] entity whose coming into being is independent of the Logos, which evolves of itself and is thus, so to speak, immediate to God."[10] He finds this theme even in verses 10–13, which he takes not to be a reference to the incarnation but rather to the "act" (*Ereignis*) of the Logos whereby the Logos maintains his transcendence from the world even in his immanence. The notes of the Logos' "antecedent deity and sovereign liberty" are what ground the further statements Barth makes about the incarnation.[11]

Much attention has been paid to this aspect of Barth's reading. When he comes to explicate the import of the incarnation, he is concerned to stress that the term "Logos" in John 1:1 is a "placeholder," a "provisional designation of a place which something or someone else will later fill."[12] This "someone" is of course "Jesus Christ," who is not named as such in the Johannine discourse itself until verse 17, after the affirmation of verse 14 that "the Word became flesh and dwelled among us." What this means, in turn, is that Barth reads the demonstrative pronoun (οὗτος) that begins verse 2 as prospective as well as retrospective.[13] *That* one—namely, Jesus Christ (vv. 14, 17), was in the beginning with God and through *him* all things were made (vv. 2–3).

7. Karl Barth, *Witness to the Word: A Commentary on John 1*, trans. G. W. Bromiley (Grand Rapids: Eerdmans, 1986), 20.

8. Barth, *Witness to the Word*, 24–26.

9. Webster, "Witness to the Word," 80, translating Karl Barth, *Erklärung des Johannesevangeliums (Kapitel 1–8). Vorlesung Münster Wintersemester 1925/1926, wiederholt in Bonn, Sommersemester 1933* (Zurich: TVZ, 1999²), 80.

10. Barth, *Witness to the Word*, 34.

11. Webster, "Witness to the Word," 81. The roots of these moves lie deep in the Reformed, as well as the Catholic, traditions and predate the dialectical theology Barth advanced in the 1920s. See E. David Willis, *Calvin's Catholic Christology: The Function of the So-Called Extra Calvinisticum in Calvin's Theology* (Leiden: Brill, 1966).

12. Barth, *Witness to the Word*, 23.

13. As Richard Bauckham notes, "Barth seems to oscillate between saying that *houtos* refers both backwards and forwards and saying that it refers only forwards" ("Revelatory Word or

Borrowing a term from Reformed scholasticism, we may locate Barth's move as one that stresses the Logos as *incarnandus*, that is, "to be incarnate." Such a determination gives new definition to the identity of the Logos and raises the question—to which we will return below—as to whether there is an identity of the Logos (*Logos asarkos*) apart from the Logos' self-revelation (*Logos ensarkos*). As others have noted, this may be one of the first hints of a departure from the classic Reformed emphasis on the *extra calvinisticum*, the *Logos asarkos* who preexists the divine decree that the Second Person of the Trinity would become incarnate in Jesus Christ, though it is only a hint: Barth affirms, even as he pursues this unconventional exegetical course, that "the Logos as the Revealer of God . . . announces himself before and even apart from Jesus of Nazareth."[14]

Thus, in the midst of his daring construal, Barth also appears anxious that affirming the "to-be-incarnate" character of the Logos might be misconstrued as compromising the distinction of the Logos from creaturely reality. As Webster puts Barth's point, "John's ἐγένετο does not entirely abolish the distinction of Word and creature," even as the Chalcedonian "without division" remains in force.[15] Barth stresses that the incarnational becoming is a real, irreversible one: "[T]he Word is not just the divine Word, the Word of the beginning, the superior Word, the epitome of creation and redemption, but because as all these things the Word is also flesh, as all these things the Word is also what we are, how we are, on the way to us, accessible to us."[16] But this incarnational sharing in our flesh is one in which the Logos retains all that makes him the Logos: "No change takes place, no transubstantiation, no replacing of the Word's mode of being by another, no dissolution of the *logos* in *sarx*, and also no development of a mixture of both, but a full union in which nothing is added to the creaturely and sinful determination of the *sarx*."[17]

Barth's Doctrine of Election and the Johannine Prologue

Moving on from here to Barth's later 1942 treatment of a much smaller portion of the same text, John 1:1–2, in *CD* II/2, we can see that many of the earlier theological emphases have been retained. Here, however, the setting is

---

Beloved Son? Barth on the Johannine Prologue," in *Reading the Gospels with Karl Barth*, ed. Daniel L. Migliore [Grand Rapids: Eerdmans, 2017], 16–33, here 19n4).

14. Barth, *Witness to the Word*, 43.
15. Webster, "Witness to the Word," 82.
16. Barth, *Witness to the Word*, 89.
17. Barth, *Witness to the Word*, 91.

not a seriatim exposition but rather a wide-ranging discussion of the doctrine of election. Famously, the emphasis in Barth's larger reconfiguration of the Reformed doctrine of election falls on Jesus Christ as the acting *subject* of election. But with his exegesis of John 1:1–2, Barth sets out to establish a prior, underlying point that Jesus Christ is the content of God's self-determination to be for humanity in the covenant of grace; Jesus Christ is "God in God's movement towards humanity."[18] Thus, Barth introduces his exegesis by saying that it is an elucidation of the claim that "Jesus Christ is Himself the divine election of grace."[19]

The way Barth approaches his exegesis is by way of nested questions, as it were: one leads immediately to the next, so that Barth finds the answer to each question in the following clause. He begins with the Ἐν ἀρχῇ, arguing that it refers not to "one moment with others in the totality of the world" but rather to a "time" before "all being and all time."[20] The time of the Word is this "in the beginning."

But that simply raises the question of where such a paradoxical "time" could be found, if not "in or with God." And so Barth says, "The answer to this question is given in the second statement, 'And the Word was *with God.*'"[21] This cannot mean that the Word is merely *for* God, along the lines of Augustine's famous prayer, "You have made us for yourself." Nor can it simply mean that the Word is "in communication with God," as certain historical-critical readings would have it.[22] Such statements would apply equally well, or indeed better, to creatures who were not "in the beginning." Therefore, if the Word's being "with" God is to be understood in such a way that it does not contradict the previous clause, the sense must be that the Word's being with God is tantamount to the Word's belonging to God, to his sharing in "the being of God Himself."[23] But how could the Word belong to God in that specialized, differentiating sense?

The answer must lie in the third clause of John 1:1–2: "And the Word was God." Barth comments: "[The Word] participated absolutely in the divine mode of being, in the divine being itself. . . . The mode of being, and being, of a second 'He,' the Logos, is identified with the mode of being and being of

18. So David Gibson, *Reading the Decree: Exegesis, Election, and Christology in Calvin and Barth* (London: T&T Clark, 2012), 50. The quotation is from Edwin Chr. van Driel, "Karl Barth on the Eternal Existence of Jesus Christ," *Scottish Journal of Theology* 61 (2007): 45–61, here 58.
19. CD II/2, 95.
20. CD II/2, 95.
21. CD II/2, 95.
22. CD II/2, 95–96, citing Theodor Zahn.
23. CD II/2, 96.

the first 'He,' God."[24] According to Barth, this understanding is in line with the Nicene claim that there is a "unity of substance of the three distinctive divine persons, prosopa or hypostases."[25] Thus, the third clause of the passage provides the ultimate basis for what is predicated of the Word in the first two clauses.[26]

That leads to the final question Barth poses with respect to verse 1: "But who or what is the Word whose predicates are declared in John 1:1?" Here Barth repeats the move he made earlier in the 1925 lectures by regarding the Logos as a "stop-gap." "[The reference to the 'Logos'] is a preliminary indication of the place where later something or someone quite different will be disclosed."[27] Before explaining that claim further, Barth pauses to ask why then the writer bothers with the "Logos" term at all if he intends to move beyond it in the subsequent verses. Here Barth omits a discussion of the possible historical background of the term in metaphysical, epistemological, or cosmological texts. Instead, he points out that the author of John 1 himself fills out the term with specific content, so that the direction runs not from a preunderstanding of the Logos to Jesus but in reverse: "What is certain is that he had no intention of honouring Jesus by investing him with the title of the Logos, but rather that he honoured the title itself by applying it a few lines later as a predicate of Jesus." *Logos*, then, should be understood as a term denoting revelation, a revelation that is given specific content ("life," "light") in the Prologue itself: "God's supernatural communication to man."[28]

Returning, then, to the key claim about the prospective nature of verse 2, Barth says (relying on Adolf Schlatter): "The οὗτος ['*this one* was in the beginning with God'] must be understood as a reference forward and not backward." In other words, "he was in the beginning with God" is not to be read as "the Logos was in the beginning with God" but instead as "Jesus Christ was in the beginning with God."[29] Barth supports that exegetical claim by pointing to a similar prospective use of οὗτος in 1:15 when the Prologue reports the speech of John the Baptist: "This [οὗτος] was he of whom I said, He that cometh after me is preferred before me: for he was before me."[30] If the author of the Johannine Prologue is appropriating the Baptist's speech, then it

24. *CD* II/2, 96.
25. *CD* II/2, 96.
26. Gibson, *Reading the Decree*, 43.
27. *CD* II/2, 96.
28. *CD* II/2, 97.
29. The significance of this exegetical move for Barth may be gauged by noting that he repeats it eight times throughout the *Church Dogmatics*: see *CD* I/1, 137, 401; I/2, 133; II/2, 98; III/1, 54; III/2, 66, 483; IV/2, 33.
30. *CD* II/2, 98.

6 /

makes sense to read the οὗτος in verse 2 as bearing the same forward-looking sense as it obviously does in 1:15. Barth then summarizes: "[T]his reference in verse 2 shows us that verse 1 is meant as the marking off or reservation of a place, for it points us to that which fills the place indicated by the concept Logos."[31] Verse 3 then, too, with its emphasis on the Word's agency in creation—"All things were made through him, and without him was not any thing made that was made"—together with verse 10, refers to Jesus Christ. It is the incarnate Christ who is the subject of the Johannine Prologue, even from the very first verse.

Making this move requires Barth to range more widely in the New Testament as he seeks to fill out what it means to claim that Jesus Christ was in the beginning with God and was active in creation.[32] With respect to Colossians 1:17, for instance, Barth claims that the Son who is "before all things" and in whom "all things consist" is the Son *in concreto*; that is, the Son spoken of in Colossians 1 is Jesus Christ.[33] As David Gibson points out, the reason this is vital for Barth is that two verses later, in Colossians 1:19, the text speaks of the divine fullness being pleased (εὐδόκησεν) to dwell in Christ—that is to say, the text speaks of the divine choice or election.[34] The linkage of election in Colossians 1:19, the Son's pretemporal existence in Colossians 1:17, and the Word's being with God in John 1:1 provide for Barth the raw materials for the claim that the Word's presence with God and as God in the beginning is to be understood *as* election. For Barth, the divine pleasure or choice displayed in Colossians 1:19 means that "Jesus Christ is the eternal will of God, the eternal decree of God and the eternal beginning of God."[35] Or, as he puts it later, "The choice or election of God is basically and properly God's decision that as described in John 1:1–2 the Word which is 'the same,' and is called Jesus, should really be in the beginning, with Himself, like Himself, one with Himself in His deity. . . . [T]he divine predestination is the election of Jesus Christ."[36]

What are the implications of this way of interpreting John 1:1–2? The theological payoff of Barth's reading is, of course, one of the most hotly debated points in Barth scholarship today. Bruce McCormack and others have argued for a "strong" reading of the significance of Barth's reading of John

31. *CD* II/2, 98.
32. He discusses briefly 2 Cor. 4:4; Col. 1:15–16, 18; 2:10; Heb. 1:2–3; Eph. 1:10, 23; 3:9; 1 Cor. 15:20; Gal. 4:4.
33. *CD* II/2, 98–99.
34. Gibson, *Reading the Decree*, 46.
35. *CD* II/2, 99.
36. *CD* II/2, 101, 103.

1:1–2, such that "election" means something like divine self-constitution. McCormack's claim is that for Barth "election is the event in God's life in which he assigns to himself the being he will have for all eternity."[37] On this interpretation, what Barth means to achieve with his reading of John 1:1–2 is a claim about the self-determination not only of God's saving movement toward humanity but of God's own eternal being: "There is no *Logos asarkos* in the absolute sense of a mode of existence in the second 'person' of the Trinity which is independent of the determination for incarnation; no 'eternal Son' if that Son is seen in abstraction from the gracious election in which God determined and determines never to be God apart from the human race. The second 'person' of the Trinity has a name and His name is Jesus Christ."[38]

Not all readers of Barth accept this construal, however. David Gibson argues:

> In the Johannine exegesis, Barth intends to show that God's self-determination is to be a God who is turned towards the human race, so that the primary referent of "election" must be Jesus Christ as the personal expression of this "turning towards" humanity. . . . It is this movement, *in Christo*, towards humanity that for Barth counts as the election, the decree, the decision of God. But it is a movement of God outside himself, a description of who God is when he turns toward that which is not God. It is not a movement which is ontologically constitutive of the divine being.[39]

For support, Gibson points out that immediately following his exegesis of John 1:1–2, Barth comments: "Jesus Christ was at the beginning. He was not at the beginning of God, for God has indeed no beginning. But he was at the beginning of all things, at the beginning of God's dealings with the

37. Bruce L. McCormack, "Grace and Being: The Role of God's Gracious Election in Karl Barth's Theological Ontology," in *The Cambridge Companion to Karl Barth*, ed. John Webster (Cambridge: Cambridge University Press, 2000), 92–110, here 98. Many of the essays that have grown out of McCormack's work are now conveniently collected in *Trinity and Election in Contemporary Theology*, ed. Michael T. Dempsey (Grand Rapids: Eerdmans, 2011).

38. McCormack, "Grace and Being," 100 (emphasis original).

39. Gibson, *Reading the Decree*, 53. For conclusions similar to Gibson's, see the book and several essays by Paul D. Molnar, *Divine Freedom and the Doctrine of the Immanent Trinity* (London: T&T Clark, 2002); "Trinity and the Freedom of God," *Journal for Christian Theological Research* 8 (2003): 59–66; "The Trinity, Election and God's Ontological Freedom: A Response to Kevin W. Hector," *International Journal of Systematic Theology* 8 (2006): 294–306; "Can the Electing God Be God without Us? Some Implications of Bruce McCormack's Understanding of Barth's Doctrine of Election for the Doctrine of the Trinity," *Neue Zeitschrift für Systematische Theologie und Religionsphilosophie* 49 (2007): 199–222; "What Does It Mean to Say That Jesus Christ Is Indispensable to a Properly Conceived Doctrine of the Immanent Trinity?," *Scottish Journal of Theology* 61 (2008): 96–106.

reality which is distinct from Himself. Jesus Christ was the choice or election of God in respect of this reality."[40] This would seem to be a straightforward pro-Nicene and Chalcedonian affirmation that although Jesus Christ was fully and truly equal with God, his humanity as the expression in time of God's determination to be in covenant with human beings was *not* eternal. It is not as such an airtight objection to McCormack's reading, since part of McCormack's claim is that Barth was internally inconsistent. But it does suggest that *at least with respect to his exegesis of John 1:1–2*, Barth does not intend to make the strong claim McCormack attributes to him.

Furthermore, it may be worth noting in passing (since a full exploration of these themes is beyond my present scope), as Paul Molnar and others have stressed, this "weaker" reading of Barth's achievement, like McCormack's stronger one, also has wide-ranging theological implications: if the *Logos asarkos* is distinct from the *Logos incarnatus* (the incarnate Word) and also from the *Logos incarnandus* (the to-be-incarnate Word), then a certain construal of the transcendence and freedom of God in creation and redemption is maintained. For Molnar, to identify as McCormack does the *Logos asarkos* with the *Logos incarnandus* makes the creative and redemptive actions of God *ad extra* essential to the being of God *ad intra* and thus compromises divine transcendence and freedom. Although adjudicating between these various positions is not my aim, I may simply observe that such issues are raised by the exegesis Barth performs.

What Barth undoubtedly intends, on all readings of his exegesis of the Johannine Prologue, is a redefinition of the concept of "election." Before it is anything to do with the choice of specific human beings, election is "God's determin[ation of] Godself for community with humanity."[41] What Barth finds in John 1:1–2—before any possible discussion of the choice made by the subject Jesus Christ for the object of his covenant favor, namely humanity—is the choice *to be* the subject "Jesus Christ." Whether we regard this exegesis as still usable today,[42] and whether we side with Bruce McCormack or his detractors as to its theological implications, one thing that does seem certain is that Barth's wider theology of election and Christology is inextricably shaped by his exegesis. The reading he offers of John 1:1–2 is inseparable from the

40. *CD* II/2, 102.

41. Van Driel, "Karl Barth on the Eternal Existence of Jesus Christ," 56–57.

42. For some recent treatments of the Johannine Prologue, see especially Richard Bauckham, *God Crucified: Monotheism and Christology in the New Testament* (Grand Rapids: Eerdmans, 1999); Mary L. Coloe, *God Dwells with Us: Temple Symbolism in the Fourth Gospel* (Collegeville, MN: Liturgical, 2001); and Daniel Boyarin, "The Gospel of the Memra: Jewish Binitarianism and the Prologue to John," *Harvard Theological Review* 94 (2001): 243–84.

conclusions he draws and may even, as he himself thought, make those conclusions "clearer."[43] In this particular instance, at least, theology and exegesis are intertwined, and Barth may indeed be seen as an exegetical theologian.

Evaluating Barth's Exegesis

In closing, however, we may pose and attempt to answer the more difficult question not of Barth's *status* as an exegete but of his *success*. Does his exegesis of these portions of the Johannine Prologue count as *good* or not? Undoubtedly a full treatment of that question lies beyond our scope, since large-scale questions of how one defines hermeneutical success would need to be explored first.[44] But perhaps three evaluative comments may still be worthwhile.

In the first place, what we have explored of Barth's reading of the Johannine Prologue, both in the 1925–26 lectures as well as in the later *Church Dogmatics*, indicates a move toward "close" reading of the biblical text. If Barth's first forays into biblical exegesis, the first and second editions of his celebrated *Römerbrief*, were marked by an ecclesial concern for homiletical application and thus a willingness, and indeed a determination, to leave behind the "historical" sense of Paul's likely original meaning, the material on John is much more obviously attentive to "the way the words go." To read the Romans commentary is to encounter a profound set of theological meditations that appear to be *evoked by* but not *accountable to* the grammar of Paul's text, which may be partly explained by their composition during Barth's pastorate before his move into an academic post. As Francis Watson has put it, in the Romans commentary "[t]here is little or no attempt to analyze the structure of a Pauline argument, for the focus is not on the Pauline text as such but on the divine reality to which it bears witness."[45] But to read the lectures on the Johannine Prologue is to observe Barth turning to a more recognizably conventional interest in treating "small-scale interpretative decisions [about words and syntax as] integral to the attempt to articulate the substance of a text."[46] One can see this, in part, by Barth's repeated reference to Adolf

---

43. *CD* II/2, x: "I have grounds for thinking that to some my meaning will be clearer in these [fine-print exegetical excurses] than in the main body of the text."

44. I gesture toward these larger questions in my essay "The Text of Ephesians and the Theology of Bucer," in *Reformation Readings of Paul*, ed. Jonathan Linebaugh and Michael Allen (Downers Grove, IL: IVP Academic, 2015), 143–64.

45. Francis Watson, "Barth, Ephesians, and the Practice of Theological Exegesis," in Karl Barth, *The Epistle to the Ephesians* (Grand Rapids: Baker Academic, 2017), 13–30, here 9.

46. Watson, "Barth, Ephesians, and the Practice of Theological Exegesis," 20.

Schlatter, a respected New Testament exegete and theologian and contemporary of Barth's, and his reading of the force of the οὗτος in John 1:2; gone is the earlier insistence in the *Römerbrief* that such exegetes merely offer the first step toward a commentary and not a commentary itself. To quote Watson once more, "Barth does *not* proclaim [as he had earlier done in the prefaces to the Romans commentary[47]] that the theological interpreter of Scripture must rise above the pedantries and minutiae of normal exegetical practice in order to engage a theme that lies beyond the words of the text."[48] And not much later, in the second half-volume of the first volume of the *Church Dogmatics*, Barth would go on to describe in detail what the Johannine lectures appear already to presuppose: *Explicatio*, unfolding the sense of the words of Scripture, and *meditatio*, the reader's reflecting on what the words say to her or him, are the indispensable bases for *applicatio*, the appropriation and assimilation of Scripture's word such that the one who reads it today makes its concern her concern.[49]

Continuing the attempt to evaluate Barth's exegesis of the Johannine Prologue, we may observe, second, that Barth's exegesis at certain points suggests an inadequate construal of the relationship between the Old and New Testaments. Recall his insistence that the title *logos* given to Jesus in verses 1 and 2 is not an honor for Jesus, as though its meaning were accessible prior to its christological application, but rather that the Prologue's author "honoured the title itself by applying it a few lines later as a predicate of Jesus."[50] The thought appears to be that the attempt to locate some prior meaning of *logos*, whether in neo-Platonism, Stoicism, or Mandaeism or the like is a red herring; Jesus Christ himself defines what it means for him to be the Logos. But in addition to observing Barth's total failure to grasp that John 1:1–5 alludes to and reworks the account of creation in Genesis 1,[51] one may question whether his retrospective move—from Christ *back* to the Logos— does justice to the relation between the two Testaments of the Christian Bible, if the Logos title is understood as referring to God's creative word as disclosed in Genesis, as argued by many contemporary exegetes.[52] The question I would ask of Barth's exegesis is why we cannot say that the Genesis text, and the related Old Testament emphasis on God's effectual word (e.g.,

---

47. See chap. 3 above.
48. Watson, "Barth, Ephesians, and the Practice of Theological Exegesis," 23.
49. See *CD* I/2, §21, 709–40, esp. 722–28.
50. *CD* II/2, 97.
51. Bauckham, "Revelatory Word or Beloved Son?," 29.
52. E.g., Marianne Meye Thompson, *John: A Commentary*, New Testament Library (Louisville: Westminster John Knox, 2015), 28–29.

Ps. 33:6), does not honor Jesus, at the same time that Jesus newly unfolds the full meaning of Genesis and its related Old Testament tradition. The direction of Barth's thought is relentlessly from Christology *back* to the Old Testament (or rather, in this instance at least, from Christology to the *omission* of the Old Testament *logos* tradition altogether), but does this not undermine the ability of the Old Testament not only to prepare for the revelation of Jesus Christ in the New but also to bear its own discrete witness to Christ on its own terms?[53] D. Stephen Long has commented more generally about Barth's retrospective hermeneutics that he "did not always keep faith with the Old Testament tradition of the divine name. To understand who Jesus is we must have the 'preconception' of God that the revelation to Moses gives. If we do not have it, then we will not know that Jesus has the name."[54] Making Long's comment particular to our own limited focus, we may say that to understand who Jesus is in the Johannine Prologue we must have the "preconception" of God's powerful word that Genesis 1 gives; if we do not begin with Genesis and its depiction of God's *logos*, then we will not know what it means for Jesus to be designated as the Logos.[55]

Finally, I would like to join Richard Bauckham in registering a concern over what Barth's exegesis leaves out. Granting that Barth's intention was not to provide a full-scale commentary on the Johannine Prologue (though the structure of *Witness to the Word* might suggest that), we may still lament the way that Barth's use of the text *does* represent in some ways what Paul McGlasson once unflatteringly described as a "virtuoso performance"[56] in the sense that it flows from Barth's own powerfully unique theological imagination and arguably not from the text's own prioritized themes. Although Barth explains the puzzling decision of the Fourth Gospel, and indeed the remainder of its Prologue, not to continue to use the Logos title by way of its prospective function (the Logos simply *is* Jesus Christ), Bauckham has rightly criticized this approach for the way it marginalizes what the Prologue

53. For this latter concern, usually associated with the work of Brevard Childs, see now especially Christopher R. Seitz, *The Character of Christian Scripture: The Significance of a Two-Testament Bible*, Studies in Theological Interpretation (Grand Rapids: Baker Academic, 2011).

54. D. Stephen Long, *Speaking of God: Theology, Language, and Truth* (Grand Rapids: Eerdmans, 2009), 180.

55. Cf. Bauckham: "[Barth] seems unable to accommodate the idea that the Prologue's strategy is to say to its Jewish readers: 'This Word you already know about from Genesis is the Word that has become flesh in Jesus Christ.'" "Revelatory Word or Beloved Son?," 29.

56. Quoting McGlasson, Brevard Childs laments that virtuosi cannot be imitated or duplicated and thus, as an instance of theological virtuosity, Barth's biblical exegesis "left little lasting impact either on the biblical academy or on the church" ("Toward Recovering Theological Exegesis," *Pro Ecclesia* 6 [1997]: 16–26, here 19), a judgment which I understand but also consider to be overstated.

foregrounds—namely, Jesus's *sonship*. When the Logos becomes flesh, what is revealed is not simply that the Logos is Jesus Christ God incarnate but that the Logos is the only *Son* of the Father. As Bauckham notes, the Prologue begins and ends similarly: The Word who is "with God" in verse 1 is eventually identified in verse 18 as "God the only Son, who is close to the Father's heart" (NRSV). This structural parallelism or *inclusio* seems designed to reinterpret the Old Testament depiction of God's relationship to his powerful word with a fuller depiction of the Father's relationship to his Son.[57] If Bauckham is right, then Barth's exegesis of the Prologue represents a powerful theological conceptuality that has seized upon certain features of the Johannine text without noticing or caring to explore those features' integration within a larger literary and theological design.

---

57. Bauckham, "Revelatory Word or Beloved Son?," 31.

SEVEN

Karl Barth on Ephesians 1:4

STEPHEN FOWL

Introduction

In the interest of full disclosure, I am not a Barth scholar, nor the son of a Barth scholar. Like many young exegetes (and I mean exegetes as opposed to theologians), I started to work through Barth's commentary on Romans as a beginning graduate student. I had been told that this commentary's publication was an earthshaking event. It seemed like an obvious thing to do. Without really understanding the context and the ecclesial situation Barth was addressing, however, reading the Romans commentary was a frustrating experience. He seemed to get Romans so badly wrong. What was worse was that he did not even seem to care.

I now have a much deeper appreciation for Barth as a theologian who loved Paul's letters and brought his great theological insights into an ongoing conversation with Paul's writings. Indeed, at their best, Barth's various engagements with Paul's letters represent a thoroughgoing attempt to bring theological concerns to bear on the interpretation of Scripture and to keep those concerns primary in the face of other more historically or philosophically focused concerns.[1] Nevertheless, although I am much more comfortable

---

1. Writing in relation to *Church Dogmatics*, Francis Watson claims, "Barth's biblical interpretation is not a particular item, but the foundation and principle of coherence of his entire project, and interpreters who overlook this biblical foundation, or who refer to it only in passing

with Barth's handling of Scripture than I was in my early encounters with his work, I am still not a Barth scholar, and I fear some of my comments about Barth's treatment of Ephesians 1:4 will reflect my amateur status.

The focus of this chapter is quite narrow—Barth's treatment of Ephesians 1:4. This text plays a central role in Christian reflection on doctrines of election and salvation, matters in which Barth took a keen interest. These doctrinal concerns would certainly outstrip any theologian's concerns with Ephesians 1:4, and I am not able to offer anything like an adequate account of Barth's views on election.[2] Instead, I plan first to discuss Barth's comments on Ephesians 1:4 in his university lectures on Ephesians. I will offer some comments about these and then move on to selected parts of the *Church Dogmatics* where Barth also engages Ephesians 1:4. I have to say that I do find some significant differences between the early lectures on Ephesians and the treatments of Ephesians 1 offered a couple decades or more later in *CD* II/1 and II/2. I know that there are serious arguments among Barth scholars about whether and to what extent the later Barth changed from the earlier Barth. I do not think anything I say here will resolve that.

Instead, I will try to raise some questions about Barth's claims that may or may not be reflective of wider arguments in Barth scholarship. I realize that in this part of the chapter I am wandering through a minefield with only the most rudimentary map. If I naively replicate at an overly simple level points raised by scholars of Barth's work, I beg your indulgence. At various points in the chapter I will offer some of my own comments on Ephesians 1:4. I take these to be compatible or potentially compatible with Barth's views even though Barth does not make them himself or does not offer them in any sort of developed way. Rather, I offer these as a way of bringing different theological approaches to Ephesians 1:4 into conversation with one another.

Barth's Lectures on Ephesians

Barth lectured on Ephesians in Göttingen in the winter semester of 1921–22. I am, and perhaps all of us are, deeply indebted to Ross Wright's 2007 St.

---

will radically misinterpret that project." "The Bible," in *The Cambridge Companion to Karl Barth*, ed. John Webster (Cambridge: Cambridge University Press, 2000), 57.

2. See the essay by Bruce L. McCormack, "Grace and Being: The Role of God's Gracious Election in Karl Barth's Theological Ontology," in *Cambridge Companion to Karl Barth*, 92–110. For an accessible collection of responses to McCormack, see *Trinity and Election in Contemporary Theology*, ed. Michael T. Dempsey (Grand Rapids: Eerdmans, 2011). See also Scott Bader-Saye, *The Church and Israel after Christendom: The Politics of Election* (Boulder, CO: Westview, 1999).

Andrews dissertation, which provides a critical annotated translation of these lectures.[3] Of the fourteen lectures, thirteen are devoted to Ephesians 1, with the final lecture summarizing the rest of the epistle. I take this both to reflect the strengths of Barth's theological approach to Ephesians 1:4 and to foreshadow some of the problems in his approach. In addition, Barth reflects on Ephesians 1:4 in various discussions of election and predestination in *CD* II/1 and II/2. Ephesians 1:4 appears a few other places in the *Church Dogmatics*, but there is little that adds to or changes the picture one gets in II/1 and II/2. The material in the lectures on Ephesians and the *Church Dogmatics* will form the basis for my comments.

The lectures are a bracing combination of Barth's theological energy and passion with an admirable grasp of scholarly literature on Ephesians. The theology is always to the fore, as I think it should be. He takes Paul to be addressing both first-century Christians in Ephesus and Christians in Germany in the early 1920s. There is no sharp distinction between first century and twentieth, no false chasm between what the text meant and what it means. If I were to offer a small criticism at this point, it would be that the biblical scholarship is often noted, but not particularly integrated into the theological argument. It reads more like an attempt to demonstrate that he did indeed read the secondary literature on Ephesians.

The center of Barth's treatment of Ephesians is his detailed account of 1:3–14. If I may quote from Wright's abstract at length here:

> Barth made a material discovery in his study of Ephesians that fundamentally shaped his subsequent theology. He observes in Ephesians 1:3–14 a train of thought which witnesses to God's action to the creature in Christ and the creature's subsequent movement to God. He concludes that we have come *from* God, who has chosen us in eternal election, and we are moving *toward* the glory of God, our divinely appointed goal. The exposition's central theme is expressed in Barth's claim that "the knowledge of God is the presupposition" and "the goal" of human existence.[4]

This is a fair, if highly abstract, assessment of Ephesians and Barth's comments on it. As Barth moves to discuss Ephesians 1:3–14 in detail, he begins with a strong assertion of his dialectical perspective, a perspective he attributes to Paul. This allows him to assert God's incomprehensibility and

3. Ross M. Wright, "Karl Barth's Academic Lectures on Ephesians (Göttingen 1921–22): An Original Translation, Annotation and Analysis" (PhD thesis, St. Andrews University, 2007). Wright's translation is now published as Karl Barth, *The Epistle to the Ephesians*, ed. R. David Nelson (Grand Rapids: Baker Academic, 2017).

4. Wright, "Barth's Lectures on Ephesians," "Abstract" (emphasis original).

Christ's surprising and unanticipated invasion of the cosmos and how deeply this destabilizes all of Paul's talk about God. In reference to Paul's initial call to bless the God and Father of our Lord Jesus Christ in 1:3, Barth says, "ευλογειν refers to a divine act which is non-contingent, unexpected, and free, an absolute act of revelation."[5] I find this claim quite plausible. Things become harder to follow when he claims that when Paul speaks of God, "the communication is always intended differently than it is spoken, and the more truly God is spoken about, the greater the difference between what is spoken and its intended meaning."[6] I have checked the German here, and this is a fair translation.

As a corrective moment to the theological complacency of his day, this may be just the right tone to adopt. Our claims about God must always be provisional. Christians must always seek to hear new things from the Spirit. Nevertheless, to claim that Paul's assertions about God are always different from what he intends is difficult to fathom. First, how could one know this about Paul or anyone else? If it were true, it would risk making any of Paul's claims about God so malleable as to make them useless for doctrine or ethics. If it is true for Paul, presumably it is also true for Barth. This also raises questions of what his students were to make of Barth's claims about God. I propose that rather than try to make further sense of this claim, we simply move on.

When Barth comes to an exegesis of Ephesians 1:4 he treats the verse as the theme for the rest of verses 4–14: "There is the blessing of God from which we *come* ἐκλογή (vv. 4–6). There is the blessing of God in which we *stand* ἀπολύτρωσις, the forgiveness of sins (vv. 7–10). And there is the blessing of God to which we *are heading* κληρονομία for which we hope, developed in two different expressions (vv. 11–12 and vv. 13–14)."[7] Barth goes to some pains to avoid separating these things too sharply. He wants readers to see this passage as reflecting a single eternal act of God. Barth's initial concern with verse 4 and with verses 4–6 more generally is that we should not move too quickly from questions of election and predestination to assertions that such election necessarily entails double predestination.[8] At the same time he warns against trying too hard to avoid this implication. He notes several commentators who

5. Wright, "Barth's Lectures on Ephesians," 43.

6. Wright, "Barth's Lectures on Ephesians," 44–45.

7. Wright, "Barth's Lectures on Ephesians," 51 (emphasis original).

8. As Bader-Saye notes, despite rejecting the idea of predestined nations (Barth even claims that Israel is only a transitory form of the community in *CD* II/2, 313), Barth was unwilling simply to leave election and predestination as a purely individual matter, though Barth was only partially successful in this (*Church and Israel*, 74).

try to do this. Both of these interpretive tendencies reflect what Barth calls "anthropological concerns," concerns that come from a set of human-focused and human-centered questions about God's election.

As Barth sees it, these anthropological concerns miss Paul's point that the notion of God's choosing believers is primarily a way of saying something about God and God's relationship to human creatures. God chooses and God alone in freedom and sovereignty. Moreover, God chooses in Christ eternally—before the foundation of the world.[9] Thus, there is nothing contingent in God's choice. Barth claims that "Paul's doctrine of predestination is more sharply formulated than both Augustine's and the Reformers.' It is not a question of a second being chosen by a first; rather, God chooses as the One and Only; as the eternal One, he chooses the human creature who lives in time."[10]

The rest of Ephesians 1:4–6 spells out the goal of that choosing. In Barth's words:

> It is thus a self-enclosed circle that Paul has in view: God's intention for us proceeds from the mystery of his own counsel and will and goes forth to us known, perceptible human creatures who are utterly finite; as soon as it does, it also goes beyond us and returns to the mystery itself. We, his children, should be holy and blameless before him so that the glory of his grace might be praised. The human creature is the scene of action of the Unique One [*Einzigen*] who is his own purpose and goal; *we* are only the scene; nevertheless, we are the *scene*; that is what is promised to us here.[11]

For Barth, the key thing to understand about this vocation to holiness is that such holiness should not be understood primarily in terms of one's relationship to God, not in terms of piety and good works. These have some significance, but this holiness is holiness in the presence of God. "Everything by which the human creature has been shaken and wounded, all good works, even the greatest prophetic or apostolic holiness as human work, is at once called into question and relativized."[12]

As the rest of his discussion of verses 5–6 unfolds it becomes clear that Barth wants to build an unbreachable wall between what he calls domesticated bourgeois piety on the one hand, and the Pauline Reformation on the

9. As Bader-Saye argues, by focusing on Christ as both the subject and object of election, Barth is trying to chart a path between notions of election that are too focused either on individuals or on communities. See *Church and Israel*, 75.

10. Wright, "Barth's Lectures on Ephesians," 59.

11. Wright, "Barth's Lectures on Ephesians," 60 (emphasis original).

12. Wright, "Barth's Lectures on Ephesians," 61.

other hand. He firmly plants himself on the Reformation side and calls on his audience to abandon the other and to see things as he does.

In terms of his sustained exegetical work as reflected in the lectures on Ephesians, it is clear that for Barth Ephesians 1:4–6 is about election and predestination as dogmatic categories. Election emphasizes God's sovereign, free, eternal, and Christ-focused choosing of humans. Barth relentlessly draws his students' attention off themselves and onto God. He does so with a passion that must have been quite striking to listen to.

If I could be transported back to those lecture halls and had the chance to ask some questions and make some observations, I would offer the following: unlike many of Barth's or my own historical-critical peers, I am not in principle opposed to reading Paul's discussion of election and predestination through dogmatic lenses. I do not think that Barth is an example of someone who simply imposes a dogmatic schema on the text of Ephesians heedless of any of the textual detail. Nevertheless, it does seem to me that when Barth reads Paul's discussion of God's election and predestining in Christ, he seamlessly assumes that this basically means the Reformers' understanding of election and predestination, particularly Calvin's. Given his prior comments about the inherent instability of any truthful speech about God—comments I do not agree with to the extent that I can understand them—I would ask why Barth does not question his own move here. To press this question further, I would also note that the language here in Ephesians is so redolent of Old Testament allusions that it is striking that Barth never cross-references or notes a single Old Testament text in his discussion of Ephesians 1:4–5. He relies on Calvin, Luther, and other Pauline texts with great regularity. He never refers to the election of Israel, to God's commission to the people of Abraham to be holy and blameless, or to language that speaks of Israel as God's inheritance. I will say a bit more about this later, but it would seem to me that the dogmatic questions about election among the Reformers might appear different if one first engaged the dogmatic questions of the relationships between the election of Israel and the election of the Ephesians, almost all of whom are Gentile. At the very least, the rest of Ephesians 2 and 3 seems interested in unpacking this question.[13] Thus, I would want to suggest that in his lectures on Ephesians the problem is not that Barth imposes dogmatic categories onto Scripture. Rather, he has not sufficiently allowed the Old Testament echoes of Paul's comments to inform his Reformed dogmatic interests. This is not to say that

---

13. In this regard Bader-Saye offers a telling argument that any doctrine of election that is not sufficiently Jewish is not sufficiently trinitarian (*Church and Israel*, 73).

there is a single way in which these echoes must inform dogmatic interests, only that they should do so.

Ephesians 1:4 in the *Church Dogmatics*

To a limited degree Barth addresses this concern in his later writings on election and predestination in the *Church Dogmatics*. In *CD* II/2 Barth has a discussion of election in what is ostensibly a larger discussion on the role of Scripture as a foundation for doctrines about God. That leads into a rather extensive small-print reflection on election and various Reformation debates. Ephesians 1:4 plays a limited direct role in these pages. Nevertheless, Barth does sharpen the picture one gets from the Ephesians lectures by emphasizing the centrality of Christ for any doctrine of election. In the Ephesians lectures Barth sets anthropological concerns with God's choosing and what that choosing says about us humans in contrast with what he takes to be Paul's theological emphasis. That is, election primarily tells us something about God. For reasons that seem explicable given Barth's context in the early 1920s, his discussion in the Ephesians lectures is relentlessly theocentric. He treats the anthropological questions as distractions.

In *CD* II/2 Barth uses a christological approach to hold the theocentric and the anthropological together. Christ becomes the way of uniting two truths: "on the one hand the electing God and on the other the elected man."[14] In this way Barth does not contradict anything he says earlier about Ephesians 1:4. Instead he brings the phrase "in him" to the forefront. The intersection of God's electing and our election is found in God's self-revelation in Jesus Christ. It is worth noting, however, that in this part of *CD* II/2 the central biblical text for Barth is John 1:1–2, not Ephesians 1:4.

The fact that this election in Christ was "before the foundation of the world," coupled with Barth's christological unpacking of election in this passage, does seem to raise questions about the eternality of the incarnation of the Word. I know enough to know that Barth's views on this were both complex and controversial. I, therefore, know enough not to venture too far into this thicket.

It does seem that here in *Church Dogmatics* Barth is working much harder to let the doctrine of election be shaped by more directly scriptural concerns.[15] This becomes even clearer when he says, "As we stated in our own introductory

14. Wright, "Barth's Lectures on Ephesians," 59. See also *CD* II/2, 103.
15. In addition, as many have noted, he is now operating in a context in which German exceptionalism is on the rise.

observations, in the Bible the concept of election stands decidedly in a direct and indissoluble union with that of the people of God, the people which is called Israel in the Old Testament and the Church in the New. The divine election is the election of and to this people."[16]

This account still leaves the relationships between the people of Israel as elect and the church as elect underdeveloped. Nevertheless, I would suggest that this account is more scriptural than the account in the earlier Ephesians lectures. I don't mean to drive a sharp wedge between doctrinal and Scriptural accounts here. Rather, it is simply to note that what I might have expected to find in the lectures on Ephesians I find much more in the *Church Dogmatics*.

I did say that I would try to offer some further theological and exegetical observations about Ephesians 1:4 as a way of supplementing Barth's comments. I want to move to this now. My aim is not to trump Barth. Instead, I want to initiate a conversation between different theological emphases that one might bring to an engagement with Ephesians 1:4.

Further Thoughts on Ephesians 1:4

In the Ephesians lectures Barth uses the language of election or choosing to move fairly directly and immediately to Reformed notions of predestination. It is only later in the *Church Dogmatics* that he unpacks and develops the point that God's choosing is not like any form of human choosing. God does not consider the alternatives and then pick the best option. Rather, God's choosing is absolutely free, unconditioned, and eternal.[17] Paul makes none of these points himself. They all have their roots in Old Testament depictions of God, however, and Paul would have presumed them even if he did not use this vocabulary.

The vocabulary Paul does use in Ephesians 1:4–5 is deeply rooted in Old Testament accounts of God's election of Israel. Listen to Deuteronomy 7:6–8 (NRSV): "For you are a people holy to the LORD your God; the LORD your God has chosen you out of all the peoples on earth to be his people, his treasured possession. It was not because you were more numerous than any other people that the LORD set his heart on you and chose you—for you were the fewest of all peoples. It was because the LORD loved you and kept the oath that he swore to your ancestors."

16. *CD* II/2, 83. To the extent that Barth does talk about this earlier in *CD* II/2, it is no more developed than his account here. Moreover, Eph. 1:4 plays no role in the discussion.
17. *CD* II/2, 100.

In the course of telling the Ephesians that God has chosen them in love to be holy and blameless before him, Paul is telling or reminding the Ephesians that through Christ they have become participants in God's election of Israel, fulfilling God's promise to bring a blessing to the nations through Abraham. That this fulfillment happens through the life, death, and resurrection of Christ is the great mystery that Paul discusses later in Ephesians 3. In this respect Barth's comments in *Church Dogmatics* seem closer to the mark, though one might want to press the question of whether Barth thinks there are two elections or a single election in which Gentiles are enfolded through Christ.

Further Paul indicates that God's choosing is directed to rendering the Ephesians holy and blameless. Again this language reminds one of passages such as Deuteronomy 7:6. Exodus 19:6 and Leviticus 11:44; 19:2; 20:26 all indicate that God's choosing of Israel is also a call to holiness. Thus, those brought into this elect group through the life, death, and resurrection of Jesus are called to be "holy and blameless." The great surprise is that holiness here does not require Gentiles to be circumcised and to take on the yoke of Torah. That is taken up in greater detail in Ephesians 2.

The language Paul uses to reflect on God's election of believers in Christ, whether in Ephesus or anywhere else, is deeply and intricately tied to his understanding of God's election of Israel. First, Paul does not think this election or the covenant has been abrogated. To think that would be to call God's righteousness into question. Second, Paul's description of election both here in 1:4–5 and throughout the rest of Ephesians rests on an account of how God fulfills the promise to Abraham by drawing Jews and Gentiles into one body in Christ without requiring the Gentiles to become Jews.

This would be an account that would be unacceptable to most of Paul's Jewish contemporaries. Yet it is an account Paul is compelled to offer in the light of God's unanticipated and surprising invasion of the world in the life, death, and resurrection of Jesus. Nevertheless, Paul points out in Ephesians 1:13–14 that the presence of the Spirit in the lives of both Jews and Gentiles in the church confirms that they have been accepted by God as full members of the covenant people. I take this to be the assertion that animates all of Paul's thinking about election and toward which almost all of the Letter to the Ephesians is directed. Indeed, it is one of Paul's central claims in his Letter to the Galatians as well. The presence of the Spirit is confirmation of God's acceptance of believers. It is all the confirmation they need. This pneumatological component of election seems distinctively Pauline and largely absent from subsequent discussions of election.

To the extent that Barth misses these issues in Paul, he shows that he is certainly a scholar of his time. It is not as if there were a large number of contemporary German scholars deeply committed to understanding Christianity's deep roots in Judaism and in Jesus's and Paul's unstinting identification with the people of Israel. Hence, if one is to criticize Barth at this point, one also has to say that he is far from alone. Perhaps a more interesting question to conclude with, one that Barth does not answer, concerns how to develop the doctrinal links in the relationships between God's election of Israel, the election of Gentiles, the making of the two into one new person in Christ, and later Christian doctrines of predestination, either patristic, medieval, or Reformed. Taking on such an enterprise today would require the cooperation of biblical, historical, and dogmatic theologians. Such cooperation is rare in the contemporary highly disciplined academy, and my sense is that this, as much as anything else, would have frustrated Barth as it would have short-circuited the intimate connection between Scripture and historical and dogmatic theology that Barth's work at its best exemplifies.

EIGHT

Karl Barth and Isaiah's Figural Hope

MARK GIGNILLIAT

Introduction: "Jesus Christ Is Manifested in the Old Testament as the Expected One"[1]

Karl Barth resists any residue of Marcionite or Socinian rejection of the Old Testament. Adolf von Harnack, for example, comes under Barth's critical scrutiny on this matter.[2] Rejection of the Old Testament is an attenuation of the gospel itself and a relinquishing of the Protestant church's historical continuity with its two-Testament canon. Barth cites Ignatius of Antioch approvingly.[3] With Ignatius we "[take] refuge in the gospel as the flesh of Jesus and in the apostles as the council of presbyters of the church. And we also love the prophets, because they anticipated the gospel in their preaching and set their hope on him and waited for him; because they also believed in him, they were saved, since they belong to the unity centered in Jesus Christ, saints worthy of love and admiration, approved by Jesus Christ and included in the gospel of our shared hope" (*Philadelphians* 5.2).[4] Ignatius's voice is

1. *CD* I/2, 72.
2. *CD* I/2, 74.
3. *CD* I/2, 74.
4. This quotation differs slightly from Barth's and is from *The Apostolic Fathers: Greek Texts and English Translations*, ed. and trans. Michael W. Holmes, 3rd ed. (Grand Rapids: Baker Academic, 2007), 241.

joined to a chorus of sympathetic voices from the church's tradition such as Irenaeus, Augustine, Calvin, and Luther.[5] Barth concludes, "To a more formal difference between the Old Testament and the New Testament (say in contrast between them from the standpoint of law and gospel), no one within the sphere of early Protestantism ever actually gave serious thought."[6] The Old Testament and New Testament differ in their moment in the divine economy—*expectation* and *recollection* respectively—but not in their shared subject matter.

Barth retains, therefore, a distinction between the divine economy that gave rise to the Old Testament and the Old Testament's continuing role as Christian Scripture. In other words, because the Old Testament is promise or expectation, the singularity of the incarnation as a particular moment in time is maintained, and necessarily so. At the same time, the Old Testament's verbal character participates in the subject matter of the New Testament in its own idiom, providing a constraining and continuing voice in the church's grappling with God's being and identity. The Old Testament's ontological horizons are not collapsed into the epistemic reach of the authors and tradents of the Old Testament in their moment of the divine economy.[7] The Old Testament speaks as Christian Scripture in its own right and beyond the ways in which the New Testament hears it. Such hermeneutical instincts are evidenced in the early church's exegetical debates, for example, between Athanasius and Arius on Proverbs 8.[8] Barth shares much in common with his patristic forebears on this interpretive front.

The focus of this essay is not hermeneutical per se, though exegetical practice and hermeneutical instincts resist easy dissolution. Rather, this essay focuses on Barth's reading of Isaiah, particularly his reading of the Immanuel texts and Isaiah's most famous and possibly most revered text, Isaiah 53. My intention with Barth is modest. I do not aim to provide a sweeping account of Barth and the Old Testament, though some of the groundwork for this is laid out in the previous paragraphs. The question I bring to Barth is straightforward: How do you engage these texts in their literary/verbal form while paying heed to their theological subject matter? How do these twin and necessarily related concerns work themselves out in practice for

---

5. *CD* I/2, 74–78.

6. *CD* I/2, 78.

7. Truth be told, Barth could have been a bit clearer about this distinction in his formal account of the Old Testament as Christian Scripture (*CD* I/2). Nevertheless, the distinction becomes apparent in Barth's actual exegesis of the Old Testament, particularly with Isaiah, as will be seen.

8. See Donald Collett, "A Place to Stand: Proverbs 8 and the Construction of Ecclesial Space," *Scottish Journal of Theology* 70 (2017): 166–83.

Barth? The Immanuel texts of Isaiah 7–9 provide the first probing point for these questions.[9]

Isaiah 7:14 and the Hope of Immanuel

In *CD* I/2 Barth makes a brief appeal to Isaiah 7:14 in concert with Matthew 1:18–25.[10] He does so in order to demonstrate that the church's dogma on the virgin birth is grounded in the teaching of Holy Scripture, though Barth admits the teaching is not as extensive throughout Scripture as one might expect. Barth wiggles his way through a complex field of theological options, situating the dogma of the virgin birth on a "different level" of testimony than the New Testament's witness to Christ as *vere Deus vere homo*. For Barth, the virgin birth is not a "repetition or description" of Christ's full deity and humanity. Rather, the virgin birth speaks to the boundless "hiddenness" and the boundless "amazement of awe and thankfulness" derived from Jesus Christ as *vere Deus vere homo*.[11] Barth's appeal to Isaiah 7:14 within his discussion of "The Miracle of Christmas" is more ad hoc or illustrative than exegetically substantive. Isaiah 7:14 and Matthew's reception of it provide the biblical warrant for the virgin birth's dogmatic affirmation.

A more substantial engagement with the Immanuel tradition is found at the beginning of *CD* IV/1 in the section titled "God with Us." Barth is aware of the difficulties associated with this passage. Within the literary context of Isaiah itself, identification of the Immanuel figure is an elusive enterprise. Historical-critical instincts tend to proximate the figure to some identifiable person or entity within Israel's own history. Barth refers to Martin Noth's *The History of Israel* at the beginning of this small-print section. Noth ascribes these three independent oracles to the Syro-Ephraimite debacle in Israel's life. Barth affirms without reservation the result of Noth's form- and tradition-critical instincts. Yet upon closer examination of Barth's reading, this appeal to tradition criticism's handling of these oracular traditions holds no material significance for his exegesis. Other than showing an awareness that the Isaianic texts he associates together originated outside the context in which they are now found, Noth's insights bear little on the substance of Barth's exegesis. In other words, Barth recognizes that Isaiah's canonical portrayal differs from

---

9. For a fuller account of Barth's reading of Isaiah, see Mark S. Gignilliat, *Karl Barth and the Fifth Gospel: Barth's Theological Exegesis of Isaiah*, Barth Studies (Aldershot, UK: Ashgate, 2009). I have taken the opportunity to rework some of the material from that book for this chapter.

10. *CD* I/2, 174.

11. *CD* I/2, 177.

the political and religious life of Israel's history "behind the text." In fact, Isaiah's account of these historical events / literary traditions subverts the political and religious life of Israel by relaying a different narrative than the one proffered within Israel's historical milieu of the time. What is also observed here is Barth's canonical instinct to allow the final form of the text the privileged adjudicatory role when answering the question: Who is Immanuel?

The Immanuel passages relate to the changed dynamic between God and Israel. Barth defines this shift as the movement from the divine Yes to the divine No. Ahaz aligned himself with Pekah and Rezin to deflect the onslaught of the Assyrians. His failure of faith is, according to Barth, the final form of Israel's unfaithfulness and opposition to Yahweh. Here again, one sees Isaiah rehearsing a different narrative than the one taking place within Israel's empirical political history.[12] The prophets understood God's providence underlying the historical situation they inhabited not by intuition, insight, or an immanent law. Quite to the contrary, it was revealed to them. In the context of Isaiah 7–9, the prophet weaves a different narrative than the one found on the surface of Israel's political history conceived in abstraction from God's providence. The Word of God via the prophet constructs these events on a different plane than observable political philosophy or an abstract philosophy of history. As has been mentioned, Isaiah's prophetic concern is the divine move from Yes to No.

Within the Isaianic context, Isaiah 7:14 arises as both a word of hope and a word of judgment. It is a word of hope because, before the year is over, the threat of Pekah and Rezin will end. God will be with them. It is a word of judgment because the greater threat, Assyria, will confront Judah before this child knows the difference between good and evil. In a short time, the child of promise will be eating curds and honey, the diet of the nomad.

The duality of grace and judgment is the central subject matter of this passage in Barth's exegesis. He makes a passing statement that the controversy over the translation of עלמה bears little weight on the "real sense" of the text.

---

12. Similarly, and in a different theological context, Barth appeals to Isa. 8:11 in his engagement of the relationship of providence to various competing philosophies of history (*CD* III/3, 24). After Barth briefly rehearses various approaches to history, e.g., Lessing, Hegel, and Marx, he makes a categorical distinction between these various philosophies—which may have good and important things to say, falling themselves under God's providence—and God's providence per se. Paradigmatic in this distinction between philosophy of history and God's providence are the Old Testament prophets. "What makes them prophets is not that they can rightly perceive and publicly appraise past and present and future history, but that the hand of the Lord seizes them (cf. Is. 8:11), that He says something to them which in relation to the thoughts of their contemporaries and even their own is always new and strange and unexpected and even unwanted, a 'burden' laid upon them (Hab. 1:1), a fire kindled and burning in them (Jer. 20:9), even a superabounding joy filling them (Jer. 15:16)" (*CD* III/3, 24).

What one observes in this passing comment is Barth's attentiveness to Isaiah's literal sense and canonical context. The sign given in Isaiah 7:14 is not the virginity of the woman giving birth. The lexical matters so often debated on this text are, for Barth, inconsequential to the text's central concern.[13] The sign given is the birth of the child who witnesses both to the grace and the impending judgment of God.

From this, Barth pursues his identification of Immanuel by placing Isaiah 7:14 in concert with the Immanuel passages of Isaiah 8:6–10. Barth does not make an appeal to the ongoing wrestling of the tradents with the Immanuel mysteries of 7:14: a diachronic scheme for proper interpretation. This is the tradition-historical move most often associated with Noth and von Rad. He simply places these texts together as a collective witness to the Immanuel idea in Isaiah. In Isaiah 8:6 the judgment side of the Immanuel mysteries is present—Assyria will sweep over your banks—while 8:9–10 presents the word of grace and hope. Even though Assyria's onslaught will be swift and destructive, Assyria is nothing other than a means of judgment in the hand of God. In the end, Assyria's destruction will not stand because Immanuel ("God is with us"). Judah will survive the Assyrian threat not because of its political prowess but because God's presence is promised in its midst. Again, Immanuel.

Taking the larger Immanuel context into account, Barth now asks, "Who is 'Emmanuel'?"[14] When Isaiah 7:14 is juxtaposed to 8:6–10, the answer to this question, according to Barth, is "[h]ardly a historical figure of the period."[15] The elusory historical background of the text and the development of the Immanuel material into chapter 8 necessitates pause when identifying the figure historically. Any identification of this kind requires the preface "perhaps." Here are the "perhaps" options given by Barth. Immanuel could be a traditional name or a *novum* selected by the prophet as a descriptor of the eschatological redeemer-king. Or, Immanuel could refer to an understanding of God's nature by a remnant within Judah: either in the real or as a charge by the prophet of what they should believe about God. Perhaps it is all these at the same time. Barth describes the mysterious nature of God's relationship to Israel. God is present with them both in prosperity and in the days of adversity. Immanuel is always true despite the variegated historical contingencies of Israel's existence. These are the "perhaps" options Barth offers, though they remain at bay because of the text's elusive nature.

13. *CD* IV/1, 5. This comment takes place without an elongated word study on the differentiation between עלמה and בתלה along with the LXX translation παρθένος.
14. *CD* IV/1, 5.
15. *CD* IV/1, 5.

Barth follows these thoughts with a move he will make later in his discussion of the servant's identity in Isaiah 53. He relativizes the question of historical proximity or precision when identifying the Immanuel figure by moving to the larger theological implication of the canonical material before him. "No matter who or what is concretely envisaged in these passages, they obviously mean this: Emmanuel is the content of the recognition in which the God of Israel reveals himself in all His acts and dispositions; He is the God who does not work and act without His people, but who is with His people as their God and therefore as their hope."[16] Barth privileges the canonical intention of the text's final form and its semantic horizon. Though he is willing to try his hand at identifying the figure historically, he does so only with the preface "perhaps." Nor does his speculation about the historical possibilities of Immanuel's identification bear any material weight on his exegesis of the text itself. The central concern of the Immanuel tradition in Isaiah 7–8 is as follows for Barth: God is with his people and reveals himself to them in all his gracious and judgmental acts. Immanuel is their hope. Here we observe Barth's tendency to relativize the historical "perhaps" in an effort to gain a maximal hearing of the text's theological "therefore."

Also, it can be argued that Barth's canonical sensibilities did not go far enough. That is, he allows the interpretation of Immanuel to be framed only in the context of Isaiah 7 and 8 with no recourse to Isaiah 9. At this point, one might see Barth possibly falling prey to the problems associated with a concordance approach to interpretation. That is, Barth seizes on the verses where the lexeme "Immanuel" is visible rather than extending the Immanuel idea into chapter 9's "unto us a child is born." In Isaiah 9:6, the language of a child being born is contextually linked with the promised child of 7:14.[17]

Brevard Childs associates Isaiah 9:6 with the Immanuel material of chapters 7 and 8. For Childs, the predicates for the child—Wonderful Counselor, Mighty God, Everlasting Father, Prince of Peace—now in canonical

---

16. *CD* IV/1, 5.

17. This literary association between the "child" concept in Isa. 7–9 and chaps. 36–39 has led Christopher Seitz et al. to identify the child with Hezekiah. The language is royal in connotation, possibly reflecting form-critically "a traditional accession piece" (Christopher R. Seitz, *Isaiah 1–39*, Interpretation: A Bible Commentary for Teaching and Preaching [Louisville: Westminster John Knox, 1993], 84–87). Brevard Childs is not inclined to find much merit in the attempt to identify 9:1–6 with Hezekiah, nor does he find much help with Alt's form-critical thesis that Isa. 9:6's form is a royal accession *Sitz im Leben*. "Yet at this juncture it is crucial to distinguish between the conventional language of the oracle and its biblical function within the book of Isaiah" (Brevard Childs, *Isaiah* [Old Testament Library; Louisville: Westminster John Knox, 2001], 80). What Childs is seeking to deflect is the ontological attenuation of the claims made in 9:6 on the basis of ancient Near Eastern hyperbole in literary forms of this type. This would be to overly historicize the material and make light of its semantic reach.

association with the Immanuel figure of 7:14 "make it absolutely clear that his role is messianic."[18] Childs understands the canonical intentionality of the text as eschatological in nature, and this despite the diachronic religious or tradition history leading to the text's final form. As such, "The language is not just wishful thinking for a better time, but the confession of Israel's belief in a divine ruler who will replace once and for all the unfaithful reign of kings like Ahaz."[19] Special note should be made of the phrase "kings *like* Ahaz," for here Childs states again the eschatological/messianic implications of his reading. It is not merely Ahaz who is replaced by Hezekiah as the promised child. Why? One can surmise the answer as follows: wicked kings came after Ahaz too. This is an eschatological hope for the day when God's royal child will rule and reign replacing all kings *like* Ahaz.

Barth does not associate Isaiah 7:14 and 8:8–10 with 9:6. In fact, Barth does not make substantial reference to Isaiah 9:6 anywhere in the *Church Dogmatics*. This is unfortunate, because the move to Isaiah 9:6 would have furthered Barth's case. God's promise to be with his people in their moments of bounty and judgment is fulfilled in the royal promise of Isaiah 9:6. In Isaiah's final form, this text is best understood eschatologically. The coming royal figure is the unique means by which God will be "Immanuel."

Barth makes an important hermeneutical move in the final paragraph of this small-print section. His attention is drawn to the New Testament's adoption of the Immanuel material in Isaiah. Whereas in Ahaz's day the promise of Immanuel is located in the change of direction from the divine Yes to the divine No, in Matthew, for example, the change of direction between God and his people is the opposite case—from No to Yes. At this juncture Barth allows Isaiah's construal of the Immanuel material a coercive, pressuring voice in his reading of the New Testament material. Points of comparison are drawn between the Immanuel sign and Jesus. For in the person of Jesus, both "the deepest extremity imposed by God (as in Isa. 8.6f.) and also of the uttermost preservation and salvation ordained by God (as in Isa. 8.9f.)" are found.[20] Jesus appears in humanity's deepest extremity and is God's means of uttermost preservation and salvation.

For Barth, Jesus fulfills Isaiah's Immanuel material. He is the concrete reality of God's promise to be with his people both in their dejection and salvation. What is of special interest at this juncture is Barth's allowing the Isaiah material itself to create the contours for his New Testament discussion

18. Childs, *Isaiah*, 81.
19. Childs, *Isaiah*, 81.
20. CD IV/1, 5.

of the issue. The elusive Immanuel material of Isaiah, along with the difficulty
of ostensive identification, opens up to the future of God's work within the
discrete voice of Isaiah's own idiom. Isaiah's literal sense plays a constraining
role on Barth's figural extension of it in light of christological fulfillment. The
figural presentation of Immanuel in Isaiah remains in substantial relation to
the person and work of Jesus Christ, with Isaiah's portrayal pressuring our
understanding of its New Testament reception.

Barth's reading of the Immanuel material of Isaiah is faithful to the canonical material, not allowing historical reconstruction or speculation to cloud
the *res* of the text at hand. Barth makes a similar move in his figural exegesis
of the servant figure in Isaiah 53.

Isaiah 53: Servant Israel, Servant Jesus Christ

Barth's reading of Isaiah 53 in various quarters of the *CD* proves interesting.
As is well rehearsed elsewhere, the challenge of Isaiah 53's canonical presentation is its backward-looking character. In other words, and on analogy
to Hosea 11:1, Isaiah 53 is not given as forward-looking prophecy. Rather,
Isaiah 53 presents something of a historically ambiguous account of the suffering of Israel and/or the suffering of an individual who is acting on Israel's
behalf. There is little room for doubt that Isaiah's servant is wrapped up
in the identity of Israel in some way.[21] Yet after Isaiah 49:1–6, the second of
the so-called servant songs, the servant's relation to Israel is problematized
because 49:3 identifies the servant as Israel with 49:6 revealing the servant
as having a mission *to* Israel. The new things promised in 48:6, created now
and not long ago, are enmeshed in this peculiar development in the servant's
literary portrayal in 49:1–6: the servant is Israel and the servant cannot be
identified as empirical Israel simpliciter. The servant's suffering in Isaiah 53
is for Abraham's offspring and for the nations.[22]

With the church's long interest in and reception of Isaiah 53, Barth refers to Isaiah 53's servant figure as Jesus Christ without any hermeneutical throat clearing. For example, in his discussion on beauty in *CD* II/1
Barth refers to Isaiah 53 in his attempt to show how a Christian concept
of beauty requires space for the ugliness of Christ in his atoning work. The

---

21. See especially Peter Wilcox and David Paton-Williams, "The Servant Songs in Deutero-
Isaiah," *Journal for the Study of the Old Testament* 42 (1988): 79–102; Christopher R. Seitz,
"You Are My Servant, You Are Israel in Whom I Will Be Glorified," *Calvin Theological Journal*
39 (2004): 117–34; Childs, *Isaiah*, 410–26.
22. See Mark S. Gignilliat, "Isaiah's Offspring: Paul's Isaiah 54:1 Quotation in Galatians
4:27," *Bulletin for Biblical Research* 25 (2015): 205–24.

transcendentals—truth, goodness, and beauty—have Jesus Christ as their source and resist abstraction from this concrete source. The beauty of God must be on display in the person and work of Jesus Christ. If this is so, then God's beauty entails within it "the human suffering of the true God and the divine glory of the true man."[23] Barth clarifies, "If the beauty of Christ is sought in a glorious Christ who is not the crucified, the search will always be in vain."[24] Barth continues, "God's beauty embraces death as well as life, fear as well as joy, what we might call the ugly as well as what we might call the beautiful."[25] God's beauty and humanity's exaltation include "the self-humiliation of God for the benefit of man."[26]

While Barth's discussion of Christian aesthetics—along with his aniconic asides—fascinates, his appeal to Isaiah 53 is of special interest to our present concerns. For Barth, Isaiah 53:2–3 keeps us from "going astray" in our attempts to speak of God's beauty apart from the self-humiliation of Jesus Christ. This aspect of Christ's person is always present with the beauty of God shining through it. Isaiah 53's presentation of the servant in his suffering is directly predicated on the person and work of Jesus Christ. With figures like Calvin before him, Barth makes no argument for this figural reading. He simply does it. The servant's portrayal in Isaiah's most famous text bears weight on the subject matter of God's beauty revealed in Jesus Christ. Barth understands Isaiah 53's verbal character as sharing in the subject matter of a two-Testament canon. In doing so, Isaiah 53's literal sense witnesses to Jesus Christ, full stop. Such a move testifies to the ontological dimension of the Old Testament's witness. While recognizing the different moments of the divine economy respective of the Old and New Testaments, the Old Testament canonical witness is not christotelic or relegated to a progressive account of revelation somewhere along the way. Quite to the contrary, Isaiah 53's verbal character bears on our characterization and identification of God's beauty in Jesus Christ in its own literal sense.

Elsewhere, Barth leans into the critical problems of identifying Isaiah's servant and does so for the sake of creating interpretive space for the subject matter at hand. For example, in Barth's biblical-theological rehearsal of covenant at the beginning of CD IV/1, Isaiah's servant appears again. Barth understands Isaiah's servant figure as an enduring witness to the "active cooperation of the human partner and Yahweh."[27] Barth follows this claim by

23. CD II/1, 666.
24. CD II/1, 665.
25. CD II/1, 665.
26. CD II/1, 665.
27. CD IV/1, 29.

raising the following critical questions: "The question whether this partner, the servant of the Lord, is meant as collective Israel or as a single person—and if so, which? a historical? or an eschatological?—can never be settled, because probably it does not have to be answered either the one way or the other."[28] Barth then provides an important clarifying phrase, indicative of the logic of figural reading. "This figure may well be both an individual and also the people, and both of them in a historical and also an eschatological form."[29] Whether or not Isaiah 53 speaks collectively or individually, historically or eschatologically is somewhat beyond the point given this text's participation in the history of the covenant, a history that not only includes but is also shaped in its entirety by God's human partner, Jesus Christ. Isaiah 53 is historical and eschatological at the same time. These two need not be played over against each other as if biblical prophecy's sole sense is predictive prophecy. Isaiah 53's eschatological reach entails the effects of the servant's work on the nations (52:13–14) as the whole of Scripture affirms the centrifugal motion of God's covenant with Israel. As such, the figure of the servant—historical, eschatological, both—participates in this singular covenantal history whose "nerve and centre" is "an event which will terminate all history and all times, a history of the end."[30]

In the final example of Barth's Isaiah 53 reading, he presses more deeply into the figural logic already on display in the preceding example. The critical concerns Barth mentions in *CD* IV/1 lean in to the historical identity of the servant as an individual or collective entity and this figure's participation in the eschatological shape of the covenant of grace. Barth does not engage the matter of Israel's identity as the servant, though the question lingers somewhere under the surface of these literary and historical concerns. Now, Barth follows after "The Glory of the Mediator" in *CD* IV/3 by means of engagement with the threefold office of Jesus Christ as prophet, priest, and king. Having briefly rehearsed Jesus Christ's role as priest and king, Barth turns his attention to the *munus propheticum Jesu Christi* (prophetic office of Jesus Christ).[31]

Isaiah's servant makes his appearance within the theological space Barth is making for Christ's prophetic office. What precedes Barth's engagement with Isaiah 53 is an explanation of his reticence to see any prophetic figure of the Old Testament per se as a proper type or figure of Jesus Christ. The discontinuity between type and antitype is too much, on Barth's account. For

28. *CD* IV/1, 29.
29. *CD* IV/1, 29.
30. *CD* IV/1, 31.
31. *CD* IV/3.1, 38.

what prophet is both Yahweh and an Israelite at the same time?[32] So where is Christ figured in the Old Testament? Barth points in the direction of the whole history of Israel and rightly so.[33] Israel's history, according to Barth, is prophetic history in its entirety. In line with the Hebrew canon's placement of Samuel and Kings within the *Nebi'im*, Barth identifies the history of Israel as a "prophetic one."[34] As Israel is to be a city on a hill, a light to the nations whose covenant presence brings an end to the "blindness of all eyes," so too does Jesus Christ share in this common history with Israel.[35] Within a catena of Old Testament texts called upon as witnesses to Israel's missional identity, the servant songs of Isaiah make a cameo appearance as well.[36] Barth offers little explanation, allowing their force to be felt prima facie. He does, however, make the following laconic comment on Isaiah 53: "Note should also be taken of the great passage in Isaiah 53:1–12 concerning the suffering Servant of the Lord, concerning rejected, humiliated and unattractive *Israel*. For it is he that 'shall sprinkle many nations.'"[37] God's actions with Israel, his election and rejection of this people in a long history of transgression and forgiveness is "in compendious form, His action with all humanity."[38] What takes place on a small scale in Israel's lived history before God "prefigures" God's actions with the whole of humanity in the person and work of Jesus Christ. As Barth is wont to do, he turns again to the small print in order to provide biblical warrant for his claim. Israel is God's covenant partner. As such, "Israel's history is really a concentration of all history, and to that extent takes place in its stead, for it, as its recapitulation and prefiguration, and the way in which it does this, are brought out with startling clarity in Is. 53:4f."[39] Barth continues by quoting Isaiah 53:4–6 and 12 in full. These verses affirm that God's covenant history with Israel is in synecdochal relation to the whole history of the world.[40] As such, Israel's history is prophetic history. As Barth

32. As an aside, I believe Barth overplays his hand here as all figural or typological readings have discontinuities between type and antitype. Reading Jeremiah's solidarity in the judgment suffered by means of his own prophetic word figures much for us in our understanding of Christ's prophetic office. While at the same time, discontinuities between Jeremiah and Christ exist as well. Jeremiah is not both Word and proclaimer of the Word at the same time as Christ is, for example.
33. *CD* IV/3.1, 53.
34. *CD* IV/3.1, 53.
35. *CD* IV/3.1, 56.
36. *CD* IV/3.1, 58.
37. *CD* IV/3.1, 58 (emphasis added).
38. *CD* IV/3.1, 64.
39. *CD* IV/3.1, 64.
40. I am consciously borrowing from Ephraim Radner's pregnant idea of "incarnational synecdoche" in his *Time and the Word: Figural Reading of the Christian Scriptures* (Grand Rapids: Eerdmans, 2016), chap. 5.

summarizes so well, "But we do say that in and with the prophecy of the history of Israel there takes place in all its historical autonomy and singularity the prophecy of Jesus Christ Himself *in the form of exact prefiguration.*"[41]

Much more could and should be said about Barth's penetrating analysis of the figural relation between Israel's history and Jesus Christ. Nevertheless, it is Barth's figural logic that I wish to highlight at this juncture. What one observes in the preceding comments is Barth's understanding of the insoluble relation between the identity of Isaiah's suffering servant and Israel's covenantal history. Such a reading is in accord with the logic of Isaiah's own literal sense. It is my understanding that within Isaiah's redemptive movements, a singular, unidentified figure emerges who takes on Israel's identity and mission for the sake of Israel and the nations.[42] Despite this, and however one reads Isaiah 40–55's redemptive movement, detaching the servant of the Lord from the identity of Israel is a textual dead end. Barth recognizes this aspect of Isaiah's prophetic witness and makes responsible use of it as he organically relates Isaiah's literal sense with its figural sense.

On Barth's reading, the integrity of Israel's history is maintained—"in all its historical autonomy and singularity." In other words, Israel's prophetic history does not become superfluous or absorbed into that which it prefigures in such a way as to attenuate the integrity of the figure itself. Israel's covenantal history as witnessed to in Holy Scripture retains its autonomy and figural shape both at the same time. Textual *fixity*, figural *potentiality*, and christological *actuality* are necessarily related to one another in a shared relation of mutual reciprocity. Moreover, Israel's history provides canonical pressure in our continued efforts to order our thoughts and prayers to the person of Jesus Christ. Rather than a placeholder whose figural role becomes redundant in the light of christological fulfillment, Israel's canonical history continues to bear witness to the nature and character of God's covenant partner. Christological fulfillment does not swallow the Old Testament's enduring figural capacity.[43]

Conclusion

The examples on offer in this essay reveal a range of reading strategies Barth brings to Isaiah 7 and 53. In all of the examples, the verbal character of Isaiah's

41. *CD* IV/3.1, 65 (emphasis added).
42. See Childs, *Isaiah*, 385. See also Robert Jenson, "The Bible and the Trinity," *Pro Ecclesia* 11 (2002): 334–35.
43. See especially Mike Higton, "The Fulfillment of History in Barth, Frei, Auerbach and Dante," in *Conversing with Barth*, ed. J. C. McDowell and M. Higton (Aldershot, UK: Ashgate, 2004), 120–41, esp. 122–23.

own canonical presentation lays a claim on Barth's theological handling of the text. Barth's figural reading is in accord with the text's letter.[44] Regarding Isaiah 53, Barth can speak of the text's referent as Jesus Christ without an elongated hermeneutical runway to get there. The figure is read in view of its fulfillment, and such a reading is responsible in its own right. It would be an unfortunate achievement for a Christian reader to detach Isaiah 53 from its liturgical setting on Good Friday.

At the same time, Barth can allow the figural logic of Isaiah's own self-presentation to pressure his christological readings in other fruitful directions. Isaiah's servant and Israel are forged together within Isaiah 40–55. To speak of the one necessitates speech of the other. Barth's reading does not require reading Isaiah 53 as prophecy in the traditional sense of clairvoyant claims about the future (though this need not be ruled out). Barth's figural logic is on display as he situates together Israel's empirical history with eschatological history, keeping figure and fulfillment or type and antitype within the same frame. As such, the history of Israel in all its integrity participates within God's providential ordering of history toward the one who would in time recapitulate Israel's history—a microcosm of world history—in his own narrative of election, rejection, and glory.[45] The servant is Israel, and at the same time, Christ is the servant.

---

44. It is worth noting Barth's brief comment on Isa. 53 in *CD* IV/1, "The Judge Judges in Our Place." There Barth admits that the New Testament does not link Christ's atoning work to a punishment suffered on our account. Nevertheless, Isa. 53 does. Because it does, "We can say indeed that He fulfils this judgment by suffering the punishment which we have all brought on ourselves" (*CD* IV/1, 253). See Shannon Nicole Smythe, "Karl Barth," in *T&T Clark Companion to Atonement*, ed. A. J. Johnson (London: Bloomsbury T&T Clark, 2017), 237–55.

45. Erich Auerbach provides an insightful definition of figural interpretation:
Figural interpretation creates connection between two events or persons in which one signifies not only itself but also the other—and that one is also encompassed and fulfilled by the other. The two poles of the figure are separate in time, but they both also lie within time as real events or figures. As I have repeatedly emphasized, both figures are part of the ongoing flow of historical life. Only the act of understanding, the *intellectus spiritualis*, is spiritual. But this spiritual act must deal with each of the two poles in their given or desired concrete reality as past, present, or future events, respectively—and not as abstractions or concepts.
Erich Auerbach, "Figura," in *Selected Essays of Erich Auerbach: Time, History, and Literature* (Princeton: Princeton University Press, 2014), 96.

NINE

Israel and the Church

Barth's Exegesis of Romans 9–11

SUSANNAH TICCIATI

Introduction

Karl Barth is famous for having urged preachers and theologians to do their theology with the Bible in one hand and the newspaper in the other. But his interpreters divide into those who find his mature theology to be in close and constant dialogue with the pressing social and political issues of his day[1] and those who find it to be at one remove from those issues as a theological system that "hovers above us like a cathedral resting upon a cloud," in Richard H. Roberts's words.[2] In this essay I will explore and diagnose the odd disjunction in Barth between theological pertinence and theological aloofness as it manifests itself in his exegesis of Romans 9–11 within the

---

1. For a paradigmatic example of such an approach, see Timothy J. Gorringe, *Karl Barth: Against Hegemony* (Oxford: Clarendon, 1999).
2. Richard H. Roberts, *A Theology on Its Way: Essays on Karl Barth* (Edinburgh: T&T Clark, 1991), 57. Roberts uses these words specifically to describe Barth's "dogma of the Incarnation."

context of his doctrine of election in volume II/2 of the *Church Dogmatics*.[3] Specifically, I will show how, on the side of theological pertinence, Barth pinpoints and addresses the contemporary problem of anti-Semitism and thereby strikes at the root of the classic Christian supersessionism of which it is a disfigured relative. And on the side of theological aloofness, I will show how Barth so abstracts "Israel" from the contingent reality of Jews and Judaism in his own day (while consistently identifying Israel with "the Jews") that he forecloses the possibility of receptive attention to that reality.[4]

This will make way for a correspondingly twofold characterization of Barth's exegesis. On the one hand, the latter is offered in repair of a contemporary problem (Christian anti-Semitism). In Peter Ochs's words, Barth "[returns] to the plain sense of Israel's story and [rediscovers] . . . what it *now* means in the light of the Gospel narrative of Jesus Christ."[5] On the other hand, Barth's repair is limited by his over-schematization of the relation between Israel and the church. Repair and over-schematization pull in opposite directions, rendering his exegesis both profoundly nonsupersessionist and intractably supersessionist in the same measure.

After outlining the "replacement theology" to which Romans 9 has almost invariably been yoked, I will offer a close but necessarily selective reading of Barth's exegesis of Romans 9–11, following its contours so as to bring out the interplay between repair and schematization. I will draw the findings together in a subsequent section so as to offer a full diagnosis of the problems inherent in Barth's doctrine of Israel. Finally, I will address head-on the question of supersessionism in Barth's exegesis, acknowledging both his important achievement and its serious shortcomings.[6]

---

3. *CD* II/2, §34, "The Election of the Community," 195–305. The paragraph is divided into four subparagraphs, each of which treats a section of Rom. 9–11, which Barth follows sequentially.

4. Daniel Weiss has been a crucial dialogue partner during the conception and writing of this essay: my thanks to him.

5. Peter Ochs, *Another Reformation: Postliberal Christianity and the Jews* (Grand Rapids: Baker Academic, 2011), 43 (emphasis added). Ochs is characterizing a nonsupersessionist Christian theology in the context of an exposition of the postliberal theology of George Lindbeck.

6. R. Kendall Soulen's critical appraisal of Barth's supersessionism in his landmark *The God of Israel and Christian Theology* (Minneapolis: Fortress, 1996), developed with further precision in "Karl Barth and the Future of the God of Israel," *Pro Ecclesia* 6 (1997): 413–28, provides an important broader context for the present essay. I seek, on the one hand, to complement Soulen's analysis by focusing on the details of Barth's exegesis. On the other hand, my analysis will issue in the identification of a more insidious supersessionism in Barth, resulting in a potentially more devastating critique.

Replacement Theology

"For they are not all Israel which are of Israel" (Rom. 9:6b).[7] This is a classic proof text for a crude replacement theology according to which Paul redefines Israel so as to defend God against the charge that he has rejected his people: "they were never really his people anyway." More elaborately (as the following verses expound), God never had in view a people defined by mere descent (9:7). He always exercised freedom to elect from among the descendants of Abraham (first Isaac and then Jacob, 9:7–13), and just as he had the freedom to exclude some, so he had the freedom to include others, finally gathering a people "not from the Jews only but also from the Gentiles" (9:24). And who else is this new people but the church? Thus the church, as true, spiritual Israel, replaces Israel according to the flesh as the covenant partner of God.

This reading provides us with an initial definition of supersessionism: the church replaces Israel as the covenant people of God. Supersessionism is replacement, and the latter is the paradigmatic form of it—although we will find that there are other kinds of replacement that instantiate the logic of supersessionism in more subtle ways.[8] A replacement reading of Romans 9–11 will act as a helpful foil against which to read Barth, since it will highlight both his innovative moves away from replacement as well as what is arguably his replication of it at deeper levels.

Barth's refreshing abandonment of a classic replacement model is signaled right from the outset by his characterization of Israel and the church as paired forms of the one community of God, which has as its task to witness to Christ. Israel is the community in its passing form, which (merely) hears the promise and thus represents the divine judgment, while the church is the community in its coming form, which believes the promise and thus represents the divine mercy.[9] While Israel figures negatively in this pairing, such negative characterization never amounts to its exclusion from the people of God. Indeed, it performs an indispensable function in that people, whose twofold determination is patterned after Christ as both the elect and the rejected. In Christ, not only is rejection for the sake of election, but rejection is also included in election, and vice versa. Thus Israel's correspondence to rejection in Christ is inextricable from its ultimate election in Christ. Barth's pairs are

---

7. As it reads in the English translation of Barth, CD II/2, 214.

8. I follow Peter Ochs here, both in the initial definition, and in the intimation that replacement can take more subtle forms. For the initial definition, see Ochs, *Another Reformation*, e.g., 1 and 257. I will return to Ochs's more intricate account below.

9. CD II/2, 195.

never dichotomies or even straightforward distinctions; they are dialectical relations in which the opposite poles of a pair contain one another.

Barth's Exegesis

"The Church in Israel": Division, Inclusion, and Reversibility

Barth's Israel-church dialectic is given flesh in his exegesis of Romans 9–11. He interprets Paul's distinction between "Israel" and "Israel" in 9:6 as a distinction between Israel (as God's elect) and the church (as God's special elect). Israel is characterized as the "race [*Stamm*] of Abraham," "Jews . . . by birth," distinguished by their "Jewish blood."[10] And the church is characterized, by virtue of its special election, as the true, spiritual Israel.[11] While this echoes a replacement reading, the logic unfolds very differently. The church cannot leave Israel behind since God's "special election" takes place within Israel, constituting (in the history to which Paul alludes in the following verses) the "pre-existent Church in Israel," and confirming the election of all Israel.[12] Barth reads 9:6–13 as a display of the fact that God's election takes the form of *division* or *separation*,[13] in which those falling on either side of the division are both included within the sphere of election, even if on one side in manifestation of the divine judgment. Judgment is not to be equated with exclusion,[14] but is rather a necessary counterpart to the divine mercy, being ultimately for the sake of mercy.[15] Thus, beside Moses stands Pharaoh, as

10. *CD* II/2, 214. I read Barth differently here from Katherine Sonderegger in *That Jesus Christ Was Born a Jew: Karl Barth's Doctrine of Israel* (University Park: Pennsylvania State University Press, 1992). The critical claim is the following one: "Not one of them is so [i.e., specially elected in Christ] by nature; not one in virtue of his Jewish blood; not one as a self-evident consequence of his membership of this people" (*CD* II/2, 214). I understand Barth to be describing God's *special election* here, as that which distinguishes "true Israel" from Israel, and thus (implicitly) to be affirming that *Israel* as an elect people is defined (among other things) by its blood. Sonderegger, by contrast, applies the claim to the election of Israel as such, concluding that Barth embraces the language of *Volk* but not race (*That Jesus Christ Was Born a Jew*, 108n31). If "blood" belongs on the side of race, then I contend that she is wrong here. It is true that Barth elsewhere takes the opposite line, claiming that "an idea of a specifically Jewish blood is pure imagination" (*CD* III/3, 213, cited in Sonderegger, *That Jesus Christ Was Born a Jew*, 156). I suggest that we acknowledge contrary tendencies in Barth on this question. I will return to the question of Barth's understanding of Jewishness below.

11. *CD* II/2, 214.

12. *CD* II/2, 214–16.

13. *CD* II/2, 216–17.

14. That is, exclusion from the one elect community of God. Barth does in fact say that "separation . . . means exclusion" (*CD* II/2, 217), but goes on to say that this does not mean forsakenness. I am wielding the terminology slightly differently for the sake of clarity.

15. *CD* II/2, 221.

"Ishmael stands fittingly beside Isaac, Esau beside Jacob, and to-day the refractory Synagogue beside the Church."[16]

The asymmetry between judgment and mercy is definitively exposed, according to Barth, in 9:22–24 (as indicated by the purpose clause of 9:23), in which it becomes clear that God's purpose does not consist in an "abstract duality," but is a unified purpose with a determinate trajectory whose goal is divine mercy.[17] That purpose is realized at the goal of Israel's history in Jesus Christ, in relation to whom Israel as a whole, as it delivers him to death, becomes a witness to the divine judgment.[18] Thus, in the parable of the potter, Israel is the "vessel of dishonour," interpreted as "a single 'vessel of wrath.'"[19] But in one and the same deed, Israel's rejection is "superseded and limited; it is characterised as a rejection borne by God," which has its goal in God's mercy on humankind.[20]

Moreover, the Yes spoken in Christ is not only the goal of the No spoken to Israel, but it is also veiled under that No (just as the Yes of the resurrection not only follows upon the No of the crucifixion but is also already veiled within it).[21] Judgment both leads to mercy and includes or hides mercy within it. The special elect within Israel are precisely a sign of that inclusion—vessels of mercy within Israel that indicate the ultimate goal of Israel's election.[22] These special elect are not so by nature, but only insofar as they prefigure Christ, who is, strictly speaking, the only true special elect.[23]

So far we have a principle of division (between judgment and mercy) supplemented by a principle of inclusion (mercy under judgment). Both principles are rooted in Christ as the elect and rejected, whose election is hidden within his rejection on the cross and revealed as its goal in his resurrection. But the centrality of God's action in Christ also serves to render all other divine divisions provisional. Barth reads Paul's vessels of wrath and mercy as *witnesses* to God's wrath and mercy, and ultimately both to God's mercy.[24] "Witness" is his primary category throughout for all human beings other than Christ. This renders those divisions dynamic and reversible. Not only, then, are those

16. *CD* II/2, 221. It is noteworthy that Barth thereby characterizes Pharaoh, as well as Ishmael and Esau, as representatives of "reprobate Israel" (*CD* II/2, 220). More surprising still, perhaps, is his addition of the final pairing of synagogue and church. We will return to this in the light of further developments below.
17. *CD* II/2, 225.
18. *CD* II/2, 226.
19. Rom. 9:21–2; *CD* II/2, 224–26.
20. *CD* II/2, 226.
21. *CD* II/2, 226.
22. *CD* II/2, 224–25.
23. *CD* II/2, 214.
24. *CD* II/2, 227.

on the side of judgment still included within the one elect community, and not only does the judgment under which they fall both witness to and hide within it the divine mercy, but as those on the side of God's judgment they can become those on the side of God's mercy. Let us plot this reversibility as we have encountered it so far.

The division between the elect and the special elect within Israel is superseded by the division between Israel (as witness to judgment) and Christ (as the only true special elect), which in turn is superseded by the division between Christ (as the one who bears the rejection of all humankind) and all Israel, and indeed all humankind (as the recipient of God's mercy). One might stop here (and there would be good reason to do so), but Barth, taking his lead from Paul,[25] does not, instead arriving at that most surprising reversal of all, in which Israel (now as witness to divine judgment) is paired with the church (as witness to divine mercy). Romans 9:24 is, for Barth, the first "express" identification of the goal of God's election of Israel, or the goal of God's Yes: as "the Church gathered from the Jews and Gentiles."[26] The church is, in virtue of Christ its Head, the "vessel of honour" that witnesses to the divine mercy.[27] It is the concrete goal to which Israel is called: where Israel is obedient, it enters the church. In other words, Israel in its natural constitution as the race of Abraham can only witness to God's judgment of human sin, and thus to human incapacity, but insofar as it is obedient to its election, it proclaims the mercy hidden in this judgment, as revealed in Christ's resurrection, and thereby enters the community of the risen Lord Jesus Christ, the church.[28] The twofold determination of God's elect community as Israel and the church is the enduring provisional form that God's division takes this side of the eschaton.

The emergence of the church at this crucial point in Barth's exegesis raises some important questions—questions that Barth in his own way raises. God's election as narrated in 9:6–13 consisted in successive divisions *within* Israel. How can the goal of this election be the church of Jews *and Gentiles*, which on no account could be reckoned a division *within Israel*? Put differently, how does the preexistent church in Israel flower into the church of Jews and Gentiles? Division might mean inclusion of both sides of the division, and it might be reversible, but the remit of God's election has all along been Israel, and Gentiles have been nowhere in the picture. A second question follows hot on the heels of this first one. Even assuming that room is found for Gentiles

25. Although it is significant that Paul does not mention the church in the present context.
26. *CD* II/2, 226–27.
27. Rom. 9:21; *CD* II/2, 224.
28. *CD* II/2, 208–10.

within God's elect purposes, why does the goal of God's election involve the constitution of another distinct assembly alongside Israel? An answer to the second question will have to wait until we reach Barth on Romans 11, but an answer to the first unfolds in the course of Barth's exegesis of the rest of Romans 9.

Remarking on the potentially unexpected character of Paul's conclusion in 9:24, Barth goes on to consider Israel's history from the perspective of the Gentiles.[29] Serving merely as "the dark foil to Israel's history," they have appeared to have no share in the divine election even under the auspices of God's judgment. Barth finds them, however, to be introduced into Israel's history "at the eleventh hour," as they too become complicit, in the figure of Pontius Pilate, in the handing over of Christ to death, and in this way "they participate concretely in the fulfilment of Israel's hope."[30] How so? Barth has earlier referred to Israel's sanctification as its "separation" from the Gentiles, but has avoided pairing the Gentiles with Israel as the rejected in relation to the elected.[31] Indeed, the Gentiles are merely said to be "not elected," and they are later called "the non-elected peoples."[32] However, what the cross of Christ does is shed retrospective light on that history, and by "unit[ing] what was divided, the elected and the rejected," it reveals the separation he spoke of (although this is only implicit in Barth) precisely to be a separation of election, functioning according to the logic of division we have uncovered. In other words, the election of Israel has not only taken the form of division *within* Israel, but from the start was also a division of Israel *from* the Gentiles. And both kinds of division operate according to the same logic, including each pole of the division within God's one elective purpose, provisionally and reversibly paired as elect and rejected, witnesses to mercy and judgment. The shock of 9:24, on Barth's reading, is that the Israel-nations pair has been reversed so as to produce the new pairing of the church and Israel, with Israel now figuring on the side of judgment rather than mercy.

This conclusion is at once corroborated and further complicated in the Scripture quotations in 9:25–29, as Barth reads them. Barth notes that Hosea's prophecy (Hosea 2:25 and 2:1 [Hebrew], cited in Rom. 9:25–26), fulfilled for Paul in the calling of the Gentiles, originally concerned Northern Israel as the *Lo' 'Ammi* (not my people) in contrast to Judah, who would one day again be addressed as *'Ammi* (my people).[33] To circumvent a replacement reading,

29. *CD* II/2, 228.
30. *CD* II/2, 229.
31. *CD* II/2, 229.
32. *CD* II/2, 228–29.
33. *CD* II/2, 230.

Barth argues that we have to do with an implicit conclusion "*a maiori ad minus*": if the promise is fulfilled in the "ten times rejected" Gentiles, how much more will it be fulfilled in the rejected Israel? The present gift of mercy to the Gentiles looks forward to the future gift of mercy to rejected Israel, and indeed contains the latter anticipatorily within it.[34] On the one hand, division within Israel is writ large in the division of the Gentiles from Israel, and the pattern of reversal within Israel allows the same to occur in relation to the Gentiles, who as a "no-people" become "my people." It is precisely their pairing with Israel that enables this, and thus the fulfillment of the prophecy in them depends on Israel's election. On the other hand, as will become explicit in Barth's comments on Romans 11:11–15, God shows mercy to the Gentiles in order ultimately to show mercy to Israel. Thus, Israel's election remains the presupposition and ultimate horizon of God's dealings with the Gentiles, whatever one might otherwise conclude from the Israel-church pairing, and Barth's claims that Israel has its goal in the church. We will return to this apparent tension below.

If the Hosea prophecy concerned the Gentiles, then the remnant spoken of by Isaiah (Isa. 10:22–23 and 1:9 [LXX], cited in Rom. 9:27–29), on Barth's reading of Paul, is to be identified as the Jews called to the church (as spoken of in 9:24).[35] Barth's conclusion, this time "*a minori ad maius*," is that if grace is the operative principle of the election of the Jews, then all the more so will it be in respect of the Gentiles. Alternatively, what the "remnant logic" does is to highlight the fact that Israel's election consists in its being marked out as a *rejected people* from whom God has committed always to save a remnant. In Barth's words, Israel exists "as this remnant which is saved and to be saved again."[36] Thus, once again, Gentiles figure on the map of God's elective purposes only insofar as they are paired with the elect Israel—as the rejected peoples from whom God saves a remnant. From the other side, if only a handful of Jews enter the church, they serve (as a remnant of Israel) to confirm rather than undermine God's election of Israel as a whole.

These developments lend greater intelligibility to the culmination of Barth's earlier list of rejected-elected pairs—Pharaoh-Moses, Ishmael-Isaac, Esau-Jacob—in the pairing of the "refractory Synagogue" and the church.[37] We now know that the unspoken beginning of that list is the pairing of the nations and Israel, which is reversed in the final pairing. But a further word of

34. CD II/2, 231.
35. CD II/2, 232.
36. CD II/2, 233.
37. CD II/2, 221.

explanation is needed. The church is a gathering of Gentiles *and Jews*. Thus the reversal is a qualified one. Israel, insofar as it comes to belief in Christ, becomes the church—not so as to lose its special witness to God's judgment, but so as to carry out that witness as "the undertone to the Church's witness about God's mercy."[38] Disobedient Israel—"Israel in itself and as such"[39]— witnesses only to judgment, thus witnessing to its divine election despite itself. The synagogue is disobedient Israel ("refractory" explicating rather than qualifying it). There are thus only two options for Israel (i.e., the Jews): to be obedient by entering the church or to remain disobedient by adhering to the synagogue in its separation from the church, thereby creating schism within the one elect community.[40]

From the foregoing exposition, we can draw out two aspects of the logic of Barth's reading so far. First, it should be clear that Israel is in no way replaced or superseded. The election of Israel, in no way undermined by Israel's disobedience to that election, remains the baseline of Barth's whole exposition and is the premise upon which grace is extended to the Gentiles. The church, even as the goal of Israel, depends for its existence on the election of Israel. Second, however, the "Israel" of Barth's account is in some ways merely a mirror image of the church: in and of itself, insofar as it does not become the church, it is by definition disobedient, refractory, a vessel of wrath capable only of witnessing to divine judgment, and therefore a rejected people. Any obedience exhibited by Israel in its history with God, even before Christ, is claimed by the church, being defined as the "pre-existent Church in Israel." And any Jews who obediently enter the church can only be the exception that proves the rule that Israel, "in itself and as such," is the disobedient binary opposite of the church. This, I suggest, is a sign of Barth's over-schematization, which is in danger of rendering Israel a Christian projection that lacks any dynamic reality of its own.

"Israel in the Church": The Uniqueness of Israel

So far we have explored the way in which Israel has its goal in the church, which nevertheless remains tethered to Israel as the elect people of God. We have noted that Israel thereby faces a choice between obediently entering the church and disobediently remaining aloof from it as the synagogue. All this can be captured under the head of "the Church in Israel," one pole

38. *CD* II/2, 208.
39. *CD* II/2, 210.
40. This dynamic is outlined by Barth with minor variations in each of the large-print summary sections preceding his exegesis (except the very first): *CD* II/2, 207–10, 235–36, 261–64.

of Barth's dialectic.[41] But if that pole focused our attention on the choice before Israel (to become or not to become the church), what about the choice before the church regarding its attitude toward Israel? We will find that this knotty issue—which is in many ways the buried focus of Barth's whole exposition—comes to the surface in the opposite pole of Barth's dialectic: "Israel in the Church." This pole has its theological center in the claim that the church has its ultimate horizon in the election of Israel. We will examine this claim in the context of Barth's exegesis of Romans 11:11f., where it goes together with his persistent affirmation of the uniqueness of Israel as the people of God, and a negative judgment on the church that questions Israel's election.

Commenting on 11:11, Barth claims that "God has so little forsaken [the hardened Jews] that it is for their sake that He has stretched out His hand to the Gentiles." He elaborates on this in the course of his exegesis of 11:11–15, arguing that God's whole purpose in extending salvation to the Gentiles is to reissue Israel with a summons to conversion, making the Gentiles entirely a means to this end. The glory of Paul's ministry to the Gentiles (11:13), and thus the glory of the Gentile church, consists entirely in its service of Israel. The Gentile church, Barth stresses, has no glory of its own, but only that which it has by sharing vicariously in Israel's. He concludes that "the Church can be what it is . . . only as it is absolutely referred to Israel's future glory."[42]

This sounds like a straightforward reversal of his claim that Israel has its goal in the church. And it is only eschatologically that the tension is resolved. On the one hand, the church in its present form, with the synagogue outside it, is only provisional; eschatologically, the church will consist in "*all* Israel," including those who are presently hardened, and "*all* the Gentile world," including those who do not yet believe.[43] On the other hand, Barth reads the "all Israel" of 11:26a as "the whole Church . . . together with the holy root of Israel."[44] It is in Israel so understood that the church has its goal. Eschatologically, in other words, Israel and the church become one.

The eschatological arc of Barth's reading is confirmed in his twin claims (in respect of verses 12 and 15) that the salvation of all Israel—its participation in the church—will coincide with the eschaton, and that insofar as the church loses its concern with the synagogue, it no longer really looks forward to the

41. See CD II/2, 210, for Barth's claim that "the Church lives in Israel," as well as his complementary claim that "Israel . . . lives in the Church."
42. CD II/2, 281.
43. CD II/2, 280.
44. CD II/2, 300.

second coming.[45] We can conclude that if Israel has its goal in the church, then the church has its goal in its eschatological unity with Israel.

This may be the eschatological horizon of Barth's interpretation, but we must not let it smooth out the real and awkward distinction of Israel from the church in the interim—a distinction that is not necessarily evacuated of meaning at the eschaton. If the church's election is foreign to it, being realized only in its eschatological unity with Israel, this is because Israel is and remains the one people of God, a fact the church ignores at its peril.

The uniqueness and irreplaceability of Israel as the people of God is first highlighted in Barth's exegesis of 9:4–5. This culminates in his claim that "the Church leads no life of its own beside and against Israel."[46] The church's dependence on Israel has been fleshed out in respect of Paul's list of Israel's privileges in 9:4–5: the church "lives by" all these aspects of Israel's life, its covenants, its law, the promises made to it etc., and decisively by the fact that Jesus Christ is "an Israelite out of Israel," the one who fulfills "everything that is pledged to Israel as promise."[47] The dark side of this affirmation is that the church, insofar as it "disputes Israel's election," commits a sin that is the "Gentile repetition" of Israel's unbelief.[48] Barth makes the stronger claim elsewhere that in doing so the church "ceases to be the Church."[49] By contrast, Barth affirms "the eternal election of Israel,"[50] implying that Israel cannot, even by its unbelief, undo its election, thereby ceasing to be Israel.

The theme of Israel's uniqueness returns in force in the context of Barth's exegesis of the olive tree analogy developed by Paul in Romans 11:16–24. While he identifies the root with Jesus Christ,[51] it is presupposed that the tree is Israel and its natural branches the Jews. Barth contrasts the holiness of the Jews, which accrues to them as "ancestors and kinsmen" of Christ, with that of the Gentiles, who share by grace in a holiness which is not their own.[52] Even once grafted in against their nature, they do not themselves become an elected people: "apart from Israel, no people as such is God's people."[53]

45. *CD* II/2, 283–84.
46. *CD* II/2, 205.
47. *CD* II/2, 204.
48. *CD* II/2, 205.
49. *CD* II/2, 234. This is one instance of a refrain repeated in each of Barth's summary sections and reiterated in different ways in the context of his exegesis.
50. *CD* II/2, 204.
51. *CD* II/2, 285.
52. *CD* II/2, 287.
53. *CD* II/2, 296.

Nevertheless, Barth grants that Gentiles, despite their nature, and without becoming Jews, do genuinely "become Israel."[54] Indeed, he goes so far as to call Gentile Christians "the true Israel."[55] This is a subsidiary note within Barth's exegesis, in which "Israel" gains a transferred or expanded meaning. We have already encountered an expanded Israel in Barth's reading of "all Israel" in 11:26a. A transferred meaning is entailed here in Barth's implicit identification of the true Israel with the (non-eschatological) church. In both cases, shift in meaning coincides with the use of a qualifier. Thus Barth safeguards the unqualified name "Israel" for the Jews. In this and other ways, Barth counterbalances any morphing of Israel by way of an emphasis on the uniqueness and distinctiveness of the people of Israel as the natural kinsmen of the Messiah.

The olive tree analogy is also an apposite context in which to develop the negative counterpart of that uniqueness: that in denying it the church ceases to be the church. The target of 11:16–24 is specifically Gentile Christians. Commenting on verses 20b–21, Barth suggests that Gentile Christians who are presumptuous toward unbelieving Jews betray their own unbelief. Indeed, they "reject [Jesus Christ] by rejecting His ancestors and kinsmen the Jews."[56] It becomes clear in his exegesis of 11:19–22 more broadly that Barth has his eye (anachronistically) on the church of his own day. He discerns in the posture of the speaker in verse 19 the fundamental stance of Christian anti-Semitism "right up to our own time."[57] And further on, commenting on verse 22, he implicitly casts the Gentile Christians addressed by Paul as the members of his contemporary church, who understand Christianity to have succeeded Judaism, separating them into two separate religions. In doing so, he reasons, they repeat the error of the synagogue and share in its fate of being "cut off" (thus Barth directly links the consequence of verse 22 to the presumptuousness being critiqued in verses 19–22).[58]

This anachronism is a sign of the reparative thrust of Barth's exegesis—at least insofar as the anachronistic categories gain acute, critical purchase in his own context. An anti-Semitic church is, regrettably, far from being a hypothetical entity for him but has substantial and horrifying reality in the German national church under Hitler—the *Deutsche Christen*.[59] That the critique of

54. *CD* II/2, 297.
55. *CD* II/2, 288.
56. *CD* II/2, 292.
57. *CD* II/2, 290.
58. *CD* II/2, 293.
59. According to Tommy Givens, Barth not only writes his doctrine of election against the background of the rise of National Socialism—in which context the Jewish Question (*die Judenfrage*) takes undeniably pressing form—but also is responding to a wider political context

anti-Semitism (as manifest in the church of his day) is in fact the nerve center of Barth's exposition is suggested, moreover, both by its reiteration in each (large-print) summary subsection of his commentary, and by its singling out as *the* sign of the church's unbelief. To recall, Israel's disobedience or unbelief consists in its refusal to enter the church, thereby creating schism within the one community. The church's unbelief is located, correspondingly, in its negative attitude toward Israel, which likewise creates schism within the one community and (more seriously) cuts the church off from its own lifeblood—the source of its election. In each subsection, after outlining Israel's special service within the one community of God and emphasizing the church's need for Israel's contribution, Barth issues the corresponding negative warning—which has a cumulative force in its varied iterations. A couple of instances will serve to capture the thrust: "If . . . the Church has become estranged from its Israelite origin . . . its name 'Church' may well be on the point of becoming sound and fury";[60] "A Church that becomes anti-semitic or even only a-semitic . . . ceases to be the Church."[61] Moreover, not only does Barth return to the charge of anti-Semitism at various points within his small-print exegesis, but also his whole exposition culminates with the following urgent call: "What this striking second νῦν [in Rom. 11:31] makes quite impossible for Christian anti-semitism (he that has ears to hear, let him hear) is the relegation of the Jewish question into the realm of eschatology. . . . [I]n relation to Israel the responsibility of the Church . . . is already a wholly present reality."[62]

The theological pertinence and contemporary bite of Barth's exegesis lies in this reparative focus. However, if we probe a little, we find that repair is inseparably yoked with over-schematization. In the previous section, Israel, as a disobedient and rejected people, was found to be merely a mirror image of the church, defined as the obedient, specially elected people. The over-schematization in the present section takes a different (apparently more innocent) form. Israel is emerging, in Barth's understanding, as a *natural* people, defined in terms of kinship and ancestry. This might appear unsurprising

---

of colonialism and racism in the aftermath of the First World War, in which Barth identifies the Jewish Question as *the* issue (Tommy Givens, *We the People: Israel and the Catholicity of Jesus* [Minneapolis: Fortress, 2014], 178–79).

60. *CD* II/2, 206.

61. *CD* II/2, 234.

62. *CD* II/2, 305. In "'They are Israelites': The Priority of the Present Tense for Jewish-Christian Relations," in *Between Gospel and Election: Explorations in the Interpretation of Romans 9–11*, ed. F. Wilk and J. R. Wagner (Tübingen: Mohr Siebeck, 2010), 497–504, R. Kendall Soulen makes an analogous case from the present tense of Rom 9:4–5 and 11:28, albeit with his own rather different theological inflection.

and unproblematic—until one notices the fixity of Barth's construal of these categories.[63]

On the one hand, Barth emphasizes again and again that Israel, even by its unbelief, cannot undo its election.[64] But he parses this ineluctability in terms of nonnegotiable, natural kinship: "[Membership of the one elected community of God] is something that none of this race [*Stamm*] can be deprived of; ... this is what Jews, one and all, are by birth."[65] And (as we have seen in the context of the olive tree analogy) the holiness of the members of Israel is something they have by nature, as part of a people that is uniquely holy by nature.[66] However it acts and whatever befalls it, Israel, as an immutable, natural people, ineluctably remains Israel. On the other hand, and by the same token, it is only by an impossible miracle that Gentiles can become the object of God's election, and thereby become part of Israel; their way is barred by their lack of natural kinship. Barth emphasizes that as members of other peoples they can never be God's elect, that prerogative falling to the people of Israel alone: "For from no people except Israel has the Son of God come forth as man."[67] Israel, as a natural ancestral people, can neither be left nor joined. The fluidity of the church—which can cease to be the church—is unmatched on Israel's side.

It might be noted that Barth's ancestral definition of Israel goes hand in hand with his identification between Israel and "the Jews." The consequence is not only that he "fixes" Israel on the one side but also that on the other side he presupposes what looks like an essentialized understanding of Jewishness, embracing under one banner ancient Israelites, Jews of Paul's time, early rabbinic Jews, Jews of Barth's own time, and so forth, thus homogenizing Jews who are temporally, geographically, and culturally diverse.[68] The anachronism in the case of the ancient Israelites should be evident.[69]

63. In *Why This New Race? Ethnic Reasoning in Early Christianity* (New York: Columbia University Press, 2005), Denise Kimber Buell employs the categories of "fixity" and "fluidity" to expound the ways in which early Christian theologians wield genealogical reasoning in order to out-narrate their ("Jewish") opponents. A key aim of her book is to undermine an assumed binary between ethnic Judaism and universal Christianity. Barth is emerging as a clear victim of her critique.

64. This is a refrain in each of the large-print summary sections (see *CD* II/2, 208, 236, and 261).

65. *CD* II/2, 214.

66. *CD* II/2, 287.

67. *CD* II/2, 296.

68. Cf. Sonderegger, *That Jesus Christ Was Born a Jew*, 170–71, where Sonderegger suggests that the problem with Barth lies not in his denial of historical reality to Jews but rather in that he had living and historical Jews too much in mind, "[drawing] too close an alignment . . . between the Jews of Pauline communities and the Jews of modern Europe" (171).

69. Givens is stridently critical of appeals to "ethnic" Israel (*We the People*, 244–56). He notes not only their ubiquity in recent theological and biblical scholarship but also the fact that they

Even if Barth means to reject the racial theories of his day (and at points explicitly does so[70]), his appeals to natural kinship allied with his apparently essentialized understanding of Jewishness bring into question his success in doing so. Indeed, his exegesis of Romans 9–11 potentially reinscribes an analogous logic. Barth's critique of anti-Semitism takes the form of an equal and opposite (albeit highly qualified) "philo-Semitism." While emphasizing the eternal election of Israel, and the church's irrevocable dependence on and unity with Israel, he continues to "other" the Jews, as a fixed, natural people. In the culminating moment of Barth's commentary, to which we now turn, this characterization of Israel as a natural people gains special theological emphasis.

Nature and Grace

The final step in our exposition of Barth will be to address the question that has been hanging over us since we left off at the end of his exegesis of Romans 9: Why does the goal of God's election of Israel involve the constitution of a distinct assembly—the church of Jews and Gentiles—alongside Israel? The answer, we will discover, depends on and reinforces Barth's characterization of the Jews as a natural ancestral people. We have already learned that the inclusion of Gentiles within God's elective purposes abides by the logic of division operative within Israel, and remains bound to the election of Israel insofar as the Gentiles are cast as the rejected peoples over against Israel as the elect people. The anomaly of the church, however, is more specifically the anomaly of an upsurge of Gentile believers over against large-scale rejection of Jesus among Jews.[71] And it is just this anomaly that Paul appears to be explaining in Romans 11:25–27. According to Barth, the "mystery" Paul speaks of is the inversion in the natural ordering of events in respect of the conversion of Israel and the conversion of the Gentiles, the latter "incomprehensible thing" having been inaugurated while the former "natural and necessary thing" is still outstanding.[72]

---

are made by some to guard against supersessionism and by others to reinforce it. The "myth" he seeks to expose, implicit within many of the uses of the term, is that of Israelite ethnicity as a "pure substance . . . passed on from parents to children . . . from a mythologically purified and common ancestor (i.e., Abraham)" (245). Givens does not mention Barth in this context, but his critique would seem to apply, despite the fact that Barth does not employ the word "ethnic." Givens's critique complements Buell's argument in *Why This New Race* insofar as Buell offers a constructivist account of ethnicity which similarly undermines the "myth" exposed by Givens.

70. See *CD* III/3, 213, and n. 10 above.
71. *CD* II/2, 288.
72. *CD* II/2, 299.

And the reason for this inversion, according to Barth, is that the first shall be last and the last shall be first—in order to show forth the divine mercy.[73] Grace can only be grace, Barth implies, if it is not nature. This "solution" reveals an extraordinary tension in Barth's doctrine of election: between the absolutely gracious character of that election on the one hand, and the natural constitution of Israel as the elect people of God on the other hand. His account of election as division is arguably a creative way of dealing with just this tension. Might one sum up the resultant dynamic by saying that the Gentile becomes by grace what the Jew is by nature (a kinsman of Christ), but in doing so reveals Israel's election ultimately to have been by grace too?

The more insidious side of this "solution"—in which Israel becomes the last in order to witness to the ultimacy of grace—is that Israel at the same time becomes the rejected. In other words, if grace is to be upheld, then the only place a natural people can ultimately have is as a rejected people, a people who reflect human incapacity and the sins of the world. In short, by insisting on the uniqueness and endurance of Israel as a natural people, Barth also singles this people out as uniquely rejected.

Repair and Over-Schematization

Having plotted the contours of Barth's commentary, we are now in a position to draw together our findings in order to offer a full diagnosis of the persistent problems in Barth's doctrine of Israel. I have suggested that the combination of pertinence and aloofness can be accounted for by the relation between repair and over-schematization. I will now fill out the picture by way of these categories, before returning in the next section to the question of Barth's supersessionism.

We noted above an important symmetry in Barth's treatment of Israel and the church: that both exhibit unbelief to the extent that they deny their unity with one another, creating schism within the one community of God. But there is a deeper symmetry to be noted. While Israel in its unbelief is a mirror of human sin, witnessing on the left to divine judgment, and the church in its faith reveals the new human being elected for eternal fellowship with God, witnessing on the right to divine mercy, they are both, as such, ideal types—types of the twofold determination of Christ as rejected and elected. As paired types they are mirror images of one another. This observation is an extension of the first kind of over-schematization diagnosed above: that Israel, as a mirror image of the church, is a Christian projection with no dynamic reality of its own.

73. CD II/2, 300.

But the symmetry between Israel and church ends at the moment when ideal type hits empirical reality. And this is where the second kind of over-schematization rears its head. Both Israel and the church are, for Barth, not just ideal types but also empirical realities. The asymmetry lies in the relation between type and reality in each case. Israel, as a natural ancestral people—kinsmen of the Messiah, Jews by birth—can never forfeit or be robbed of its identity. However it lives, even if it denies its God, Israel cannot stop being Israel. Because the empirical people is fixed, the ideal type (which is by definition fixed) must always coincide with it. It is easy to see how the conclusion might be drawn—and Barth does all but draw it—that the natural ancestral people is *by nature* disobedient, stiff-necked, and hard-hearted.

In the case of the church, by contrast, ideal type and empirical reality do not coincide. The church, says Barth, can cease to be the church; and it does so whenever it denies its unity with Israel. One can parse this refrain as follows: the church (as empirical reality) ceases to be the church (as ideal type) when it lapses into unbelief, since the church as ideal type is by definition character-ized by faith. However, from the shape of Barth's critique of the empirical church—which so clearly seems cast in terms of the pressing problems of his own time—it would seem that "faith" is not fully defined in advance as an ideal, to which the empirical church might or might not live up, but is rather filled out contextually, as Barth draws a posteriori conclusions on the basis of the observable events of his own day. In short, I surmise, Barth's Israel-focused doctrine of election and his critique of the anti-Semitism epitomized by the *Deutsche Christen* mutually inform one another. Thus the gap between ideal type and empirical reality in the case of the church (absent in the case of Israel) is so construed as to enable repair of the contemporary church.

By closing the gap in the case of Israel, Barth forecloses the possibility of engaging with the Jews and Judaism of his day in an a posteriori way.[74] The church's precarious, fluid, and contingent identity over time is not paralleled on the side of Israel. Defined a priori, Israel coincides with a fixed, (pseudo-) empirical "Jewish people." Thus Barth leaves himself no room for contextual definition of Israel's "unbelief." It is either defined in advance and imposed on the empirical people willy-nilly or filled out by way of empirical description. In practice, Barth ends up with an unhappy combination of the two. As type, Israel's unbelief is fleshed out as its resistance to election, its "refusal" to join

---

74. Cf. Sonderegger, *That Jesus Christ Was Born a Jew*, 177–79, where Sonderegger notes Barth's complacent ignorance of Judaic thought and emphasizes, contra Barth, the obligation for Christian theology to familiarize itself with Judaism in its integrity and difference from Christianity.

the church and consequent creation of schism,[75] its character as "rebellious" and "hardened,"[76] being epitomized by the delivering up of its Messiah to death[77]—in all of which it embodies the wrath of God, witnessing to the divine judgment. These are theological descriptions determined by the Israel-church contrast pair; they are not (first and foremost) a psychological and sociological portrait. But Barth also indulges in pseudo-empirical description, speaking of "Jewish or clerical phantasy and arrogance,"[78] Israel's "sectarian self-assertion," "the [joyless] Jews of the Ghetto,"[79] "Jewish obduracy and melancholy . . . caprice and phantasy,"[80] and Israel's "carnal loyalty."[81] Such empirical claims give his theological portrait a worrying psychological and sociological counterpart. This is just the result one would expect from his equation between ideal and empirical people.

If Barth had left himself room for contextual definition of Israel's "unbe-lief," he may have discovered that the synagogue does not fit his type, revealing it to be a Christianly devised foil for the church. But as it is, Barth is not open to learning from the contingent realities of Jews and Judaism in his day (or indeed in earlier times); absorbed into his Christian framework they become a mere cipher. It follows that his critique of the church, being insulated from what it might learn from Jews as genuine others, can only be one-sided.

Supersessionism and Nonsupersessionism

In this final section, I will draw out the consequences of Barth's combina-tion of repair and over-schematization for the character of Barth's superses-sionism, or more specifically, the interplay between nonsupersessionism and supersessionism in his exposition.

Barth comments that "the doctrine of predestination has only too often been presented without a coherent consideration of this *locus classicus* [i.e., Rom. 9–11]."[82] True, the passage may have been scavenged for its predesti-narian language. But what Barth does is to take seriously, in the context of a radical reworking of the doctrine of predestination, the controlling concern of Paul in these chapters: the fate of Israel in the light of its large-scale rejection

75. *CD* II/2, 208.
76. *CD* II/2, 220, 228.
77. *CD* II/2, 226.
78. *CD* II/2, 196.
79. *CD* II/2, 209.
80. *CD* II/2, 236.
81. *CD* II/2, 262.
82. *CD* II/2, 202.

of Christ and the anomalous place of Gentiles in the elect people of God. This is at once to anticipate the arguments of those associated with the New Perspective on Paul, for whom Paul's driving question is how Gentiles can enter the people of God (not, contra the "Lutheran Paul," how the human being can be righteous before God),[83] and at the same time to keep the passage rooted in its traditional locus. The result is a transformation of that locus. And the doctrinal ramifications are immense. Israel is given a place within the doctrine of God as the passing form of the one elect community of God. But passing does not mean ephemeral; rather, it is the shape taken by the human people most closely associated with God's fate as the incarnate one, witnessing to the divine judgment that God himself bears. As kinsmen of God incarnate, Israel is the people of God in a special and inalienable sense, beloved of God in a way that no others are or can be.

This is a radical way of overcoming traditional replacement theologies. Israel is inscribed into the eternal purposes of God, finding a pivotal place in the doctrine of God. But who is the Israel that is so inscribed? It is a fixed Israel: both a fixed type (witnessing to judgment) and a fixed people (defined as natural kinsmen of the Messiah). But is the establishment of this fixed Israel not itself the "replacement" of the living Israel of the Old Testament by a fixed form?

Peter Ochs defines supersessionism as primarily a hermeneutical failure: Christ is understood to be the answer to the Old Testament in such a way that "the Gospel narrative . . . replaces rather than interprets the Old Testament," foreclosing its ability "to be read in different ways in different contexts."[84] A nonsupersessionist Christian theology is, by contrast, a "practice of reading the gospel . . . as itself a practice of rereading the Old Testament narrative of the salvation history of Israel," a rereading characterized further as "a perennial event of returning to the plain sense of Israel's story and rediscovering every day what it now means in the light of the Gospel narrative of Jesus Christ."[85] This means that "the story of Israel remains open," and that "the place of Israel [within salvation history] is not yet fully defined."[86] This does not mean that the Christian cannot claim definitively that "Jesus Christ is the Messiah of Israel" (indeed she must), but that the meaning of that claim

83. For classic accounts of this contrast, see Krister Stendahl, "The Apostle Paul and the Introspective Conscience of the West," *Harvard Theological Review* 56 (1963), 199–215, which famously calls Rom. 9–11 "not an appendix to chs. 1–8, but the climax of the letter" (205); and E. P. Sanders, *Paul: A Very Short Introduction*, new ed. (Oxford: Oxford University Press, 2001), esp. 58 (which serves as a popular introduction to some of his earlier groundbreaking work).

84. Ochs, *Another Reformation*, 210.

85. Ochs, *Another Reformation*, 43, commenting on George Lindbeck's theology.

86. Ochs, *Another Reformation*, 43–44.

remains vague and thus open to renewed interpretation in each rereading (of the Gospel and Old Testament in the light of one another).[87]

In some respects, Barth's reading of Romans 9–11 is precisely a rediscovery of the meaning of the plain sense of Israel's story in the light of the gospel for his day: it is by appealing to the history of Israel as the elect people that Barth says a forceful "no" to anti-Semitism. But just as Israel's story is redis-covered, it is fixed in its relation to Christ and the church. By equating Israel with "the Jews,"[88] moreover, Barth also fixes Jews of all ages in their relation to the church. He thereby masks not only the ambiguity of Israel's story as narrated in the Old Testament, reductively capturing it within the dialectic of mercy and judgment, but also the ambiguity of Jewish identity both in history and in the present. Specifically, Barth seals off the church from encounter with Jewish self-definition as Israel in appropriation of biblical Israel's history to itself. It is this that results in the insular character of the church's self-critique, as highlighted above.

In response to a history of the occlusion of Israel from the Christian story, Barth reads the canon of Old and New Testaments so as to bring Israel right to the center of that story, as the natural kinsmen of Christ and uniquely chosen people of God. This is the mammoth achievement in which his read-ing of Romans 9–11 plays such a crucial part. However, it is an ambivalent achievement insofar as the Israel with which Barth is concerned is a Christian creation into which he shoehorns "the Jews," who as such can only be another fabricated entity that has little, if anything, to do with real Jews. It is precisely the combination that is so lethal, "Israel" being wrested from Jews in order to be given back to them, Christianly redefined. If, instead, Christians were to own the "Israel" of their making, recognizing it to be the product of a Christian retelling of Israel's story with its culmination in Christ,[89] drawing

87. Ochs, *Another Reformation*, 44.
88. In *Another Reformation*, Ochs implicitly does this, too, by naming American and British brands as two complementary wings of Christian postliberalism (e.g., 28), the American focus being on the biblical Israel while the British focus is on the dialogue between Christians and Jews. "Biblical Israel" in the one wing implicitly corresponds to "Jews" in the other wing. I am indebted to Nicholas Adams for this observation. In corroboration of this inference, Ochs lists as entailed in the new relationship of Christian postliberal theologians "to the people Israel," their new relationship "with the Old Testament, with Israel's ancient covenant with God, and with the Jews as a religious people during the time of Jesus and into the rabbinic period that continues today" (17–18). Such conflation, I suggest, forestalls consideration of the contested character of the term "Israel."
89. One way to do this is boldly but nonexclusively to identify the church as Israel. This is what both George Lindbeck and Robert Jenson do, avoiding supersessionism by denying that "the church owns the identity of Israel in such a fashion as to exclude any other divinely willed Israel-after-Israel" (Robert Jenson, "Toward a Christian Theology of Judaism," in *Jews and*

on Romans as part of Christian Scripture, they would be in a better position to acknowledge the existence of other ways of telling the story of Israel and thus to allow their telling to be interrogated by those other tellings. If Barth raised the stakes for Israel, the next step will be to raise the stakes for the many afterlives of Israel, bringing into the limelight the contested and ambiguous character of biblical Israel and its manifold futures among Christians, Jews, and others.[90]

Christians: People of God, ed. Carl E. Braaten and Robert W. Jenson [Grand Rapids: Eerdmans, 2003], 5). Cf. Lindbeck's characterization of the supersessionism that he rejects as the claim that "Christians alone are now the true Israel, the chosen people, because God rejected the Jews" (George Lindbeck, "The Church as Israel: Ecclesiology and Ecumenism," in *Jews and Christians*, 79). He goes on to claim, by contrast, that the Bible "is a capacious instrument of God's Spirit: it bestowed its unity-and-community-building power on both [i.e., both early Christians and rabbinic Jews]" ("The Church as Israel," 87).

90. This is just what Givens does in *We the People*, in critical engagement with both John Howard Yoder and Karl Barth (among others), and in a culminating chapter on Rom. 9–11, in which he reads Paul, contra Barth and most others, not to be contrasting one Israel with another, "true" Israel, but to be narrating the trajectory of the one divinely constituted Israel, inclusive not only of those Gentiles who have recently been grafted in, but also of those Jews who are presently hostile toward the Christ-movement. The upshot is an Israel that (nonexclusively) includes Christians today, alongside Jews and various potential others. Crucial to Givens's account is its self-consciously Christian telling of the story of Israel in such a way as nevertheless not to occlude the possibility of other (non-Christian) tellings.

PART 4

Barth's Doctrine of Creation in Exegetical Perspective

TEN

Creation and Covenant

Karl Barth's Exegesis of Genesis 2:8–17

ANDREW B. TORRANCE

Introduction

Creation, for Barth, is the realization of God's purpose to establish the history of the covenant. It is both the expression of God's covenant purposes and the condition for their fulfillment. So, to understand what creation is, we cannot simply look to historical and natural-scientific observations of the immediate world. We must look to Scripture, where we find a witness to those features of creation that cannot be known directly. There we are afforded an opportunity to learn about the covenant of grace within which God creates and sustains the creature. Also, we are given a chance to learn about the doctrine of election, which testifies to God's "eternal, free and unchanging grace as the beginning of all the ways and works of God."[1] For Barth, it is from Scripture that we learn about the God who elects himself to be Creator: to be the only Creator, who creates with a purpose that is neither constrained nor conditioned by the dynamics of the contingent. As a witness to God the Father, Scripture tells us: "[God] constitutes [*setzt*] Himself the Lord of the covenant. He is, therefore, its free author. He gives it its content and determines its order. He maintains

1. *CD* II/2, 3; *KD* II/2, 1.

it. He directs it to its goal. He governs it in every respect. It is His decision that there is a covenant-partner. It is also His decision who this partner is, and what must befall him."[2]

Scripture, however, does not only tell us about the God who is lord of the covenant. It also tells us about the God who wills, expects, and demands something from his covenant partner. God seeks fellowship with the creature and requires that creatures should realize their humanity in obedience to God. This does not change. God's eternal plan does not waver and is not conditioned by fickle phenomena and random occurrences that characterize the contingent order. The final consummation of God's creative purposes is thus identical with the fulfillment of election—because God's purpose for creation remains constant. "There is no such thing as a created nature which has its purpose, being or continuance apart from grace, or which may be known in this purpose, being and continuance except through grace."[3] For Barth, creation and covenant are inseparable.

What does this opening glance at a fragment of Barth's theology have to do with his exegesis of Genesis 2:8–17? It is not the intention of this essay to examine how Barth arrives at this theological understanding, by way of exegesis or otherwise. So why start in this manner? Barth's reading of Scripture is conditioned by his awareness of what Scripture is: a witness to God and the works of God. In turn, his reading of Scripture is shaped by his understanding of God and the works of God. And, as we shall see, his reading of Genesis 2 assumes and is influenced by the theological vision that I have just outlined.

An awareness of the interrelationship between Barth's exegesis and this theology is key, therefore, to understanding his reading of the Genesis creation narratives. In particular, it is key to understanding how and why the drama of covenant history shapes his exegesis of these narratives. As this chapter will demonstrate, Barth's recognition of the connection between creation and covenant is at the core of his exegesis of Genesis 2:8–17. While this may raise eyebrows for some historical-critical exegetes, for those who share Barth's conviction there is an exceptional coherence to Barth's exegesis of this text.

Before turning to focus specifically on Barth's reading of Genesis 2:8–17 in *CD* III/1, it will be helpful to take a moment to come to terms with his understanding of the genre of the Genesis creation narratives, "saga" (*Sage*), which he adopts from Hermann Gunkel. By so doing, we shall find that his understanding of this genre is itself shaped by a deep appreciation for the interconnection between creation and covenant.

2. *CD* II/2, 9; *KD* II/2, 8.
3. *CD* II/2, 92; *KD* II/2, 99.

The Creation Accounts as Saga

For Barth, the Genesis creation stories are to be associated with the genre of saga. "Saga," he describes, refers to "'historicised' myth" (*"historisierter" Mythus*).[4] More specifically, it refers to "an intuitive-poetic image [*ein divinatorisch-dichterisch entworfenes Bild*] of a concrete prehistoric historical reality [*praehistorischen Geschichtswirklichkeit*] that is within the limits of space and time."[5] There is a lot going on in this statement. So, for the sake of clarity, it will be worthwhile unpacking three aspects of this statement.

1. The Genesis creation sagas refer to events that occur "within the limits of space and time." In a certain sense, the opening chapters of Genesis tell us about actual events that took place at the beginning of creation's history. They tell us about the beginnings of spatiotemporal reality. They present creation as a reality that is wholly distinct from God and yet contained within his purposes. But they also tell us more. For Barth, they provide insight into the nature of God's purpose for creation: it is to serve as the "presupposition" on the basis of which God's purposes of love can be realized."[6]

This is where interpreting Barth becomes thorny. There is a sense in which Barth wants to say that the creation sagas tell us about the divine purpose that is enacted "within the limits of space and time." God creates the world to realize a particular purpose from the very outset—one that is imaginatively described in the opening chapters of Genesis. This, we find, is a fixed purpose that fills every substantive aspect of the contingent order, and follows from God's creative and providential purposes. There are no other ends for the cosmos. The world is created in order to "enable" the history of the covenant.[7]

This finds famous expression in Barth's understanding of creation as the external basis of this covenant. For him, creaturely existence is "meaningful" rather than accidental because it represents the realization of "a purpose, a plan, an order."[8] As the external basis of the covenant, "creation is the road to the covenant."[9] The covenant itself is thus the "internal basis of creation"

---

4. CD III/1, 87; KD III/1, 95.

5. CD III/1, 81; KD III/1, 88 (my translation). (I should clarify that the reason I have offered my own translation at various points in this essay is not necessarily because I think my translation is more accurate—although sometimes I think it is. It is also because of "fair use" limits on how much of CD I am able to quote.) Garrett Green offers another helpful translation of this definition of "saga": an image conceived in visionary-poetic fashion of a concretely unique, spatio-temporally limited, prehistoric temporal reality. Garrett Green, "Myth, History, and Imagination: The Creation Narratives in Bible and Theology," *Horizons in Biblical Theology* 12 (1990): 24.

6. CD III/1, 96; KD III/1, 105.

7. CD III/1, 42; KD III/1, 44 (my translation).

8. CD III/1, 229–30; KD III/1, 260.

9. CD III/1, 231; KD III/1, 261.

in that creation "was foreordained for the establishment and the history [*Geschichte*] of the covenant."[10]

> The fact that the covenant is the goal of creation is not something which is added later to the reality of the creature, as though the history of creation might equally have been succeeded by any other history. It already characterizes creation itself and as such, and therefore the being and existence of the creature. The covenant whose history had still to commence was the covenant which, as the goal appointed for creation and the creature, made creation necessary and possible, and determined and limited the creature.[11]

Mindful of this connection between creation and covenant, Barth views the creation sagas as an integral witness to the "prehistory" [*Vorgeschichte*] of Israel, which traces back to the "history" [*Geschichte*] of Adam, and is thus irreducibly integrated with "actual history [*eigentlicher Geschichte*] as it begins in Gen. 12:1."[12] So, for Barth, when God tells Abram about God's purpose for his people, God is speaking of a purpose that has already been established in and with the very beginning of creation's history. This purpose is not an optional extra that may arise should creation choose to take it on for itself. Nor is it merely an order that God decides to introduce later, in an attempt to improve the circumstances of the fallen creation. Rather, it is bound up with every facet of created reality: it is every bit as fundamental to creation's history as the physicality, temporality, and spatiality of creation. As we approach Barth's exegesis of the Genesis creation narrative, it will be critical for us to bear this in mind.

Perhaps the main reason that it is not assumed that God's purposes are fundamental to created reality is that they are not directly visible. The hiddenness of God's purposes promotes the illusion that creation is able to exist for itself, without the will of God. This is why the witness of Scripture is so vital to our understanding of created reality. "To encounter Scripture," as John Webster notes on Barth, "is to stand before a witness to something which is not simply part of the immanent historical world."[13] Scripture is a witness to the purposive activity of God, who determines the nature of created reality, and does so from beyond the immediate phenomena of the contingent order.

---

10. *CD* III/1, 231; *KD* III/1, 261–62.

11. *CD* III/1, 231; *KD* III/1, 262.

12. *CD* III/1, 63; *KD* III/1, 67 (my translation). For clarification regarding the meaning of the term "history" in *Church Dogmatics* as a translation of either *Geschichte* or *Historie*, see n. 17 below.

13. John Webster, *The Domain of the Word: Scripture and Theological Reason* (London: T&T Clark, 2012), 70.

To be this witness, Scripture does not need to provide an accurate record of natural-historical occurrence—even the most accurate record of natural history will fall absolutely short of providing a direct testimony to the invisible operations of God. If, therefore, a prophetic reimagining of history is able to provide a more succinct and meaningful witness to God's relationship to creation, then there is no reason why revelation could not happen in this way. It would be no less true for God to reveal himself through such a medium. Therefore, while Barth would be the first to recognize the importance of Scripture's being considered an accurate witness to certain historical actualities, such as the resurrection, he also understands that Scripture is, first and foremost, a witness to the eternal God who transcends contingent reality and whose purposes can be revealed every bit as much through a prophetic reimagining of history as they can through historical record. On this point, Barth quotes Adolf Schlatter approvingly:

> With all the obscurities of his historical hindsight and his prophetic foresight, the biblical narrator is the servant of God, the one who awakens the recollection of him and makes known his will. If he doesn't do it as knower, he does it as dreamer; if his eye should fail, his imagination [*Phantasie*] steps in and fills the gaps as needed. In this way he passes on the divine gift that entered into the course of history and makes it fruitful for posterity. The fact that he has to serve God not only as knower and thinker but also as poet and dreamer is grounded in the fact that he is human and we human beings are unable to arrest the transition from thought to poetry.[14]

For Barth, Scripture is held together, and made appropriate to creation, by the activity of the one God who unites all things. God's "once and for all" activity is first enacted "within the confines of space and time" with his initial act of creation. It then continues throughout the history of creation with the divine acts of providence and revelation, which are united with the act of creation by virtue of the oneness of God. Given the unity that exists in all God's activity, the communicative activity that inspires the writing of creation sagas is able to make them representative of God's actual act of creation.

2. Barth uses the term "saga" to present the creation narratives as referring to events that are prehistorical. Since creation involves the origins of time itself, it "eludes" the tools associated with historical observation and description.[15] In creation, the eternal God creates ex nihilo in a way that gives rise

---

14. Adolf Schlatter, *Das Christliche Dogma* (Stuttgart: Calwer, 1923), 337; cited in *CD* III/1, 83; *KD* III/1, 91 (I am here using Garrett Green's translation from "Myth, History, and Imagination," 28–29).

15. *CD* III/1, 42; *KD* III/1, 44.

to history. This act, therefore, is inseparable from the history that it creates. Clearly, God does not have the freedom to create without bringing something contingent into existence—there can be no creation without a subsequent history. As such, God relates to creation in a relationship that is "essentially," and not merely accidentally, "historical" [*geschichtliche*].[16] Yet, at the same time, creation is not created by a God who somehow already finds himself caught up in the history of creation, or somehow finds himself constituted by the act of creation. There is no contingency within the eternal life of God. For Barth, God is *a se*; God is God in, of, and from himself prehistorically. As such, while the act of creation is inextricable from creation history, the act itself is not historical; it is only creation as it comes into existence ex nihilo that is historical. The act of creation does not take place in time. Rather, it is out of God's act of creation that creation comes to be in time.

The creation narratives, therefore, cannot be made subject to the criteria of historical criticism because, quite simply, there were no temporal (let alone human) witnesses to observe and record the events of creation, as they are determined by God. So, while the creation narratives serve as a witness to the events that took place at the beginning of creation, it would not be possible for them to provide an actual record of these events.

    3. Barth uses the term "saga" to present the creation narratives as an intuitive-poetic image of a historical reality (Geschichtswirklichkeit). For Barth, "the concept of saga must be distinguished from that of myth, not only that of history [*Historie*]."[17] On the one hand, as we have seen, the creation sagas are intuitive: they are designed (*entworfenes*) by God's self-revelation in a way that makes them true to the nature of creation, as it exists before God. They "try to say how things actually were."[18] Unlike "godless

---

    16. *CD* III/1, 66; *KD* III/1, 71.

    17. *CD* III/1, 84; *KD* III/1, 91 (my translation). It is important here to be aware of the distinction between the German terms *Geschichte* and *Historie*, both of which are translated as "history" in the *Church Dogmatics*. Garrett Green offers an extremely helpful account of this distinction, which I would strongly endorse ("Myth, History, and Imagination," 25–29). But let me here offer a brief account of this distinction. *Historie* refers to visible history: history that can be known directly by the "objective" eyes of modern historical-critical interpreters. *Geschichte*, however, refers to the reality of history in the much broader sense, as it is created by God. This account of history can only be known with the eyes of faith, as they are given to perceive history as created history. As such, *Geschichte* includes those "non-historical" (*unhistorisch*) features of history that cannot be directly observed by modern historians or natural scientists, such as the being and purpose of the world. At the same time it also includes those features of history that can be known by modern historical criticism. For Barth, "it is necessary and imperative" for the faithful theologian to recognize "that in actual history [*Geschichte*] the 'historical' [*Historische*] and 'non-historical' [*Unhistorische*] accompany one another and belong together" (*CD* III/1, 81; *KD* III/1, 88 [my translation]).

    18. *CD* III/1, 87; *KD* III/1, 95.

myths,"[19] they depend upon God revealing himself in history. That is, they depend upon God revealing himself both to the authors of the creation sagas and also to the readers of these sagas. For Barth, therefore, "we are no less truly summoned to listen to what the Bible has to say here in the form of saga than to what it has to say in other places in the form of history [*Historie*]."[20] The Genesis sagas should be read neither as the story of a fantastic order nor as the story of an order that has been lost following the fall of Adam. Again, they are a witness to God's purposes that continue to encompass creation. For Barth, as Nathan MacDonald points out, the first two chapters of Genesis must be taken to refer to "genuine events"; otherwise we end up denying "the connection between Israel's pre-history and her history."[21] On the other hand, the sagas cannot be understood as "history in the historicist sense [*historische Geschichte*]."[22] The creation sagas do not offer an account of natural-historical phenomena that could be verified by scientific observation. Rather, they are a poetic rendering of history.

While Barth does not think that the Genesis creation narratives offer a report of natural history, he does think that they offer a true witness to the way that God relates to the history of creation. As sagas, they are to be read as historical (*geschichtlich*) narratives that speak to us of the nature of creation's history. Further, they are to be interpreted as the beginning of Scripture's narrative of God's engagement with history. Reflecting on Genesis 2, Barth writes: "What happens there is narrated wholly in the manner and with the colors of this following history [*Geschichte*]."[23]

As we turn now to look at Barth's exegesis of Genesis 2:8–17, it will be important to be aware of the way in which he interprets this text as a historical witness to God and his purpose for creation: God's purpose to "enable" a covenant history with humanity.[24] For Barth, "the history of this covenant is as much the goal of creation as creation itself is the beginning of this history."[25] As we shall notice, Barth's understanding of the relationship between creation and covenant exerts a clear influence on his exegesis of Genesis 2:8–17.[26]

19. 1 Tim. 4:7; cf. 1 Tim. 1:4; 2 Tim. 4:4.

20. CD III/1, 83; KD III/1, 90.

21. Nathan MacDonald, "The Imago Dei and Election: Reading Genesis 1:26–28 and Old Testament Scholarship with Karl Barth," *International Journal of Systematic Theology* 10 (2008): 312.

22. CD III/1, 78; KD III/1, 84.

23. CD III/1, 232; KD III/1, 263 (my translation).

24. CD III/1, 42; KD III/1, 44 (my translation).

25. CD III/1, 42; KD III/1, 44.

26. That said, it is interesting and perhaps surprising to note that while, for Barth, "the history of God's covenant with man has its beginning, its centre and its culmination in Jesus

Barth's Exegesis of Genesis 2:8–17

The second passage of the second creation saga (Gen. 2:8–17) deals with the planting of a Garden in Eden as the dwelling place of the man,[27] with its trees and rivers, with the divine commission to the man, with the permission and prohibition given to him.[28]

One of the things that, for Barth, distinguishes the Yahwist saga of creation (Gen. 2:4–3:24) from the Priestly saga (Gen. 1:1–2:3) is that, in the Yahwist saga, "we find that we are here, from the very beginning, in *mediis rebus* [in the middle of things]."[29] In the Yahwist saga, we are told of the way that the creature exists meaningfully within creation: as the work of God who creates the world to have purpose, plan, and order. For Barth, the creature cannot escape God's purposes for creation any more than it can escape its created-ness. The creature is limited by this fact. However, as Fergus Kerr remarks, the creature is not limited in a way that implies curtailment, impoverishment, or deprivation.[30] As the creature finds itself limited by the grace of God, it is limited by the eternal truth; it is limited by the life that it has been given to live within creation.

As we turn now to Barth's exegesis of this passage, we shall learn what these limits mean to human existence within the Garden. We shall also learn how they anticipate what is to come in the subsequent narrative. In engaging Barth's exegesis, we shall reflect the way in which he himself dissects this passage, as this is key to his approach.

Verse 8

In his exegesis of verse 8, Barth takes special care to think about how we should interpret the nature of the Garden in Eden. He interprets "Eden" to mean "delight," and interprets the Garden in Eden as a kind of "pleasure garden" (*Wonnegarten*).[31] But, being meticulous, he notes that readers need to be careful not to jump too quickly to accept the Greek translation of the Garden as "Paradise" (παράδεισος).

Christ" (*CD* III/1, 42; *KD* III/1, 44), Christology exerts very little influence on his exegesis of this passage—although, as one would expect, it is never far from his mind.

27. Given the particular passage with which we are dealing, there will be a tendency for this essay to refer to "man" or "the man." The reason for this gender-exclusive language is that "the woman" is not yet on the scene.

28. *CD* III/1, 249; *KD* III/1, 283.

29. *CD* III/1, 232; *KD* III/1, 263 (my translation).

30. Fergus Kerr, *Immortal Longings: Versions of Transcending Humanity* (London: SPCK, 1997), 38.

31. *CD* III/1, 250; *KD* III/1, 284.

What is it that distinguishes a "pleasure garden" from a "paradise"? In his exegesis of this verse, Barth is concerned to recognize the precise meaning of the term "garden." Drawing on the original Persian and then also on the Hebrew, he points out that the term "garden" refers to "a walled-in and therefore an enclosed and limited place, e.g., a royal park."[32] Also, he points out that the Garden in Eden is elsewhere referred to as the "Garden of Elohim" or the "Garden of Yahweh" (Ezek. 28:13; 31:8–9). Bearing these two things in mind, Barth interprets the Garden of Eden as an enclosed and limited space that God purposefully plants in Eden.[33] This Garden is holy land: it belongs to God, it is defined by God, and it is governed by God.

In contrast to Barth's reading here, a number of commentators, including Terje Stordalen, Gerhard von Rad, and Claus Westermann, have played down the association of the Garden of Eden with the "Garden of God." They have done so in order to make it clear that the Garden of Eden is not to be misinterpreted as an eternal dwelling place of God.[34] Barth would agree that such an overly literal interpretation would be problematic and is careful not to invite such a reading. However, he also thinks that it is important that readers are alert to the close connection between these two descriptions of the Garden in order to help them recognize the close relationship that God has with the Garden.

We can begin to see here a few ways in which Barth's deep appreciation for the connection between creation and covenant may be influencing his exegesis. That is, we are able to notice some ways in which his interpretation of the Garden aligns (conveniently) with his interpretation of God's covenant. First, Barth recognizes that God's covenant establishes an enclosed and limited space like the Garden, within which the creature's purpose is defined in the world. Second, both the Garden and the covenant belong to God, and God determines what it means for humanity to belong to God within creation. Third, humanity was created, from the beginning, to be placed within the history of God's covenant, just as Adam was created to be placed in the Garden. Again, the covenant was not a later development that God introduced to establish order within creation.

For Barth, God places the man in the Garden to realize a particular purpose within a particular space. The Garden is a place where the man finds

---

32. CD III/1, 250; KD III/1, 284.

33. As Gordon Wenham points out, this verse is the only place where the phrase "in Eden" occurs. Gordon Wenham, *Genesis 1–15*, Word Biblical Commentary 1 (Dallas: Word, 1998), 61.

34. Terje Stordalen, *Echoes of Eden: Genesis 2–3 and Symbolism of the Eden Garden in Biblical Hebrew Literature* (Leuven: Peeters, 2000), 298; Gerhard von Rad, *Genesis: A Commentary* (Philadelphia: Westminster, 1972), 78; Claus Westermann, *Genesis 1–11: A Commentary*, trans. John J. Scullion, SJ (London: SPCK, 1984), 208.

pleasure and delight in the sanctuary of God's presence.[35] It is a place where he finds fulfillment not in a life that he makes for himself but in the life that he is given by God. The paradise of the Garden, therefore, is not defined by subjective human caprice: it is not paradise in the sense that it conforms to the human's idea of paradise. Having said that, Barth does think that the Garden may well correspond to a person's mental image of paradise. Indeed, he compares the Garden to the well-watered plain of the Jordan (Gen. 13:10) and the future Zion (Isa. 51:3), and he also describes it as an oasis that would have conformed to many people's idea of paradise.[36] The paradisiacal nature of the Garden is not to be defined with recourse to some subjective aesthetic value. Rather, for Barth, it requires to be interpreted theologically. The Garden in Eden is a place where the man is given to repose in the presence of God and thereby find joy and fulfillment. Importantly, this interpretation is not merely the product of "free theologizing,"[37] but would appear to be true to the ancient Near Eastern context of its author. As John Walton notes, "When we consider the Garden of Eden in its ancient context, we find it is more sacred space than green space . . . and its significance has more to do with divine presence than human paradise."[38]

In sum, Barth's reading of verse 8 does not differ dramatically from other readings. It does, however, have its own particular character that is distinguished by his recognition of the connection between creation and covenant—between the creation sagas and the later accounts of covenant history. If Barth is right to approach the text with this in mind, the distinctive moves he makes are not only appropriate but also illuminating.

Verse 9

Verse 9 makes it clear that God made both the tree of life and the tree of the knowledge of good and evil. Later, in verses 16–17, God commands that the man may "freely eat of every tree of the Garden; but of the tree of the knowledge of good and evil you shall not eat, for in the day that you eat of it you shall die" (NRSV). With these verses in mind, verse 9 could be seen to

35. In alignment with Barth, K. E. Greene McCreight insightfully refers to the Garden as a "spatial Sabbath which corresponds to the 'temporal sanctuary in the first saga' which introduces the Sabbath." K. E. Greene McCreight, *Ad Litteram: How Augustine, Calvin, and Barth Read the "Plain Sense" of Genesis 1–3* (New York: Peter Lang, 1999), 195; see *CD* III/1, 254; *KD* III/1, 288.

36. *CD* III/1, 277; *KD* III/1, 316.

37. *Romans II*, ix.

38. John Walton, *The Lost World of Adam and Eve* (Downers Grove, IL: InterVarsity, 2015), 116.

raise a difficult question: Why would God make the tree of the knowledge of good and evil if he intended to prohibit the man from eating from it? For Gerhard von Rad, such speculation is "not permissible; the question cannot be discussed." He continues: "Nothing is said to indicate that God combined pedagogical intentions with this prohibition (in the sense of a 'moral' development of man). On the contrary, one destroys the essential part of the story with such rationalistic explanations. Man in his original state was completely subject to God's command, and the question, 'Who will say to him, What doest thou?' (Job 9.12; Dan. 4.35b) was equally out of place in Paradise."[39]

Barth would agree about the impropriety of such speculation. However, if we are to interpret Genesis 2 as saga rather than historical report, then Barth thinks that we can ask what God's placing the two trees there tells us about the nature of the Garden. It is also appropriate to ask about what it contributes to the message of the saga.

Like most readers of Genesis 2, Barth's exegesis of verse 9 anticipates verses 16–17. For him, the presence of the tree of knowledge indicates that the Garden is not free from "serious problems."[40] Yet he does not think that the tree endangers man.[41] By making this tree, God does not turn the Garden into a threatening situation. As Bill Arnold notes, the Garden still remains a place of "peace and tranquility," so long as the man is willing "to hear God's command to stay away from a single tree."[42] The presence of the two trees simply turns the Garden into a place where the man finds himself at a crossroads; the presence of the tree of knowledge means that obedience to God is not inevitable. For Barth, the two roads that the man faces in the Garden prefigure the two roads that are faced by the people of Israel. As Nathan MacDonald points out: "For both [the man and the people of Israel] continued existence in the land depends on obedience to the divine law. The presence of the two trees in the garden 'prefigures' (*vorbildet*) the alternative possibilities of Israel's existence: on the one hand, life through the law and the tabernacle, on the other, destruction and ruin. This is the mark of its election."[43]

But Barth has more to say about each of the trees. To appreciate fully his exegesis of verse 9, it will be helpful to look more closely at the way in which he thinks that the description of each of these trees prefigures the history of

39. Von Rad, *Genesis*, 80–81.

40. *CD* III/1, 250; *KD* III/1, 284.

41. *CD* III/1, 263; *KD* III/1, 299.

42. Bill T. Arnold, *Genesis*, New Cambridge Bible Commentary (Cambridge: Cambridge University Press, 2008), 59.

43. MacDonald, "*Imago Dei* and Election," 319.

Israel's participation within God's covenant. To start, let us first look at his interpretation of the tree of life.

For Barth, the tree of life "has a special relationship with the Lord of this Garden."[44] He writes:

> The tree of life has the position and function that the tabernacle will later have in the camp of Israel in the wilderness, and the temple in Jerusalem in the promised and given land, and the Holiest of Holies in the tabernacle and the temple. In the midst of the Garden, in the special place of the tree of life, what is tangibly prefigured is that there can and will be only one sanctuary in the holy land and on the whole earth: that which is chosen by God Himself.[45]

By making the tree of life to grow in the midst of the Garden, God gives the Garden a center: a heart that is a sign of the life that God breathes into the Garden. In the center of the Garden, the tree gives form to the Garden in the way that the tabernacle gives shape to Israel's camp in the desert, in the way that the temple gives shape to Jerusalem, and in the way that the holiest of holies gives shape to both the tabernacle and the temple. With this form, the Garden is given to be a place of worship, in which life is oriented toward God, and in which fullness of life is found in obedient fellowship with God. As Dietrich Bonhoeffer writes on this verse (referring to the man as Adam): "Adam has life in the unity of unbroken obedience to the Creator—has life just because Adam lives from the center of life, and is oriented toward the center of life, without placing Adam's own life at the center."[46]

To be clear, the form that the tree of life gives to the Garden is a visible form: a form that is able to reveal to the man the shape for which God created the Garden. The created form of the Garden—to which the visible form corresponds and witnesses—is established by the "wholly invisible operations of God."[47] So, for Barth, the primary purpose of the tree is to be a visible sign that tells the man where he is, to whom the Garden belongs, what he should expect, and who he is in this place.[48] The tree reveals the nature of life in the Garden by telling the man that his life revolves around its source: the God who creates and gives life. It provides a sign that he needs to look to God to

---

44. *CD* III/1, 282; *KD* III/1, 322 (my translation).

45. *CD* III/1, 282; *KD* III/1, 322 (my translation).

46. Dietrich Bonhoeffer, *Creation and Fall: A Theological Exposition of Genesis 1–3*, ed. Martin Rüter and Ilse Tödt, English ed. John W. de Gruchy, trans. Douglas Stephen Bax, Dietrich Bonhoeffer's Works 3 (Minneapolis: Fortress, 1997), 84.

47. W. Zimmerli, *1. Mose 1–11* (Zurich: Zwingli Verlag, 1943), 27, cited in *CD* III/1, 78; *KD* III/1, 84.

48. *CD* III/1, 256; *KD* III/1, 291.

understand his life.[49] It tells him that he does not live simply because he has a beating heart and the ability to breathe; he lives by virtue of his special relation to God and, as such, in virtue of his special purpose. The tree of life points to God, who is beyond the immanence of the Garden, and tells the man that God determines his life in the Garden, and so he must look to God to understand his humanity. By so doing, the tree of life prefigures the voice of God, which is heard and witnessed by Moses and the prophets.[50]

To elaborate on what I have said so far, there are three things in particular that Barth thinks the tree of life tells us about the nature of created reality.

First, the tree of life is a sign that God is present for the man in the midst of the Garden as the one who is the source of his life.[51] Why is this the case? Clearly, the tree itself is not itself the source of life; God is the source of life. However, the fact that this tree is named "the tree of life" means that it is in some way representative of God. The tree is the visible sign of the invisible God. One of the key reasons that God makes and names this visible sign, for Barth, is to give the man a constant reminder that human life is to be lived in gratitude to God. Life in the Garden should not be taken for granted but should be known and enjoyed as a God-given life. To be clear, this does not mean that human life is burdened by a need to thank God continuously. Rather, it is a sign that human life finds fulfillment in gratitude: human beings discover their humanity in grateful response to "the good news of this life."[52]

Second, the tree is "the sign that [the man] can live."[53] Interestingly, Barth suggests that the tree prefigures the sacrifice that would take place in the midst of the Israelite community so that the Israelites might know of their deliverance and salvation. The connection that Barth points out between this tree and the later sacrifices in Scripture appears slightly forced. However, Barth does not overstate this connection. This connection makes some sense, he

49. For Barth, v. 9 prompts readers to think about why God would make a tree and call it the tree of life when it does not appear that the man needs to eat from this tree in order to live (see *CD* III/1, 256; *KD* III/1, 291). The obvious answer, for him, is that God creates it to be a sign. However, not all commentators would agree that the man does not need to eat from the tree of life to live. James McKeown, e.g., thinks that the presence of the "tree of life suggests that the human beings were mortal but that eternal life was within their grasp while they lived in Eden" (*Genesis* [Grand Rapids: Eerdmans, 2008], 33). That said, it is hard to see why Barth would have any major difficulties with McKeown's reading. The major difference between their two readings would seem to be that McKeown primarily interprets the tree of life as the source of life, whereas Barth would primarily interpret God (whom the tree of life represents) as the source of life.

50. CD III/1, 269; KD III/1, 307.
51. CD III/1, 257; KD III/1, 292.
52. CD III/1, 257; KD III/1, 292 (my translation).
53. CD III/1, 269; KD III/1, 307.

suggests, if we recognize the tree as a sign "that all that could happen and had to happen for its [the man's or Israel's] sake is done and accomplished."[54] He continues: "The sign represents the accomplished fact of its deliverance and salvation. God has made it a nation; God has brought it to this place; God is present to it in this place: the wholly distant God is wholly close to it."[55]

Third, the tree indicates that the Garden is God's sanctuary.[56] It is a sign that God is present with and for the creature, as the co-inhabitant who offers and guarantees life and peace to the man.[57] As such, the Garden is the man's proper "home": it is a place that is true to the life that God created him to live.[58] In return, the presence of the tree indicates that the Garden is a home in which God wishes to be "known, honored, and loved."[59] In this way, as suggested above, it prefigures "the tabernacle and later the temple and the special ministry entrusted to it":[60] in the temple and the tabernacle, God "dwells in the midst of Israel and possesses a definite place."[61]

For Barth, the purpose of the tree of the knowledge of good and evil is very different. Anticipating the rest of chapter 2, he notes that the tree of knowledge "is not, according to its name and thus by virtue of its nature, . . . the sign of a reality given to man by God."[62] Rather, it is "the warning sign of a possibility which, if he were to realize it, would be the opposite of the life and salvation promised to him, which would be his ruin and his downfall."[63]

As we saw in Barth's exegesis of verse 8, God creates the man to live a particular kind of life in the Garden of Eden, which conforms to the covenant in which he was elected to participate. He "lives by the fact that God alone has given him this land according to His wisdom and justice."[64] That is, God decides to create the man to live in covenant fellowship with God, so it is within this covenant that he finds the promise and hope that characterize the humanity for which he was created. For Barth, "everything depends

---

54. CD III/1, 269; KD III/1, 307.

55. CD III/1, 269; KD III/1, 307 (my translation).

56. CD III/1, 282; KD III/1, 322.

57. Barth points out that the book of Proverbs deploys the idea of a tree of life in various proverbial images related to flourishing human existence (CD III/1, 282; KD III/1, 322).

58. CD III/1, 257; KD III/1, 292.

59. CD III/1, 282; KD III/1, 322 (my translation).

60. CD III/1, 269; KD III/1, 307.

61. CD III/1, 480; KD III/1, 540. This connection is also pointed out by a number of other commentators, such as Gordon Wenham, who notes: "There are many other features of the garden that suggest it is seen as an archetypical sanctuary, prefiguring the later tabernacle and temples" (Genesis 1–15, 61).

62. CD III/1, 257; KD III/1, 292–93 (my translation).

63. CD III/1, 270; KD III/1, 308 (my translation).

64. CD III/1, 270; KD III/1, 308 (my translation).

upon its [the creature's] acceptance of the sovereignty and uniqueness of this decision."[65]

So, again, God's covenant purpose for the creature is central. It is fundamental to the created (or real) nature of the human being. The fact that creation is brought into being with the express purpose of establishing the covenant relationship (held forth in the history of God's dealing with Israel) means that there is no room for the man to possess his own independent knowledge of good and evil. Any such knowledge would stand over against the knowledge that is appropriate to the particular life that God gives to him in the Garden. For Barth, God does not create the man with a capacity to choose another life or another humanity for himself, based on his own judgment. There is no other humanity; there is no other life. Nor is there any middle ground between humanity and inhumanity, between life and death. The fruit of the tree of knowledge is poisonous precisely because it directs the human subject away from his life-giving purpose—and, as such, it is the alternative to the tree of life. The saga of the two trees, for Barth, as we shall see further below, indicates an "order in which Yahweh Elohim and His revelation will encounter man, and in which man will always and everywhere encounter Him."[66]

Why is this? Barth explains with both the man and the people of Israel in mind:

> This is not because God envies it the joy of its own choice and therefore its own decision, but because He knows that it can find true joy only in His divine choice and decision; that with every act of self-choice and self-justification, with every attempt to understand and to that extent accomplish its own distinction, even if only secondarily, it simply pronounces its own death sentence instead of living in it. Its distinction from other nations is that it is elected without having elected itself, without being able even secondarily to base its election on its own goodness and strength or other excellent attributes. The power of the promise given to it is that its content is the goodness of God, resting on Himself alone and not on anything else. To rejoice in it, Israel had to live on this goodness of His election which has no basis except in God, on the ground of His knowledge of good and evil.[67]

The connection that Barth draws between the underlying God-given purpose and the nature of human life is not picked up to the same extent by many other commentators. This is because Barth's theological reasoning has

65. *CD* III/1, 270; *KD* III/1, 308.
66. *CD* III/1, 272–73; *KD* III/1, 311.
67. *CD* III/1, 270; *KD* III/1, 308.

a clear influence on his interpretation of this verse. Indeed, at various points in his exegesis of verse 9, Barth "brings" a series of theological insights to the text. This encourages him to "see" a great deal more in the verse than might be apparent from a more direct exegetical process. What drives this is his conviction that the Genesis creation narratives prefigure so much that is to come. For him, "all that happened later could only be the unfolding of the wisdom already at work there [in the Garden]."[68]

Verses 10–14

Reflecting on this passage, Barth notes that the Garden of Eden is presented as "a real place on earth," insofar as it seems to refer to the physical earth in which we now find ourselves.[69] For Barth, it is an important feature of the second creation narrative that it offers an account that seems "so close to the 'historical' [*historischen*] . . . that the inquisitive question, Where was Paradise situated? is continually raised and can never be wholly silenced."[70] This means that "like the land of Canaan, it is [presented as] a definite earthy space"; it is not merely "an elysian wonderland."[71] However, he also adds that "to be true to this passage, we must drop the question [of its geographical location] as soon as it is raised."[72] And he goes on to describe the river system as "hydrographically impossible and geographically indefinite."[73]

One of the primary roles of this passage, for Barth, would seem to be its attempt to connect the second creation narrative with the real world. If this is the case, this passage provides support for his reading of this narrative as saga ("historicized" myth) rather than pure myth.[74]

68. *CD* III/1, 282; *KD* III/1, 307.
69. *CD* III/1, 253; *KD* III/1, 287.
70. *CD* III/1, 253; *KD* III/1, 287.
71. *CD* III/1, 267; *KD* III/1, 305.
72. *CD* III/1, 253; *KD* III/1, 287.
73. *CD* III/1, 280; *KD* III/1, 320. Another point that Barth touches upon (*CD* III/1, 277; *KD* III/1, 316) but could have developed further, in line with his concern to emphasize the connection between creation and covenant, is the possibility that the source of the four rivers corresponds to the "holy mountain of God" (Deut. 33:2; Pss. 3:4; 15:1; 24:3; 43:3; 48:1; 99:9; Isa. 11:9; 27:13; 30:29; 56:7; 57:13; 65:11, 25; 66:20; Ezek. 20:40; 43:12; Zech. 8:3), the mountain where God dwells or is present.
74. Claus Westermann is another exegete who takes note of the author's attempt to link the "information" about paradise with geography. Westermann, however, has his own view as to why the author does this (although there are definitely connections between the two readings). For Westermann, the role of this passage "is to state that the rivers which bring fertility (= blessing) to the world have their origin in the river which brings fertility (= blessing) to the garden of God." He continues: "The intention of the author in inserting 2:10–14 was not to

Something else that Barth finds interesting about this passage is what it has to say about water. Reflecting on the first saga (and elsewhere in Scripture), he notes that water is presented as "the dangerous element of chaos and death hemmed in and held back by God."[75] But, in the second saga (and, again, elsewhere in Scripture), it is also presented as a necessary requirement for life, given to human beings by God. And what we see in this passage is God controlling the waters in ways that prevent chaos: "the water is no longer averted and restrained but is called forth by God; it is no longer the subdued enemy of man but his most intimate friend; it is no longer his ruin but his salvation; it is not the principle of death, but that of life."[76]

For Barth, the description of the way in which God engages with water symbolizes the way in which God orders creation in the history of the covenant. God's "purpose is not only the preservation but the transformation of man and the cosmos."[77] In this way, the second creation saga builds on the first by telling the reader a bit more about what it means for God to enact his purposes vis-à-vis creation. Indeed, for Barth, the bestowal of order on the waters (creating a life-giving force out of formless chaos) projects forward to the culmination of history, in which "life will consume death, in all its serious danger, and death itself, in spite of its dangerousness, will become life."[78] For Barth, when we take some of these nuances and symbolic pointers into account, these verses (10–14) "are better not described as 'sterile Paradise-geography' (Zimmerli). They are full of prophetic content."[79] So much so that if these verses were indeed a later addition to the text, as a number of commentators suggest, then "one cannot be grateful enough that they were added."[80]

Verse 15

Barth has very little to say about verse 15, but, like most commentators, he thinks it warrants attention as a stand-alone verse. This verse tells

---

determine where paradise lay, as the majority of interpreters hold, but rather to point out—by way of parenthesis and at the place where a land (Eden) with its garden is first mentioned—that the 'life-arteries' of all lands of the earth have their source in the river that watered paradise." Like Barth, Westermann then goes on to note: "It does more justice to the text to distinguish clearly what is significant and what is not and to set aside hypotheses that are not soundly based" (*Genesis 1–11*, 215–16).

75. *CD* III/1, 279; *KD* III/1, 318.
76. *CD* III/1, 280; *KD* III/1, 320 (my translation).
77. *CD* III/1, 280; *KD* III/1, 320.
78. *CD* III/1, 281; *KD* III/1, 320 (my translation).
79. *CD* III/1, 281; *KD* III/1, 321.
80. *CD* III/1, 281; *KD* III/1, 321.

readers that the man was ordained to work in the Garden and that, prior to the fall, "perfect joy and work are not . . . divorced."[81] In the Garden, God gives the man a vocation in which he finds fulfillment by taking care of the land that God has prepared for him. The Garden is not a place of idle relaxation, "of leisure or luxury but a glorious sphere of activity" that corresponds to God's purposive creative act.[82] The man was not created and then given a purpose; rather, he was intentionally created with a purpose. In alignment with Barth, Claus Westermann notes: "Human work then, is a mandate from God to his creatures, is a necessary part of the exchange between God and his people. Work is a determining factor in a God-created person. The dignity which belongs to civilization rests on the mandate of God to his creatures."[83]

Barth's interpretation of this verse aligns with most other exegetes, although he adds a comment that others may implicitly assume: namely, just as it is useless to inquire as to the Garden's geographical location, so it is useless "to ask about the practical necessity of 'cultivation,' and the enemies or dangers from which man is to 'defend' the Garden of God."[84] For Barth, readers should recognize that the specific reference to cultivation is meant to have a broader significance, that of representing the variety of ways in which human beings may be called to serve God. This is a point that finds further support when Gordon Wenham notes that the verb עבד, "to serve, till," is also "commonly used in a religious sense of serving God (e.g. Deut. 4:19), and in priestly texts, especially of the tabernacle duties of the Levites (Num. 3:7–8; 4:23–24, 26, etc.)."[85]

Verses 16–17

When human beings eventually disobey God and choose to eat from the tree of the knowledge of good and evil, Barth notes that there is an intermediate stage, before death, in which their eyes are opened to the knowledge of good and evil. Most of Barth's engagement with verses 16–17 attends to the question of why God would command human beings not to eat of the tree of knowledge.

There is much debate among biblical scholars and theologians as to what precisely it means for a person to gain the knowledge of good and evil—

81. *CD* III/1, 278; *KD* III/1, 317.
82. *CD* III/1, 277; *KD* III/1, 316.
83. Westermann, *Genesis 1–11*, 222.
84. *CD* III/1, 278; *KD* III/1, 317 (my translation).
85. Wenham, *Genesis 1–15*, 67.

and Gordon Wenham offers a helpful examination of the variety of interpretations of this.[86] Some scholars have interpreted it to mean moral dis-
cernment.[87] This interpretation is largely dismissed, however, because the
author seems to assume that the man already possesses this by virtue of
recognizing that it is wrong to eat from the tree of knowledge. Other scholars
have interpreted it to mean omniscience. However, there is no indication that
one becomes omniscient by eating from the tree.[88] The interpretation that
Wenham considers most promising is the interpretation of the knowledge
of good and evil as divine wisdom: "a wisdom that is God's sole preserve,
which man should not aspire to attain (e.g., Job 15:7–9, 40; Prov. 30:1–4),
since a full understanding of God, the universe, and humanity's place in it
is ultimately beyond human comprehension."[89] He continues: "To pursue
it without reference to revelation is to assert human autonomy, and to neglect the fear of the LORD which is the beginning of knowledge (Prov. 1:7)."[90]
W. Malcolm Clark also interprets the knowledge of good and evil as referring to a moral autonomy whereby individuals illegitimately take it upon
themselves to distinguish between what is right or wrong, and do so apart
from the command of God.[91]

Barth's interpretation of the knowledge of good and evil would seem to
align with Wenham's and Clark's. For Barth, the knowledge of good and evil
entails that the man can differentiate between "what is and what should not
be."[92] In this way, it "is to be like God, to be oneself the Creator and Lord
of the creature."[93] For Barth, God distinguishes himself from the creature by
the fact that it is God alone who orders creation, according to his covenant
purposes, and thereby distinguishes between good and evil. The man is thus
created to accept and respond to God's command about what should and
should not be done—regardless of his own view on the matter. He is not
created with his own basic ability to judge God's judgment according to his
own knowledge of good and evil. As Augustine puts it, God does not create
humanity to possess its own capacity for knowledge with which it can proudly

86. Wenham, *Genesis 1–15*, 63–64.
87. See Karl Budde, *Die biblische Urgeschichte (Gen 1–12, 5) untersucht* (Giessen: J. Ricker, 1883).
88. See von Rad, *Genesis*, 80–81; Howard N. Wallace, *The Eden Narrative*, Harvard Semitic Monographs (Atlanta: Scholars Press, 1985), 128; and Frederick Eiselen, "The Tree of the Knowledge of Good and Evil," *The Biblical World* 36 (1910): 104.
89. Wenham, *Genesis 1–15*, 63.
90. Wenham, *Genesis 1–15*, 63.
91. W. Malcolm Clark, "A Legal background to the Yahwist's Use of 'Good and Evil' in Genesis 2–3," *Journal of Biblical Literature* 88 (1969): 266–78.
92. *CD* III/1, 257–58; *KD* III/1, 293 (my translation).
93. *CD* III/1, 258; *KD* III/1, 293.

"turn to itself with its back to God."[94] For Barth, the tree of the knowledge of good and evil reveals the "possibility of an unheard of exaltation of the creature."[95]

As already noted, the final consequence of eating of the tree is death. So, for Barth, eating of this tree "would be to him as if he had taken poison and only had minutes or hours before it came to take necessary effect. It is because of this existing danger that the prohibition is made."[96] The prohibition to eat from the tree, therefore, for Barth, is "revealed as an act of God's fatherly care."[97] He qualifies: "The meaning is not, therefore, that God first prohibits and then adds a threat in order to give the prohibition weight, but that God prohibits because He wants to safeguard man against the threat connected with the doing of what is prohibited."[98] What happens when the man breaks the commandment and eats of the tree of the knowledge of good and evil? For Barth, the presence of God becomes "intolerable."[99]

The prohibition, therefore, serves to protect the man from trying to realize something for himself that is only appropriate for God. If he is to function properly in the Garden, for Barth, he needs to respect the appropriate place of his creatureliness before the Creator. Death is not simply a punishment for transgressions but a description of what happens after transgression. God's purpose is life-giving; just as blood must flow through human veins, and oxygen through human lungs, God's purpose must be realized in human life. So, for human life to be sustained, human beings need to correspond to the tree of life and the purpose it represents. The human creature needs to obey the one who is the source of life.

Conclusion

Barth approaches his exegesis of Genesis 2:8–17 with a faithful perception of the one God who holds creation and covenant together, and who knits Scripture together as a witness to him. Not for a moment does he think that he should cease to refer back to the divine acts of grace. Never does he pretend that God does not exist and act in history, nor does he think that theological commitments should be set aside for the purposes of historical exegesis. Such

94. Augustine, *On Genesis: A Refutation of the Manichees*, in *On Genesis*, ed. John E. Rotelle, trans. Edmund Hill (New York: New York City Press, 2013), 79.
95. *CD* III/1, 258; *KD* III/1, 293.
96. *CD* III/1, 259; *KD* III/1, 294 (my translation).
97. *CD* III/1, 259; *KD* III/1, 294.
98. *CD* III/1, 259; *KD* III/1, 294.
99. *CD* III/1, 283; *KD* III/1, 324.

maneuvering would be improper to the proper object of his exegesis; it would be improper not only to his faith but also to his intellectual commitment to the scientific pursuit of truth. Instead, his exegesis is conditioned by his faithful awareness of the way things really are: an awareness that is awakened by the grace of the God who speaks into creation history—both to the authors and readers of Scripture.

As God speaks into history, God tells creation about its history. God does this through the words of Scripture, through which creatures are given a way to develop a more complete picture of created reality—with which we can then return to Scripture to develop a more complete understanding of its message. But when God designs Scripture, he allows the human imagination to play a part in the reception of God's communicative presence. This means that the genres of saga, poetry, and psalmody each have a role in testifying to God and the works of God, and thereby to the true nature of created reality. As we have seen, Barth's exegesis of Genesis 2:8–17 provides a prime example of the way in which a reimagined account of history can serve as such a witness to the nature of created reality as it is determined and purposed by God. With a faithful attentiveness to the text, Barth is not only able to help us understand the direct meaning of the text but also able to help lay bare a deeper meaning of the text that is only illumined once we have seen the allusions that point to the profound interconnection between God's intention in creation and his overarching covenant purpose.

ELEVEN

Barth on God's Graciousness toward Humanity in Genesis 1–2

CHRISTINA N. LARSEN

Introduction

This essay evaluates Karl Barth's exegesis of Genesis 1–2 in *Church Dogmatics* III/1 with respect to conclusions he finds there concerning God's graciousness toward humanity in creation. Taking up the bulk of the part-volume, §41 ("Creation and Covenant") supplies Barth's predominant discussion of the passage and, curiously, does so as a rare candidly exegetical passage of the *Dogmatics* not relegated to the fine print. Here Barth begins to unfold the economic implications of the bold supralapsarianism of *CD* II/2, finding Genesis to present a pair of "sagas" that together clarify the relationship between creation and the eternal covenant of grace. In this, Barth finds Genesis 1–2 to be the ideal text for initiating his discussion of true humanity as the covenant partner of God, so much so that he allows the text to provide the outline for this initiation. The result is a full-bodied analysis of "creation as the external basis of the covenant" and "the covenant as the internal basis of creation" that climaxes in a profound account of the glory of God's free love in creation.[1]

1. On the relationship between creation and the covenant of grace in Barth, see Kathryn Tanner, "Creation and Providence," in *The Cambridge Companion to Karl Barth*, ed. John Webster (Cambridge: Cambridge University Press, 2000), 111–26; and John Webster, *Barth's Ethics of Reconciliation* (Cambridge: Cambridge University Press, 1995), 59–98.

While relatively few engagements with Barth's theology grapple with *CD* III/1 at length, the familiar theological disputes in Barth studies are deeply concerned with what Barth establishes in §41. However, recognizing that an awareness of a passage's dogmatic location is vital for a comprehensive interaction with any portion of the *Dogmatics*, the modest goal of this essay is to appreciate Barth's exegesis in §41 on its own. Specifically, this essay will appreciate particulars of his exegesis that are often passed over in dogmatic-level discussion in order to evaluate the exegetical integrity of what he finds concerning God's graciousness toward humanity in the creation narratives.[2]

Despite this intentionally limited focus, such an appreciation is nonetheless challenging given *how* Barth's commitment to know creation by faith in Christ complicates his exegetical approach toward Genesis 1–2 within §41. Barth's commitment to such a knowledge of creation leads him to reject a historical-critical reading of the creation narratives, eschewing a dominating concern with *Historie* for a focus on *Geschichte* that entails that he read the passage as the revealed prehistory of God's dealings in the covenant of grace. However, perhaps owing to his belief that an attempt to interpret Scripture detached from a sufficient understanding of Scripture's historicity will not comprehend the fullness of Scripture's witness, he nonetheless utilizes historical criticism in service to this focus throughout §41.[3] The closest Barth comes in §41 to articulating how he ensures the fidelity of the ensuing approach is his insistence that he must attend to the creation narratives (1) as part of the prehistory of Israel, recognizing that they depict "genuine events" rather than "timeless, metaphysical, or physical explanations" and must be understood in light of the history of Israel and its fulfillment in Christ;[4] and (2) as saga, recognizing that they are prehistorical and thus poetic, yet, unlike myth, deeply literal, so one must attend to their details as such.[5]

2. Barth is clear that God's work of creation is not identical with the covenant of grace, but that it is gracious insofar as it "points" and "prepares for" his work in the covenant (*CD* III/1, 97).
3. On these commitments and their developments, see Richard E. Burnett, *Karl Barth's Theological Exegesis: The Hermeneutical Principles of the* Römerbrief *Period* (Grand Rapids: Eerdmans, 2001); and George Hunsinger, "Postcritical Scriptural Interpretation: Rudolf Smend on Karl Barth," in *Thy Word Is Truth: Barth on Scripture*, ed. George Hunsinger (Grand Rapids: Eerdmans, 2012), 29–48. For a detailed theological account of Barth's views, see Donald Wood, *Barth's Theology of Interpretation* (Aldershot, UK: Ashgate, 2007).
4. *CD* III/1, 64. See also 63–65. For Barth, it is in this way that the creation narratives, no less than the rest of Scripture, ultimately witness to Christ.
5. *CD* III/1, 81–87. On Barth's preference for reading Gen. 1–2 as saga in light of his *Historie-Geschichte* distinction, see David F. Ford, *Barth and God's Story: Biblical Narrative and the Theological Method of Karl Barth in the Church Dogmatics* (Eugene, OR: Wipf & Stock, 2008), 105–9; and Garrett Green, "Myth, History, and Imagination: The Creation Narratives in Bible and Theology," *Horizons in Biblical Theology* 12 (1990): 19–38, esp. 24–29.

Recognizing that a full analysis of Barth's discussion of God's graciousness toward humanity in the creation narratives would need both to evaluate the merits of his complicated relationship with historical criticism in *CD* III/1 and to engage at length his theological program in order to address the merits of his espoused criteria (and adherence to them), the hope of this brief essay remains to appreciate the particulars of Barth's approach that might be missed in such an expansive discussion. For this reason, aside from noting the initial exegetical framework that allows Barth to read the creation narratives as a unified whole, this essay will limit its modest engagement to how Barth lets the "literal" details of Genesis 1–2 shape his preliminary discussions of God's graciousness toward humanity in creation. In practice, it is only after this initial, crucial step of listening to the details of the presented narrative that Barth seeks to understand these revealed details in connection with the history of Israel and its fulfillment in Christ, so an awareness of his observations at this initial level, while not sufficient, is necessary for a full understanding of Barth's exegetical practice (and is perhaps more readily appreciable by those who might not follow Barth's manner of connecting the passage with the history of the covenant).[6] With God's graciousness toward humanity in mind, the following will first review the basic contours of the two sagas Barth finds in Genesis 1–2, then suggest that Barth's overarching understanding of this graciousness is more obviously directed by the text's details than is his specific discussion of God's gracious creation of the human as male and female.

Saga I (Genesis 1:1–2:4a)

At the beginning of his exegesis, Barth finds that the first saga presents creation as the external basis—or "formal presupposition"—of the covenant of grace because he finds that it presents this creation as the possibility of covenant history. Here, creation is no more and no less than "one long preparation, and therefore the being and existence of the creature [is] one long readiness, for what God will intend and do with it in the history of the covenant." Consequently, creation "promises, proclaims and prophesies the covenant" whereby God loves humanity in freedom.[7]

6. For discussion of how Barth ultimately includes the entirety of Scripture in his "plain sense" reading of Gen. 1–2, see K. E. Greene-McCreight, *Ad Litteram: How Augustine, Calvin, and Barth Read the "Plain Sense" of Genesis 1–3*, Issues in Systematic Theology 5 (New York: Peter Lang, 1999), 174–240.

7. *CD* III/1, 230–32. Where III/1 adopts the language of "man" in discussion of God's preparation for humanity in the first saga, the following uses the language of "humanity" while

Owing to the proleptic orientation of the first saga, Barth finds it to offer a "prophetical" account wherein creation is finally known according to its ultimate goal in Christ as the one in whom the covenant of grace is achieved.[8] So Barth finds that his reading of the saga must approach it backward from the institution of covenant history in God's Sabbath rest (wherein creation finally enjoys the grace of God's covenantal presence), and thus notes this consummation at the outset in order that his understanding of creation's telos might appropriately inform his interpretation of the rest of the saga as a unified account of creation aimed toward this end.[9] By following this approach, Barth ultimately finds the saga to present an incredible view of the depths of divine graciousness in creation, each detail contributing toward a demonstration of how it is that the possibility of covenant history "depends wholly on the fact that the creature is in no position to act alone as the partner of God, that it is thrown back wholly and utterly on the care and intercession of God Himself, but that it does actually enjoy this divine care and intercession."[10] It is in this context that the first saga presents a remarkable picture of God's gracious preparation of an incredibly contingent humanity for the covenant of grace.

Once Barth begins his exegesis of the saga, he finds the saga to present a series of ten successive points: three introductory points in the initial three verses of Genesis 1, and seven points corresponding to the days that follow. Barth first finds that the first word of Genesis 1:1 could not be more central to a proper understanding of creation: by establishing the astonishing fact that God's will alone "stands at the beginning," the saga shows creation and its history to begin as a reality "chosen, willed, and posited" by God and, consequently, "'very good,' in His sight." From the onset, creation is "at the disposal of His grace," finding its end as a theater of the covenant in service to his purpose alone.[11] Barth then finds that Genesis 1:2 depicts that which is rejected by God, a point equally vital insofar as it establishes the freedom of God's faithfulness. Recognizing "the threatening curse" of such chaos, God pitied what he had made and so created "in harmony and at peace with Himself," rejecting chaos by banishing all that is hostile or even neutral to his will. In this, it is God's will that protects the creature from the possibility of failing to fulfill God's purpose.[12] Finally, Barth finds the point concerning the

---

maintaining III/1's use of "male" and "female" in discussion of their creation in Gen. 1:26–27 to reflect the text's terminology.

8. *CD* III/1, 232–33.
9. *CD* III/1, 98–99.
10. *CD* III/1, 231.
11. *CD* III/1, 99. See also 99–101.
12. *CD* III/1, 102. See also 101–10.

"And God said" of verse 3 to elaborate upon the first, establishing both the freedom of God's creative act as a person ("One who knows and wills and speaks") and the intimacy of the creature's disposition for God's grace because creation's coming into being corresponds to the Word of God. Here, it is by God's Word that he freely creates, by God's Word that the creature is made free, and by "obedience" to God's Word that it will "be free, and remain free, and again become free."[13] In short, Barth's examination of the introductory points anticipates God's grace toward humanity in the covenant, finding a basic sense of the creature's contingence upon a free act of divine grace and purpose that by the providence of God will attain its good end in freedom.

When Barth then outlines the saga's remaining points in the seven days, he finds God's creation of light and darkness on the first day to set the stage, as it were, for God's preparation for humanity in the remaining days. While Barth finds God to freely affirm the life of creation in the first three points, here Barth finds God to reveal this affirmation, with the light proclaiming that God's will is the "irrevocable declaration of life," and the darkness serving as a reminder of what is rejected by God. Given that the works of the remaining days echo this proclamation, it is fitting that God calls the light "day" and the day becomes the location of all of God's future works; as his "Yes to the creature," light is a sign of God's covenantal faithfulness and so all of God's future creations consist in "works of light" as repetitions of this Yes.[14]

From this binding of the ontic and noetic in the creation of these light-days, Barth finds the unfolding of a Yes-No dialectic over the following days, climaxing in the creation of humanity with whom God would finally covenant on the seventh. In their respective separations of cosmos from chaos, God's works on the second and third days reiterate God's free and gracious Yes to humanity by completing the creation of the earth as a theater of the covenant suited to the life of humanity.[15] And God's work on the fourth day initiates three days of this free and gracious Yes in the earth's furnishing, no longer ensuring the endurance of the cosmos but its bounty.[16]

However, besides establishing the wealth of humanity's earthly dwelling place, Barth finds that the details of the sixth day—as the day of humanity's creation—nuance the uniqueness of God's gracious preparation of humanity beyond what is established in the details of the preceding days. On one hand, insofar as both the land animals and humanity are created on the sixth day, Barth finds that the saga establishes the kinship of humanity with the land

---

13. *CD* III/1, 110–11. See also 110–17.
14. *CD* III/1, 117–19. See also 117–33.
15. For Barth's discussion of the second and third days, see *CD* III/1, 133–56.
16. For Barth's discussion of these days, see *CD* III/1, 156–81.

animals and, consequently, that it establishes that any precedence humanity has over the rest of creation as God's covenant partner is a precedence that humanity has as part of creation. As part of the animal kingdom, humanity's blessing includes a blessing held in common with the animals: humanity is dependent upon the Word for its life and fecundity on earth, and is indeed blessed with this life and fecundity. On the other hand, insofar as humanity is the final creature created, Barth finds that the saga establishes that humanity's precedence is one that entails humanity's unique dependence upon the rest of creation, "whereas they for their part have no need of him whatever."[17] There is a sense that humanity is more needy than the rest of the animal kingdom, and so more blessed as its need is met by the Word's sustenance of the other animals.

It is after noting the saga's depiction of humanity's complicated relationship to the other animals that Barth finally finds the saga to climax with the creation of humanity as the "true occupant" of creation in whom creation fulfills its end. The sixth day concludes the work of creation insofar as "this whole has aimed and moved towards man as the true occupant of the house founded and prepared by God."[18] Given the saga's indication that it is as the divine plural that God creates humanity in his image and likeness, and then its subsequent interpretation of the creation of humanity as the creation of male and female, Barth finds humanity to be the true occupant of creation suited to share in an independent covenant history with God as God's "true counterpart," bearing a correspondence to God, in part, in the I-Thou "confrontation" that is bestowed in the "differentiation and relationship" between male and female. Barth finds that the differentiation and relationship between male and female is at the center of God's gracious preparation of humanity because it is part of the divine gift of the *analogia relationis*, providing the formal possibility of humanity's I-Thou relationship with God in covenant history. In the creation of a humanity in "natural fellowship" with its Creator, creation is finally equipped for the grace of a covenant history between humanity and God (humanity's subsequent dominion and fecundity following from this grace).[19]

17. *CD* III/1, 177. See also 176–81.
18. *CD* III/1, 181.
19. *CD* III/1, 184–85. See also 181–206, 212–13. For a helpful introduction to Barth's understanding of the relationship between the *analogia relationis* and Jesus Christ as the image of God, see Ryan S. Peterson, *The* Imago Dei *as Human Identity: A Theological Interpretation*, Journal of Theological Interpretation Supplement 14 (Winona Lake, IN: Eisenbrauns, 2016), 42–46. Nathan MacDonald suggests that despite Barth's discussion of the *imago* in *CD* II/2, Barth seems to retain a traditional *imago-similitudo* distinction in III/1. Nathan MacDonald, "The *Imago Dei* and Election: Reading Genesis 1:26–28 and Old

While the work of creation is "finished" in the creation of humanity on the sixth day, Barth finds that the saga does not present creation's "completion" until God's final free and loving act of rest on the seventh day. Rather, in God's act of rest, God "confirmed" the conclusion of creation, and confronted it with himself, inaugurating the history of the covenant so that it was at this time that "with man and his true humanity, as His direct and proper counterpart, that God now associated Himself in His true deity."[20] Barth finds this finishing of creation tremendously significant for the saga's depiction of God's graciousness toward an incredibly contingent humanity insofar as it establishes that once all is created it is still God who affirms the goodness of creation and then initiates the covenant history for which it was made. Here, humanity's final end is not truly work but rest. Not the rest of recovery, but the Sabbath rest of God who "was satisfied with what He had created and had found the object of His love."[21] It is thus that Barth finds the first saga to reveal God's gracious preparation of a "wholly and utterly" contingent humanity for the covenant of grace.

Saga II (Genesis 2:4b–25)

Whereas Barth finds the first saga to present the prehistory of Israel by establishing the possibility of covenant history in creation's equipment for grace (and, in this, God's graciousness toward contingent humanity), he finds the second saga to do so by prefiguring the covenant, establishing that the covenant is the internal basis—or "material presupposition"—of creation.[22] In this difference Barth finds the second saga to possess not a prophetic but a "sacramental" character, its aim being to establish the "purpose and plan and order" of creation.[23] By establishing that the creature exists with "meaning and necessity" and, because of this, is "a unique sign of the covenant and a true sacrament," the saga attests to the glory of "God's free love."[24]

Prior to exegeting the second saga Barth clarifies that, while the sagas address a common theme, he must resist the urge to read the second as a "supplement" or "commentary" on the first, but rather read each saga on its own in order to attend to the details of both sagas in full and then appreciate

Testament Scholarship with Karl Barth," *International Journal of Systematic Theology* 10 (2008): 303–27, here p. 319.
    20. CD III/1, 213–14, 217. See also 213–28.
    21. CD III/1, 217.
    22. CD III/1, 232.
    23. CD III/1, 233, 229.
    24. CD III/1, 230, 232.

the "higher harmony" between them.[25] Because of the second saga's sacramental character, Barth finds that he cannot approach it in the same way as the first saga because "if we ask what the story is really leading up to, a general answer is given by its direct connexion with the ensuing account of the fall." In the second saga "we are already at the goal" where creation is "the sign and witness" of the ensuing history of the covenant.[26] So, instead of reading the second saga as a narrative to be read strictly backward or forward, Barth identifies three sequences in the second saga that introduce motifs integral for the apprehension of creation's sacramental character. He finds this approach no less christologically oriented than his approach in the first saga because for the second, sacramental, saga the concern is "not Jesus Christ as the goal, but Jesus Christ as the beginning (the beginning just because He is the goal) of creation."[27] By following this approach, Barth finds the second, sacramental, saga to show God's gracious blessing of an indispensably humble humanity with meaning, given that the creature "was not created other than to be the recipient of this gift [of meaning and necessity], and that it does not exist otherwise than as the recipient of this gift."[28]

Barth finds his first sequence in the three points of Genesis 2:4b–7. First is the astonishing revelation of God's name as Yahweh Elohim—the LORD and covenant partner of Israel—establishing that the God of creation is the God of covenant history, and is known as such in the creation that is the presupposition of this history. Second, verse 4b inverts the order of terms in verse 4a, finding that God is Creator of "the earth and the heavens."[29] Here, Barth finds that the second saga moves beyond the first in its concern to emphasize the value God finds in the earth independent of its relation to heaven (even, in a qualified sense, independent of its relation to humanity), given that the saga shows that the human is significant first as that which will serve the earth in order that the earth's own vegetation might thrive.[30] At least initially, the human is valued only as a servant of the earth, necessary for the good of the earth because earth in its barren state is not good; there is no suggestion that the human might be in any way superior to the creation for which it exists to serve.

The third and final point of this sequence develops the implied anthropology of verse 4b, asserting the "indispensable humility of man's existence."[31]

25. CD III/1, 229. Barth is especially leery of how a superficial synthesis might treat them as merely complementary attempts to speak of a timeless truth (CD III/1, 84).
26. CD III/1, 233–34.
27. CD III/1, 232.
28. CD III/1, 230.
29. CD III/1, 234.
30. CD III/1, 234–35.
31. CD III/1, 235.

While the first saga might have effectively portrayed humanity's utter contingence upon God's gracious preparation, Barth finds that the second saga establishes the overwhelmingly humble state of this gracious existence. The human is taken from dead and barren earth: "he has no independent position in the totality of creation." Recognizing that "he is more than this," the second saga nonetheless insists that "he is this too." Thus, the second saga shows that the human has no intrinsic "claim" over the beast: both belong to the earth, sharing the same complete dependence upon God for their life. All that sets the human apart is that the dust from which it is made is freely elected by God and enlivened by his breath. In this, the first sequence establishes that the human's existence is "problematical, threatened and transitory," yet the fact that God continuously wills humanity's existence testifies that God is humanity's "refuge and hope" and thus the hope of creation.[32]

As Barth moves on to the second sequence (Gen. 2:8–17), he finds that the saga progresses from a place of barren earth to an abundantly fruitful Garden in Eden, a Garden of delights because, "specially planted by God," it "specially belongs to Him." Given that the fruits of this land are those pleasing to a gardener, it is evident that "the earth which man is ordained to serve is also ordained to serve him" and to be for the human a home given by God toward the completion of its "task and perfect satisfaction."[33] Barth finds the detailed account of the river that waters the garden to describe the source of the garden's fruitfulness, indicating the totality of the "divine favour" that flows from within Eden to the ends of the earth.[34] And when the human is introduced as placed in the garden for its work, Barth recognizes that this work in the already thriving garden prepared and watered by God is nothing less than the gift of "the rest of his normal existence in relationship to his Creator and to the earth as the creaturely sphere."[35]

Barth takes particular interest in the tree of life and the tree of the knowledge of good and evil. The tree of life is a sign of humanity's life in the Garden, what it has been given to be and do in this Edenic rest, whereas the tree of the knowledge of good and evil is a sign of the possibility that humanity might know and will good and evil for itself and, in this, die in its attempt to hold the judicial office that belongs only to God: "It is with reference to them that man is allotted his place and receives a permission and prohibition."[36] Barth finds that the existence of the latter establishes humanity's freedom

32. CD III/1, 235–37. See also 235–49.
33. CD III/1, 251. See also 249–51.
34. CD III/1, 255. See also 249–56, 278–81.
35. CD III/1, 251. See also 249–56.
36. CD III/1, 256.

for "fellowship with God" by its obedient participation in Yahweh's judicial wisdom over its own; thus the presence of these trees and God's prohibition to eat of the tree of the knowledge of good and evil are themselves a gift in the freedom they bestow for humanity to fellowship with God in the fullness of creaturely freedom.[37]

Barth finds the "third and most explicit" sequence (Gen. 2:18–25) to be the "climax and conclusion" of the second saga, giving "life and substance" to what was introduced in the previous sequences. While the third sequence accounts for the origin of animals and human language, he finds that its singular theme is "the completion of the creation of man by the adding to the male of the female."[38] Noting that in the saga God decides to create a helpmeet because he does not find the solitary human good, Barth argues that it is in this third sequence that the human created in the first sequence is completed by the creation of the woman because it is as "male and female that God will have dealings in the history which follows" for, "if created man were solitary, creation as a whole would not be good, because it would then lack its internal basis in the covenant."[39] Although humanity's creation as man and woman is established in the first saga, it is significantly detailed in the second's emphasis on the man's free recognition and acceptance of the woman as his God-given completion and helpmeet over and against the animals: Barth concludes that it is by the man's joyful affirmation of his humanity, in his declarative choice of "the fact that he is elected," that he finally freely "says Yes to God," and thus creation achieves its goal. That the man was in a state of sleep when God made the woman indicates that the completion of the human is entirely a work of God, and that the man's knowledge and affirmation of her is a matter of confession—man does not judge what he does not see, but confirms his own creation in the secret that he is given.[40] And that the silent woman is given to be joyfully recognized and then named as made from the man's rib indicates the initiation of their relationship and its ordering in light of the unity and differentiation implied: the woman is the one in whom the man finds his glory insofar as she "belongs" to the man "in her being and existence"; she "is ordained to be his helpmeet," and "without detriment to her independence she is the part of him which was lost and is found again," while the man is the one who freely chooses the completion of the human in her.[41] Finally, Barth finds that the conclusion of the saga confirms the reality

37. CD III/1, 260. See also 255–78, 281–88.
38. CD III/1, 288.
39. CD III/1, 290.
40. CD III/1, 293, 300. See also 290–300.
41. CD III/1, 301. See also 296–97, 299–303.

of this relationship in covenant history: because of the creation of humanity as man and woman, it is now only in this ordered relationship between "man to whom woman belongs" and the "wife of man" that God will henceforth deal with humanity.[42] It is thus that Barth finds the second saga to reveal God's graciousness toward an "indispensably humble" humanity in creation.

Barth on God's Graciousness toward Humanity in Creation

The above has outlined how, broadly speaking, Barth's attention to the first saga draws out God's gracious preparation of a contingent humanity for the covenant of grace, whereas his attention to the second saga draws out God's gracious gift of meaning for an indispensably humble humanity in creation. Of the many things that might be observed, Barth's work seems particularly notable in the way that his overarching discussion is more clearly directed by his sustained attentiveness to the details of the text than by theological convenience. Consider the dialectic that Barth allows to emerge in his overarching understanding of God's graciousness toward humanity in creation because of the way the text presents itself.

As reviewed above, Barth finds the first saga to establish God's graciousness toward humanity in his bestowal of the divine likeness and in his provision of a creation suited to its fullness of life with God, creation existing for the sake of this blessing. Barth finds that the basic contingence of this blessed existence upon God's free and gracious provision for humanity is initially established in Genesis 1:1–3: God alone is "at the beginning of all things"; God has rejected "the world fashioned otherwise than according to the divine purpose"; and God creates by his Word as a "divine Person," the creature existing in "no other way" than by this Word. And the subsequent discussion of the light-days reveals the abundant depths of this provision, and the extraordinary freedom and graciousness with which it is made.[43] However, Barth's understanding of the uniqueness of God's graciousness toward an utterly contingent humanity is complicated by the text's allusion to a kinship between humanity and the land animals, so Barth finds he must uphold a sense that humanity's precedence as God's chosen covenant partner does not elevate humanity above creation (if anything, humanity's precedence highlights its unique contingence upon the rest of creation!).

This sustained attention to the text's details is even more pronounced in Barth's treatment of the three sequences in the second saga wherein God's

---

42. *CD* III/1, 308. See also 303–29.
43. *CD* III/1, 99, 102, 110–11.

gracious bestowal of meaning and purpose to an indispensably humble humanity is established. Barth finds that the first sequence of the second saga introduces the humility of humanity's purpose in its depiction of a creation valued as good independent of humanity: the human's purpose is that of a servant and, in this, the human is necessary for the goodness of creation only insofar as since a barren creation is not good, a gardener is required. And Barth finds that the sequence insists on the humility of humanity's mere existence when it reveals the human to be made of dead dust. In this, the second saga presents an understanding of God's graciousness toward humanity that is not only rather different from the first but also at least appears to contradict the first at this point. Here, humanity is not so much a part of creation that God blesses through the earth as it is a blessed part of the humble earth that is blessed by God to bless the rest of creation. Barth notes this—"how different this is from the first account, which is far more anthropocentric at this point, suggesting that the world of vegetation was ordained and created only to be the food of men and animals. For in this [second] account it is a kind of end in itself"[44]—but in his attention to the text he neither rejects the first saga's view nor downplays the view of the second because the details of the text demand this tension.

Of course, Barth then allows this dialectic to continue when he observes the second sequence of the second saga's view of the abundance lavished upon humanity in its service as gardener of the earth. Consequently, Barth finds the sequence to present a view of how it is through the earth that God blesses the indispensably humble human with its task. However, while he finds that the theme of the first saga "emerges at this point" insofar as the sequence shows that the earth in its abundance serves the blessedness of humanity, the details of the sequence lead him to recognize nonetheless that its illustration neither simply reiterates the first saga's view nor abandons the stress upon humanity indispensable humility in the first sequence of the second saga.[45] When the human is brought to a fruitful Garden, the sequence shows that humanity's God-given service to creation is itself humble insofar as it is a work of resting with God that is vivified by the Garden's bounty because Eden—and through it the rest of creation—is, in fact, watered by God: "man is really at rest in respect of nourishment, and his work . . . is the permitted minimum of the Sabbath which does not disturb the freedom, joy and rest of his existence."[46] Barth again attends to the text rather than

44. CD III/1, 235.
45. CD III/1, 251.
46. CD III/1, 254.

smoothing over unresolved tensions or, as he might have also done in this case, brushing past details that are not in obvious tension, in order that he might not lose the texture of God's graciousness toward humanity that the text describes.

Finally, when Barth observes that the presence of the trees, animals, and woman in the last two sequences of the second saga shows that humanity's choice plays a role in receiving God's blessings, Barth again allows the text to further the dialectic within his discussion of God's graciousness toward humanity. In the presence of the trees, animals, and woman the sequences are clear that the human is not only tremendously blessed by them, but that it receives these blessings freely, the possibility of human freedom being itself a divinely bestowed blessing given in these three. Yet, in this, the sequences are also clear that this freedom is a supremely humble one, consisting in no more (yet no less!) than the freedom to participate in the will of God by accepting that which is given. Again Barth, attending to the text, insists upon stressing God's graciousness in both the freedom of humanity's blessing and the narrowness of true human choice because it would be misleading to include one without the other.

In the end, Barth's overarching understanding of God's graciousness toward humanity in creation is wonderfully attuned to the details he finds in the sagas. After explicating the first saga's nuanced view of this graciousness toward a wholly and utterly contingent humanity, Barth allows the second saga's view of God's graciousness toward an indispensably humble humanity to complicate the first saga one sequence at a time. While Barth ultimately harmonizes the sagas in light of their respective concerns with the creation–covenant relationship and connection with the history of the covenant of grace, the dialectical understanding of God's graciousness apart from this harmonization is nonetheless profound: humanity is the object of divine love for whom the rest of creation takes its shape, yet is never elevated above its state as a servant made of dust, dependent on Yahweh for all. But insofar as this humanity lives in its freedom of resting in the wisdom of God, humanity is blessed to be the one through whom God fulfills the hope of creation.

Whether others might follow Barth's interpretations of the text is a difficult question to answer given his idiosyncratic attitude toward conducting word studies or utilizing extratextual means to defend many of the key interpretive decisions that go on to texture what he finds in the details of the text.[47] However,

47. For a sampling of these idiosyncrasies in §41, see Greene-McCreight, *Ad Litteram*, 200–213, 217–26; and MacDonald, "*Imago Dei* and Election," 320–27.

one need not entirely agree with the manner in which Barth analyzes details to find his conclusions concerning God's graciousness toward humanity in the text compelling. This is so particularly because Barth's broad-stroke observations are mostly not unique to him (even if their particular dialectical connection is), and also because his conclusions about humanity's overarching blessedness by God fit well with a wide range of interpretations (especially those open to reading the two sagas as constructing distinct narratives to be explored separately but eventually understood in connection with one another).[48] Although Barth does not explicitly articulate the "higher harmony" between the sagas' respective presentations of God's graciousness toward humanity, beyond his broad harmonization of the sagas as a whole, even one who rejects his broad approach could easily argue that by his attendance to the details of each saga in turn, he does indeed find a high harmony between them that offers a view of this graciousness much richer than a view taken from either saga on its own.

Barth on God's Graciousness in the Human as Male and Female

Contrasting with Barth's overarching understanding of God's graciousness toward humanity in creation, Barth's specific discussion of God's gracious creation of humanity as male and female—a reality that, in both sagas, Barth finds especially vital for the grace of covenant partnership with God—appears to go far beyond the textual details in its interpretation of the text.

In the first saga Barth looks at the creation of humanity as male and female, finding that it is (in part) in this differentiation and relationship that humanity is gifted with an *analogia relationis* and finally equipped for the grace of covenant history. Then—while the first saga is "simply content to mention the fact" that it is as male and female that God created humanity in his image and likeness, establishing the "central position" of this fact—the third sequence of the second details this equipment in the sequence's establishment of creation's internal basis in the covenant.[49] Barth finds that together the sagas provide a complex view of God's grace toward humanity in the male-female differentiation and relationship that contributes to the formal possibility of humanity's covenant relationship with God. However, Barth's discussion does not so much allow the sagas' details to direct so

---

48. By "broad-stroke observations" I have in mind that in the first saga, (1) creation takes its shape to serve the life of God with humanity. And in the second saga that (2) the human serves the good of creation; (3) the human is mere dead dust unless animated and given its vocation by God; (4) watered by God, the fruitful Garden serves the life of humanity; and (5) the trees, animals, and woman depict the human's choice given by God.

49. *CD* III/1, 187, 288.

much as it allows them to open the door for imposing his own understandings onto the text.

In the case of the first saga, there is a sense that Barth's finding that the saga limits the primary significance of humanity as male and female to the differentiation and relationship therein imposes onto the text his own detailed understanding of humanity as male and female rather than resisting the urge to speak where the text does not. Numerous arguments have been mounted against Barth's exegesis at this point. However, even if one dismisses (1) the broad consensus among Old Testament scholars that, given the ancient Near Eastern context, the *imago* in Genesis 1:27 is clearly functional rather than relational,[50] (2) arguments against finding the third line of Genesis 1:27 to continue the thought of the previous two (a central move in Barth's argument),[51] (3) arguments for the connection of the third line with the mention of Adam's likeness and image in Genesis 5:3 (a connection Barth's argument rejects),[52] or (4) arguments against the notion that Genesis 1:26–27 intends to clarify the content of the *imago Dei*,[53] one still wonders what details in Genesis 1:26–27 can sufficiently ground Barth's insistence that the differentiation and relationship between the male and female is the primary significance of humanity's creation as male and female in this passage,[54] and ground his detailing of this differentiation and relationship to the extent that he does so. Does the mere mention of the creation of the male and female, following a sequence of the divine plural and the decision to create humanity in the divine image and likeness, obviously clarify the male-female relationship beyond its introduction of sexual difference, and qualify as an undeniable ancient recognition of the relatively modern I-Thou concept?[55] Even if Barth were to suggest that there is a much more modest account of this relationship in the text (perhaps by toning down his claim of its obvious distinction from the I-Thou

50. See J. Richard Middleton, *The Liberating Image: The* Imago Dei *in Genesis 1* (Grand Rapids: Brazos, 2005).

51. See James Barr, *Biblical Faith and Natural Theology* (Oxford: Clarendon, 1994), 160; and Middleton, *Liberating Image*, 49–50.

52. See Peterson, Imago Dei *as Human Identity*, 48–49.

53. See, for instance, Claus Westermann, *Genesis 1–11: A Commentary*, trans. John J. Scullion, SJ (Minneapolis: Augsburg, 1984), 155–58. Like Barth, Westermann finds reference to the image in the passage to be relationally significant, but not because it explains in what the image consists.

54. This of course recognizes that, for Barth, this is the primary significance only because it is in this relationship that the male and female ultimately point to the relationship between Christ and the church (*CD* III/1, 191).

55. On these concerns, see Phyllis A. Bird, "'Male and Female He Created Them': Gen 1:27b in the Context of the Priestly Account of Creation," *Harvard Theological Review* 74 (1981): 129–59.

confrontation within the Godhead,[56] and from the male-female relationships elsewhere in the animal kingdom[57]), it is difficult to see how he might find that these two verses on their own support much more than a basic equality in this relationship insofar as both the male and the female are made in the image and likeness of God.

Barth is certain that this conjunction establishes the divine likeness as the *analogia relationis* given partially in the creation of humanity as male and female, and he considers the tradition's numerous attempts to import into the text understandings of the *imago Dei* from beyond the details of the passage to be one of the church's great exegetical embarrassments. He rehearses the tradition's wrongful importations at length, reiterating that the divine likeness to which the saga refers must be understood as an *analogia relationis*, this being "the definitive explanation given by the text itself," such that those before him "ought to have kept to this point" because nothing could "be more obvious" when "we agree that we must keep close to the wording and context of the passage."[58] Perhaps it is, ironically, Barth's fear of imposition that drives him to develop his understanding of the divine likeness from Genesis 1:26–27 before showing how the passage might be interpreted given references to the image and likeness elsewhere in Scripture. (His exegesis might appear more promising to some if he had worked this the other way around.[59]) As it stands, it is hard to avoid the conclusion that Barth's discussion of God's gracious creation of humanity as male and female imposes its own view onto the text's details rather than attending to what the text presents.

Barth's discussion in the second saga is more obviously textured by the details of the text while also more obviously imposing meaning on them. For instance, Barth's finding that the woman's creation from the man's rib, together with the man's jubilant recognition of her, establishes unity and differentiation in the male-female relationship (and the necessity of both for the human's completion) seems drawn from the text's description of God's taking of the rib from man to create the woman to be his helpmeet.[60] Even if

56. *CD* III/1, 196.

57. *CD* III/1, 186–87. See John McIntyre, *The Shape of Christology: Studies in the Doctrine of the Person of Christ*, 2nd ed. (Edinburgh: T&T Clark, 1998), 111–12.

58. *CD* III/1, 195, 192.

59. Indeed, when Barth himself goes on to develop his understanding of this likeness in light of the history of Israel and its fulfillment in Christ, MacDonald argues that this development itself appears partial to Barth's initial interpretation of Gen. 1:26–27 (MacDonald, "*Imago Dei* and Election," 320–21). For a favorable interpretation of Barth's canonical approach at this point, see Craig A. Carter, "Karl Barth on the *Imago Dei*: Typology and the *Sensus Literalis* of Holy Scripture," in *Go Figure! Figuration in Biblical Interpretation*, ed. Stanley D Walters, Princeton Theological Monograph Series 81 (Eugene, OR: Pickwick, 2008), 121–36.

60. *CD* III/1, 296–97.

one disagrees with Barth's interpretation of the text, it is nonetheless clear that Barth's approach here at least presents as allowing the text's details to guide. However, one wonders how the silent woman's completion of the man in his acceptance of her guides Barth's inference that "it is her glory to be his glory" and that the man's "recognition and acknowledgement imply hers as well."[61] Regardless of the serious appreciation and offense Barth's understanding of the male-female relationship has elicited, it is difficult to escape a sense that Barth again imposes much more onto the saga than the details themselves require.

Conclusion

As is evident from this brief appreciation of Barth's exegesis in §41, his interpretation of Genesis 1–2 is rather convenient for his larger theological program. If Barth is correct, it is surely to his credit that latent in the creation sagas of Genesis is an incredibly Barthian world, and quite appropriate that his exegesis of Genesis 1–2 takes up the majority of *CD* III/1, providing an intuitive unfolding of *CD* II and anticipation of the remaining volumes of the *Dogmatics*. Of course, regardless of convenience, Barth's primary contribution to the exegete is nothing less than his attentive contemplation of the world he finds the text's details to construct, and what theological conclusions must be drawn from those details.

Idiosyncrasies and all, Barth clearly attempts to *notice* details in the creation narratives, to contemplate them, and only then to discern the picture they provide and the theology that must necessarily follow. However, as the above has shown, in Barth's discussion of God's graciousness in the creation of the human as male and female, he appears to import more into the details than he takes from them; it is unfortunate that he insists on developing his preliminary discussion on such narrow ground given the importance of his view for his prehistory of Israel and theology to follow. That said, in his overarching understanding of God's graciousness toward humanity in creation, the view that emerges is quite impressive in its sensitivity to the ever-shifting world of the text, offering dialectical nuance far beyond what his program requires, but enriching his program immensely.

---

61. *CD* III/1, 302–3.

TWELVE

"Worthy Is the Lamb"

Karl Barth's Exegesis of Revelation 4–5

CHRISTOPHER GREEN

Introduction

It is somewhat curious that Karl Barth, who understood himself as a careful student of Scripture, attracts much more attention as a dogmatic theologian. Of course, for him, these are not exclusive vocations.[1] Barth's readers may be captivated and satisfied by his theological exposition given in the large print of the *Church Dogmatics*. This kind of reading searches Barth for an assumed or implicit "system" and risks overlooking his exegetical work, which is frequently embedded in his excurses in small print or given in his freestanding commentaries on Scripture.

In the *Wirkungsgeschichte* of the *Church Dogmatics*, it is now frequently noted that Barth's readers have to a significant extent treated his disciplined commentary on Scripture as an aside, an outworking of his "doctrine of Scripture," or have pressed it into more broadly based hermeneutical discussions.[2]

---

1. In 1935, just prior to his official dismissal from his post at Bonn, Barth states, "Take now my last piece of advice: Exegesis, Exegesis and once more, Exegesis! If I have become a dogmatician, it is because I long before have endeavored to carry on exegesis." "Das Evangelium in der Gegenwart," *Theologische Existenz heute* 25 (1935): 17 (my translation).

2. "Properly speaking . . . Barth does not have a doctrine of scripture, but more a scripture principle." John Webster, "Karl Barth," in *Reading Romans through the Centuries*, ed. Jeffrey P. Greenman and Timothy Larsen (Grand Rapids: Brazos, 2005), 206.

More recently, a number of careful treatments have pointed out this short-coming. Quite simply: readers of Barth's *Church Dogmatics* should look to, instead of away from, the small print. This acknowledges his stated purpose to continually return to the Bible.[3]

My aim here is to evaluate Barth's exegetical treatment of the fourth and fifth chapters of the Apocalypse, searching out its importance for the rest of *Church Dogmatics* III/3. This study should not be taken as an uncritical endorsement of Barth's, as he says, both "reading out and reading in."[4] In some places I do find Barth's treatment of this portion of Scripture wanting, especially with regard to his avoidance of any angelic ontology.[5] However, as the most significant exegetical aside in III/3, this section deserves extended commentary. It is also tempting—but would be supererogation—to begin by providing an outline summary of Barth's discussion of divine providence and evil in the whole of §§48–50.[6] Instead, I attempt to summarize the place that Barth's exegesis of this passage has within the whole of III/3 with three

3. A brief survey of approaches to Barth's exegesis: Paul McGlasson, *Jesus and Judas: Biblical Exegesis in Barth* (Atlanta: Scholars Press, 1991); Mary Kathleen Cunningham, *What Is Theological Exegesis? Interpretation and Use of Scripture in Barth's Doctrine of Election* (Valley Forge, PA: Trinity Press International, 1995); David E. Demson, *Hans Frei and Karl Barth: Different Ways of Reading Scripture* (Grand Rapids: Eerdmans, 1997); Richard E. Burnett, *Karl Barth's Theological Exegesis: The Hermeneutical Principles of the Römerbrief Period*, Wissenschaftliche Untersuchungen zum Neuen Testament 2/145 (Tübingen: Mohr Siebeck, 2001); Donald Wood, *Barth's Theology of Interpretation*, Barth Studies (Aldershot, UK: Ashgate, 2007); Bruce McCormack, "The Significance of Karl Barth's Theological Exegesis of Philippians," in *Orthodox and Modern: Studies in the Theology of Karl Barth* (Grand Rapids: Baker Academic, 2008), 89–105; Mark S. Gignilliat, *Karl Barth and the Fifth Gospel: Barth's Theological Exegesis of Isaiah*, Barth Studies (Aldershot, UK: Ashgate, 2009).
4. *CD* I/1, 106. See also Burnett, *Barth's Theological Exegesis*, 112–14.
5. The being of Barth's angels is in their becoming, which is both a hallmark of his work in §51 and a point of vulnerability. Barth defends his own approach to the angels in saying that this subject is the "most remarkable and difficult of all" for him (*CD* III/3, 369). His effort in §51.1, "The Limits of Angelology," to distinguish his approach from both medieval and modern approaches (e.g., demythologizing) is fascinating but falls a bit short, given that this part of §51 is the least exegetical portion of the whole section. While he gives pride of place to Scripture in his critique of his opponents, his retreat from any angelic ontology as speculative creates a difficulty that returns back to him in his exegetical dealings with different *kinds* of angels, such as the "angel of Yahweh" (*CD* III/3, 486–93) or the demonic, which he demythologizes (*CD* III/3, 519–31). See G. C. Berkouwer, *The Triumph of Grace in the Theology of Karl Barth* (Grand Rapids: Eerdmans, 1956), 76–80; Timothy Gorringe, *Against Hegemony: Christian Theology in Context* (Oxford: Oxford University Press, 1999), 174–78.
6. Regarding the question of the overall unity of *CD* III/3, see two recent studies: Darren Kennedy, *Providence and Personalism: Karl Barth in Conversation with Austin Farrer, John Macmurray and Vincent Brümmer* (Frankfurt: Peter Lang, 2011); Christopher C. Green, *Doxological Theology: Karl Barth on Divine Providence, Evil and the Angels* (London: T&T Clark, 2011).

theses. This, in turn, positions us for some attention to Barth's exegetical work, which follows.

My argument in summary: Barth's exegesis in Revelation 4–5 is focused on the angels and the manner in which they exemplify a performative and holy theology. Heaven has a special role within creation because, as a created space, it comprises the "whence" of God's being and action with respect to the creature. Heavenly witness is, therefore, a theology that resides in this space perpetually, and acknowledges the kingly office of Christ "analytically."[7] This heavenly chorus exemplifies the proper response to divine providence that the holy will of God expects because it is focused specifically on the risen Lamb, who alone is able to "open the scroll" that clarifies the Father's will (Rev. 5:1–7). This heavenly theology acknowledges the enfleshed and risen Christ as the subject of divine governance, which sets Barth's theology, which is patterned after that of the angels, apart from other approaches.

Three Theses

1. In Barth's exposition of divine providence in CD III/3 *there is a correspondence between the holy, self-electing will of God and the fulfillment of that will in the praise of his creatures.*[8] In CD III/3, Barth first maintains that his doctrine of providence is unique on account of its being placed subsequent to his doctrine of election. His view of predestination concentrates the will of God on an expansive soteriology, which has the whole of creation in its purview. Barth's placement of his doctrine of election anterior to divine providence is, I think, what he calls his "radical correction" of the Reformed position in his preface to *CD* III/3.[9] Second, Barth sees his doctrine of providence as set apart in that it culminates in the praise of the creature.[10] This clearly redemptive will of God ends in doxology, and so divine providence—which Barth insists is not trapped in a heavenly "frozen immobility"—must also eventuate in praise.[11] Angels find their importance for Barth's treatment here; they themselves are "an eternal hymn of praise."[12]

7. CD III/3, 468.
8. Holiness is a prominent interest of Barth's in *CD* III/3; Green, *Doxological Theology*, 28, 210–20.
9. CD III/3, xii. For further argument, see Green, *Doxological Theology*, 10–41. See also CD II/2, 144 and §33.2.
10. Green, *Doxological Theology*, 131–52, 210–20.
11. *CD* III/3, 438.
12. CD III/3, 486. Timothy Gorringe describes angels in Barth's theology as having a "liturgical existence," *Against Hegemony*, 176.

The angelic host belongs to heaven and not earth, so Barth makes a distinction between both kinds of witness.[13] Angels are, by necessity, perfect witnesses. As heavenly creatures, they exist in a genitive relationship with God in Christ. There is no taint of self-interest, fear, or anxiety in angelic praise. Angels do not focus on "causal" concepts or raise anxious questions about concursus. Rather, they concentrate on and extol the risen Lamb, who demonstrates that he is the ruler of the universe in his opening of the scroll (Rev. 5:1–7). In this manner, the angelic host exemplifies theology-as-praise as it directs its attention exclusively to Christ.

Now, for earth: given that providence involves God's sustaining of earthly creatures, the praise that Barth's doctrine expects is historically extended. Providence does not look to a momentary praise on the part of the creature but to the whole of a human life before God. Divine providence takes seriously that life is intended by God to be characterized by prayer without ceasing (1 Thess. 5:17).[14] This means that heaven's praise also has bearing on the theological witness of the earthly creature. As with the angels, earthly theology should also take off its sandals. This focus anticipates Barth's subsequent volume on the ethics of creation, CD III/4.

Any doctrine of providence, if it is to be understood as a *holy* work of God, must first be summoned by the praise of heaven. All praise on earth is summoned by heaven. "This expectation of God makes the praise of God necessary."[15] When the human creature ceases to pray, this does not subvert God's providential will.[16] When and where earthly praise falls short, the praise of heaven always exists without fail. When earth lacks holy witnesses to God's glory, heaven "makes up" for this deficiency.[17] The heavenly host eulogizes the risen Lamb at all times.

2. *Heaven is constituted by the career of Jesus Christ.* Barth states in his section on the kingdom of heaven in §51.2 that he is dealing with the "climax" of his treatment of the doctrine of creation.[18] In his exposition, heaven takes up a completely transcendent position *within* creation. Heaven and earth

13. Angels offer "thanksgiving" in relation to God and "proclamation" in relation to other creatures (CD III/3, 461).
14. Michael Thomas Dempsey's noteworthy study of Barth's doctrine of providence makes this argument; "Fully Divine, Fully Human: The Mystery of Divine Providence in the Theology of Thomas Aquinas and Karl Barth" (PhD dissertation, University of St. Michael's College, Toronto School of Theology, 2004). For an appreciative critique, cf. Green, *Doxological Theology*, 96–108.
15. CD III/3, 461.
16. Theology is implicated and self-directed when it makes decisions that move the creature to the "left hand" of God. Such theologies fail to take the holiness of God seriously with the advent of what Barth calls "the Christian decision" (CD III/3, 112).
17. "Even where [wo] the earthly creature seems to be sadly lacking" (CD III/3, 462; cf. Green, *Doxological Theology*, 199).
18. CD III/3, 428.

are paired and share an "intracosmic relationship."[19] But why, we ask, must there be such a place?

Barth's answer is that the exaltation of Christ makes it necessary that we give a name to this upper sphere of creation. Heaven is a predicate of the will of God, which distinguishes God's movement toward the creature with an "above" and a "below."[20] Heaven, then, is a space that uniquely belongs to the presence of God.[21] It is a transcendent space; however, it is a created space.

While heaven is part of creation, it is constituted by the primal determination of God that he should be God in Jesus Christ.[22] In this self-electing movement, the suffering, death, resurrection, exaltation, and parousia that define the name "Jesus Christ" also define the *whence* of these moments as belonging to a sphere the Bible calls "heaven." Heaven belongs to the external basis of the covenant.[23] For this reason, it is a servant and instrument of Christ's exaltation and not vice versa.[24]

Barth focuses in on Colossians 3:1, alongside a conglomeration of other texts, for exploring the ontology of this part of creation.[25] This section provides his definitive statement on the constitution of heaven. "Where is this heaven?" he asks. "The answer is that it is where Christ is," seated at the right hand of the Father.[26] Reminiscent of his doctrine of predestination, which focuses on Christ's role as active subject, Barth's aim in this section is to demonstrate that Christ is not a mere "spectator" but has a complete share in the exercise of divine governance.[27] "Jesus Christ shares fully in this transcendence of God over heaven."[28]

The reality of the resurrection in particular is what makes heaven not only real but also relevant.[29] Christ's resurrection is absolutely inaccessible from

19. CD III/3, 421. Paula Gooder deserves some mention here as she comes to a similar conclusion regarding the nature of heaven in the Bible in *Heaven* (Eugene, OR: Cascade, 2011), 1–11.
20. CD III/3, 418–33; see also CD II/1, 474–76.
21. Barth argues this against "the old error of God's non-spatiality," CD II/1, 486. See Kennedy, *Providence and Personalism*, 289.
22. CD III/3, 371, 433–41.
23. CD III/3, 54–55. See also §41.2, "Creation as the External Basis of the Covenant," in CD III/1, 94–228.
24. CD III/3, 46–48, 440–42.
25. CD III/3, 438–41; II/1, 475. For some comment on how Barth conglomerates texts in his exegetical practice, see Cunningham, *What Is Theological Exegesis?*, 19–44.
26. CD III/3, 438.
27. "As the object of this divine action He has been made its Subject" (CD III/3, 439). See also §33.2, "The Eternal Will of God in the Election of Jesus Christ" (CD II/2, 145–94).
28. CD III/3, 441. The exaltation of the resurrected Lord from earth to heaven demonstrates that Jesus is Lord "in the whole cosmos" (440).
29. Brevard Childs notes that the resurrection of Christ is an "eschatological confirmation" of the new creation, which is the aim of the biblical account of creation in Barth's theology. *Biblical Theology of the Old and New Testaments* (Minneapolis: Fortress, 1992), 405.

the standpoint of earth because this moment in God's economy belongs specifically to heaven. Heaven is the created space—completely inscrutable to human capacity—where God's will to be God in Jesus Christ is vindicated in the resurrection. Heaven stands above earth in asymmetry.[30] The angels are the first to stand next to, and point to, the empty tomb. As such, they are the preeminent witnesses to the vindication of God's will in human history.[31] All such realities that comprise the mystery of God reside on this inaccessible side of creation.

3. *Heavenly praise is the prototype of all theology on earth that acknowledges the saving work of Christ the King.* Heaven is the place where the sovereign determination of God's providence is initially commended by the angelic host. It is here that Jesus Christ is first apprehended as he is, as the self-electing God and subject of God's reconciling work. Essentially, heaven is the birthplace of all doxological theology. The existence of angels is "exemplary,"[32] and "the angels are the originals of the prophets and apostles."[33]

Heaven does not initiate but shapes earthly praise. It does not dispense grace but exemplifies its end.[34] The praise of heaven is meant to form theology, which is to be free of the fear that focuses on relating God and the creature in terms of causality.[35] Rather, the praise of earth takes its cues from heavenly theology when it responds to the initial angelic heralding of the resurrection. In doing so, heavenly theology expels fear. Barth focuses on a discontinuity between the theologies of heaven and earth in stating that John the seer, whom Barth (alongside many others) gives the appellate ὁ θεολόγος, "would have been most surprised, and the 4 living creatures, and the 24 elders and the many angels in heaven, must surely have been surprised, at most of the things which have since been given the name of theology."[36]

In his exegesis of Revelation 4–5, Barth's focus is on how the praise of the angels should have an impact on the praise of God's creatures on earth. It is the *theology* of the angels that interests him, in that their knowledge of God should have an impact on earth as well—"on earth as it is in heaven."

---

30. The angelic host praises God for his manifold wisdom demonstrated in the church (Eph. 3:10). See *CD* III/3, 467.

31. *CD* III/3, 507–8.

32. *CD* III/3, 463.

33. *CD* III/3, 497.

34. "They do not mediate between God and human beings but they constitute the 'atmosphere' in which there can be a creaturely witness." Gorringe, *Against Hegemony*, 177.

35. Barth sees the Christian appeal to secondary causality in providence as the expression of a "fear complex" (*CD* III/3, 146).

36. *CD* III/3, 476.

For this reason, Barth states that the actions of the four living creatures are "proper to all creatures."[37]

Revelation 4

I now turn to Barth's section on Revelation 4–5 specifically (found in CD III/3, 463–76). He begins with a summary statement that immediately divides the two chapters. Chapter 4 depicts what the seer sees as the "throne of God," its "immediate entourage," and chapter 5 depicts "the Lamb."[38] With reference to the Lamb as the one given the scroll that proclaims coming events, Barth draws attention to the importance of these chapters for the book as a whole. The divine courtroom uncovers the events that must take place (Rev. 4:1). Barth signals that here we are investigating heaven, which is the "invisible background of world history."[39]

After his brief gesture to the importance of these chapters, Barth draws attention to the fact that the one who sits on the throne in chapter 4 is unnamed. This divine namelessness is clearly intentional. Richard Bauckham confirms: "There is nothing in [Revelation] chapter 4 which could not have been written by a non-Christian Jewish visionary."[40] Invoking 1 John 1:5, Barth indicates that this must be the Holy One in whom there is no darkness.

The accent in chapter 4 is apophatic as the seer glances into the transcendence of the divine majesty. Read apart from the fifth chapter, Barth's exegesis of the fourth might promote a picture of providence he elsewhere aims to reject. This crux underscores the importance of the connection between the two chapters for developing a christologically focused doctrine. It is the joining of these two chapters, and the involution of both forms of praise elicited by the self-same God in both accounts, that draws Barth's interest.

Barth next turns his attention to the heavenly entourage. He focuses on the nature of the twenty-four πρεσβύτεροι. Are these "elders" angels or sanctified humans? Barth finds several indicators in the text to be unhelpful, especially the number twenty-four. He prefers to understand this as inclusive of

37. CD III/3, 466.
38. CD III/3, 464.
39. This is J. T. Beck's statement, quoted by Barth with approval at CD III/3, 464.
40. "Only in the continuation of the vision in chapter 5 . . . [does the] Jewish *Christian* character of Revelation's theology become apparent." Richard Bauckham, *The Theology of the Book of Revelation* (Cambridge: Cambridge University Press, 1993), 32. Gordon Fee echoes this sentiment, indicating that the prophets and psalmists from whom John is borrowing his imagery "showed no such reluctance" to name God. *Revelation* (Eugene, OR: Cascade, 2011), 68.

numerous possibilities.[41] Rather, the decisive factor is that these elders are clothed in white, which connotes the "appropriate response" of the creature to the multifaceted glory of God (citing Rev. 1:14 and 19:14).[42] Whiteness does not indicate anything ontological, but only that these creatures actively reflect the divine glory. In effect, by sidelining the question of ontology, Barth artfully opts to understand the twenty-four πρεσβύτεροι as angels, without requiring too much of the text.[43]

While commentators differ on this question, and Barth sees a number of available solutions, he is still undecided. If he had understood the twenty-four elders as glorified persons or as representatives of the church, this perhaps would have pressed his reading of the heavenly choir in the direction of personal eschatology.[44] However, Barth finds it very important to indicate that these are all angelic beings. His solution here is congruent with his refusal to speculate about heaven as a framework for the afterlife.[45]

Barth confirms his actualistic reading of the heavenly host with reference to the "seven lamps" before the throne (Rev. 4:5). While there are some indicators that this could be the Holy Spirit, still "we cannot rule out the possibility," he says, that this is a reference to heavenly creatures.[46] He also sees these λαμπάδες πυρὸς καιόμεναι in the same way as the elders, with their function pointing away from any angelic ontology.[47]

Following these statements, Barth highlights the four living creatures with greater interest. In doing so, he observes that they are made up of a combination of the visions of Ezekiel 1, which represents earthly creatures, and Isaiah 6, which reflects the doxology of the seraphim.[48] Unlike the other participants in the heavenly song, the four living creatures are definitely connected with the earthly, "sub-lunary" spheres of creation, although it is not specified how.

41. "Something of all of [these possibilities] ought to be found in the number 24" (CD III/3, 465).

42. CD III/3, 465.

43. Barth's demurral from speculating about angelic ontology becomes important for his exegetical argument in Rev. 4–5 at this point.

44. Joseph Mangina's commentary on Revelation cites Rev. 7:1–8; 12:1, 12 as demonstrative for the number 12 as the ecclesial number in the book, denoting the church of the 2 Testaments. Joseph L. Mangina, *Revelation* (Grand Rapids: Brazos, 2010), 77. Richard Bauckham and Robert Mounce disagree, seeing these as angelic beings. See Bauckham, *Theology of Revelation*, 34; and Robert Mounce, *The Book of Revelation* (Grand Rapids: Eerdmans, 1977), 121. David Aune's observation would resonate with Barth the most—that the "literary *function* of the 24 elders within Revelation is far more important than any speculation regarding their supposed identity." *Revelation 1–5*, Word Biblical Commentary (Dallas: Word, 1997), 288.

45. Berkouwer, *Triumph of Grace*, 157–65; Green, *Doxological Theology*, 216–19.

46. CD III/3, 465.

47. Barth writes, "in analogy to the white clothes of the elders" (CD III/3, 465).

48. Cf. also CD II/1, 124–25.

As he understands it, these creatures are still "definitely" heavenly beings, and so he remains interested in Isaiah 6 throughout this section.[49]

The four living creatures praise God by acknowledging his absolute lordship in a reference to the "threefold Sanctus" of Isaiah 6:3. Barth notes that this threefold praise exemplifies the holiness of these angels. They acknowledge God by deferring to him as the only one who is holy. Intertextual conversation with Isaiah 6:5 confirms that the four living creatures in the vision of Revelation 4 are a "people of clean lips."[50]

It is important to read this section with Barth's polemical counterpart in mind, Erik Peterson. Peterson's *Das Buch von den Engeln* provides the background for what Barth has to say about angels here.[51] Barth's contention with Peterson begins as early as the onset of §51, where he asks: "But how can the task of a messenger consist decisively in the singing of hymns?"[52] He continually keeps in focus the notion—which he fully intends to repudiate—that angels offer only a unique form of worship to God and that this worship is somehow ossified in an eternalized expanse and so is indifferent to the salvation of earth.[53] This would bracket the angels by consigning them to heaven alone, making them irrelevant to the economy of salvation. Barth's main concern is to say that angels not only worship the Lamb around the throne but that they also serve the rest of the cosmos as witnesses who proclaim. The ministry of angels is "thanksgiving" in relation to God and "proclamation" in relation to other creatures.[54]

The four living creatures give Barth an opportunity to demonstrate that the angelic host does proclaim. These creatures initiate the heralding of God's eschatological plan in the midst of an unresolved tension. This heralding is also what theology should be like on earth. In extolling God as holy, the four

49. CD III/3, 465.
50. CD III/3, 466.
51. Cf. Joseph Mangina, "Apocalypticizing Dogmatics: Karl Barth's Reading of the Book of Revelation," *Journal of Theological Studies* 1 (2007): 202. Barth describes the "basic error of Peterson" as the thought that the angels have turned "their back on earth and man" in a kind of gnostic elevation (CD III/3, 483). According to Barth, Peterson believes he has found an "enhancement and intensification of his own being" in the angelic chorus (CD III/3, 483). On the role of Barth's encounter with Erik Peterson in the development of his early theology, and in terms of the wider reception of Eberhard Jüngel's thesis, see Keith Johnson, "A Reappraisal of Karl Barth's Theological Development and His Dialogue with Catholicism," *International Journal of Systematic Theology* 14 (2012): 4–6.
52. CD III/3, 384–85.
53. Heaven's theology cannot be understood as being made up of "spiritual truths" or "eternal ideas" because heaven is not an extension of earth. Rather, "the angels in heaven do already what will also be done on earth by earthly creatures" (CD III/3, 468).
54. CD III/3, 461.

living creatures do what is proper for all creatures. Earth is meant to join in with the praise that extols God as "ὁ παντοκράτωρ" in the same way as is already found in Isaiah 6:3: "The whole earth is full of his glory."[55]

Next, and most importantly, Barth indicates that the song of the four living creatures is "broken" with the third appellation given in praise to God: "who was, and is, and *is to come*" (Rev. 4:8).[56] That is, as the one who comes, this Lord is not only the Lord of creation but is also its Savior. With this assertion, Barth reads both chapters as depicting a continuous movement of worship that commends God as Father and Son, Creator and Savior, the Almighty and Holy One. The praise of the angels is, then, an act that extends across both chapters and is to be understood as *one* developing chorus. Barth does not dismiss the discontinuity between these two accounts, but indicates in chapter 4 "an anticipation of" the new song of Revelation 5: "The song in 5:9 is, of course, a new song in the sense that it explicitly proclaims this coming of the Lord, or rather the fact that He has already come in what the Lamb has done on earth. But even so it only confirms what is implicitly declared and proclaimed to the heavenly and earthly world by the four living creatures."[57]

Barth's focus on both chapters unpacks the God of Revelation 4 as "the One who comes," allowing him to center his doctrine of divine providence on the Lamb in Revelation 5. The four living creatures are responsive to the work of salvation that occurs on earth, and so they exemplify a movement that extols divine lordship for this particular reason. Barth wants us to see this character of angelic doxology, which begins by getting its soteriology right, to be an example of correct recognition of God's transcending rule over human history.

In their representation of the lower, earthly sphere, Barth notes that the four living creatures also lead the heavenly chorus. That is, the doxological action of the twenty-four elders follows that of the four living creatures in Revelation 4:9–10 and 5:8. He says this is due to the fact that the four living creatures stand in a particular relation to the "depths of the earth." With a quotation of Ephesians 3:10, he notes that they search the manifold wisdom of God in the church. The four living creatures proclaim the "evident mercy of God" in the lower spheres.[58] This allows the angels with the soteriological insights to take up the lead.

Barth concludes his section on Revelation 4 with a description of this praise as "analytic" [*analytisches*].[59] That is, he indicates that angelic praise

---

55. CD III/3, 466.
56. CD III/3, 466 (emphasis added).
57. CD III/3, 467.
58. CD III/3, 467.
59. CD III/3, 468.

here will simply acknowledge that δόξα, τιμή, and δύναμις all belong to God originally. Ascribing these perfections to God does not "add" anything to him, but it recognizes and extols the fact that God is the one to whom these perfections belong.

In the first volume of the *Church Dogmatics*, Barth maintains that "God reveals himself as the Lord" is an "analytic" [*analytisches*] statement.[60] That is, in response to the revealed Word of God, Christian theology must acknowledge the Lordship of God in his saving and self-revealing movement.[61] This is what the angelic praise of Revelation 4 does: it acknowledges, in worship to God, that God alone is worthy (ἄξιος εἶ). In saying that God is the One who is worthy, the angels ascribe to God something that is not "a title conferred by others."[62] Rather, what Barth is about to uncover in his section on Revelation 5 is that the one who opens the book stands at the beginning of all events in history "as their Lord."[63]

Revelation 5

As Barth's evaluation moves into Revelation 5, he consistently keeps the relationship between these two chapters in view. The vision of the Lamb is introduced, and from that standpoint Barth evaluates the relationship between the two chapters. He says he has in mind "the specific relationship" between the first two articles of the creed.[64] Barth describes this relationship as one between the "implicit" and "explicit"[65] or between "shadow" and "reality."[66] If we read only the fourth chapter of Revelation, we might be left with a formless account of God. The transition between these two chapters constitutes a crossover from angelic worship that addresses a hypothetical *deus absconditus* to the risen Lamb.

In Revelation 5:5, the prevailing of the Lamb is announced. Barth identifies this proclamation as the Easter message.[67] This Christ, who has taken

60. *CD* I/1, 306. See also *KD* I/1, 323.
61. Colin Gunton maintains that this statement in I/1 reiterates Barth's volume on Anselm: "Barth is . . . making the point that the assertion of the lordship of God in revelation is made necessary for the theologian by revelation . . . 'to act as Lord *means* to act as God in His revelation acts on man' (*CD* I/1, 306)." *Becoming and Being: The Doctrine of God in Charles Hartshorne and Karl Barth* (London: SCM, 1978), 129.
62. *CD* III/3, 468.
63. *CD* III/3, 470.
64. *CD* III/3, 466.
65. *CD* III/3, 469.
66. *CD* III/3, 471.
67. *CD* III/3, 470.

on human flesh, is the one who is worthy to open the scroll of history and stands "at the beginning of these events" as the only providential Lord. This passage focuses very specifically on the fact that this Jewish man, who stands before and presides over all of history, is the *enfleshed* Christ. The one who "had been slain" is alone able to open the scroll (Rev. 5:6). The content of this book is "what takes place in history," or the will and counsel of God.[68] The transition between the two forms of worship, from the general to the more specific, identifies the object of angelic worship as the one who is, at once, Creator and enfleshed Redeemer:

> The depths of the earth have the advantage over heaven that it was here below that the decisive event took place, that the Lamb gained the victory as the Lion which He is now seen to be in heaven. . . . It is for this reason that the angels can and must sing that the Lamb is worthy to take the book and open the seals. It is for this reason that they can and must see and praise Jesus Christ (*vere Deus vere homo*) as the one who stands in the power and wisdom of God at the beginning of all cosmic occurrence and who will initiate and control all cosmic occurrence.[69]

Barth's engagement with the heavenly praise in the Apocalypse requires that the providence of God be directed by the mercy displayed at Golgotha. The event that takes place there is an act that redeems "out of every kindred, and tongue, and people and nation."[70] Whatever slavery may have initially or hypothetically held these creatures captive, their redemption expresses God's mercy. Also, and on this account, the "second" act, which derives from Golgotha, is "creation."[71] The divine counsel, aiming to move outward to create and redeem, is made possible by the slaying of the Lamb.

The qualities ascribed to Christ in Revelation 5 are expanded into a "greater number of predicates" than in the previous chapter.[72] Omnipotence is an attribute emphasized here because, with the advent of chapter 5, we see that the "Lamb is the Lion."[73] The perfections of God are on display at Golgotha, and Barth finds this praise directed to the Lamb to be the most important and final clarification of how these perfections are to be apprehended.

This God who elicits worship in both chapters is one and the same "true and genuine" God.[74] Barth is concerned to indicate that the angels have no

68. CD III/3, 469.
69. CD III/3, 473–74.
70. CD III/3, 473.
71. CD III/3, 473.
72. CD III/3, 474.
73. CD III/3, 470.
74. CD III/3, 476.

confusion about these two choruses being directed to the same God. This is Barth's primary claim. The worship in chapter 4 is open to the eschatological vindication of the will of God provided by the one who elects himself in Christ, dies at Golgotha, and rises again. Thus, there is a "confluence" of the two chapters and, importantly, also the heavenly praise to the selfsame, self-electing God.[75]

Barth's preceding paragraph in *CD* III/3 focuses on the difficult problem of *das Nichtige*. This is, as he describes it—and with some shorthand—the problem of the unification of the divine attributes of holiness and omnipotence in God's economy.[76] Barth's volume brings this problem into proximity with a resolution in the praise of the angels in §51, which does not resemble the "broken thoughts and utterance" that attempt to adjudicate this break between the Creator and the creature.[77] Rather, the praise of the angels in chapter 4 sees the omnipotence of God as brought into alignment with the disclosure of the Lamb as the Lord of providence in chapter 5. As the one who executes mercy at Golgotha, he is: "as the Holy One . . . the παντοκράτωρ."[78] Majesty and mercy combine in this heavenly *visio Dei* of God in Jesus Christ.[79]

In §51, Barth answers his own question by pointing to the praise of heaven. The angelic doxology acknowledges that the holiness and sovereignty of the Son is also that of the Father. In the heavenly chorus, the angelic acknowledgment of honor and glory and power does not pretend to "add" anything to God, but to simply acknowledge, with thanksgiving, what qualities belong to God *in se*. This form of worship puts Barth's initial statement in §48.2 into practice: "The object of the belief in providence can only be God Himself, as God Himself in His revelation in Jesus Christ is its only basis."[80]

In *CD* III/3, Barth is resolved to explicate a doctrine of providence that does not leave the first article to stand on its own.[81] The doctrine of providence can give due credence to the God of Christian confession only if it points to a holy God who expels evil and so leads us to praise him. This theological confession of the angels leads us full circle for the whole of *CD* III/3 in that it acknowledges—beyond the dilemma of the problem of evil—that Jesus Christ is the omnipotent and holy subject who governs the world providentially.

75. *CD* III/3, 475.
76. *CD* III/3, 292, 294.
77. *CD* III/3, 294.
78. *CD* III/3, 467.
79. "The majesty of God as His mercy was the outline and shadow of the divine mystery as indicated already in Rev. 4. And now at the climax of Rev. 5 we are confronted by the form and reality of the same mystery" (*CD* III/3, 471).
80. *CD* III/3, 20.
81. *CD* III/3, 428.

The theology of heaven finds its resolution to the problems that beset doctrines of providence in an active commending of the Lamb on the throne. This doxological commendation on the part of God's heavenly witnesses is a practical separation of light from darkness, which fulfills God's holy expectation that his creature should praise him.[82] It is the angelic host that first recognizes that the "multiplicity and confusion of the lines of creaturely occurrence" apparent in world history are resolved in the triune God.[83] In Barth's exegesis of Revelation 4–5, then, he gives deference to the theology of the angels for establishing his own performative approach to divine providence.

Revelation 4 as Angelic "Placeholder"

Barth's focus here is upon worship directed to the man Jesus who, as the Word of God, stands above history and presides over it. For this reason, as well as due to Barth's bringing his doctrine of providence into close alignment with his doctrine of election, it may be instructive to briefly compare his section on Revelation 4–5 with his approach to the Johannine Prologue in the context of his doctrine of predestination, which has attracted some attention.[84] A few points of continuity and discontinuity between these two exegetical treatments deserve comment.

In Barth's weighty excursus on the introduction to John's Gospel in CD II/2, he uncovers his exegetical argument for establishing the enfleshed Word of God as the electing God.[85] Barth's procedure in this section is to describe the Logos of the Johannine Prologue as a "stopgap," which does not immediately refer to extrabiblical thought forms. Rather, he maintains that this Logos, who is God, is identified with the man Jesus Christ, narrated in John's Gospel. The "Logos" is, then, a forward-looking reference that is unidentifiable on its own. The reference is precisely this man who does the electing work of God. With this in mind, it is interesting that Barth's volume on election first illustrates the notion of a "stopgap" by drawing an explicit connection with

82. Gorringe states it well: "In thanking God, we confirm the divine separation of light from darkness in Barth's theology" (*Against Hegemony*, 208).

83. *CD* III/3, 44.

84. See *CD* II/2, 96–99; Karl Barth, *Witness to the Word: A Commentary on John 1*, ed. Walther Fürst, trans. Geoffrey W. Bromiley (Grand Rapids: Eerdmans, 1986), 23–29; Cunningham, *What Is Theological Exegesis?*, 22–26; John Webster, "Barth's Lectures on the Gospel of John," in *Thy Word Is Truth*, ed. George Hunsinger (Grand Rapids: Eerdmans, 2012), 140–47. See also Wesley Hill's essay, chap. 6 in this volume.

85. Bruce McCormack, "Grace and Being: The Role of God's Gracious Election in Karl Barth's Theological Ontology," in *The Cambridge Companion to Karl Barth*, ed. John Webster (Cambridge: Cambridge University Press, 2000), 93–101.

the nineteenth chapter of the Apocalypse. This use of the book of Revelation is meant to illustrate what he means with his term "stopgap": "In Revelation 19:13 it is said of the Rider on the white horse that one of the diadems on his head bears a name which no one knows . . . and this name, which can be read but which only He can understand, this ideogram which only He can decipher, is as follows: 'ὁ λόγος τοῦ θεοῦ.'"[86]

This gesture shows Barth's interest in the fecundity of the Apocalypse for establishing the theologian's proper movement toward the *who* of God in Jesus Christ. In the statement above, Barth selects this particular text because it serves as a quick illustration for how the Johannine Prologue refers to the "Logos," which is a term without meaning until the reader comes across the Word-made-flesh in John 1:14.[87] The term's reference is located subsequent to its introduction because it only points forward to the Incarnate One.

Barth's exegesis of Revelation 4–5 also provides an example of a similar interpretive movement in the heavenly sphere. The angelic *visio Dei* in Revelation 4 looks forward to the enfleshed Christ for clarification in Revelation 5. Angelic worship is good theology because its attention to God as Creator, as the "one who comes," cannot be understood apart from his forthcoming self-disclosure as the enfleshed Messiah who opens the scroll of history. While he makes no direct reference to the Johannine Prologue in this section, Barth similarly maintains that Scripture focuses on the enfleshed Word of God as the one who clarifies the divine will. This move transitions from a general form of worship to a much more specific focus on the Lamb who "had been slain."[88]

As with his doctrine of election, Barth places emphasis in §51.2 on Scripture granting a position to the enfleshed Word within the eternal council of God. The Lamb is already slain prior to the onset of creation. The risen Lamb who opens the scroll is still "bearing the marks of . . . immolation."[89] A rejection of the *Logos asarkos* can be discerned here, but without laboring over the use of such theological terms. Rather, Barth aims to closely reiterate the text. He wishes to communicate what this text implies for providence by continually returning to what it says about "the book." In this respect, Barth challenges his readership to adequately wrestle with the biblical text and its description of God in Jesus Christ (read: *Logos ensarkos*) as the active subject of divine providence.

Second, Jesus is the subject of divine providence in an analogous way to his establishment as such in the context of predestination. Barth concentrates

86. CD II/2, 96.
87. Barth, *Witness to the Word*, 84–102.
88. CD III/3, 471.
89. CD III/3, 470–71.

on the fact that it is the Lamb who, in taking the scroll, becomes the "all powerful . . . Executor of His [God's] will and plan."[90] This is, of course, reminiscent of Jesus Christ being counted as, on account of Barth's exegesis of the Johannine Prologue, the electing God in an active sense.[91]

Of course, between the two treatments of Scripture important discontinuities remain. Barth's specific focus in this section is on the importance of heaven's praise for the locus of divine providence. Barth is not concerned here with retracing a description of Jesus Christ as the subject of predestination. Rather, his focus is on the *ordo cognoscendi*. He seeks to describe the praise that is elicited, and exemplified for us, by the God who elects himself in Christ and his heavenly entourage. The angels offer praise to the risen Lord who stands at the onset of "all cosmic occurrence" as its Lord.[92]

Conclusion

Barth states in *CD* III/3 that he finds a joyful embrace of divine providence largely lacking in the theological tradition. He sees his forebears, especially— but not exclusively—the Reformed, as more speculative and focused on an all-encompassing understanding of omnipotence.[93] Barth's exegesis of Revelation 4–5 attempts to strengthen his case by appealing to terms deployed in the text of Scripture and not straying too much by discussing the conceptual entailments. In this sense, he aims to juxtapose his theology over against his predecessors—as well as his contemporaries, such as Peterson—by appealing to the text of Scripture.

Taken directly, Barth is challenging his readership with his exegesis of these two chapters in the book of Revelation. He is indicating that all theology must be done in a manner that is expected by the praise of heaven. In addition, Barth is focused on the nature of theology itself and how to secure the harmony of omnipotence with holiness in God's economy. He resolves this by juxtaposing one kind of theology over and against another, making his

90. *CD* III/3, 471.
91. The term "Logos" points "to an eternal happening and to a temporal: to an eternal in the form of time and to a temporal with the content of eternity" (*CD* II/2, 97). Later, Barth says that "the Prologue is not speaking of an eternal Son or divine Logos *in abstracto*, but of a Son and Logos who is one with the man Jesus" (*CD* III/2, 483).
92. *CD* III/3, 474.
93. The Reformed tradition is one of Barth's many dialogue partners throughout *CD* III/3. To a significant extent, his exposition affirms the position established within his own tradition. His understanding of the providence of God is "as sovereign as the Calvinist teaching describes" (*CD* III/3, 131). He states this in spite of his own criticisms of the Reformed with his "radical correction," which places the doctrine of predestination as anterior to providence (*CD* III/3, xii).

own approach mandatory. He tells all other approaches that they have yet to take off their sandals.

In this exegetical aside, the angelic chorus provides Barth with an implicit critique of any generic doctrine of God in the context of the locus of divine providence. Angelic praise eschews impersonal causal schemes in favor of a thoroughgoing awareness of the God who elects himself in the enfleshed man, Jesus Christ. Rigid questions regarding causality are considered by the angels to be a distraction. Their praise, which extols God "analytically," disallows such questions from interrupting their outcry, "Worthy is the Lamb who was slain" (Rev. 5:12).[94] The doxology of the angels looks beyond the problem of primary and secondary causality and exemplifies how a theology of providence should properly terminate in praise. In this, Barth sees a concrete answer to the frequent dilemmas that emerge in the doctrine of providence and deploys the chorus of the angels to outrun the abstract questions of his readers.

94. *CD* III/3, 468.

PART 5

Barth's Doctrine
of Reconciliation
in Exegetical Perspective

THIRTEEN

Barth on Christ and Adam

GRANT MACASKILL

Introduction

This essay concerns Barth's treatment of the contrastive parallel of Christ and Adam in Romans 5 and the question of how this is to be evaluated in relation to the alternative approaches found in much biblical scholarship. I will focus on Barth's 1956 work *Christ and Adam: Man and Humanity in Romans 5*,[1] which represents a slender but mature reflection on the topic, with some further reference to the *Church Dogmatics*. It is undoubtedly important to ask how this mature material is related to Barth's earlier commentaries on Romans, but that is a question that may be investigated elsewhere by Barth specialists who can comment on elements of development in his thought and also on elements of tension with his wider theology. As a biblical scholar, my interests and competencies are more usefully directed toward evaluating Barth's reading of the Christ-Adam comparison in Romans in relation to alternatives more usually encountered in my own discipline. Barth's distinctive approach is at once radically at odds with some of the common approaches to the Christ-Adam comparison that see

---

1. Karl Barth, *Christ and Adam: Man and Humanity in Romans 5* (New York: Harper, 1956). Translated by T. Smail from *Christus und Adam nach Römer 5* (Zurich: Evangelischer Verlag, 1952). The page numbers here correspond to the 1962 reprint by Collier (New York).

it as key to Pauline soteriology, notably those that support some kind of "Adam Christology," while at the same time sharing an underlying logic with some of the alternative approaches to Pauline soteriology, particularly the one often now labeled "apocalyptic." In fact, recognizing the significance of this common underlying logic for how the surface detail of the text is interpreted is critically important for a proper understanding of the debates around the apocalyptic Paul in New Testament scholarship: much of the confusion around those debates stems from a failure among both onlookers and some participants to recognize the fundamental issues that shape the presenting surfaces. This essay will outline some of the distinctive features of Barth's developed reading of Romans 5 and will give some consideration to how these are shaped by his programmatic decisions about directions of correspondence and contingency, offering some concluding reflections on how this relates to current apocalyptic Paul debates.

The nature and significance of these decisions about correspondence and contingency, particularly with respect to Romans 5, are made clear if we isolate the issues at stake with reference to a series of linked questions, the first of which is programmatic for all that follow: What or who conditions what or whom? Does the significance of Adam, in Paul's theology or in mature Christian theology, condition how we think about Jesus, or does the significance of Jesus condition how we think about Adam? Might there be something more reciprocal, if perhaps asymmetrical, in their relationship? Further, is this simply a matter of interpretive conditioning—in which the story of one is "read" or "understood" in the light of the story of the other—or is there something more basic, something ontological, at stake? Are the being, nature, and experience of Jesus determined by Adam, or that of Adam determined by Jesus? And is the evaluation of all of this shaped, consciously or not, by assumptions about human nature—about anthropology—that are external to the biblical material? The issues at stake are rather more live in current biblical studies than may at first be recognized, notably in the debate around apocalyptic readings of Paul. Some of what I highlight in Barth's reading of Romans 5 may allow a greater degree of mutual understanding to characterize that debate and perhaps a sharper sensitivity to some of these underlying issues.

In the first part of the essay, then, I am going to explore some recent and contemporary approaches to the Christ-Adam parallel in biblical studies, highlighting the way that the scholars in question understand the direction of conditioning (or, perhaps better, what they presume it to be). I will then explore Barth's contrastive approach, noting some of its theological and textual motivations.

Variants of Adam Christology

At the time when Barth wrote his commentaries, one of the dominant approaches to the Adam-Christ parallel in Romans 5 and 1 Corinthians 15 understood it to reflect a form of gnostic theology or Hellenistic mystery religion.[2] While it is now largely out of favor, it is important to give some thought to this approach in order to highlight some easily overlooked parallels that exist between it and some of the alternatives still popular today. The gnostic approach is most famously associated with Bultmann, who writes: "The contrast 'psychic-pneumatic' (man of soul, man of spirit) to designate two basically different classes of men . . . is an especially clear indication that Paul's anthropological concepts had already been formed under the influence of Gnosticism."[3] Bultmann, importantly, sees this Pauline anthropology as framed principally in cosmological and not salvation-historical terms: "The thought of two mankinds (or two epochs of mankind), and their determination each by its originator, is a Gnostic idea which is conceived cosmologically and not in terms of salvation-history."[4] Elsewhere, he shifts the terms slightly, identifying the Hellenistic mystery cults as the immediate background, but the basic terms of his approach are still the same. Similar approaches are found in Schmithals[5] and Brandenburger,[6] who also pursue a gnostic background to Paul's handling of Adam. All, of course, have been widely criticized, in particular for the lateness of the evidence that they use in support of their reconstruction of the place of Adam in gnostic beliefs and for the extent to which their theories rest on an arguably speculative reconstruction of the beliefs of Paul's theological opponents, particularly in Corinth. Those criticisms are well documented elsewhere,[7] and I will not cover them again here.

Instead, I want to draw attention to the way in which the correspondence of Christ and Adam is conceived by Bultmann and by the others who share

2. For an excellent discussion of this, on which I draw here, see Felipe de Jesús Legarreta-Castillo, *The Figure of Adam in Romans 5 and 1 Corinthians 15: The New Creation and Its Ethical and Social Reconfiguration* (Minneapolis: Fortress, 2014), 4–12. The quotations from Bultmann that I discuss throughout this section are identified by Legarreta-Castillo, and I cannot improve upon his perceptive selection of readings.

3. Rudolf Bultmann, *The Theology of the New Testament*, vol. 1, trans. K. Grobel (New York: Scribner, 1951), 174.

4. Rudolf Bultmann, "Adam and Christ according to Romans 5," in *Current Issues in New Testament Interpretation: Essays in Honor of Otto A. Piper*, ed. William Klassen and Graydon F. Snyder (London: SCM, 1962), 154. See also Bultmann, *The Old and the New Man in the Letters of Paul*, trans. Keith R. Crim (Richmond: John Knox, 1967).

5. Walter Schmithals, *Die Gnosis in Korinth* (Göttingen: Vandenhoeck and Ruprecht, 1956).

6. Egon Brandenburger, *Adam und Christus: Exegetisch-Religionsgeschichtliche Untersuchung zu Romans 5, 12–21 (1 Kor. 15)* (Neukirchen: Neukirchener Verlag, 1962).

7. See Legarreta-Castillo, *Figure of Adam*, 4–12.

this approach. Clearly, Adam and Christ are understood within a dualistic framework, but it is one in which, in certain senses, the problem of Adam is determinative for how the Christ event is presented, and not vice versa: "Paul says nothing about the possibility of our recognizing in retrospect the ordering principle of the kingdom of Christ also in the world of Adam."[8]

The second is the key role that the concept of "anthropology" plays within this. Paul is understood to work with a set of categories about "human being" shaped by gnostic thought or mystery cults, within which Adam and Christ are considered. While Adam may not, in this scheme, directly condition the representation of Jesus so much as parallel it, both figures are understood in terms of a prior category of anthropology, which the program of "demythologization" now exposes and requires to be translated. The point highlights something important: for Bultmann, at least, what is pursued is not simply the historical backdrop to Paul's thought and its theological development, but rather an account of "authentic human existence" set in terms of theological anthropology.

While the gnostic approach is now rather marginal to Pauline scholarship, another family of approaches continues to be quite influential and, indeed, to be seen as the key alternative to the gnostic thesis, since it is seen as locating Paul's theology within Jewish thought rather than Hellenistic. This family might appropriately be identified with the label "Adam Christology," for what holds the divergent contributions together is some agreement that the representation of Jesus in Romans 5 and 1 Corinthians 15 is conditioned by the story of Adam, and further agreement that these texts are merely the explicit surfacings of an underlying theology that is far more widespread in Paul's thought and quite fundamental to it. Well-known representatives of this approach include Robin Scroggs, James Dunn, Morna Hooker, and N. T. Wright, all of whom have developed their Adam Christology in the context (primarily, at least) of the study of Paul.[9] Further representatives might be noted whose work has been rather more oriented toward questions of biblical theology, with the significance of Adam represented as a driving theme in the development of biblical narrative. So, for example, Beale's *The Temple and the*

8. Bultmann, "Adam and Christ," 163.
9. See Robin Scroggs, *The Last Adam: A Study in Pauline Anthropology* (London: Blackwell, 1966); James D. G. Dunn, *Christology in the Making: A New Testament Inquiry into the Origins of the Doctrine of the Incarnation* (Grand Rapids: Eerdmans, 1989), 98–128; Dunn, *The Theology of Paul the Apostle* (Grand Rapids: Eerdmans, 2003), esp. 200–204, 241–44; Morna D. Hooker, *From Adam to Christ: Essays on Paul* (Cambridge: Cambridge University Press, 1990); N. T. Wright, *The Climax of the Covenant: Christ and the Law in Paul* (Minneapolis: Fortress, 1993), 18–40, 56–98. See my discussion in *Union with Christ in the New Testament* (Oxford: Oxford University Press, 2013), 128–43.

Church's Mission,[10] while primarily concerned with the trajectory of temple imagery in the Bible, traces this imagery back into the representation of Adam in the Garden and some of the evidence from Jewish literature of the time that Adam was considered the prototypical priest and Eden the prototypical temple. For Beale, the temple and cult recapitulate the reality lost at the fall and themselves anticipate the ultimate recapitulation or recovery of this in the incarnational narrative and those realities consequential to it: the church and the cosmic eschatological reality still to be seen. Elements of Beale's account parallel some of the fine detail of Wright's work, notably in terms of the Adamic overtones in, for example, Daniel 7 and its influence on Mark 13 and parallels: the vindication of the Son of Man is really a matter of the fulfillment of Israel's commission—which, as a nation, it failed to realize—to be the true humanity in which is recovered what was lost by Adam.

While the various accounts diverge in their detail, this element is common to all of them, and it involves a number of further common decisions or assumptions. First, the wider influence of the Adam story is identified by the presence of less explicit allusions to it, which are typically constituted by the presence of words and images that are synonymous to (or antonymous to) those found in the accounts of Genesis 1–3. So, for example, the use of *harpagmos* in Philippians 2:5 ("who . . . did not count equality with God a *thing to be grasped*," RSV) is understood to represent Jesus's self-emptying in terms that are implicitly contrasted with Adam's taking of the fruit.[11] It is assumed without much question that Jewish readers would make such allusive use of the Old Testament texts, though the dedicated study of Jewish reading strategies in the Second Temple period suggests that quite different principles seemed to govern exegesis.[12]

Second, this family of approaches tends to affirm a narrative that is held to lie behind the biblical text, one that moves from Adam to Israel to Christ, in which the direction of conditioning is always forward. Often this narrative is labeled as one involving "recapitulation": Israel recapitulates Adam, Christ recapitulates Israel; Christ, hence, ultimately recapitulates Adam. The term is used with reference to Irenaeus and Athanasius, often explicitly taking warrant from these figures, but in a way that—as we shall see—departs quite

10. Gregory K. Beale, *The Temple and the Church's Mission: A Biblical Theology of the Dwelling Place of God* (Downers Grove, IL: IVP Academic, 2004).

11. N. T. Wright, "Harpagmos and the Meaning of Philippians 2: 5–11," *Journal of Theological Studies* 37 (1986): 321–52.

12. See the excellent overview and analysis of scholarship in William Tooman, *Gog of Magog: Reuse of Scripture and Compositional Technique in Ezekiel 38–39* (Tübingen: Mohr Siebeck, 2011), 4–22.

significantly from their usage. One of the points that is rather important within this is the significance attached to "glory" language. Rather than being seen as principally a designation of Jesus's divinity, this is seen as a designation of his truly human humanity, of his recovery of the original Adamic condition. A corollary of such a narratival arrangement is that law and covenant are typically understood in positive terms, and their relationship to the Christ event is understood to have a preparatory significance that is fulfilled in his coming. So, we are in the territory of what is often labeled "salvation history," and it is unsurprising that some of the advocates of such an approach have also been part of the recent debate around the apocalyptic approach to Paul.

A third point is, in some ways, an outworking of the second: there is a widely shared assumption that this way of thinking about the relationship of Adam and Israel is characteristic of Second Temple Judaism, so that to read the New Testament through Jewish eyes inevitably involves seeing a host of ways in which the story of Jesus is seen truly to be the conclusion of the story of Adam *ha-rishon*, the resolution of the biblical story that began with that figure. Part of the evidence that is adduced for this is found in a cluster of writings that appear to reflect an underlying Adam myth with some fairly stable features, particularly in relation to the glory of the protoplast. He was a glorious figure, having either a glorious form or glorious garments, which were lost with the fall. Even here, there is a real risk of confusing somewhat variant categories: in the case of the former, what is in view is some kind of ontological change (even if it is not labeled as such), something intrinsic to the being of Adam; in the case of the latter, something more extrinsic or even functional is in view. But there is also a more basic problem, which is the question of how much of this material may be legitimately admitted to exegetical discussion of the New Testament and how it is used. I have argued elsewhere,[13] on the basis of the work of others, that much of this material is probably later than the New Testament—although some fresh scholarship has emerged in recent years that presents a stronger case for the earliness of the pseudepigraphical *Life of Adam and Eve*—and that what is demonstrably early presents a significant level of diversity. Significantly, that diversity reflects the fact that, rather than Adam being the controlling factor in the stories, actually the controlling or conditioning elements are precisely the things that come later: Israel, the temple, the covenants, and so on. The Adam myth itself is quite elastic, able to be bent to fit the controlling ideas of the narrator.

13. See *Union with Christ*, 128–43.

Given these three points, among others, the critics of the Adam Christology approach argue that what is labeled as exegesis is, in fact, quite creative interpretation—interpretation, indeed, that unwittingly projects some very modern ideas of narrative, coherence, and anthropology back onto the biblical text. Bultmann's approach, by contrast, is quite *consciously* modern: he seeks to retrieve from the text something about authentic human existence based on a set of decisions about the character of religion, even if he does so in a way that now appears to us to be historically naive, given what we know today about the lateness of the evidence for gnosticism, and even for the mystery religions. The alternative approaches consider themselves to stand in sharp contrast to this, being warranted by their Jewishness and by their sensitivity to ancient premodern categories, but their critics see them as inattentive to key details of the text that point in the direction of discontinuity and disruption, not that of continuity and conditioning.

Included among the critics of this approach are those who represent what is now often labeled as the "apocalyptic Paul" school. Their reading of Paul sees the Christ event as something radically contrastive to Adam and Israel, rather than as something the meaning of which is conditioned by the Adam story. The gospel is an invasive reality, one that comes from outside the machinery of our world: it is radically new, and no line can be traced from Adam through Israel to it. As the new Adam, Jesus is "the paradigmatic eschatological *anthrôpos*";[14] his death brings an end to the old order and constitutes a fundamental disruption that is perceived by those who have received this apocalypse. There is, for the apocalyptic school, no sense in which the anthropology of Jesus is contingent upon that of Adam.

As we shall see, this corresponds in key ways to Barth's approach, and, indeed, the influence of Barth on this approach is recognized and acknowledged:[15] proper reflection on this is helpful for our understanding of the major debate in Pauline scholarship around the apocalyptic interpretation. As we shall also see, however, those elements of Barth's reading that are attentive to the significance of Israel have rather vanished from the Pauline scholarship.

14. J. Louis Martyn, *Galatians: A New Translation with Introduction and Commentary*, Anchor Yale Bible 33 (New York: Doubleday, 1997), 280. The comment concerns the language of co-crucifixion encountered in Gal. 2:19.

15. For an excellent analysis of the relationship between the apocalyptic Paul school and Barth's thought, see Philip Ziegler, "Some Remarks on Apocalyptic in Modern Christian Theology," in *Paul and the Apocalyptic Imagination*, ed. Ben C. Blackwell, John K. Goodrich, and Jason Maston (Minneapolis: Fortress, 2016), 203–10.

Barth's Account of Christ and Adam

Barth's understanding of the formal parallel between Christ and Adam involves first a basic acknowledgment of the retrospective dimension of Paul's treatment of the figure of Adam. Adam is understood on the basis of Paul's understanding of Jesus, his story read through that later story and the significance that Paul now attaches to it. The problem of sin is necessarily approached from the standpoint of the one who considers himself to have been forgiven and saved, including the account of the first sin to be described in the final form of the canon. This decision is obviously not arbitrary on Barth's part, either in relation to the critical position of Christ or in relation to that of Adam. In relation to Christ, I do not think I need to say much on a hermeneutical commitment that has been covered in depth elsewhere; in relation to Adam, though, some comments may be helpful (in general terms, before we come to look more closely at the formal parallel). For Barth considers it important that there are only two points in the Pauline corpus where Adam is explicitly identified and, indeed, few further such points in the canon.[16] Given the scarcity of references, Adam's importance should not be overplayed and must be properly identified in relation to the comparison with Christ.

The identification of Adam's representative character, as Barth describes it here, is linked to a decision about the genre of the biblical creation story, that it is saga:

> It is not history but only saga which can tell us that he came into being in this way and existed as the one who came into being this way—the first man. We miss the unprecedented and incomparable thing which the Genesis passages tell us of the coming into being and existence of Adam if we try to read and understand it as history, relating it either favorably or unfavorably to scientific paleontology, or to what we know with some historical certainty concerning the oldest and most primitive forms of human life. The saga as a form of historical narration is a genre apart. And within this genre biblical saga is a special instance which cannot be compared with others but has to be seen and understood in and for itself.[17]

This move is important, for it means that Adam's sin—understood now in the light of the pardon that has come through God's work in Christ—may not be considered straightforwardly as the original cause of subsequent sin; it is not, in other words, understood etiologically, but rather paradigmatically.

16. See CD IV/1, 507–8.
17. CD IV/1, 508.

Here, Barth offers some distinctive reflections on Adam as "first among equals":

> He simply did in the insignificant form of the beginner that which all men have done after him, that which is in a more or less serious and flagrant form our own transgression. He was in a trivial form what we all are, a man of sin. But he was so as the beginner, and therefore as *primus inter pares* (first among equals). This does not mean that he has bequeathed it to us as his heirs so that we have to be as he was. He has not poisoned us or passed on a disease. . . . We and he are reached by the same Word and judgment of God in the same direct way. The only difference is that what we all are and do he was and did at the very gateway of history, and therefore he was reached first by the Word and judgement of God in a way which is typical for all his successors.[18]

Barth's account of "the original sin," then, in moving away from any notion of etiology or transmission, results in an intense view of our personal culpability for the sins that we have committed. We have no excuse: we cannot blame them on our genetics, or excuse ourselves on the basis of our background. They are *our* sins. We have put ourselves under this yoke. Sin "came in to the world through the one act of Adam" only in the sense that there had to be a first instance, and that first instance establishes a gateway of sorts: all subsequent acts correspond to the shape of that original act and share in its fatal outworkings. Significantly, then, our solidarity with Adam is constituted not just by our common and shared human nature but also by our common and shared practices, our mutual active subjecthood of verbs of sin. "Death spread to all, because all have sinned" (Rom. 5:12, NRSV).

This has implications for how Barth goes on to read Romans 5 and 1 Corinthians 15 and for the nature of the formal parallel between Christ and Adam. If Adam is considered to be first among equals in the agency of sin rather than as the originator of the problem, then the formal parallel is necessarily shaped and interpreted somewhat differently. Christ's relationship to Adam corresponds quite directly to his relationship to us, to other sinners; it does not *first* address the problem that Adam represents and *then* address the problem that we represent as heirs.

As an aside, but an important one, an approach that understands Adam in this way, framed by concepts such as saga (whether or not we think that is the right category for Gen. 1–3), allows us also to speak of Eve. In Barth's account, Adam retains a certain primacy in representing sinful humanity simply because of his name: he is "man" (we have seen this already in the

18. *CD* IV/1, 509–10.

quotation above from *CD* IV/1). Within such an account, Eve is not marginal. She simply does not have this etymologically universal representative function. There is, I think, an interesting point of contrast for us to reflect on with the Adam Christology approaches that involve some notion of etiology, for there Eve is truly marginal, squeezed out of the story by the dominance of the male characters whose actions are represented as essentially determinative for those who follow them.

These observations serve to embed and contextualize Barth's particular handling of the formal parallel between Adam and Christ and allow us to understand the more specific moves that Barth makes concerning the constitutive character of the humanity of Christ. For Barth's understanding of the priority of Christ is not simply a matter of hermeneutical principle—that we now interpret Adam in the light of Christ—but of something basic to the very existence and being of the first earthly man: that his being was always contingent upon the being of Christ, that he was never an independent reality, and that, as such, his sin was never an independent reality. Adam's reality is a provisional one, and consequently our relationship to Adam is itself a subordinate one: "because the guilt and punishment we incur in Adam have no independent reality of their own, but are only the dark shadows of the grace and life we find in Jesus."[19]

Barth's statements to this effect involve a combination of close attention to the text and more systemic decisions. Within the text of Romans 5 itself, a pivotal role is played by the contrasts, the dis-analogies, established in verses 15–16: the gift is *not like* the trespass, the gift is not like the effects of the one sin. The key to the contrast or to the dis-analogy lies specifically in the identity of the giver of the gift: it is given by God. Precisely because it is given by God and is determined by his goodness and plenitude, it "abounds" (5:15) with an "abundance" (5:17) and does so for "the many" (5:17). It stands, therefore, in sharp contrast to any human act or work that proceeds from the finitude of the individual in question. This is where Barth's close attention to the text meets a set of systemic considerations about God and about the contingency of human existence that we have already seen highlighted in *CD* IV/1: "Adam appears in the Genesis story as the man who owes his existence directly to the creative will and Word and act of God without any human intervention." Adam's original existence is already to be understood as graced directly by the creative will of God and is conditioned by nothing outside of that will.

This same emphasis on the immediate, unconditioned, radically free will of God emerges in Barth's understanding of the contrast between the trespass

---

19. Barth, *Christ and Adam*, 48.

and the gift. The trespass and its consequences are linked by a certain logic, even if the situation that results from them is truly a senseless one of death and despair.[20] Sin incurs guilt, guilt incurs death; there is a logic to such correspondences. But no logic external to the free decision of God is determinative of the gift, even if its outcome is entirely meaningful;[21] Barth uses invasive language of the gift because nothing incurs it, or requires it, or determines it, apart from the radically free decision of God himself.

> Thus, when the work of Christ is compared with the work of Adam, though they are formally identical, yet the difference between them is the radical, final and irremovable difference between God and man. That is why verse 15b said that the grace (*charisma*) was not to be measured by the transgression (*paraptoma*). That is why the opposite alone is possible. Paul is not denying that Adam's sin still brings death to all men, but he is affirming that the grace of Christ has an incomparably greater power to make these dead men alive. He is not saying that there is no truth in Adam, but he is saying that it is a subordinate truth that depends for its validity on its correspondence with the final truth that is in Christ.[22]

This involves a further decision about the genuine correspondence and genuine disparity between Christ and Adam that will go on to have implications for how Israel is to be understood. That Paul draws the parallel between Christ and Adam at all is, for Barth, significant. There is a sense in which their stories intersect, and this is important: Adam's story is no longer readable as one of despair and tragedy, but must now be read within the story of Christ. The point of relating the story of the trespass is precisely that it is overcome by the story of the gift, that it does not condition but is itself conditioned by the story of God's decision to save. Barth reflects extensively on the significance of πολλῷ μᾶλλον ("all the more") in Romans 5:15 and 17 in these terms: God's grace is always decisive for the evaluation of human trespass; it always exceeds the capacity of the latter to disrupt, always circumscribes it. By divine grace, by gift, Jesus makes himself present as a friend with those who live in the darkness of Adam's sin and its consequences, an act that requires his solidarity with them in death.[23] Here, again, Barth's

---

20. "On the one hand, the logical connection between sin and death is unmistakeably obvious, but the practical outcome of the rule of death is impossibly strange." Barth, *Christ and Adam*, 56.

21. Following from the quotation in the last footnote: "on the other hand, the logical connection between sin and pardon is completely miraculous and the material outcome of men living their true life is natural and true to the fundamental nature of man." Barth, *Christ and Adam*, 56.

22. Barth, *Christ and Adam*, 50.

23. Barth, *Christ and Adam*, 69–72.

representation of the primacy of Adam in terms of "first among equals," and not in terms of origination or etiology, allows that solidarity to be extended to him: it is not merely that Christ's story is determinative for the heirs of Adam, but it is determinative for Adam and his race. The retrospective dimension of the hermeneutic itself rests on a more basic identification of the truly determinative reality.

What this means is that there is an essential disparity between our relationship with Adam and our relationship with Christ, as well as an essential disparity between these two. Hopefully Barth's statement will now make sense within its logical context:

> Our unity with Adam is less essential and less significant than our true unity with Christ. On both sides, there are the same formal relationships between the one and the many, so that both sides have the same ordering principle. But within that formal identity, Adam is subordinate, because he can only be the forerunner, the witness, the preliminary shadow and likeness, the *typos* (type) [v. 14] of the Christ who is to come. . . . For Christ, who seems to come second, really comes first, and Adam, who seems to come first really comes second. In Christ, the relationship between the one and the many is original. In Adam, it is only a copy of that original. Our relationship with Adam depends for its reality on our relationship to Christ. And that means, in practice, that to find that true and essential nature of man, we have to look not to Adam the fallen man, but to Christ in whom what is fallen has been cancelled and what was original has been restored.[24]

There is a certain idealism to the language that Barth uses here that is similar to and different from certain patristic treatments of recapitulation. There,[25] the idea is developed with reference to images or texts that Barth neglects to treat (at least in his study of Christ and Adam), particularly those places where Christ is specifically designated as the very image of God (2 Cor. 4:4; Col. 1:15; 3:10), which is in contrast to the representation of Adam as made "after (*kata*) the image" and those places where the redemptive identity of Christ is represented in pretemporal or atemporal terms (Col. 1:15–18; Eph. 1:4; 1 Pet. 1:20; Rev. 13:8). Recapitulation is not simply a matter of early elements in a narrative being recovered at later stages: it is about a single figure whose personal identity and narrative are determinative for the entirety of the story, in whom all things are "summed up." Adam's humanity is patterned on Christ's, and not vice versa.

24. Barth, *Christ and Adam*, 74–75.
25. Notably, Irenaeus. See, e.g., *Against Heresies* 3.18.7; 3.21.9–10.

There is one further matter that needs to be discussed before we move toward our concluding reflections, and that is the significance of the people of Israel in relation to the formal correspondence between Christ and Adam. Barth represents the story of Israel in correspondence to both figures, but with the asymmetry and prioritization that we have seen to shape his account as a whole. Israel's story instantiates the sin and death of Adam; indeed, it abounds in this, but is itself determined by the grace that abounds all the more. "What does it mean to say that grace became much greater at the very place where sin became great? From the whole context of the chapter, Paul must have been thinking here of one thing. The people of Israel. . . . Out of Israel comes the Christ who bears but also bears away the guilt of Israel and the guilt of all men in his death."[26]

Israel becomes the place where the simultaneous but disproportional realities of Christ and Adam are seen to obtain. Hence, for Barth, the fact that Jesus was a Jew "at one stroke makes a nonsense of all Jewish pride and all anti-Semitic scorn."[27] Within this, the condemnatory function of the law is important for Barth. The law functions negatively, to condemn evil and to keep that wound open,[28] in order that it might be healed: "Adam had to remain Adam or he could not be reconciled."[29] A particular significance is then attached to the Jewishness of Jesus:

> Jesus Christ was a Jew and so he also was subjected to the Law. He also was set in the place where God's grace reveals man's sin. But there is more to it than that. He was the only one who completely and genuinely stood in that place; he was *the* Jew. There was no other Jew like him because he alone, of his own free will incorporated in his own person the man who rebels against God and has to bear God's wrath. There is a substitution of Israel for other peoples. But what is that compared to the substitution of Christ for Israel, beside his acceptance of the mission of the Jews. . . . [He chose to be] the Israel that was subject to the Law and that through the Law was accused and convicted of its sin.[30]

The Adamic dimension emerges in a way that is quite contrastive with much contemporary Adam Christology: Jesus corresponds to Adam precisely by taking the place of Israel under the judgment of God, standing under that judgment as those who re-instantiate the sin of Adam, the sin that abounds in her midst. He is *the* Jew because he is the representative of sinners exposed

26. Barth, *Christ and Adam*, 91.
27. Barth, *Christ and Adam*, 91.
28. Barth, *Christ and Adam*, 87.
29. Barth, *Christ and Adam*, 87–88.
30. Barth, *Christ and Adam*, 91 (emphasis original).

by the law. But his capacity to save does not correspond to any fulfillment of the law, taken by itself; rather, it corresponds to his identity as God himself.

> And yet he was a Messiah whom no Israelite could beget as his son, for he could only be God's son and as such had to be engrafted into Israel from the outside as the beginning of the new, true Israel of God. In this preeminent way, he was a Jew. . . . He took that sin and that punishment upon himself when he was pronounced guilty and put to death and because it was as Son of God that He bore them, he took away the sin and punishment from men.[31]

Further, for Barth, this necessarily involves the "notorious" event of the rejection of Jesus by the Jews. The cross is the point where the abounding of Adam's sin in Israel formally parallels and intersects with the superabundance of divine grace: "Nothing else could have happened. . . . The time when God sealed the covenant with Israel by himself intervening on man's behalf, and so made his grace to overflow, was bound to be the time when Israel finally disowned the covenant and proved itself absolutely unworthy of the grace of God."[32]

The correspondence of Jesus to Israel to Adam, then, is for Barth not a matter of Jesus fulfilling Israel's commission to fulfill Adam's commission (although there are hints of this in Barth's language of Jesus as true humanity); rather, it is a matter of Jesus taking up the abundance of Adam's failure in Israel, carrying it away as an act of superabundant grace. Adam Christology, if we can speak of such a thing, is a subordinate and negative element within a constitutive gracious theological anthropology. If there is a "glory of Adam," it is but a derivative correspondence to the true glory of Christ, in whom the glory of God is present with us as Immanuel.

Concluding Reflections: Barth's Reading of Christ and Adam and the Apocalyptic Paul

As a general point, Barth's treatment of the formal parallel in Romans 5 is intimately connected to what is now commonly represented as the apocalyptic approach to Paul and the related movement of apocalyptic theology, which have their common root in Barth. Some reflection on the elements that we have outlined here might be helpful for those participating in the debate around this, for often what occupies the surface of that debate—particularly

31. Barth, *Christ and Adam*, 92–93.
32. Barth, *Christ and Adam*, 94.

concerning the question of salvation history—reflects a deeper set of decisions, frequently overlooked, about how the elements of the biblical texts are to be aligned. That, of course, is true on both sides: often what is presented as a historical or a Jewish reading of the text is determined by a set of equally theological decisions about God (and how he is known), about the coherence of the canon, about the place of human agency. If the debate is to mature, this must be recognized; reflections on Barth's treatment of Adam in Romans 5 and its connection to the representation of Israel may be helpful in advancing that conversation. At the same time, there needs to be some careful evaluation of the quality of Barth's exegetical activity and the implications that this may have for his eventual conclusions. I offer the following observations in relation to the apocalyptic Paul debate by way of conclusion to this chapter.

First, it would be a serious mistake to see Barth's ordering of the Christ-Adam correspondence—reflected in the priority of Christ's name in the title of the book—being made *apart from* exegetical factors. Barth's resistance to what may seem to be the surface meaning of the text involves genuine sensitivity to a number of features in Romans 5 and in the canon more broadly: the relative scarcity of explicit references to Adam, his appearance only now in the flow of Romans, the diminutive significance of Adam and the trespass when compared to Christ and the gift, the use of contrastive language in Romans 5—all of these lead Barth to his decisive identification of disparity in our relationships to each. It is attention to these textual details that leads him to an interpretation that seems to be so basically at odds with the surface detail of the text: that Christ is truly the first Adam.

Having said this, the exegetical component of Barth's interpretation is actually quite thin, even allowing for a general disinterest in matters of background, of things behind the text. While the Greek of the text is often noted, there is little engagement with the language that moves beyond simple quotation. There is little (if any) lexical work, even by way of comparison of the usage of terms here and elsewhere in Paul. And this means that there is a certain legitimacy to the criticism that while Barth is attentive to certain features of the text, and exploits them powerfully, he is so neglectful of others that his reading cannot be considered a responsible one. Barth's heirs, particularly in the apocalyptic Paul school, have sought to address precisely this lack, and it is, I think, helpful to consider some of their contributions in such terms: they are seeking to refine Barth's theological reading with exegetical detail.[33] Thus, while many of the core moves parallel those in Barth, notably in their attention to the language of contrast and disruption, they also move

---

33. Perhaps most notably, J. Louis Martyn's *Galatians*.

into discussions of background and context that are more obviously the stuff of modern biblical studies.[34] The question we are left with is whether these contributions are constructive exegetical developments of Barth's penetrating theological insight or strange hybrids of exegesis and theology, afflicted in the end by the genes that they have inherited.

Second, Barth's reading of Romans 5 is quite explicitly set against attempts to approach Christology with any kind of predetermined anthropology, any account of human nature that is not itself determined by Christ's own humanity. This orients Barth's approach against the basic directions of much modern theology, where christological questions are approached through modern categories of human being, but it also orients it against much modern biblical study. While the latter will often position themselves against "modern thought," they often share with that thought the idea that there is a self-subsistent or isolable category of human nature, even if they demand that this be derived from the biblical material. The account of Adam's creation and fall, coming as it does at the beginning of the Bible, is taken to be the starting point for this. Barth is critical of such an approach for its willingness to start anywhere other than with Christ, and this ultimately involves a decision about what we are doing when we read Scripture theologically: we are seeking to talk properly about God (a task now understood through the apocalypse of the gospel to involve talking properly about Jesus), not merely to talk about Paul. Properly understood, this helps to cast light on why the proponents of the apocalyptic reading of Paul consider this to provide pathways by which we might move past dualistic readings and theologies, and past supersessionist approaches to the relationship of church and Israel.[35] By starting our analysis with proper talk of God-in-Christ, the dualisms that always afflict theologies and philosophies developed from below are resisted from the beginning.

Third, as a corollary of this, Barth's exegesis is determined by prior theological decisions shaped by classical theological tradition: divine aseity, divine goodness/perfection, stringent monotheism, understood in trinitarian categories. Barth's handling of this text, then, is determined by what he understands to be the tradition itself determined by the canon of Scripture as a whole. It

---

34. The various excurses in Martyn's *Galatians* commentary exemplify this well, as does in general the work of Martinus de Boer, who has sought to locate Paul's apocalyptic in the complex of Second Temple apocalyptic thought. For an evaluation of both, see James P. Davies, *Paul among the Apocalypses? An Evaluation of the "Apocalyptic Paul" in the Context of Jewish and Christian Apocalyptic Literature*, Library of New Testament Studies 562 (London: Bloomsbury T&T Clark, 2016).

35. See Joshua B. Davis, "The Challenge of Apocalyptic to Modern Theology," in *Apocalyptic and the Future of Theology: With and beyond J. Louis Martyn*, ed. Joshua B. Davis and Douglas Harink (Eugene, OR: Wipf and Stock, 2012), 1–50.

is marked by his particular species of the rule of faith. This means that the task of exegesis is not to identify the thought of Paul the apostle as an isolable thing but to understand how God renders himself known in that thought, in this text, within the canon of Scripture.

This leads to one of the key points of contrast between Barth's handling of the Christ-Adam parallel and the apocalyptic reading of Paul. Functionally, if not intentionally, the emphasis on disruption and discontinuity that is a key element in the apocalyptic approach leads to particularly negative engagement with the wider canon of Scripture, and particularly the Old Testament.[36] I would suggest that the principal factor in this is the loss or lack of the concept of "correspondence" (*Entsprechung*) that marks Barth's own thought widely[37] and is manifest throughout his discussion of Romans 5. Barth, as we have seen, identifies a real value in Adam and Israel that they enjoy by their correspondence to Christ. This same concept is maintained and developed in other families of biblical scholarship shaped by Barth's theology, such as the figural approach developed by scholars such as Christopher Seitz[38] and Richard Hays.[39] It is a concept, however, that seems largely underdeveloped or even absent from the apocalyptic approach to Paul. Some reflection on this point might open fresh avenues for constructive discussion in the debate around the apocalyptic Paul, for those (such as Wright) who are resistant to the apocalyptic reading are most concerned by the apparent dislocation of Paul's theology from its biblical frameworks. Brought into the debate, Barth's categories of correspondence provide alternative ways of conceiving the coherence of the biblical material and its dramatis personae without conceding the necessary emphasis on disruption that the gospel entails.

36. See my comments on Douglas Campbell's *The Deliverance of God: An Apocalyptic Rereading of Justification in Paul* (Grand Rapids: Eerdmans, 2009) in Grant Macaskill, "Review Article: *The Deliverance of God*," *Journal for the Study of the New Testament* 34 (2011): 150–61.

37. For a discussion of this concept in Barth's theology, see Kimlyn Bender, *Confessing Christ for Church and the World: Studies in Modern Theology* (Downers Grove, IL: InterVarsity, 2014), 33–34.

38. Christopher R. Seitz, *Word without End: The Old Testament as Abiding Theological Witness* (Grand Rapids: Eerdmans, 1998); *Figured Out: Typology and Providence in Christian Scripture* (Louisville: Westminster John Knox, 2001).

39. Most obviously, see Richard B. Hays, *Echoes of Scripture in the Letters of Paul* (New Haven: Yale University Press, 1989). The concept of figuration is developed further in Hays's more recent work on the Gospels, *Reading Backwards: Figural Christology and the Fourfold Gospel Witness* (Waco: Baylor University Press, 2015).

FOURTEEN

"We, Too, Are in Advent"

Barth's Theological Exegesis of Hebrews 11

R. DAVID NELSON

Introduction

During the spring of 1922, Barth, still somewhat green in his first full-time academic appointment as honorary professor of Reformed theology at Göttingen, scheduled two lecture series for the upcoming summer semester: a main cycle, meeting four times each week, on Calvin and a secondary cycle, meeting three times per week, on Hebrews. By early April, and after "reach(ing) a crisis in [his] work in preparation for the summer lectures," Barth had made the decision to drop the Hebrews series in order to concentrate his energies on Calvin, commenting to Thurneysen that "Calvin and all that is involved with him alone claims me *wholly*."[1] While he had made some headway in the exegesis of the epistle,[2] the possibility of negotiating the complexities of Calvin's thought and Hebrews at the same time had become for Barth "really quite

1. Karl Barth, letter to Eduard Thurneysen (circular letter), April 2, 1922, in *Revolutionary Theology in the Making: Barth-Thurneysen Correspondence, 1914–1925*, trans. James D. Smart (Richmond: John Knox, 1964), 96.
2. So reports Eberhard Busch in *Karl Barth: His Life from Letters and Autobiographical Texts*, trans. John Bowden (London: SCM, Philadelphia: Fortress, 1976), 138.

incomprehensible."[3] In particular, Barth apparently had grown nervous that he would give the epistle's textual, historical, and theological issues short shrift, an especially treacherous prospect given the quality of the New Testament faculty at Göttingen during the period. Remarking to Thurneysen on the scrapped lecture cycle, he anticipates the embarrassment that might have come his way had he moved forward with the lectures: "Oh! I will yet make myself beautifully ridiculous in this university with the crumbs that I have scraped together and my historical *far*sightedness which makes all the contours become blurred for me no matter how interesting and important each figure as such is to me."[4]

It is an unhappy chance of history that Barth's planning for the aborted series on Hebrews fell on the calendar during the same season that he was intensely wrestling with Calvin, whom he famously described to Thurneysen in a letter written in early June of 1922 as "a cataract, a primeval forest, a demonic power, something directly down from Himalaya, absolutely Chinese, strange, mythological."[5] Sapped by Calvin of his energies for the epistle during the spring and early summer of 1922, Barth never returned to it in the context of a formal lecture cycle. We thus can only speculate what Barth would have made of the broad concerns of the letter and of the sophisticated architecture of its argument. It is, however, demonstrable that Hebrews continued to serve as a significant interlocutor for Barth as his theological journey unfolded following the early Göttingen period. Citations from the epistle can be traced throughout the lectures on dogmatics he delivered in Göttingen during 1924–26.[6] Barth also draws from Hebrews with some frequency in the exegetical sections of the *Church Dogmatics*, devoting focused attention to a number of the epistle's key passages, including the prologue (1:1–4), the comparison of the high priesthoods of Jesus and Melchizedek (5:5–9), the description of the completion of Christ's atoning sacrifice in the heavenly

3. Barth, letter to Thurneysen, April 2, 1922, *Revolutionary Theology in the Making*, 97.

4. Barth, letter to Thurneysen, April 2, 1922, *Revolutionary Theology in the Making*, 97 (emphasis original).

5. Barth, letter to Eduard Thurneysen, June 8, 1922, *Revolutionary Theology in the Making*, 101. The Calvin lectures from 1922 are available in English as Barth, *The Theology of John Calvin*, trans. Geoffrey W. Bromiley (Grand Rapids: Eerdmans, 1995).

6. Published in the Gesamtausgabe as Karl Barth, *"Unterricht in der christlichen Religion" I: Prolegomena 1924*, ed. Hannelotte Reiffen, GA II 17 (Zurich: Theologischer Verlag Zürich, 1985); Karl Barth, *"Unterricht in der christlichen Religion" II: Die Lehre von Gott / Die Lehre vom Menschen 1924/25*, ed. Hinrich Stoevesandt, GA II 20 (Zurich: Theologischer Verlag Zürich, 1990); and Karl Barth, *"Unterricht in der christlichen Religion" III: Die Lehre von der Versöhnung / Die Lehre von der Erlösung 1925/26*, ed. Hinrich Stoevesandt, GA II 38 (Zurich: Theologischer Verlag Zürich, 2003). The first volume of the English translation is available as Barth, *The Göttingen Dogmatics: Instruction in the Christian Religion*, vol. 1, ed. Hannelotte Reiffen, trans. Geoffrey W. Bromiley (Grand Rapids: Eerdmans, 1991).

tabernacle (9:9–15), the employment of the athletic metaphor of the marathon to illustrate faith's endurance (12:1–12), and the author's assertion that "Jesus Christ is the same yesterday and today and forever" (13:8). Theological themes prominent in the *Church Dogmatics*, such as the word of God, the supremacy of Christ, atonement, eschatology, and the Christian life, all find exegetical support in passages from Hebrews.

This chapter examines Barth's theological exegesis of Hebrews 11, the epistle's great exposition of *faith*. Barth hones in on this passage in three sections of *The Doctrine of Reconciliation*: namely, in *CD* IV/1, §59; IV/2, §66; and IV/3.2, §73. We will concentrate our analysis on the first passage, making brief forays into the second and third. At all points we will find Barth turning to chapter 11 for help in articulating an account of eschatology in light of the divine verdict pronounced in the history of Jesus Christ. After framing the main passage, I demonstrate that Barth couches chapter 11's eschatological signposts (e.g., the "seen-unseen" and "visible-invisible" pairings dispersed throughout the chapter, the imagery of wandering, the author's metaphorical use of the comparative "better," and so on) in a description of what he calls the "human situation" (the already of "waiting" and the not yet of "perfection"). In doing so, Barth suggests that the author's conceptions of faith and hope can be properly understood only when the exegete acknowledges that humanity is now "in Advent," awaiting the eschaton. Further, I unpack Barth's argument that Hebrews 11 confirms the identity-in-difference of faith and hope. Based on his exegesis of chapter 11, Barth describes faith as the "basis and presupposition" of Christian hope and, just so, inseparable from it. Finally, I consider Barth's engagement with chapter 11 for the sake of an eschatological account of divine and human agency. For Barth, Hebrews 11 makes clear that human acts of obedience are grounded externally in the "great acts of God" that give plot to the drama of reconciliation.

Listening to Scripture's Witness—Barth's Theological Exegesis in the *Church Dogmatics*

Before addressing Barth's interpretation of Hebrews 11, it is worth considering some salient features of the theological exegesis he employs throughout the *Church Dogmatics*. In particular, it is critical to orient ourselves to what we might say is, for Barth, the appropriate *posture* of the interpreter vis-à-vis the Bible. From beginning to end, we discover that Barth is relentlessly occupied in the *Church Dogmatics* with the task of *listening to* Christian Scripture. This commitment to the basic posture of hearing stamps Barth's approach to the entirety of Scripture's witness, and also animates his exegesis of particular passages from the Old and New Testaments. "If I understand what I am trying to do in the *Church Dogmatics*," he once told a group of inquisitive students, "it is to listen to what Scripture is saying and tell you what I hear."[7] As Francis Watson puts it, Barth's project "is nothing other than a sustained meditation on the texts of Holy Scripture, in all the richness and diversity with which these texts elaborate their single theme: a divine-human action constitutive both of divine and human being, a particular action that is nevertheless all-inclusive in its scope."[8] For our purposes here, we must unfold in two directions this emphasis on the theological and exegetical virtue of listening.

1. Barth's basic posture toward the Bible emerges from his understanding of the relations between the speaking God, Scripture, and the listening interpreter. Bruce McCormack summarizes Barth's account of the correspondence between the first two—the word of God and the biblical text, here especially with the problem of Scripture's historical sense in mind. For Barth:

> God continually takes up the witness of the biblical writers and bears witness to himself in and through their witness. In that he does so, the human words of Scripture are made to conform or correspond to the divine word. A relationship of analogy between the Word and the words is established. But only in the event of divine speaking! . . . If God did not speak again and again through these words in an active way, they would snap back into their old connotations. Again, it is the biblical language which is made to conform to God's speech about himself. It is not that God's speech conforms itself to this language.[9]

The key words in McCormack's summary for our reading of Barth are "witness," "conform," and "analogy." According to Barth, God has spoken decisively, singularly, and finally in Jesus Christ, and the authors of Scripture are *witnesses* to this event of self-disclosure, whether as contemporary eyewitnesses to the history that unfolded in Jesus's life, death, and resurrection, or as those who testify to God's act of revelation through prophetic anticipation or apostolic anamnesis. Barth insists, though, that it is God alone who mobilized the witnesses of the Old and New Testaments to testify, and this mobilization, in turn, authorized the compositions of the various texts of Scripture. The writing of Scripture, the encapsulation of the original witnesses in the Bible's

7. This story is recounted by Robert C. Johnson in "The Legacy of Karl Barth," *Reflection* 66 (1969): 4.

8. Francis Watson, "The Bible," in *The Cambridge Companion to Karl Barth*, ed. John Webster (Cambridge: Cambridge University Press, 2000), 57.

9. Bruce McCormack, "Historical Criticism and Dogmatic Interest in Karl Barth's Theological Exegesis of the New Testament," *Lutheran Quarterly* 5 (1991): 220.

literary forms and words, was, for Barth, an act of *conformation*, occurring from above to below, in which human language is commandeered[10] by God for the sake of communicating God's self-revelation.

At play in this conception of Scripture is a relation of identity-in-difference of God's Word and human words, which leads us directly to the problem of *analogy*. According to Barth, Scripture's words and God's Word are related neither univocally nor equivocally, but analogically.[11] A univocal understanding suggests that Scripture and God's Word correspond to each other as sheer identification, an equation that assumes that "human language is intrinsically capable of referring to God."[12] On the other hand, equivocation posits a sheer disparity between Scripture's words and God's Word, the basis of which is the thesis that the symbols of human language can refer to God only at a distance, since God—so it is presupposed here—resides beyond the grasp of human thought and speech. Analogy allows Barth to chart between the pitfalls on both sides by describing the linguistic relation as one of *both* similarity *and* dissimilarity. But the analogy that Barth envisages here is not an *analogia entis*, a linguistic correspondence between God's Word and human words grounded in some primal and overarching ontological structure uniting Creator and the creaturely. Such an analogy would at least tacitly entail a step toward univocity, as it would allow for (though not necessarily demand) a direct ontological correspondence between the text of Scripture and God's self-revelation. By contrast, in Barth's use of analogy the linguistic correspondence is always grounded in God's free decision of self-revelation. God lovingly wills to be known by creatures, and, in an act of gracious condescension, conscripts human language for the sake of self-communication.

If nothing else, Barth's analogical approach to Scripture in light of the priority of God's self-revelation liberates the Word of God from becoming enclosed within the text of Scripture, and yet accomplishes this without in any way fully divorcing revelation from the biblical witnesses. In turn, analogy becomes a key for understanding how, for Barth, Scripture's words are the

10. *CD* I/1, 340. In his incisive analysis of Barth's doctrine of revelation, ensconced as it is in the conceptual language of the New Hermeneutic, Eberhard Jüngel seizes upon this notion of "commandeering" as critical for Barth's approach to the relation of divine and human language. See Jüngel's comments in *God's Being Is in Becoming: The Trinitarian Being of God in the Theology of Karl Barth*, trans. John Webster (Grand Rapids: Eerdmans, 2001), 21–25. As Jüngel puts it, for Barth, God's act of self-revelation always both precedes and makes possible human speech about God, including Scripture's language. The "commandeer" metaphor expresses this prioritization.

11. On univocity, equivocity, and analogy in Barth's hermeneutics, see George Hunsinger, *How to Read Karl Barth: The Shape of His Theology* (New York: Oxford University Press, 1991), 43–49.

12. Hunsinger, *How to Read Karl Barth*, 43.

means through which God speaks "again and again." Barth's much maligned idea (at least in some quarters) of the "threefold" form of the Word of God is really an effort to plot out a differentiated account of God's communicative acts that resists the ossification of revelation in objects of knowledge.[13] At all points Barth is concerned with God as the God who speaks—*Deus dixit*. God's *former* speech, preserved in the text, participates in God's active (as it were) *ongoing* communicative agency. The entailments of this for interpretation are far-reaching. For Barth, the exegetical task of listening to the text amounts to neither literalism (which would dovetail to a univocal orientation of the relation between the text and the Word of God) nor expressivism (corresponding to equivocity), but rather to the *realism* of Scripture.[14] Correspondingly, to listen to Scripture means neither to search it out for factual reports of God's past activities nor merely to appreciate its latent aesthetic or emotive potencies, but to be addressed by the speaking God.

We now arrive at the second and third elements of the nexus of relations listed above—that is, the relation of the text to the interpreter. Barth's analogical approach, with its focus on Scripture's realism, suggests that "the role of the reader [of Scripture] becomes primarily passive. The text addresses us as a demand for faith. Faith, however, is no natural capacity but that which is worked in the reader by God."[15] This entails, in turn, that reading "is characterized (at the individual level) by obedient receptivity and (at the communal level) by a complex process of mutual deference and free responsibility in the interpretation and application of Scripture."[16] In contrast to most critical and pietistic modes of exegesis and interpretation, which, as a general rule, locate Scripture as an object of historical or spiritual information to be searched and processed by the exegete, in Barth's hermeneutical vision the reader is passive

---

13. See Richard E. Burnett's excellent summary of this theme in "Word of God," in *The Westminster Handbook to Karl Barth*, ed. Richard Burnett (Louisville: Westminster John Knox, 2013), 223–27; also Trevor Hart, *Regarding Karl Barth: Toward a Reading of His Theology* (Downers Grove, IL: InterVarsity, 1999), 28–47.

14. These words—literalism, expressivism, and realism—are Hunsinger's and are both appropriate and helpful for parsing the distinction between the various hermeneutical approaches that correspond to three broad ways of understanding the relation of Scripture and God's speech—namely, univocity, equivocity, and analogy, respectively. See Hunsinger, *How to Read Karl Barth*, 43–49. For a slightly different take on analogy and realism, pivoting on the "stories" of Scripture, see David F. Ford, "Barth's Interpretation of the Bible," in *Karl Barth: Studies of His Theological Method*, ed. Stephen W. Sykes (Oxford: Clarendon, 1979), 55–87, esp. 76–82.

15. John Webster, *Barth*, Outstanding Christian Thinkers (New York: Continuum, 2000), 33. Webster here summarizes the hermeneutical principles undergirding the second edition of *Romans*. He later shows, though, that Barth remained committed to this theology of reading Scripture in the early volumes of the *Church Dogmatics* (see 65–68).

16. Webster, *Barth*, 65.

and acted upon by the text. As Barth put it as early as 1916 in his famous paper on "The Strange New World within the Bible," Scripture disappoints our efforts to pry loose from it the answers to our historical and religious questions, for these are merely *our* questions posed to God, rather than *God's* questions posed to us. Scripture communicates the latter: "It is not the right human thoughts about God which form the content of the Bible, but the right divine thoughts about men. The Bible tells us not how we should talk with God but what he says to us."[17] Barth never departed from this commitment to the passive posture of the interpreter vis-à-vis the text. Indeed, we contend that it is the key ingredient of the exegesis Barth undertakes in the *Church Dogmatics*.

2. Related to all of this is our second point, which we can canvass more succinctly; namely, that Barth was perennially wary of ceding too much ground to historical-critical methods in the pursuit of Scripture's meaning. To be sure, Barth was keenly aware of the various debates taking place in contemporaneous biblical studies, and his exegesis is marked by interlocutions with Old and New Testament scholars. But Barth is relentless in his refusal to allow his exegesis to become bogged down or railroaded by the preoccupations of historical-critical research. For Barth, critical biblical study is of value to the exegete only when it is located subordinately to the passive interpretative practice of listening to the text. The point is both methodological and theological. McCormack tidily summarizes the former aspect, here in a reflection upon the "revolution in biblical hermeneutics" instigated by the publication of the first edition of *Romans*. Barth, McCormack argues, "was seeking to show the limits of historical-critical study of the Bible in the interests of a more nearly theological exegesis. He was not at all interested in setting historical-critical study aside, as some of his early critics thought. In fact, he was quite convinced that historical criticism could itself play a role in establishing its own limitations."[18] Far from merely endeavoring to dispense with the scientific study of Scripture, Barth instead sought to appropriately situate such study for the sake of "more nearly theological exegesis."

McCormack later expounds Barth's arrangement of the theological and critical modes of exegesis by commenting upon his understanding of historical

17. Barth, "The Strange New World within the Bible," in *The Word of God and the Word of Man*, trans. Douglas Horton (Gloucester, MA: Peter Smith, 1978), 43.

18. McCormack, "Historical Criticism and Dogmatic Interest," 211. McCormack argues in this essay that Barth elaborated these commitments in the foreword to *Romans II* and that subsequently his basic position remained unchanged, even as "the framework in which that hermeneutical strategy did its work" (214) evolved as Barth's theology pressed into new areas. See especially 211–14.

criticism's necessary self-limiting function. For Barth, an accurate historical reconstruction of, say, Paul would ineluctably reveal that the apostle was never concerned with religion or some sociocultural context or his own self-understanding or piety, but at all points with the God of the gospel, to whom Paul had been called as a witness.[19] That is to say, if done properly and without the influence of any driving agenda, the application of historical-critical methods will reveal the *theological commitments* of Scripture's authors, commitments that are themselves beyond the grasp of scientific study since they have to do with the speaking God, whose being, action, and speech, for Barth, are not objects manipulatable by the scholar. To put it in one of Barth's earlier idioms, historical-critical study inevitably breaks down because, in due course, it butts up against the "strange new world" of Scripture. When it fails to recognize that it will necessarily reach an interpretive boundary beyond which its exegetical methods are, simply, out of place, historical criticism becomes mired in the absurd game of attempting to render Scripture's striking otherworldliness as, in fact, all too familiar. Such is the great irony of exegesis affected by the spell of historical criticism's more abjectly ostentatious gestures.

We see, then, that Barth's uneasiness with historical criticism's penchant for unchecked methodological overreach is tied to the same theological concern we encountered above—namely, the proper negotiation of the relation-in-distinction of *Deus dixit*, the biblical text, and the listening interpreter. For Barth, historical-critical biblical study is useful for exegesis, but only to a certain extent. While it is helpful for uncovering and collating significant historical, political, religious, cultural, and linguistic data, it is always secondary and subordinate to hearing the God who speaks, which, according to Barth, is ultimately the true task of biblical exegesis. By navigating the tension between these modes of exegesis, Barth's hermeneutical program, as Webster has it, "replaces suspicion by consent; it makes historical reconstruction a mere preliminary; it requires *spiritual* skills of the interpreter."[20]

Situating the Verdict of the Father—The Eschatological Framework of Barth's Exegesis of Hebrews 11

If the foregoing comments on Barth's exegetical posture constitute a plausible assessment, then the question before us as we shift to the Hebrews 11

---

19. McCormack, "Historical Criticism and Dogmatic Interest," 214–15.
20. Webster, *Barth*, 67 (emphasis added).

material in the *Church Dogmatics* is: What exactly does Barth *hear* in this passage?

Barth's major exegetical engagement with chapter 11 occurs about two-thirds of the way through the third subsection of §59, "The Obedience of the Son of God." Having addressed in the first subsection "the person of Christ and especially the doctrine of His true deity," and in the second "the work of Christ and especially His 'high priestly' work,"[21] Barth now turns to a somewhat labyrinthine unfolding of the theme of "The Verdict of the Father."[22] At the outset of the subsection he identifies his present task as a "transitional discussion between the problems and answers we have just given and the further questions we will now have to add to them."[23] In particular, he devotes the bulk of the subsection to disentangling the problem of the *pastness* of the actualization of God's reconciling work in the crucifixion and resurrection of Jesus Christ.

Barth concedes that, at least at first glance, the dilemma of the pastness of the Jesus events relative to any present appears to be an instantiation of the general problem of the relation between God and *time*.[24] Contemporaneous theology had expended copious amounts of energy and ink attempting to leap Lessing's "ugly ditch" between historical contingency and the truths available to reason,[25] and this expenditure both funded and foregrounded the issue of the proper framework for conceiving the relation between God and human history. Barth, however, contends that such discussions are off base: "The question of Lessing, the question of historical distance, is not a genuine problem."[26] For Barth, the legitimate issue at stake here, we might say, is *eschatological* rather than sheerly historical. It is the problem of "the real distance in which the God appearing in the human sphere . . . confronts us to whom He turns and for whom he acts." The judgment of God, that is, comes to us as a radical contradiction, as the violent collision of "two opposite world-structures, two worlds opposing and apparently excluding one another."[27] The issue of God and time is grounded in this eschatological crisis, not vice versa. To put it in another vein: far from being merely an epistemological problem (say, how do we know God with historical certainty since the putatively supernatural

---

21. *CD* IV/1, 283, referencing the first two subsections of §59 on pp. 157–210 and 211–83.
22. *CD* IV/1, 283–357.
23. *CD* IV/1, 284.
24. See *CD* IV/1, 287–94. Bultmann, whom Barth mentions in the fine-print comments just after he broaches the issue of God and time, is likely in mind here as Barth elaborates the "problem" of history just in order to show that it is not, in fact, problematic.
25. See Barth's comments in this subsection in *CD* IV/1, 287, 292.
26. *CD* IV/1, 292.
27. *CD* IV/1, 290.

acts of God bend the rules of reason and scientific objectivity?), in play here, according to Barth, is the disquieting—dare we say *existential*—question of whether humanity is not altogether decimated by the coming of the God who brings a terribly gracious and graciously terrible verdict, which we can hear—at least at first—only as a "deep-seated No."[28]

The predicament of the divine verdict, as Barth has just sketched it, becomes pivotal for his argument in the rest of the subsection. For our purposes here, we can focus on his reintroduction of the problem of history and eschatology in the elaboration of "the connexion between the death of Jesus Christ and His resurrection."[29] This is the third of five clarifying statements Barth offers to explain the sense in which the crucifixion of Jesus actualizes the judgment of God. In his brief road map of the five "conditions" necessary for understanding the crucifixion as judgment,[30] Barth provides a clue for how his exposition of the third condition will unfurl. The relation between the crucifixion and resurrection, he writes, is characterized by a *sequence*: the resurrection has in the crucifixion "its presupposition" and "must affirm" the crucifixion. Hence, "both events must be independent and complete, but both must stand to one another in a relationship which is concealed but which is none the less real and unbreakable."[31] Later on, Barth seizes upon the concrete "temporal sequence" between the two events, which, he notes, is described in the New Testament as "the gulf between the first and third days."[32] Further, alongside the three holy days, he argues, theology must address the "forty days" between the resurrection of Jesus and his ascension, and also "the time of the community in the world," which begins at the ascension and thus shows that, in fact, its roots stretch all the way back to the resurrection.[33]

Barth proposes that these distinct periods from the narrative of the New Testament serve as a framework for eschatology. What is narrated by the Evangelists as a sequence of temporal events epitomizes the existence of humanity beneath the judgment of God. In a breathtaking passage, Barth shows that humanity's eschatological situation in the time commencing with the ascension relates analogically to the three days between the crucifixion and Easter Sunday. The time between the ascension and the parousia

28. CD IV/1, 290. See the entirety of Barth's argument in 287–97 for his nuancing of the historical and eschatological questions.

29. CD IV/1, 309. The entire passage runs from 309 to 332.

30. CD IV/1, 297–98.

31. CD IV/1, 298.

32. CD IV/1, 318.

33. CD IV/1, 319. See the entirety of the passage that runs from 319 to 324 for Barth's interesting engagement with the three days, four days, and post-ascension temporal periods.

is a "time between the times"[34] during which the community is both "*still in the world . . .* in the sphere of human perception" and "*still hidden . . .* [in] an altered world only in relation to Jesus Christ" and "perceptible only by faith and not by sight." It is the time of the "*already,*" marked by "the comprehensive alteration of the human situation which has already taken place," and also the "*not yet,*" as the "fulfilment" of that alteration will not be completed until the parousia. It is the time of *looking backward* "to the life and death of Jesus and also to the happening of the forty days," and *looking forward* "in the light of the consequences of these two related events, first to its own time and then to all the times that follow."[35] This strange season oriented to two eschatological events bears "an unmistakable similarity with the being of Jesus Christ Himself with his death and resurrection, with His being buried in the tomb."[36] Just as on Holy Saturday Jesus lay awaiting the completion of the crucifixion in the resurrection, humanity too awaits the consummation of the events of Jesus in his glorious second advent.

According to Barth, all of this points to the ineluctably "provisional" character of the human predicament in this present eschatological season. The verdict of the Father has been definitively spoken in the events of Jesus Christ. However, even as we look back on those events as having occurred in the past and in their narration hear the definitive Yes! of the gospel, the completion of God's saving action lies ahead of us. "For now we see as in a mirror, dimly," says Paul, "but then we will see face to face" (1 Cor. 13:12 NRSV). And just here Barth draws an additional parallel that points directly to his use of Hebrews 11: in the "time between the times," "the men of the New Testament . . . have not ceased to look forward to Him *with the men of the Old.*"[37] For Barth, the Old Testament narrates the stories of faithful individuals who lived eschatologically in light of God's promised, forthcoming deliverance. As such, those who line the ranks of the Old Testament faithful are "predecessors" of those who live after the ascension and before the second advent. Indeed, as Barth puts it, both groups find themselves in "the Advent situation," waiting for God's coming as the fulfillment of the divine promise. And the sign of living in advent is *faith*; the sort of faith that is "essentially bound up with *hope*, with the confidence that the reality which is now believed will be seen."[38]

---

34. *CD* IV/1, 323.
35. *CD* IV/1, 319 (emphasis added).
36. *CD* IV/1, 323.
37. *CD* IV/1, 323 (emphasis added).
38. *CD* IV/1, 331 (emphasis added).

Faith, Hope, and Obedience in Advent—Barth's Exegesis of Hebrews 11

The cascading exposition of eschatology that constitutes the first half of the subsection on "the verdict of the Father" sets up Barth's major exegetical engagement with Hebrews 11. Barth is attuned to chapter 11 in this context precisely because he *hears* Hebrews bearing witness to the eschatological situation of advent and, concomitantly, to the relation between faith and hope. We will follow Barth's exposition through these two steps to reveal the key moves of his interpretation of the chapter. We will then briefly consider a passage from *CD* IV.3.2, where Barth augments his reading of chapter 11 by considering the eschatological entailments of obedience motivated by faith.

1. Hebrews 11, as commentator Harold W. Attridge puts it, consists of an "encomium on faith," a "catalogue of *exempla fidei*."[39] The author extols for the epistle's original audience the virtues of faith, which he defines at the outset as "the substance (ὑπόστασις; Vulgate: *substantia*) of things hoped for" (11:1), pointing to exemplars taken from the overarching narrative of the Hebrew Scriptures. D. Stephen Long perceptively observes that chapter 11's emphasis on the personal and communal forms of the exercise of faith marks "something of a turn" in Hebrews. "Until 10:22," he comments, "Hebrews primarily explains the faithfulness of Jesus and why it offers a better sacrifice than that of the Levitical priesthood. . . . The emphasis was never on our faith, but on Christ's."[40] This change in focus concerning the nature of faith is tied to a broader shift in thematic material, which, as I see it, following one approach, takes place at 10:32, where the author commends his original audience to "call to remembrance the former days."[41] But no matter where we draw the major pivots in the argument of Hebrews, it is beyond dispute that chapter 11 extends the theme introduced at the end of chapter 10, where the author reminds his original audience of a bygone episode of social upheaval during which this community, animated by compassion (10:34), confidence (10:35), endurance (10:36), and faith (10:39), "cheerfully accepted the plundering of [their] possessions" (10:34) while caring for those who had been (by implication) wrongfully imprisoned. The author seizes upon this concern

---

39. Harold W. Attridge, *The Epistle to the Hebrews: A Commentary on the Epistle to the Hebrews*, Hermeneia (Philadelphia: Fortress, 1989), 307.

40. D. Stephen Long, *Hebrews*, Belief (Louisville: Westminster John Knox, 2011), 176.

41. See James W. Thompson, *Hebrews*, Paideia (Grand Rapids: Baker Academic, 2008), 13–20, where Thompson argues that 10:32 marks the commencement of the third and final unit of the epistle, an extended *peroratio*. The locations of divisions in the text have long been a matter of debate among interpreters. On this, see the survey in George H. Guthrie, *The Structure of Hebrews: A Text-Linguistic Analysis* (Grand Rapids: Baker, 1998), 3–41.

that his audience has lost their confidence and become anemic in faith, offering in chapter 11 a sweeping survey of examples of faith, beginning with the narrative of Abel and continuing all the way up to the Maccabean revolts (at least by way of allusion).[42]

In our passage from the *Church Dogmatics*, Barth adds a significant exegetical insight to what we have already stated concerning the account of faith in Hebrews. Perhaps surprisingly at first, nowhere here does Barth suggest that the list of figures constituting chapter 11 serves as some sort of manual for how to believe and act today. Rather, for Barth, Hebrews 11 is interesting precisely in that it testifies to the eschatological orientation common both to the faithful ones of the Old Testament and to those who now await the second advent in faith. Barth, that is, observes here that, for Hebrews, both before the first coming of Jesus and now in advance of his second coming, the life of faith is determined and motivated by advent. The call of chapter 11, then, consists of acknowledging this common eschatological horizon of advent and orienting faith and action accordingly.

The character of faith as advent waiting is highlighted in 11:1, which, Barth remarks, "has the force of a definition." According to Hebrews, faith is "the conviction of things *not seen*" (NRSV); likewise, the common denominator among the figures drawn from the Hebrew Scriptures is that "in their day they were *never granted to see* that which was promised."[43] The dawning of God's coming to the world in Jesus Christ is eschatologically future to those who are waiting. The use of "unseen" must be interpreted in light of this eschatological framework, and it by no means conceals a warning against creaturely *materia*. Rather, chapter 11 calls for courage in the face of current circumstances in light of the future fulfillment that is eschatologically on its way. This, indeed, is that for which all of those in advent wait. Barth ties these strands together in the following way: "They [who awaited the first advent] will not therefore (v. 40) be made perfect without us, but with us, for whom God has laid up a new and better promise. And in the continuation in Heb. 12:1f. this is shown to mean that formally we have the same faith as this 'cloud of witnesses.' On a better presupposition we, too, are in Advent. We look forward in hope. We are on the way to the fulfillment: τελείωσις."[44]

The sum effect of this reading of Hebrews 11 is to shift the attention off faith as a disposition or a catalyst for a particular mode of existence and onto the *object* of faith. Just as the exemplars of Israel and Judaism looked

---

42. On this connection, see Attridge, *Hebrews*, 346–52.
43. CD IV/1, 331, paraphrasing Heb. 11:39 (emphasis added).
44. CD IV/1, 331.

ahead to the fullness of time that arrived with the coming of Jesus Christ, the Christian's faith fixes its sight on the as-yet-unseen consummation of all things in the coming eschaton, the arrival of which will bring an end to the "already but not yet" of the time of advent. At all points, faith's object is the promised action of God, and, just so, faith consists of eschatological foresight and insight.

2. In the course of a fascinating passage in *Romans II*, the edition of which he was preparing right around the time he initiated and then ditched his Göttingen lectures on Hebrews, Barth turns to Hebrews 11 to raise an indictment against the *easy* faith that corresponds to religion. Commenting on Romans 9:32, Barth takes his contemporaneous church to task for pursuing faith, as it were, "in the light"—that is, "oriented to what can be seen." For Barth, such faith is, in fact, not faith at all, for "its activity proceeds from works," · pursuing God through "things that are definite, observable, comprehensible, direct, and tangible." As Barth points out, since, in sharp contrast to such an easy understanding of faith, Hebrews focuses on what is *not* seen, its catalog of faithful works lists actions that are far from comfortable or unhazardous. As such, the idea of faith in Hebrews 11 "seems to the Church too unsympathetic, too loveless, too dangerous, too unpsychological, too unpractical."[45]

In our passage from the *Church Dogmatics*, Barth's consideration of the *uneasiness* of faith when it is fixed on the as-yet-unseen eschatological fulfillment of God's promises leads to a discussion of the relation of faith and *hope*. Barth's comments on hope in Hebrews 11 take up the bulk of the latter half of the exegetical section. His chief interlocutor here is Calvin, who, he contends up front, "was not always at his best when dealing with eschatology."[46] And yet, Barth seems to think that Calvin got right the nest of eschatological issues at hand. According to Calvin according to Barth, since what is promised by God will not be revealed "until the last day when . . . the books will be opened" and is thus, at least for now, "too high to be apprehended by our reason or seen with our eyes or grasped by our hands," that is, it is "invisible," "it cannot be otherwise than that faith should have hope as its *inseparable companion*."[47] Still in dialogue with Calvin and continuing his exposition of Hebrews 11, Barth goes on to define the hope that corresponds to faith as "the expectation of what faith believes as that which God has truly promised. . . . Waiting quietly for the Lord, hope restrains faith, preventing it from rushing forward in too great a hurry."[48] For Barth, Hebrews 11 stresses that faith in the

45. *Romans II*, 368.
46. CD IV/1, 332.
47. CD IV/1, 332 (emphasis added).
48. CD IV/1, 332.

as-yet-invisible fulfillment of the promises of God *requires* hope to mitigate the eagerness, weariness, and distractedness that might otherwise befall it in its relentless pursuit of its eschatological object.

And yet, faith's relation to hope is analogical, an identity-in-difference. While Hebrews brings together faith and hope into the tightest possible relation, they are not altogether identical. As Barth explains in *CD* IV/3.2, §73:

> Faith as such is the obedience which man gives to the Word and command of God by receiving and respecting this as the Word of promise quite apart from banking on its fulfilment. He does this not because he hopes, for he has no ground for hope apart from believing. But as and because he believes, putting active trust in the Word spoken to him as God's Word, he also hopes. Thus faith and hope are closely related. They belong inseparably together. Yet they are two distinct things.[49]

In the eschatological situation of advent, faith "begets" and "creates" hope.[50] Faith needs hope to come alongside it to bolster faith's trust in the promises of the Word.

3. Barth briefly returns to Hebrews 11 in *CD* IV/2, §66.5, "The Praise of Works," and his comments here on faith and obedience round out the emphases of the other passages on faith and hope in the advent situation. The broad theme of the section is "The Sanctification of Man," and in the seven smaller units Barth unfolds a complex account of the transformation of the saints into a *new humanity*, a reality that, in fact, has already transpired by virtue of humanity's participation in the reconciling work of Jesus Christ. Having worked through the identity-in-difference of justification and sanctification (§66.1), the relationship between Jesus Christ and sanctified humanity (§66.2), the character and forms of the "call" to Christian discipleship (§66.3), and the nature of Christian conversion (§66.4), in our subsection Barth turns to the question of the role of works in the Christian life. For Barth, sanctification entails works, and therefore the good works of the Christian are both obligatory and (as the title of the subsection encapsulates) praiseworthy. However, the works of the Christian do not themselves justify, nor are they produced by virtue of the independent moral agency of the Christian. On the contrary, the good works of the Christian are possible only because of God's work of converting and justifying slothful and miserable humanity.[51] Moreover, for

---

49. *CD* IV/3.2, 913.
50. See Barth's comments in *CD* IV/1, 332.
51. Barth uses these terms in §65 (*CD* IV/2, 378–498)—"The Sloth and Misery of Man"—to describe the condition of humanity apart from the justifying action of God.

Barth, since the origins of human ethical action reside in God, it is impossible to neatly distinguish the good works of the Christian and the works of God. Human good works, rather, relate to the works of God by way of "participation."[52]

Just here Barth offers a brief exegetical survey of Hebrews 11. As in the passage from §59, here he reads chapter 11 *eschatologically*, foregrounding the theme of the relation between God and history. In this instance his particular concern is to show that the good works of the saints, corresponding to their faith, participate in the unfurling history of God's "great acts" toward his creatures. Barth notes that Hebrews 11

> is dealing with faith as the confidence of things hoped for, the certainty of things not seen. But in the depiction of this faith we have to do at every point with human acts and attitude—those of Abel and Enoch and Noah and Abraham and Isaac and Jacob and Moses and Rahab the harlot and others. Of all these it is said (v. 13) that "they died in faith, not having received the promises, but having seen them afar off and were persuaded of them, and embraced them, and confessed that they were strangers and pilgrims on this earth." But it is also stated of them that . . . they worked actively and passively in obedience. Their acts are of great consequence in the context of that history, and they are thus depicted in rather extravagant terms.[53]

Three interesting exegetical insights emerge in this condensed treatment, and all of these fold back onto the larger theme of the narrative shape of God's reconciling agency. First, Barth points out the equation between, on one hand, faith's orientation toward "things not seen" and, on the other hand, the obedient actions of the faithful. It is pivotal for the interpretation of chapter 11 to catch this connection. As Barnabas Lindars put it, describing how the figures listed in the catalog act "on the basis of faith": "Each person's action is guided by a promise concerning the future at a time when it is impossible to see the outcome, so that they can only act in faith."[54] Hebrews 11:13, which Barth quotes in its entirety in the passage, is critical here, as it demonstrates that none of these figures lived to see the fulfillment of the promises. And yet, at all points in chapter 11, the exemplars of faith are depicted as having acted out of obedience in light of the as-yet-unseen promises. With this we see in full the yield of Barth's exegesis of Hebrews 11 for the doctrine of the Christian life: *faith* in the

52. CD IV/2, 595, 596.
53. CD IV/2, 597.
54. Barnabas Lindars, *The Theology of the Letter to the Hebrews*, New Testament Theology (Cambridge: Cambridge University Press, 1991), 111.

eschatological promises of God—that is, the faith of advent—necessarily leads to both *hope* and *obedience*.

Second, Barth makes explicit here that, by virtue of their obedient acts, the exemplars of chapter 11 are connected both to God's acts of reconciliation and to the communion of the saints. Barth hints at a broader vision of the relation between God and history with his assertion that the works of the exemplars "are of great consequence" to the unfolding chronology of the great acts of God. As we have already noted, Barth employs the idea of participation to explain the relation—surely, again, an analogical identity-in-difference—between the works of obedience and the works of God. Now we see a bit more clearly what the conception of participation encapsulates; namely, that the works of obedience of the faithful saints, grounded externally in the works of God, *just are* events according to which the unfolding history of God and the world is plotted.

Precisely by virtue of this, Barth's third noteworthy insight emerges, harkening back to the title of the subsection. On account of their works, the exemplars of chapter 11 are "depicted in rather extravagant terms." As 11:38 puts it, "the world is not worthy" of these faithful individuals who acted obediently in response to God's promises. The good works of the exemplars are worthy of great praise because they testified to *God*; "and it is to Him that Christians can and should and may and will bear witness with their works."[55]

Conclusion

As we argued in the first section, above, Barth's exegetical practice in the *Church Dogmatics* consists of listening to the text of Scripture and restating what he hears. In these exegetical exercises on Hebrews 11, we find Barth doing just that—retrieving the voice of Scripture for the sake of dogmatics, here specifically for a robust and nuanced account of an eschatological orientation for the Christian life. We might rightly criticize Barth for focusing on such theological concerns at the expense of fully exploring chapter 11's contextual problems; for instance, the immediate social situation to which chapter 10 alludes, the author's own exegesis of the Hebrew Scriptures in the chapter, or the comparison of Hebrews 11 to other examples of the encomium genre in ancient literature. And yet, for all of Barth's relative inattentiveness to historical-critical concerns such as these in the Hebrews materials, as we have demonstrated, his exegesis yields significant insights for the understanding of chapter 11. By hearing the voice of Hebrews as bearing witness to the

55. CD IV/2, 597.

relation of faith, hope, and obedience in the season of advent, Barth is able to highlight the participation of Christian existence in the sweep of events and actions that constitutes God's relation to his creatures.

In the end, Barth's contribution to the exegetical tradition of commentary on Hebrews 11 resides in his unremitting interest in the God who reconciles. Barth situates the narratives of the exemplars of chapter 11 alongside the advent waiting of the epistle's original hearers, showing that, at all points, anticipation of God's reconciling action gives rise to faith, hope, and obedience in correspondence to God. And Barth is convinced that this same nexus of faith, hope, and obedience oriented toward God marks authentic Christian existence at all times. Barth's reiteration of the voice of Hebrews 11—that is, his *exegesis* of the chapter—is, at heart, an act of theological proclamation, intended to persuade the readers of the *Church Dogmatics* that Scripture still speaks today.

FIFTEEN

The Compassion of Jesus for the Crowds

PAUL T. NIMMO

Introduction

This chapter focuses on the compassion of Jesus Christ as part of this volume's reflections on the way in which Barth undertook theological exegesis. The particular focus here is on how Barth engaged at a significant juncture in the *Church Dogmatics* with the text of Matthew 9:36, which thematizes the compassion of Jesus Christ. The text as it stands in the NRSV—though there will be cause to refer to the Greek and the German later—runs thus: "When [Jesus] saw the crowds, He had *compassion* for them, because they were harassed and helpless, like sheep without a shepherd" (emphasis added). Though cited at various points in the *Church Dogmatics*,[1] this verse is afforded especial attention in the doctrine of reconciliation, where it is directly thematized.[2] The purpose of this chapter is, first, to outline the dogmatic topos and immediate context in which this verse receives particular attention; second,

---

An abbreviated version of this article was first published as "The Compassion of Jesus Christ: Barth on Matthew 9:36," in *Reading the Gospels with Karl Barth*, ed. Daniel L. Migliore (Grand Rapids: Eerdmans, 2017), 67–79.

1. See *KD* II/1, 439; III/2, 252; IV/3, 885; *CD* II/1, 390; III/2, 211; IV/3.2, 774. All translations of *KD* are the author's own, and all emphasis in *KD* quotations is original.

2. The pages in question are *KD* IV/2, 205–8; *CD* IV/2, 184–87.

to exposit the core material concerns of Barth's handling of the verse in some detail; and third, to offer one primary methodological and three briefer dogmatic reflections on Barth's treatment.

The Setting

Karl Barth's most detailed exposition of Matthew 9:36 finds its place in the fourth volume of the *Church Dogmatics*, in the midst of his doctrine of reconciliation. His treatment of this doctrine in *Church Dogmatics* volume IV has three parts, each pertaining to a different focus on the subject matter. The first, in part-volume IV/1, considers the way in which "in Jesus Christ we have to do with the true *God*," while the second, in part-volume IV/2, explores the way in which "in Jesus Christ we have to do with a true *human being*"; the third, in part-volume IV/3, views this bilateral history of Jesus Christ in its *"unity and completeness."*[3] It is in the treatment of the second aspect of Christ's history, in *CD* IV/2, that Barth's exposition of Matthew 9:36 takes place—in particular, in his exploration of Jesus Christ as the one who, by virtue of the fact that God is one with him, is "the *free* human being." In his survey of this tranche of material in part-volume IV/1, Barth writes of the implications of this aspect of the history of Jesus Christ thus: "[Jesus Christ is] completely a creature, yet quite superior to his own creatureliness; completely arrested [*verhaftet*] also by sin, yet completely innocent in face of it, because utterly blameless in respect of committing it; completely mortal and thus also [someone who] really died, as we must all die—yet as he died, already superior even to death and therefore snatched from death immediately and absolutely and in this way (as a human being like us) victorious and ultimately alive."[4]

The result, Barth suggests, is that Jesus Christ is "the true human being, that is, the human being who in all his humanity is exalted above it."[5] And this exaltation is not an isolated or individual event without wider implications: in this particular human being, the remainder of humanity is also implicated. Barth continues: Jesus Christ is "exalted as a human being in *our* place, set at the side of God in exactly the same humanity as ours—*above* us, *against* us, but now also *for* us."[6] His exaltation thus includes the exaltation of all people: "Precisely what happened in him as this *one*, true human being is the

3. *KD* IV/1, 140, 143, 149; *CD* IV/1, 128, 130, 136.
4. *KD* IV/1, 143–44; *CD* IV/1, 131.
5. *KD* IV/1, 144; *CD* IV/1, 131.
6. *KD* IV/1, 144; *CD* IV/1, 131.

conversion of all people to God, the becoming true of all human being [*das Wahrwerden alles Menschseins*]."[7] This objective realization of the exaltation of all people in Jesus Christ, of their justification, sanctification, and vocation in him, is one of the most central, and most controverted of Barth's claims, though it is not a claim that serves as the principal focus of attention for this chapter.

In the second part-volume of the doctrine of reconciliation Barth elaborates this concise outline of the kingly work of Jesus Christ across a series of major sections under the primary rubric "The Exaltation of the Son of Man." After setting the scene, Barth opens with a section entitled "The Homecoming of the Son of Man," in which he sets out to consider the three doctrinal viewpoints on the basis of which he sees this concept of exaltation to have particular relevance and significance—"its initial and final foundation in God's election, its historical completion in the event of the incarnation, and its basis of revelation in the resurrection and ascension of the person of Jesus."[8] This section principally contains material on the latter two themes, with extended reflections offered first on some of the dogmatic material traditionally associated with the person of Jesus Christ and second on this material's epistemological reality and—and only then—its possibility.

The following section is titled "The Royal Man," and it is within this material that the exposition of Matthew 9:36 is found. This section sets forth a particular task—"the development of the knowledge of Jesus Christ insofar as he, as the Son of God, is also the Son of Man—the human being Jesus of Nazareth."[9] In other words, it is the person of Jesus Christ as the true, new, exalted human being that here comes into view. And it is no surprise that Barth notes that his material will proceed in a way to be explicitly informed, as was the theology of the early church, by the New Testament witness.[10] Indeed, Barth succinctly comments, "The royal human being is the Jesus of the four Gospels."[11]

There ensues, first, a series of four formal observations about the human Jesus that are drawn out of the Gospel texts. These observations concern the way that Jesus was present among his contemporaries—as one who could not fail to be seen and heard, as one who demanded and effected a decision in respect of him, as one who was present in an unforgettable and irrevocable way.[12]

7. *KD* IV/1, 144; *CD* IV/1, 131.
8. *KD* IV/2, 32; *CD* IV/2, 31.
9. *KD* IV/2, 173; *CD* IV/2, 154–55.
10. *KD* IV/2, 32; *CD* IV/2, 31.
11. *KD* IV/2, 174; *CD* IV/2, 156.
12. *KD* IV/2, 175–85; *CD* IV/2, 156–66.

At this point, the formal reflections give way to material considerations. If Jesus is "the new human being," "the royal human being," the One in whom all humanity is exalted, it remains to be seen how concretely Barth is to fill out these descriptors. His starting-point is to observe that "the royal human being of the New Testament tradition is created 'according to God' (κατὰ θεόν)." Barth offers the following elaboration of this governing thesis:

> He exists as a human being analogously [*analog*] to the way of existence of God. His thinking and desiring, his acting, and his attitude occur in correspondence [*Entsprechung*], form in the world of the creature a parallel [*eine Parallele*] to the plan and the intention, to the work and the behavior of God. He images God [*bildet Gott ab*]; he is as a human being [God's] εἰκών (Col. 1:15). . . . He does that which is demanded and expected of the human being in the covenant, corresponding [*entsprechend*] in a deed of [human] faithfulness to the faithfulness of God.[13]

This is the central statement to be explored in this tranche of material, and in three short numbered paragraphs, Barth begins to detail the specific ways in which this correspondence, this analogy or parallel, is evident. First, he observes that the royal human being—in common with God and the people of God—is "overlooked, forgotten, undervalued, despised"; second, he states that Jesus in a biased fashion preferred "the low, the small, the weak, [and] the poor to all those in the world who were high, great, mighty, [and] rich"; and third, he posits that Jesus evidenced a "markedly revolutionary character of relationship to the orders of value and life that were valid in his context."[14] In each case, the claims made here are supported by a raft of references to the text of the Gospels. In each case, one might profitably linger on these material claims, considering further the way in which Barth offers supports to each thesis from the relevant scriptural material.

But it is here that Barth indicates that the decisive material point in the analogy between God and the royal human being Jesus has not yet been identified. This decisive point is not "something accessible from the side of the rest of humanity, [not] something conceivable by us and available to us,"[15] but rather broaches new theological terrain. Barth explains: "The word which is really the first and also the last word is undoubtedly that the man Jesus, like God, is not against but *for human beings*—even and precisely for human beings in the complete impossibility of their corruption [*Verkehrung*], in their

---

13. *KD* IV/2, 185–86; *CD* IV/2, 166.
14. *KD* IV/2, 186–99, quoting 186, 188, 191; *CD* IV/2, 167–79: 167, 168, 171.
15. *KD* IV/2, 200; *CD* IV/2, 179.

form as people of the old world of Adam. . . . The royal human being Jesus reflects and images the divine 'Yes' to the human being and to their world."[16]

The person of Jesus, in his life and work, is a mirror in which there is revealed the Yes of God to humanity and to creation. Of course, the Yes of Jesus—like the Yes of God—is not without a No: it is not a word of approval bereft of the power to divide, discover, and punish. Indeed, precisely as this affirmation, it encloses and accompanies this negation. Yet the note of affirmation is the first and the last and the dominant note throughout: if there is a dialectical relationship here, it is a supplementary or unbalanced rather than a complementary one. As such, it reflects dialectical structures that are operative elsewhere in Barth's theology—for example, that of Adam and Jesus, or of law and gospel. Of Jesus as the reflection and image of the imbalanced divine Yes and No, Barth writes as follows:

> The person of Jesus is the royal human being, insofar as he is not only *one* human being with other human beings, but *the* human being *for* them: for them, just as God is for them—the human being, in whom the love, faithfulness, salvation, and glory of God is directed to them in the concrete form of a historical relationship between two human beings . . . The human being Jesus is decisively "created after God" in that he is as a human being the work and the revelation of the compassion of God [*des Erbarmens Gottes*], of God's gospel, kingdom of peace, and reconciliation, that he is in this sense God's creaturely, earthly, human correspondence [*Entsprechung*].[17]

This, then, is the decisive point of this whole section, the apex of the argument that the human Jesus corresponds to God. Jesus is the perfect analogy, the perfect image, as he shows forth the compassion of God in the proclamation and realization of the kingdom of God and its attendant blessings of peace and reconciliation.

In the following small-print material, the reader is drawn into the heart of the exegetical support for this theological position as Barth exposits in sequence four different sets of texts from the New Testament. The *first* set records human reactions to encounter with the human Jesus; here Barth observes that Jesus opposes any response of fear not only with the command not to fear but also with the command to rejoice. The cause of such joy, Barth contends, is that "what encounters them in this human being is the clear, unambiguous, and *saving compassion* of God which speaks compellingly."[18] There is no

16. *KD* IV/2, 200; *CD* IV/2, 180.
17. *KD* IV/2, 201; *CD* IV/2, 180.
18. *KD* IV/2, 203; *CD* IV/2, 182.

abstract wrath of God, no No of God divorced from this encompassing Yes. The *second* set of texts is the Magnificat of Mary and the Benedictus of Simeon from Luke 1, both of which are replete with citations of and allusions to the Old Testament and refer repeatedly to the mercy and compassion of God. In view here, then, for Barth, is the "indirect identity" between "the merciful, saving visitation of God [to Israel] in faithfulness to Godself and to Israel" attested in these hymns, and "the life, words and deeds, and passion, death, and resurrection of Jesus of Nazareth" to which Luke's presentation is oriented.[19] The phrase "indirect identity" here serves to encompass what Barth has earlier described under the terms "image" and "analogy," and here again describes as "correspondence." The *fourth* and final set of texts in view here comprises the Beatitudes of the Gospels of Matthew and Luke. Barth considers these to be "synthetic statements," emanating not from human knowledge or wisdom and expressing not human endowments or virtues, but indicating "in human words the proclamation of a judgment of God."[20] The reason for the "*Beati qui*" of the Beatitudes, the "μακάριοι οἱ" of the makarisms, is that in the person of the one proclaiming, the kingdom of God has drawn near and is now present, and the message of this kingdom is one of salvation and life and joy.

But in this survey of the exegetical material, there has been overlooked the important *third* set of texts, and it is in the three short pages devoted to it that Barth examines Matthew 9:36. It is to this detailed exposition that this chapter now turns.

The Exegesis

Of all the possible texts in the Gospels that illustrate the divine compassion, Barth selects this one, describing it as one that is "supremely instructive [*höchst lehrreich*] in respect of the matter currently occupying us."[21] Of particular material relevance is the opening statement of this Gospel text: "When [Jesus] saw the crowds, He had *compassion* for them" (Matt. 9:36a). The noun "compassion" here—a form of the verb "*erbarmen*" is used in Barth's original German—renders the Greek term ἐσπλαγχνίσθη, from the verb σπλαγχνίζομαι, meaning to have pity or to feel sympathy.[22] The verb is related to the Greek word σπλάγχνον, usually found in the plural σπλάγχνα,

19. *KD* IV/2, 205; *CD* IV/2, 184.
20. *KD* IV/2, 209; *CD* IV/2, 188.
21. *KD* IV/2, 205; *CD* IV/2, 184.
22. Frederick W. Danker, *A Greek-English Lexicon of the New Testament and Other Early Christian Literature*, 3rd ed. (Chicago: University of Chicago Press, 2001), 938, s.v. σπλαγχνίζομαι.

which literally means one's entrails, or bowels. As in the present world, so in the ancient: "inner body parts served as referents for psychological aspects," and the bowels were perceived to be "the seat of the emotions."[23] The equivalent in contemporary English, then, for such visceral language, might be to speak of the "heart" as "the seat and source of love . . . sympathy, and mercy."[24]

Barth opens his investigation by noting that this term σπλάγχνα appeared in connection with the mercy *of God* in Luke 1:78, in the text of the Benedictus, which he explored immediately before. There will be cause to recall this particular reference at the end of this chapter. In Matthew 9:36, however, the same term is used of "the person *Jesus of Nazareth*, who walks through the cities and villages of the Galilee, teaching, preaching, and healing."[25] The implication is clear: that this same Jesus is the very image of God in precisely these actions.

Barth moves immediately, however, to the observation that this term is "untranslatably [*unübersetzbar*] strong," for "the misery that was before him not only affected him, not only touched his heart—sympathy in our sense of the word would not be the word for it—but entered his heart, into his very being."[26] And the consequence of this was that "it was now completely his misery—no longer theirs, but completely his: he suffered it in their place."[27] Because Jesus had made the misery of the people his own, their lament could only be a lingering echo, in truth already obsolete and superfluous. And so Barth writes: "To the compassion [*Erbarmen*] of God which saves radically, totally, and conclusively there corresponded the help that Jesus brought to humanity by way of his radical, total, and conclusive surrender [*Hingabe*]. In this surrender [*Hingabe*], in the fact that . . . he had compassion [*es ihn erbarmte*] on seeing the people, he was on earth as God is in heaven. In this surrender [*Hingabe*], he was the kingdom of God come on earth."[28]

That which moved Jesus to compassion at this point in the Gospel narrative was the act of seeing the crowds—τοὺς ὄχλους. This term "crowds," according to Barth, is all-encompassing and indiscriminating: "Strictly speaking, there is no one who does not belong to it."[29] Barth observes that precisely this holistic perception of the crowd runs counter to the universal human desire *not* to consider oneself to belong to "the crowd" but instead "to consider oneself

23. Danker, *Lexicon*, 938, s.v. σπλάγχνον.
24. Danker, *Lexicon*, 938, s.v. σπλάγχνον.
25. *KD* IV/2, 205; *CD* IV/2, 184.
26. *KD* IV/2, 205; *CD* IV/2, 184.
27. *KD* IV/2, 205; *CD* IV/2, 184.
28. *KD* IV/2, 205; *CD* IV/2, 184.
29. *KD* IV/2, 205; *CD* IV/2, 185.

as an exceptional case."[30] It is for this crowd that Jesus has compassion, this crowd that—in contrast to his treatment of the Pharisees, the scribes, and even his disciples—Jesus never accuses or berates. Instead, there is a "solidarity" with them, a "strong solidarity," even, "grounded in his compassion [*Erbarmen*]."[31] The strength of the connection between the crowds and Jesus and between Jesus and the crowds thus rests in his response to their plight, and only in that compassionate perception.

Barth now turns to the plight of the crowds directly—their lack of a shepherd. This explanation for the compassion of Jesus invokes material from Ezekiel 34:2–6, which describes how the sheep of Israel are scattered and lost on account of the selfishness, inattentiveness, and cruelty of the shepherds appointed to take care of them. Jesus had compassion on the crowd because they "were like these sheep, who had shepherds, and yet did *not* have shepherds, because the ones they had were not true shepherds."[32] Barth proceeds to outline—with reference to and paraphrase from the passage in Ezekiel—the respective characters of the good and the derelict shepherd. In the depiction of the good shepherd, Barth suggests that they "would know themselves to be responsible for [the people] and thus completely for them"; this stands in stark contrast to the portrayal of the pretend shepherds, who would be "not there for the people [*Volk*], but basically there for themselves."[33] There is thus a gap, a vacancy, for a good shepherd. And Barth observes that this gap "became clear and hurt even more, every time one of [the people] thought *they* should be the shepherd and [the people] thought that person could indeed be it."[34]

According to Barth, "the compassion of Jesus simply steps into this gap"— "It is precisely in this place that he himself belongs."[35] It is as the good shepherd, Barth writes, that "the one human being Jesus came among all people and for all people."[36] The people to whom Jesus came were suffering, though they did not realize that they were missing a good shepherd or even that they were in misery; and thus they did not recognize the good shepherd when he arrived to take away their misery. Yet this lack of recognition, for Barth, "did not alter the actual deep and strong connectedness and solidarity of Jesus with this people, and of this people with Jesus."[37] Instead, Barth writes, "The visitation of God which confronted the people in the existence of this one

30. *KD* IV/2, 205; *CD* IV/2, 185.
31. *KD* IV/2, 206; *CD* IV/2, 185.
32. *KD* IV/2, 207; *CD* IV/2, 186.
33. *KD* IV/2, 207; *CD* IV/2, 186, 187.
34. *KD* IV/2, 208; *CD* IV/2, 187.
35. *KD* IV/2, 208; *CD* IV/2, 187.
36. *KD* IV/2, 208; *CD* IV/2, 187.
37. *KD* IV/2, 208; *CD* IV/2, 187.

person, that 'dawning from on high,' was earthly *history* in the form of the compassion [*des Erbarmens*] which Jesus had on them; the 'great joy' intended and already prepared for all people was objective *event*."[38] And so the interpretation of this particular text from Matthew concludes with a reprisal of the themes that have been seen to dominate this exegetical section: the theme of divine visitation in the person of Jesus and the theme of the compassion of Jesus as the very image of God.

With this exploration and the exegesis of the Beatitudes behind him, Barth proceeds in a third tranche of investigation in this section on "The Royal Man" to treat the relationship between the being and the activity of Jesus. Barth denounces any separation of the person and the work of Jesus as alien to the Gospel narratives,[39] and proceeds to explore the lifework of Jesus in bringing the kingdom of God to actuality by way of the mutually informing categories of speech and activity.[40] Barth concludes the section on "The Royal Man" with a reflection on the orientation of the whole life of Jesus toward the cross.[41]

However, the text of the relatively short exegesis of Matthew 9:36 provides more than enough material on which to reflect, and thus the tour of part-volume IV/2 ends here.

The Analysis

In what follows, the chapter seeks to explore a variety of distinct but interrelated points of analysis in respect of the exegesis just exposited. The first point is methodological, pertaining to Barth's use of Scripture; the following two are dogmatic and explicit in the text, relating respectively to work in the loci of theological anthropology and atonement theory. In conclusion, some thoughts on the text and the divine attributes, a locus that sits close to the text and may be implicit in its reflections, will be offered.

The Use of Scripture

Central to the theme of this volume is the matter of theological interpretation—of the relationship between dogmatics and exegesis. In this vein it is instructive to record in the first instance here the—modest yet indicative—material from this particular exegetical section, which impacts on an understanding of Barth's view of this relationship.

38. *KD* IV/2, 208; *CD* IV/2, 187.
39. *KD* IV/2, 214; *CD* IV/2, 193.
40. *KD* IV/2, 215–74; *CD* IV/2, 194–247.
41. *KD* IV/2, 275–93; *CD* IV/2, 249–64.

First, when Barth considers the reason that Matthew offers for the fact that Jesus had compassion on the crowds—namely, that the crowd had no shepherd—he observes that this is "clearly a commentary of the evangelist."[42] And in case the reader missed this level of critical awareness at the first mention, Barth observes again a few lines later that Jesus saw the crowds in this way "according to the testimony of the evangelist."[43]

Second, Barth considers explicitly the interests of the Gospel writers. On the one hand, Barth asserts that the "complete and palpable gracelessness of the ὄχλοι" is of no interest to the Gospel reports;[44] on the other hand, he contends that "what is of interest to the Gospel reports is *this fact* as such"[45]—that is, the fact of the earthly reality and the objective event of the divine compassion in Jesus Christ. Barth explains that it is only in this "fact" that the Gospel reports see "the question of faith posed: the question that the community, in which these reports arose, found answered by the work of the Holy Spirit."[46]

At the most basic level, a couple observations can be offered here. First, Barth is well aware that the Gospel writers are not only reporters but redactors and that their writings emerge in the midst of a community marked by the perspective of faith. Second, Barth is also well aware that there is no access to the mind of Jesus, such that attempts to psychologize Jesus are futile and any scriptural attempts to do so are simple commentary.

Yet venturing into the material that circumscribes this particular section of exegesis offers further material for dogmatic reflection. In the formal investigation that precedes the material consideration of the royal man in which the exploration of the divine compassion takes place, Barth writes of the "irrevocability of Jesus."[47] He writes here:

> The Gospels and so also the individual and collected documents of oral tradition which may underlie [the Gospels] are certainly written in *retrospect* of the life of Jesus, which is complete and now lying in the past: they are monuments to the *recollection* of precisely this man. . . . Yet we cannot speak [thus] . . . without raising a great question mark and exclamation mark. . . . The "Lord" whose memory they preserve is not a dead "Lord." He is not only unforgettable for the community, but it remembers him as the one who *is* who he was. It is not first the community, but he himself who ensures that he cannot be forgotten.[48]

42. *KD* IV/2, 206; *CD* IV/2, 186.
43. *KD* IV/2, 207; *CD* IV/2, 186.
44. *KD* IV/2, 208; *CD* IV/2, 187.
45. *KD* IV/2, 208; *CD* IV/2, 187.
46. *KD* IV/2, 208; *CD* IV/2, 187.
47. *KD* IV/2, 181; *CD* IV/2, 163.
48. *KD* IV/2, 181–82; *CD* IV/2, 163.

The result is, Barth observes, that "the New Testament proclamation tells of one who was there incorruptibly and therefore one who not only was there, but *is there* and *will be there*."[49] Thus the Gospel texts are not simple records or biographical portraits. Certainly, they present Jesus as a human being, yet they do this in a way that is "so singular, so out of proportion in relation to other people, so idiosyncratic and to that extent so strange that all the categories by which one might seek to grasp him fail."[50] Given the unity of Jesus with God—the divine sonship that forms the background of these events—the Gospels can attest him as a human being only in the same way that they can attest God and God's revelation and works.[51] And this indicates in turn that "the New Testament tradition has not only spoken of this royal human being, let alone simply about him, but has also spoken *from him*."[52] To attend to the New Testament witness is therefore not simply to hear it as a historic text, Barth concludes, but to hear it in its activity of issuing forth the command to obey and to follow the one of whom it speaks, the one who speaks through it.

And in the brief methodological reflection that comes after the exegetical exposition that Barth provides in this section on "The Royal Man," Barth returns to this same theme. He reiterates that the previous sections have sought to see the Son of God as the one who was also the Son of Man, and he states not only that "this is the way in which the community in which the New Testament arose saw him" but also that "we have sought to see him in the same way: according to the best of knowledge and of conscience, from the position from which the New Testament also saw him."[53] Here, Barth explains: "We have presupposed as the New Testament—not somehow naively but quite consciously!—the form of the tradition indicated by this term that is not hypothetical but is well known to us historically as a whole, and thus, again consciously, refrained from every critical-historical construction or reconstruction of this presupposition."[54] The material result of this procedure is to accept the New Testament together with the presupposition of its writers that "the position from which they saw Jesus and proclaimed him was located on the far side of the temporal boundary of his life, that they saw and witnessed from the context of the events *after* his death."[55] In

---

49. *KD* IV/2, 183; *CD* IV/2, 164.
50. *KD* IV/2, 184; *CD* IV/2, 165.
51. *KD* IV/2, 184; *CD* IV/2, 165.
52. *KD* IV/2, 185; *CD* IV/2, 166.
53. *KD* IV/2, 274; *CD* IV/2, 247–48.
54. *KD* IV/2, 274; *CD* IV/2, 247–48.
55. *KD* IV/2, 274; *CD* IV/2, 248.

other words, the rather transitory and transient responses of the crowds to Jesus in this passage from Matthew, clearly anticipating the unpredictable and unreliable behavior of the crowds throughout the passion narratives, are not their final response. The final response of the crowds arrives only in response to the living testimony of the resurrected Jesus. And this means, for Barth, as he describes the royal Jesus, that there is no recourse in respect of either the New Testament or Jesus himself to a position abstracted from the resurrection.[56]

There are perhaps two significant dogmatic points evident in these reflections. The first concerns the nature of Scripture itself: that as testimony of Jesus it is, switching genitives, testimony of Jesus—in other words, that it attests Jesus as Jesus attests himself. The Gospels are not simply narratives without qualification; they are narratives of that which cannot be narrated, placeholders awaiting the inspiration or (perhaps better) transpiration of God's revelation. As such, the texts in their written form can take the form of a witness only to something or someone lying beyond them, to a power greater than can be captured or held by the text itself. The second concerns the perspective of Scripture itself: that as testimony of Jesus, it is written a posteriori, in retrospect, with full knowledge of the resurrection to come. Neutrality in respect of reading Scripture is simply impossible: all reading of Scripture takes place with a decision having been made in advance, albeit not a decision that is immune to challenge and change. The illegitimacy of the historical-critical movement in this perspective might be cast semantically in terms of an overreaching of human authority, a pretense to control over the object, the *Sache*, which the text attests, an unwillingness to attend in the first instance to that which the text, or the one to whom the text attests, has to say and to respond with obedience.

In respect of both points, there is a clear christological intuition governing Barth's attention. The ungraspability of the encounter with Jesus as the divine Son is mirrored by the ungraspability of the thoughts of Jesus as the royal person: in respect of both, the doctrine of the anhypostasis seems to be instrumental insofar as it is aligned with the inability on the one hand to domesticate or on the other hand to scrutinize Jesus Christ in the replete fullness of his identity. A willingness to think with Barth in this way also leads one to call into question that common idiom of theological speech that seeks to speak or act *etsi Deus non daretur*—as if God were not given. The emphatic point to glean from this exegetical practice is precisely that *Deus non daretur*—that God is not given.

56. *KD* IV/2, 275; *CD* IV/2, 247–48.

But it is not simply the case that the dogmatic points are *illustrated* by the exegetical performance rehearsed above. The claim might also be advanced that the exegetical performance in some measure—however small—both constitutes *and* reinforces the dogmatic points. In other words, it is not plausible that Barth's exegetical principles are formulated independently of attention to Scripture, in absentia of exegesis itself. Nor is it plausible that Barth's principles once formulated, say in CD I/2, then stand as a monolith governing all future exegesis without constantly requiring renovation and renewal by precisely the task of exegesis that gives them life. If one is to speak of dogmatic points in this connection, then, one must do so with some such qualification. There would appear here in Barth to be a genuine and living concourse between exegesis and dogmatics—not just a unidirectional application of hermeneutical theory.

But it is time to turn, rather more briefly, to certain dogmatic implications of this text.

Insights for Theological Anthropology

Jesus's compassion has a particular object in Matthew's Gospel—the crowds. And this observation leads Barth to reflect with brevity but also with power on precisely these crowds, and to do this both in a narrative frame of reference and in a present frame of reference. In other words, the group of people who constitute "the sheep without a shepherd" encompasses— precisely by virtue of Jesus addressing the reader through the text—not only the Galilean masses but also the contemporary listener to the gospel.

The result is that Barth suggests that all people are part of the same "crowd"—that there are no exceptions. The people of today are no different from the gathering of people whom Jesus saw in first-century Palestine, and if one thinks differently, then one is wrong. There is a lovely pastoral insight here: Barth refers to the "tiresome desire" of all human beings to think of everyone except themselves as belonging to the crowd, to "the people," "but in precisely this way they show that they truly do belong."[57] The misguided quest for individuality and for uniqueness for oneself, on the one hand, and for separation and distance from others, on the other hand, renders one more than ever a part of the whole.

Yet belonging to the crowd is not merely a function of shared createdness, as if it were something that could be parsed merely through the basic denominator of common humanity. The deeper reality to belonging to the

57. *KD* IV/2, 205; *CD* IV/2, 185.

crowd lies in the fact that the reality of *this* crowd is an invidious thing. In this crowd, names become indifferent and persons become characterless—"human beings are simply no longer human beings."[58] There is a fallenness to this shared humanity, manifesting itself here in a profound lostness—one might say, an *original* lostness that is at the same time unavoidable and inescapable.

Drawing this dimension of Barth's exegesis into the open renders it within touching distance of Barth's account of original sin, an account in which God sees, addresses, and treats humanity as a unity—as a "crowd," if you like—on account of a disobedience that is radical and universal. This verdict, Barth notes elsewhere, implies "a judgment on that which is human history apart from the will and word and work of God."[59] The result, according to Barth, is that "all of us [are] concluded in disobedience."[60] This is what original sin means for Barth: that the whole of human history, including both individual human beings and the crowds, stands before the divine judgement under the sign of Adam.

The lostness of the crowds is thus not simply something external to the people involved, but something for which they are—at least in part—responsible, something to which they—at least in part—contribute. In their freedom and responsibility, they have in the past raised false shepherds from their midst, and in the present they do not recognize the true shepherd who stands before them. And the same is true of present readers of this text—their hearts are just as much a factory of false shepherds and of failure to recognize the true shepherd. The only consequence of such fallenness can be the misery of the crowd.

Insights for Atonement Theory

Yet misery is not the end of the story, and precisely here there emerges the unbreakable material connection between theological anthropology and atonement theory.

Barth reports that Jesus desires nothing from the crowds—"apart from their misery, in order to take it away from them and onto himself."[61] And this is true, remarkably, despite the fact that the extent of the crowd is not coterminous either with the disciples or with the community and indeed that the crowd "usually never believed."[62] Barth comments that the misery

58. *KD* IV/2, 206; *CD* IV/2, 185.
59. *KD* IV/1, 563; *CD* IV/1, 503.
60. *KD* IV/1, 570; *CD* IV/1, 512.
61. *KD* IV/2, 206; *CD* IV/2, 185.
62. *KD* IV/2, 206; *CD* IV/2, 185.

of being without a shepherd was precisely "that which Jesus saw, that which moved him to compassion [*es ihn erbarmte*], that which he took from [the people] and onto himself," and that on account of which the same people cried, "Crucify him!"[63] There is no member of the crowd upon whom Jesus did not, does not, have compassion—whether the crowd be understood (once again) in historical narrative or in present realization.

This universal scope of the atonement resonates with an earlier christological claim from within the bounds of Barth's theological anthropology, where he writes:

> If the divinity of the human Jesus is to be described summarily in the sentence "He is the human being for God," then it can be said just as simply and certainly of his humanity that "He is the human being *for human beings*, for the other human being and other human beings, for his fellow human being and fellow human beings . . . as he exists himself, he is related to the human being, the other human being, the fellow human being, and not just partly, not just incidentally, not just additionally, but originally, exclusively, and totally."[64]

It is in light of this claim that there can be understood in its full and majestic sweep Barth's language of the misery of the crowds not only affecting Jesus or touching his heart but also entering into his very being—indeed, one might add, constituting his very humanity.[65]

This absolute solidarity with the crowd has a twofold consequence. First, it leads Jesus into what Barth describes as the "greatest [possible] isolation over and against [the crowd]," in a way that Barth finds reminiscent of other passages that proleptically indicate the accounts of the solitude and separation of Jesus in Gethsemane and on Golgotha.[66] This isolation is a corollary of the *substitutional* nature of the atonement as evidenced in this exegesis. Jesus's assumption of human misery is such that it becomes the primary mode of its being borne and removed—it no longer belongs to them but is completely his, suffered by him for them in their place.[67] Jesus alone, therefore, was not only *with* the crowds, but truly *for* them, and this as the very image of God. Barth writes of Jesus correspondingly as the true shepherd, who did not consider that the herd was there for him, but that he was there for the herd, the truly royal human being, in whose human compassion (*Erbarmen*) the compassion (*Erbarmen*) of God was mirrored, the God who had sworn

63. *KD* IV/2, 207; *CD* IV/2, 185.
64. *KD* III/2, 248; *CD* III/2, 208.
65. *KD* IV/2, 205; *CD* IV/2, 184.
66. *KD* IV/2, 206; *CD* IV/2, 185.
67. *KD* IV/2, 205; *CD* IV/2, 184.

faithfulness to humanity and who was now in a final and complete way in the act of demonstrating it.[68]

Second, this absolute (and substitutional) solidarity with the crowd is redemptive for the crowd—in this enburdening of the Son there takes place the liberation of humanity. And this in turn leads to the reconciliation of the crowd not only as individuals but also as a collective or community of individuals. Barth writes that to the good shepherd described in Ezekiel, the people "would not be a nameless, inhuman mass, but a single group [Volk] of people: He would name and call each and every one, sustaining [geweidet] them so that all would be together and yet everyone would have their own place."[69] Jesus is precisely this good shepherd, the one in whom the individual is reconciled precisely not as an isolated individual yet in whom the reconciled community is precisely a community of individuals.

Conclusion

The dogmatic points raised above—pertaining to the use of Scripture, theological anthropology, and atonement theory—are all present on the surface of the text of this theological exegesis, and the foregoing section has sought to tease out some of their dogmatic instincts and implications, both internal and external to the passage itself. Yet there is perhaps one further area of dogmatic inquiry that merits attention at this point. It concerns the relationship between the compassion of the royal human Jesus and the compassion of God, which the former images so completely and so perfectly.

One of the most compelling moments in the whole exegesis, perhaps, is where Barth observes that the attribution of the term σπλάγχνα to Jesus represents a predication that is "untranslatably [unübersetzbar] strong."[70] The strength of this has been explored above in respect of the humanity of Jesus. Yet as an image of the divine compassion, the question arises of the extent to which this compassion touches the bowels—the heart, if you prefer—of God. And herein lies a raft of germane questions concerning the relationship between the activity and disposition of God in the economy and the eternal divine being.

There is vexed theological ground here, and so one must proceed carefully. It is certainly true that in the exegesis under review there is no detailed treatment of the divine attributes. And yet the idea that the compassion of Jesus is

68. KD IV/2, 208; CD IV/2, 187.
69. KD IV/2, 207; CD IV/2, 186.
70. KD IV/2, 205; CD IV/2, 184.

"untranslatably strong" serves as an indicator of how profoundly it registers also in the being of God, for as noted already, it is God who in a second mode of being constitutes the personhood of the royal Jesus.

Such a vivid and ineffable depth of compassion is in turn clearly evident in Barth's treatment—prior to the doctrine of election, in *CD* II/1—of the perfections of the divine loving, and in particular the perfections of grace and mercy. A brief reminder of some of the contours of Barth's position may be germane at this point.

First, on grace, Barth explicitly opposes any position that considers that grace is "only a gift of God, which God might give or also not give, [or] only an attribute which can be accorded to God or not."[71] In place of this view, Barth emphasizes that "God is gracious . . . grace is itself really and essentially divine."[72] Barth continues: "Any other conception of God, in which God is not yet or is not yet fundamentally, decisively, and comprehensively recognized as gracious, is to think, whether it is affirmed or denied, of gods or idols of this world and not of the true, living God."[73] This grace "is real in God Godself in a way which is other, hidden to us and incomprehensible."[74]

And second, on mercy (*Barmherzigkeit*), a term whose German form derives from the same etymological root as the word *Erbarmen*, which has here throughout been translated as "compassion," Barth writes as follows: "God *is* merciful [*barmherzig*] . . . because and as God has pity [*es jammert ihn*] in eternity, because God only has to call to mind God's mercy!"[75] And Barth continues: "The freedom and power of God's mercy [*Barmherzigkeit*] is thus not first that of a 'disposition in the economy of salvation,' but truly and rightly the freedom and power of God's eternal divinity."[76]

These statements about the way in which mercy and grace pertain to the eternal being of God in an ineffable way are both striking and innovative. They are not unintended: it is certain that Barth means what he says here, even if the ineffability of the subject matter results in incomplete comprehension of what he is saying. Nor are they isolated statements: the claims made are reiterated numerous times in different ways, as is regularly Barth's tendency in making clear a point that may be controverted. Instead, the trajectory of thought that Barth evidences in such material runs from the compassion of Jesus for the crowds surrounding him in the course of his earthly ministry to

71. *KD* II/1, 400; *CD* II/1, 356.
72. *KD* II/1, 400; *CD* II/1, 356.
73. *KD* II/1, 401; *CD* II/1, 357.
74. *KD* II/1, 402; *CD* II/1, 357.
75. *KD* II/1, 418; *CD* II/1, 372.
76. *KD* II/1, 418; *CD* II/1, 372.

the compassion abounding in the perfection of the eternal and ineffable being of God. And it would be uncivilized not to observe that such a trajectory collides in rather straightforward fashion with much of the magisterial tradition of theological reflection on the divine attributes—whether in Protestant, Catholic, or Orthodox guise.

This is not the place to embark upon a further trajectory of investigation. But perhaps in closing it might be observed that in the midst of the material on the divine mercy in CD II/1—at the point where Barth is relating his innovation to the tradition, and to Polanus in particular—there is a striking echo of the visceral language of Matthew 9:36 concerning the divine compassion. In particular, there is a reference to the text of Luke 1:78, which, as noted above, Barth explores in CD IV/1 just before turning to the text of Matthew 9:36. The reference draws to attention Luke's use of the term σπλάγχνα, and it cites additional references to the same as indicating a broad line in New Testament discourse indicating the divine compassion. And the result of this reflection is, Barth suggests, that "the compassion of God truly concerns his σπλάγχνα and thus no less than in the case of all God's other attributes his eternal and simple essence."[77]

In the innermost depths of the divine being, then, there is found divine grace and divine mercy. This is what is seen in the compassion of the royal Jesus for the crowds. And this is what stands for Barth, and for the crowds, at the heart of the gospel.

77. KD II/1, 416–17; CD II/1, 371.

Contributors

Carsten Card-Hyatt is a postdoctoral fellow in systematic theology at Leuphana University, Lüneburg. He completed a PhD dissertation at the University of St. Andrews on Barth's earlier exegetical work.

Stephen Fowl is professor of theology and dean of Loyola College of Arts and Sciences at Loyola University Maryland. His books include *Theological Interpretation of Scripture* and *Ephesians*.

Mark Gignilliat is professor of divinity for Old Testament at Beeson Divinity School. His books include *Paul and Isaiah's Servants*; *Karl Barth and the Fifth Gospel: Barth's Theological Exegesis of Isaiah*; and *A Brief History of Old Testament Criticism*.

Christopher Green is senior lecturer in theology and education at Melbourne School of Theology and Eastern College Australia. His books include *Doxological Theology: Karl Barth on Divine Providence, Evil, and the Angels* and *Revelation and Reason in Christian Theology*, edited together with David Starling.

Wesley Hill is assistant professor of biblical studies in the Department of Biblical Studies at Trinity School for Ministry. His books include *Paul and the Trinity: Persons, Relations, and the Pauline Letters*; *Spiritual Friendship: Finding Love in the Church as a Celibate Gay Christian*; and *Washed and Waiting: Reflections on Christian Faithfulness and Homosexuality*.

Christina N. Larsen is assistant professor in the College of Theology at Grand Canyon University. She completed a PhD dissertation on the theology of Jonathan Edwards at the University of St. Andrews.

Grant Macaskill is Kirby Laing Chair of New Testament Exegesis in the School of Divinity, History, and Philosophy at the University of Aberdeen. He is the author of *Union with Christ in the New Testament*; *The Slavonic Texts of 2 Enoch*; and *Revealed Wisdom and Inaugurated Eschatology in Ancient Judaism and Early Christianity*.

R. David Nelson is senior acquisitions editor at Baker Academic and Brazos Press. He is the author of *The Interruptive Word: Eberhard Jüngel on the Sacramental Structure of God's Relation to the World* and coauthor of *Ecumenism: A Guide for the Perplexed*.

Paul T. Nimmo is King's Chair of Systematic Theology in the School of Divinity, History, and Philosophy at the University of Aberdeen. He is the author of *Being in Action: The Theological Shape of Barth's Ethical Vision* and *Barth: A Guide for the Perplexed*.

Ben Rhodes is the director of academic engagement at the Christian Institute on Disability at Joni and Friends International Disability Center. He completed a PhD dissertation at the University of Aberdeen on Barth's doctrines of the Holy Spirit and sanctification.

Susannah Ticciati is reader in Christian theology in the Department of Theology and Religious Studies at King's College London. She is the author of *A New Apophaticism: Augustine and the Redemption of Signs* and *Job and the Disruption of Identity: Reading beyond Barth*.

Andrew B. Torrance is lecturer in systematic theology in the School of Divinity at the University of St. Andrews. He is the author of *The Freedom to Become a Christian: A Kierkegaardian Account of Human Transformation in Relationship with God*.

Francis Watson is professor of New Testament in the Department of Theology and Religion at Durham University. His books include *Gospel Writing: A Canonical Perspective*; *Paul, Judaism and Gentiles beyond the New Perspective*; and *Paul and the Hermeneutics of Faith*.

John Webster (1955–2016) was professor of systematic theology in the School of Divinity at the University of St. Andrews. His works on Barth include *Barth's Ethics of Reconciliation*; *Barth*; *Barth's Earlier Theology*; and *Barth's Moral Theology*.

Martin Westerholm is senior lecturer in systematic theology in the Institute for Literature, History of Ideas, and Religion at the University of Gothenburg. He is the author of *The Ordering of the Christian Mind: Karl Barth and Theological Rationality* and coauthor of *Reading Sacred Scripture: Voices from the Christian Tradition*.

Subject Index

and Jesus Christ, 29–30, 146–48, 155, 161, 247, 248, 251, 276
and Jews, 152
as a natural people, 163–65, 166–67
No spoken to, 155
over-schematization, 152, 159, 163, 166–68
and Paul, 153, 154, 165
rejection, 158
as servant (Isaiah), 149
story of, 170
unbelief of, 166, 167–68
uniqueness, 159–65
See also Jews; replacement theology; supersessionism
I-Thou. *See under* humanity

James (apostle) 99, 100, 106, 107–8
James, Letter to. *See* lectures (Barth): on James
Jesus Christ
    and Adam, 6, 235–36, 237–38, 241, 242–48, 249, 251
    compassion of, 6, 271, 276–77, 278–80, 286–88
    and creation, 28, 119, 204
    death, 262
    election, 27, 117, 119, 120–21, 133, 155, 228
    and ethics, 104
    exaltation, 272–73
    as free, 272
    and God, 84, 117–18, 119, 121, 219, 229, 256, 274, 276, 278–79, 286–87
    in Gospels, 273–74, 276, 280–81
    and heaven, 219–20
    and humanity, 121, 250, 267, 274–75, 285
    human nature, 38, 244, 272, 273–74
    Immanuel, 143, 144
    incarnation, 84, 115–16, 119
    irrevocability, 280
    and Israel, 29–30, 146–48, 155, 161, 247, 248, 251, 276
    Jewishness, 247
    king, 273, 274
    the Lamb, 221, 225–26, 230
    life of, 67
    Lord, 65–66
    Messiah, 66
    object of faith, 265–66
    and Old Testament, 30, 123–24, 169
    in Paul, 65–67, 135, 245
    and predestination, 229–30
    prophet, 29, 143–44
    and providence, 229–30
    resurrection, 67, 68, 219–20, 262

in Revelation, 228–29
and Scripture, 27–28, 38, 282
as servant (Isaiah 53), 144–45
solidarity with, 285–86
Son of God, 281
Son of Man, 281
sonship, 125
Spirit of, 17
threefold office, 29n97, 146
worship directed to, 228
See also Christology; Logos; Word of God
Jewishness of Scripture, 43–44
Jews, 154, 161, 162, 164–65, 167, 168, 170, 247, 248
Johannine Prologue, 4–5, 114–25, 228, 229
John, Gospel of, 22, 23–24. *See also* lectures (Barth): on John
John the Baptist, 23–24, 118–19
Judah, 141
judgment, 154, 155–56, 284
justification by faith, 99, 106, 107–8

Kant, Immanuel, 101
Kierkegaard, Søren, 15, 59
knowledge, 193

language, 257
later work of Barth, 25, 27, 93n6,113. *See also* earlier work of Barth
law, 247–48
lectures (Barth)
    on Calvin, 88, 253–54
    on Ephesians, 4, 5, 74, 75–88, 128–33, 134
    on ethics, 98
    exegetical, 93
    Göttingen, 44, 45, 46, 71–74, 83, 92, 253, 254
    on Hebrews, 253–54
    Herrmann, 101
    on James, 4, 91–110
    on John, 22, 114–15, 122
    on Scripture, 3, 11
liberalism, 71, 81
life of Barth, 9
living creatures (Revelation 4 and 5), 222–24
Logos
    and Jesus Christ, 115–16, 118, 123, 124, 125, 228
    Logos asarkos, 116, 121, 229
    Logos ensarkos, 116, 229
    Logos incarnandus, 116, 121
    Logos incarnatus, 121
    See also *extra calvinisticum*

Luther, Martin, 96
Lutheranism, 104

mature work of Barth. *See* later work of Barth
McCormack, Bruce, 119–20, 121, 256, 259–60
mercy, 155, 156, 277, 287, 288
miracle, 42n34
misery, 284–85
modern exegesis, 13–14, 15
moral action, 97, 98–99, 101–3

New Testament, 3, 5, 10, 107, 123, 138, 143, 240,
    262, 281
Noth, Martin, 139

obedience, 267, 269
objectivity, 73
Old Testament, 3, 4, 5, 10, 29–30, 123–24, 132,
    134, 137–38, 145, 147, 169, 263, 276
olive tree, 161, 162
orientation, 101
origin, 81
Otto, Rudolf, 63–64

paradise, 183, 184
parousia, 263
participation, 267, 268, 269
pastor, Barth as, 10, 17
Paul (apostle)
    Adam, 236, 238, 241, 242, 245
    anthropology, 237, 238
    apocalyptic readings of, 236, 241, 248–49, 250,
        251
    as apostle, 62, 79
    and Barth, 73, 91, 127, 129–30, 132, 135–36,
        156, 165, 241, 242, 245, 248–49, 260
    commentary on, 15, 54–55, 57–69
    election, 135
    Gentiles, 165
    gnosticism, 237, 238
    God, 64, 130
    gospel, 61, 63, 65, 107
    and Holy Spirit, 42
    humanity, 238
    Israel, 153, 154, 165
    and James, 99, 106, 107–8
    Jesus Christ, 65–67, 135, 245
    letter openings, 60
    mystery, 165
    New Perspective, 169
    and New Testament, 107

and Old Testament, 17
    wrath of God, 54–55
Paulinism, 107–8
Pekah, 140
Peterson, Erik, 223
philosophy, 59, 140n12
Pietism, 47
planes, 66–67
postliberalism, 170n88
praise, 218, 220–21, 223, 224–25, 226, 227, 231
prayer, 49
preaching, 46
predestination, 130, 131, 132, 168, 217, 229–30.
    See also election
promise, 22
Protestantism, 41, 103
Protestant scholasticism, 45
providence, 140n12, 217, 218, 226, 227–28,
    229–30
psychology, 100–102

reading of Scripture, 17–18, 122, 258–59
realism, 85
recapitulation, 239–40, 246
reconciliation, 5–6, 269, 270
Reformation, 131–32
Reformed tradition, 19, 20–21, 22, 45, 46,
    71–72, 102, 114, 230n93
repentance, 95, 96, 97–98, 103, 104, 109
replacement theology, 152, 153–54, 169. *See
    also* supersessionism
revelation, 30–31, 38, 41, 46, 82, 118, 257
Rezin, 140
rivers of Eden, 190nn73–74
Roman Catholicism, 103–4
Romans commentaries (Barth), 1, 2, 4, 10–11,
    37, 53–60, 61–69, 74, 76, 92, 122, 127, 266

sacraments, 21
sacrifice, 187–88
Safenwil, 36–37, 74
saga, 31–32, 176–81, 199–209, 242, 243
salvation history, 249
sanctification, 267
Schleiermacher, Friedrich, 13, 17, 103, 105
scholarship on Barth, 1, 2
Scripture principle, 20–21, 25
Second Temple Judaism, 240
servant (Isaiah 53), 142, 144–48
shepherd, 278
sin, 242–43, 284
Sonderegger, Katherine, 154n10, 164n68
strange new world of the Bible, 59–60, 259

Scripture Index

Author Index

Adams, Nicholas, 170n88
Aland, Barbara, 94n7
Allen, Michael, 122n44
Anselm, 225n61
Arnold, Bill, 185, 185n42
Asprey, Christopher, 83n42, 102n28
Attridge, Harold W., 264, 264n39, 265n42
Auerbach, Erich, 149n45
Augustine, 138, 194n94
Aune, David, 222n44

Bacote, Vincent, 35n1
Bader-Saye, Scott, 128n2, 130n8, 131n9, 132n13
Barr, James, 211n51
Barth, Karl, 6n1, 9n2, 10nn3–7, 11nn8–9,
    12nn10–18, 13nn19–23, 14nn24–27,
    15nn28–34, 16nn35–40, 17nn41–43,
    18nn44–48, 19nn49–50, 20nn51–55,
    21nn56–59, 22nn60–63, 23nn64–69,
    24nn70–75, 25nn76–78, 27nn85–88,
    29n97, 31n110, 33n127, 35n1, 37n3, 38n8,
    42nn33–34, 43n35, 43n37, 44n38, 44n41,
    45n46, 47nn50–51, 48n52, 49n55, 56n12,
    59nn22–23, 63n29, 71n, 72nn1–3, 73nn7–8,
    74nn10–11, 75nn12–13, 76nn14–15,
    77nn16–19, 78nn20–22, 79nn23–27,
    80nn28–29, 81nn30–31, 82nn32–38,
    83nn39–41, 84nn43–46, 85nn47–49, 85n51,
    86nn52–59, 87nn60–66, 88nn67–69, 92nn1–
    2, 94n7, 95n9, 96nn10–11, 97nn12–14,
    98nn15–16, 99nn18–19, 100n20, 100nn22–
    23, 101nn24–26, 102nn29–31, 105n41,
    106nn44–45, 107n46, 108nn47–50, 110n51,
    115nn7–13, 116n14, 116nn16–17, 118n29,
    122n45, 130n8, 133n16, 138n7, 139n9,
    140n12, 147n32, 149n44, 152n3, 152n6,
    153n7, 154n10, 154n14, 155n16, 159n40,
    160n41, 161n49, 164n63, 165n69, 167n74,
    171n90, 180n17, 181n26, 184n35, 186n47,
    187n49, 188n57, 190n73, 191n74, 198n2,
    198nn4–5, 199n6, 201nn15–16, 202n19,
    204n25, 211nn53–54, 212n59, 215n1, 216n5,
    218n14, 219n21, 220n35, 221n39, 222n43,
    222n47, 223n51, 225n61, 228n84, 229n87,
    230n91, 230n93, 235n1, 241n15, 244n19,
    245n20, 245nn22–23, 246n24, 247nn26–30,
    248nn31–32, 253n1, 254nn3–6, 257nn10–11,
    258n15, 259nn17–18, 261nn24–25, 262n28,
    262n33, 267nn50–51
Battles, Ford Lewis, 47n49
Bauckham, Richard, 115n13, 121n42, 123n51,
    124, 124n55, 125, 125n57, 221, 221n40,
    222n44
Baur, F. C., 85
Bax, Douglas Stephen, 186n46
Beale, Gregory K., 238–39, 239n10
Beck, J. T., 85, 85n50, 221n39
Bender, Kimlyn, 251n37
Berkouwer, G. C., 216n5, 222n45
Bird, Phyllis A., 211n55
Bizer, Ernst, 45n42, 103n32
Blackwell, Ben C., 241n15
Bloesch, Daniel W., 47n48
Bohnet, Jörg-Michael, 72n5, 92n2
Bonhoeffer, Dietrich, 186, 186n46
Bowden, John, 37n2, 253n2

303